ROMAN BRITAIN

About the Author

Patricia Southern has written and researched on Roman history for over thirty years. She has written twelve books on Roman history including *Ancient Rome: The Republic 753BC-30BC*, *Ancient Rome: The Empire 30BC-AD476*, *Antony & Cleopatra: The Doomed Love Affair That United Ancient Rome & Egypt*, *The Roman Empire from Severus to Constantine*, *The Roman Army* and seven classical biographies; *Mark Antony*, *Augustus*, *Cleopatra*, *Julius Caesar*, *Pompey the Great*, *Domitian: Tragic Tyrant* and *Empress Zenobia: Palmyra's Rebel Queen*. She lives in Northumberland.

ROMAN BRITAIN

A New History 55 BC – AD 450

PATRICIA SOUTHERN

AMBERLEY

This edition first published 2013

Amberley Publishing
The Hill, Stroud
Gloucestershire, GL5 4EP

www.amberleybooks.com

British Library Cataloguing in Publication Data.
A catalogue record for this book is available from the British Library.

ISBN 978 1 4456 1190 7 paperback
ISBN 978 1 4456 0925 6 ebook

Typesetting and Origination by Amberley Publishing
Printed in Great Britain

CONTENTS

Preface & Acknowledgements

The study of Roman Britain is evolving all the time as new discoveries are made, which hopefully stimulate interest in the subject. In recent years there have been some spectacular finds, mostly unearthed by people using metal detectors responsibly, of coin hoards, a lantern from near Ipswich, a face mask or cavalry parade helmet from Cumbria, and a bronze enamelled bowl with coloured patterns and the names of four forts on Hadrian's Wall. Excavations have provided evidence that Roman-style villas were built much further north than previously thought, and unexpected details have emerged from towns and cities, such as the gladiator burials discovered recently. The history of the Romans in Britain is known in broad outline, but it will never be finished, because the gaps in the broad outlines have to be shored up with informed guesswork, and new discoveries may show that older theories are not quite right. This is what makes it challenging and fascinating.

Roman Britain was never static, unchanging through the four centuries that the island was under Roman rule. In four centuries it is not just fashions in clothing, household goods, and outward appearance that change, but morals and the way people think undergo changes as well – things that cannot be properly grasped via ancient literature and archaeology. The Romans and the Britons were just like us, but then again they weren't.

Writing a book involves more than just one person pounding away at a computer, so the author would like to thank Jonathan Reeve at Amberley for suggesting the book in the first place. Jacqui Taylor produced the drawings from garbled instructions, in return for coffee and buns and not much else, so 'thank you' isn't quite adequate enough to express what I mean, unless it is chiselled in capital letters on stone – but then what would she do with it? Then there are the photos freely given by the same Jacqui Taylor, James Eden and David Reid, who have visited places that I haven't, or even if I have visited the same sites they took better photos than I did. There's lots to see and learn about in Roman Britain, and this book covers a selection of it. So thanks from the author to everyone who helped, including the cats, and Jacqui Taylor gives thanks to soulmate Jim Eden, and to Mr Jilani and Mr Ditta, who allowed free access to their photocopy machine and expressed such amused interest in the work.

In common with many other books published in recent years, the narrative in this book contains 'text boxes' on specific topics. These boxes are distinguished by slightly larger type enclosed inside solid lines marking the beginning and end of the subject. The practice allows for more detailed explanation of certain aspects that would interrupt the narrative, especially if coverage of the topic extends beyond the strict chronological parameters of the chapter.

Introduction

The sources for the study of Roman Britain include a wide variety of materials, ranging from archaeological excavations, inscriptions, ancient Latin and Greek literature, coins and sculpture, supplemented and interpreted by the vast amount of secondary literature that arises from the study of all these media.

Many of the primary sources outlined here, forming the basis of the study of Roman Britain, are accessible to the general reader in English, especially since the rate of translation has increased in recent years. For the ancient texts, the Loeb classics, originally published by Heinemann and now by Harvard University Press, are the best source because they give the Latin or Greek text on one page and the English translation on the accompanying page, with footnotes to explain the more obscure details.

Secondary sources on Roman Britain have now reached enormous totals and are continuing to proliferate. The list of further reading in this book mentions only a few of them. More detailed information can be found in the bibliographies in these selected titles. The subject is limitless, because of the widespread interest in the Romans in Britain, and in special aspects of Roman Britain, such as the Roman army, the growth of towns, the way in which villas were used, and what happened to native settlements during the Roman period. New discoveries and new thinking occasionally add to knowledge and necessitate the revision of older works.

The Romans left behind an array of archival records concerning the administration of their provinces, and these are to be found on papyrus, stone slabs, and wooden writing tablets such as those from Vindolanda. For the armies of the Empire there are even rough daily records written on potsherds, the Roman version of scrap paper, presumably for copying up later in the unit offices. These records, together with tombstones, altars, and building inscriptions, are all used in conjunction with the literary record to produce a history of Roman Britain. With new discoveries and new interpretations of older evidence, this history is, and will always be, a constantly changing one, as a comparison of older books with more recent ones soon reveals.

ARCHAEOLOGICAL SOURCES
There is a growing collection of information about Roman Britain from archaeological investigations of forts, fortresses, marching camps and civilian Roman sites. The study of Britain can also benefit from comparison with other Roman provinces, and any account of events in Britain should be set against the wider background of the Empire, where policy was decided by the Emperor and his advisers.

Archaeological data can be brought to life by the re-enactment societies that have proliferated over the last few decades, not just to recreate legions and auxiliary troops but also to investigate civilian life, clothing, cooking and medicine, to name only a few attributes of these societies. At one time it was probably only the epic film makers who reconstructed circuses, chariots, military equipment, costume, interiors of Roman houses and so on, but now many people are researching these topics in a practical way, as far as possible using authenticated sources, and putting their results on display to show how the Romans and Britons lived.

As the whole of Britain was predominantly a militarised province until the army moved north and the frontiers were created, the study of forts and fortresses is bound to occupy a large proportion of studies on Roman Britain. Not all the Roman forts in Britain have been studied in depth, and any map of military installations reflects where the archaeological work has been done as much as it illustrates the activities of the army. It is important to remember that not all the forts on a composite map of Roman Britain were occupied at the same time, otherwise it will give a distorted picture of the intensity of Roman control. Dating evidence from pottery, coins, and inscriptions helps to establish the context of a particular fort or camp, and if there are sufficient finds it is usually possible to document the broad general history of these excavated forts. Archaeology can establish the size and number of barrack blocks, the internal alterations that may have taken place, and sometimes it can be established which unit garrisoned the fort at certain times. In many older books on the Roman army, it is frequently stated that all forts across the Empire were built more or less to the same standard pattern, but as more sites are investigated in more depth, an increasing number of anomalies are discovered, revealing that although the Romans adhered to a broad general plan, they also adapted to circumstances and did not slavishly follow the pattern book.

In recent years, greater interest has been expressed in civil settlements, ranging from towns when rescue excavations can be organised, through villas in the countryside to small villages and industrial sites. These projects help to illustrate how the Britons and the Romans lived, filling the gaps in knowledge, which is too often limited to how the population died and what happened to the bodies, rather than what the people did when they were alive.

Archaeology is a fairly new and very exciting tool, but it is not one of pinpoint accuracy. Information from other Roman provinces can sometime be used to fill gaps in knowledge, with the cautionary note that there was no absolute uniformity over the whole Empire. Other corroborative information must be brought in to complement and augment the archaeology of a site, and there is always the problem of mistaken or misinterpreted evidence, as is occasionally revealed by further investigation and research.

Papyrus Records and Writing Tablets
The relevance of papyrus records to the study of Roman Britain may be

considered slight, but the chief categories of administrative records are to be found on papyrus, from Roman provinces such as Syria or Egypt, where the dry climate is conducive to the preservation of such items. Though administration in one province might not be wholly relevant to another, the background information that the papyrus records provide is useful. Several notable collections of papyri are distributed among the museums and libraries of the world. Two of the largest collections, revealing how the Romans governed their provinces and how the army operated on a day-to-day basis, are those from Oxyrhynchus, 200 kilometres south of Cairo in Egypt, and from Dura-Europos on the Euphrates. The Oxyrhynchus papyri are diverse in content, covering private documents and letters, official civilian material, and military affairs. The Dura-Europos papyri cover a much narrower field with regard to timescale and content, but they are of considerable importance for the study of the army, since they contain the duty rosters of *cohors XX Palmyrenorum*, the auxiliary unit that was stationed there in the early third century AD. These records show that the Roman army was not limited to the area of their forts, and had many duties that would classify as police work, border control, special missions to other parts of the province, guard duties, care of animals and so on, and a lot of time was taken up simply in securing supplies of food, equipment, fuel, horses and draft animals, and many other goods. Though these records apply to a province many miles from Britain, the activities documented in them are probably applicable to the troops stationed in the island province, and are corroborated by the Vindolanda writing tablets.

The persistent damp climate and the particular soil conditions of northern England have fortuitously preserved a collection of wooden writing tablets from the fort at Vindolanda (modern Chesterholm), just south of Hadrian's Wall. These tablets throw much light on the day-to-day lives of soldiers on the northern frontier of Roman Britain at the end of the first century AD. A selection of these have become justly famous, such as the party invitation from the commander's wife, the letter enquiring about what had become of the supply of hides, and the complaint that has such a modern ring to it, that the writer didn't want to collect them himself, risking injury to the animals, because the roads were very bad. It is a portrayal that would surely have been recognisable in broad general terms to other Roman soldiers stationed in other provinces, and perhaps also to soldiers of many other periods of history.

EPIGRAPHIC RECORDS

Throughout the Empire the Romans faithfully adhered to the epigraphic habit of recording significant events on stone, an ingrained practice which is useful to archaeologists and historians in reconstructing the lives of Roman military and administrative personnel. The sum total of inscriptions from Britain is not sufficient to present a rounded picture of the Roman era in the island, since many of the army officers and government officials spent only a few years in the province and then moved on, and sometimes set up inscriptions in other provinces, recording their careers. Thus inscriptions from all parts of the Roman Empire can have some relevance to Roman Britain.

INSCRIPTIONS – TEXT BOX

The Romans all over the Empire regularly set up stone inscriptions for a variety of purposes. Such documents, for this is what they are, can elucidate many aspects of life in the provinces that cannot be known from the literary evidence. Inscriptions were used to record new buildings, or the repair of old ones, predominantly by the Roman army, where the building of a fort or its repair is usually recorded with the Emperor's name and titles, and sometimes the names of the consuls of the year, providing an accurate date for the building work. Formulaic abbreviations are used, to save space on the stone and to reduce the number of characters that had to be carved. A typical inscription would begin IMP. CAES. standing for Imperator Caesar, the Emperor, Imperator signifying his command of the armies and the title used when the troops hailed victorious

Emperors. The name Caesar derives from Julius Caesar, and was used as a title. The Emperor's name followed, then his other titles such as Parthicus Maximus, or Britannicus, signifying victories over the Parthians or the Britons. These victories could have been gained by the Emperor himself fighting with the troops, but more usually they were gained via the governors of the province concerned, or specially appointed generals. Emperors assiduously collected and advertised the number of times they had been hailed as Imperator by the armies, expressed on inscriptions as IMP. IV or IMP. IX and so on. Emperors were also chief priests of the Empire, rendered as PONT. MAX. for Pontifex Maximus. More official titles usually came next, most commonly TRIB. POT., or sometimes merely TR. P. followed by a number, standing for *tribunicia potestas*, tribunician power. This rather than the consulship was the most important aspect of the Emperor's power, because among other things it gave him the right to summon the Senate and to veto proposals. It was renewed each year, hence the numbers assigned to the title, and provides useful dating evidence for the building work. The number of the Emperor's consulships was given in the same fashion as COS. III or however many times he had held the office. It cannot be assumed that the Emperor held the consulship every year, so this evidence can be used in the absence of other information, for instance when the number of Trib. Pot. years is missing, to date an inscription to sometime after the last consulship. After all the formalities the inscription would then detail what had been built or rebuilt, under named individuals, the governor of the province, the commander of the unit, or sometimes a centurion. The word for 'built this' is usually FECIT, but it is not always included.

There are only a few inscriptions from civilian buildings, showing a curious lack of the epigraphic habit in Britain, or possibly of relevant archaeological finds. Most towns possessed a Forum and basilica complex, but only a few town councils or individual benefactors seem to have recorded their building work. The most famous Forum inscription is from Verulamium, recording work done under Gnaeus Julius Agricola in the reign of Titus.

Many people erected tombstones, often with a carved portrait of the deceased and a text giving their names and ages. Religious dedications are perhaps the commonest group of inscriptions from Roman Britain, recording a multiplicity of gods and goddesses. Most of them begin with the abbreviation D. M. standing for *Dis Manibus*, to the gods and shades, in the dative case and in the plural, therefore covering all deities (and avoiding giving offence to any jealous gods). The name of the deceased was given, and the age at death, expressed as e.g. VIXIT XLI ANNOS, lived for forty-one years. For children who died young the exact number of years, months and days are sometimes poignantly stated. Sometimes the name or names of the people who set up the tombstone are given, and the relationship to the dead person, or the formula H.F.C. or HERES FAC. C. appears, for *heres faciundum curavit*, meaning that the heirs of the deceased arranged the proceedings. Sometimes the tombstone was set up according to the last will and testament of the deceased person, recorded as EX TEST., *ex testamento*, included in the phrase *heres ex testamento posuit*, the heir set this up according to the will. Military tombs usually give the name and rank of the deceased, the age at death, more rarely the cause of death, and the number of years that the soldier served in the army, e.g. STIP. XX, indicating twenty years' *stipendiorum*, or service. The abbreviation H.S.E. is used for *hic situs est*, meaning 'lies here'.

Altars to various gods were set up often as the result of making a request of the god or goddess, and having the wish granted. The opening lines indicate the deity, DEO MARTI, to the god Mars, or DEAE MINERVAE, to the goddess Minerva. Many altars were dedicated to the chief of gods of the Empire, by the formula I.O.M. for Jupiter Optimus Maximus, Jupiter (more strictly Iupiter) best and greatest. A common abbreviation at the end of the text of an altar is V.S.L.M. *votum solvit libens merito*, willingly and deservedly fulfilled his vow, indicating that in return for a favour from the chosen deity, the dedicator had promised to set up an altar, and perhaps to make a sacrifice to the god or goddess. The Romans were tolerant of other religions, often equating native gods with their own, hence the dedications to gods such as Mars Belatucadrus from forts in northern England, or Sulis Minerva from Bath.

Thanks to the labours of eminent nineteenth-century scholars there are collections of Latin and Greek inscriptions that are indispensable to historians of the Roman Empire, such as the vast *Corpus Inscriptionum Latinarum (CIL)* which was begun in 1862 and comprises many volumes, arranged roughly by regions of the Roman Empire. A smaller but no less useful assemblage is H. Dessau's collection, in most books referred to by its initials, *ILS* (Dessau, H. (ed.) 1892–1914. *Inscriptiones Latinae Selectae*. Berlin: Weidmann Verlag. 3 vols. 2nd ed. 1955). The inscriptions are classified by subject, so that all the inscriptions pertaining to government, religion, military affairs and so on are grouped together under subheadings. For Greek inscriptions with relevance to Roman history there is the *Inscriptiones Graecae Ad Res Romanas Pertinentes (IGRR)*, begun in 1906.

These collections listed above cover the whole Empire. For the study of Roman Britain, there is Collingwood, R.G. and Wright, R.P, *Roman Inscriptions of Britain: Vol. I Inscriptions on Stone*. Oxford University Press, 1965, reprinted with addenda and corrections 1995, Alan Sutton. This volume lists all the inscriptions found in Britain up to the 1960s, including those that have been lost but were observed and sometimes drawn by antiquarians from the sixteenth century onwards. The work is arranged by place, so all the inscriptions from, for instance, the forts and rural sites along Hadrian's Wall are listed under their original locations. This series is now in several volumes, covering not only inscriptions on stone but also graffiti and other media, and it now has an index.

When the Roman army built forts and fortresses, or when civilians constructed buildings, walls and gates, they usually declared who the builders were on inscriptions prominently placed for all to see, usually over the gates. The most significant information for modern dating purposes derives from the custom of noting the full titles of the Emperor together with the number of his consulships and the number of years that he had held tribunician powers. In addition the builders sometimes noted the names of the consuls of the year when they dedicated their new or repaired buildings. Since these dates are fully documented, the building dates are easy to establish.

Another form of epigraphic record, from both corporate and also personal sources, is the dedication of altars to the multiplicity of gods to be found in the Empire. Several altars are often found outside forts, usually around the parade ground, but some military dedications have come to light from towns and cities, as soldiers passed through or were stationed there for a variety of reasons. A military presence was not totally excluded from civilian locations; for instance some soldiers were detailed to guard markets and keep order, while others were attached to the governor of the province as part of his entourage.

Personal dedications from military and civilian sources include tombstones, dedications to various gods, some of them British deities, often equated with Roman ones, and some inscriptions on lead tablets, designed to curse thieves or other individuals who had harmed the author of the inscription. Tombstones in particular can tell personal stories of age at death, careers, and status, and sometimes poignant instances of the loss of children, wives or husbands. These are reminders that the people of Roman Britain were not far removed from modern inhabitants in emotional terms, and their hopes, aspirations and their way of life differed only in their outward forms.

SCULPTURE

Artistic representations of individual soldiers and the army in action

16

are found in the corpus of sculptural evidence from the Roman Empire. Most Roman military tombstones display a portrait of the deceased, not to be interpreted as an accurate depiction of the soldier, but stylised according to an accepted, Empire-wide pattern. Cavalry tombs from a wide variety of regions all over the Empire usually show the horseman with full gear and horse trappings, spear in hand, and a crouching barbarian tribesman under his horse's hooves. Legionary tombs usually display great detail about military dress and equipment. A centurion's tombstone from Colchester in Britain (*RIB* 200) depicts its subject full-length, resting his right hand on his vine stick as though it were a modern walking stick. This is the centurion of the Twentieth legion (*legio XX*), Marcus Favonius Facilis, who died not long after the Claudian conquest of Britain. His armour and military dress are shown in great detail, including the straps holding his sword on his left side, and his dagger on his right.

The accuracy of the details of the infantry and cavalry arms and armour, and of the horse trappings on military tombs, has been much debated. It is known that the portraits and the lettering of the tombs would have been brilliantly painted, so it is probable that some details that were difficult to depict in a carved relief were probably made much clearer in paint. But in general the sculptured reliefs of soldiers give us more information than any amount of words, and they can be favourably compared to the archaeological finds of weapons and armour from all parts of the Empire.

Some of the civilian tombstones provide similar details of clothing, and of household goods and furniture, and would probably have been brightly painted. Where the inscriptions have survived, much can be gleaned about family life, affection and grief, particularly from the tombs of children.

Coins

The most authoritative English-language studies of Roman coins are to be found in the multiple volumes of *Roman Imperial Coinage* (*RIC*), and the catalogue volumes published by the British Museum in London

(*BMC*): Mattingley, H. and Carson, R.A.G. (eds.). 1923–1964. *Coins of the Roman Empire in the British Museum*. London: British Museum. 6 vols. Reprinted 1976. Other more accessible studies, each in a single volume and with illustrations, include: Sydenham, E.A. 1952. *The Coinage of the Roman Republic*. London: Spink; Sutherland, C.H.V. 1974. *Roman Coins*. London: Barrie & Jenkins; and Kent, J.P.C. 1978. *Roman Coins*. London: Thames & Hudson.

The Romans used their coinage to disseminate political and military propaganda, a practice which gained considerable popularity during the various civil wars, when the Emperors issued their own coinage to pay their troops. Favourite motifs were the military standards of various legions and units, and displays of armour with shields and weapons. In times of stress, the legends running round the coins often praised the 'fidelity of the army' (*Fides Militum*) or the 'fidelity of the cavalry' (*Fides Equitum*).

The study of coins can impart much information about a particular Emperor's military policies. The find spots of multiple coins can sometimes reveal the presence of troops during wars, especially when there was a special issue to pay troops; for instance in the third century AD in Britain, Carausius issued coins naming his legions and they are found in Britain and in Gaul. The coins can indicate that troops were operating in a particular location, but cannot answer the more precise questions as to when they were there, or why.

OFFICIAL OR SEMI-OFFICIAL DOCUMENTS: THE *NOTITIA DIGNITATUM*

The late fourth-century administrative and military organisation of Roman Britain is ostensibly outlined in the *Notitia Dignitatum*, an administrative handbook listing government officials, and the headquarters of each army unit with their commanders. Its full title is *Notitia omnium dignitatum et administrationum tam civilium quam militarium*, a list of all ranks both civil and military. The four versions now available date from medieval times, all derived from a copy of the work made in the time of Charlemagne, which has been lost, so scribal errors may have been made on more than one occasion when the various copies were produced.

The *Notitia* reveals a strict hierarchy of civilian officials and military officers, all of whom wore uniforms and were graded for pay and privileges by the time the work was produced. It is divided into two parts, for the eastern Empire (*Oriens*) and the western Empire (*Occidens*), and within each half it is further divided into the Prefectures, governed by the Praetorian Prefects. The Prefecture of Gaul includes Spain and Britain. The Dioceses are listed, each with their *vicarius*, and then the provinces with the titles of the governors and military officers and their subordinates. Only ranks and titles are given, and not personal names of officials in these posts. All state-run organisations are included within each provincial list, including mints and weaving houses producing textiles.

The many problems of the *Notitia* have been much debated. The date when the whole document was drawn up is not precisely established, but is reckoned to belong to the end of the fourth century or the beginning of the fifth. The main point of contention for the British sections is that it is not known whether the list represents the current situation in Britain when the compiler of the whole document collected the data, which is very unlikely. There appear to be anachronisms within the British sections, as though the compiler was using more than one source which didn't quite match, probably being of different dates. In the *Notitia* Hadrian's Wall appears to be garrisoned by the same units attested there in the third century, including the old-style *alae* and *cohortes*, which had disappeared from other provinces. This implies that the British sections of the document dealing with the northern parts of the island must be hopelessly out of date. But the list of Wall garrisons also includes units such as the *ala Herculiana* and the *equites Crispiani*, named respectively for Maximian, the colleague of Diocletian, and for Crispus, the son of Constantine, which brings the information up to at least the beginning of the fourth century.

None of the outpost forts north of Hadrian's Wall are listed, and since they were given up after 367 it seems as though the information should be dated to the second half of the fourth century. It is generally agreed that the British sections were compiled *c*.395, but the western half of the *Notitia* was amended up to about 428, implying that the occupation of Britain must have gone beyond the traditional date of the Roman withdrawal in 410, which is hotly disputed. Another fundamental problem is that the place names of the *Notitia* cannot all be equated with known sites, and the forts in the north where fourth century occupation is archaeologically attested significantly outnumber those listed in the *Notitia Dignitatum* under the command of the *Dux*. One reason for this could be that only the headquarters forts are listed in the *Notitia*, and other troops were out-posted, which may explain why there are more archaeologically attested sites than appear in the list.

Nothing is listed for Wales, so it has been suggested that when Magnus Maximus was declared Emperor by the troops in Britain he took all the units with him. Another suggestion is that the section listing units in Wales became detached at some point from the original version.

Law Codes

There is some relevance to Roman Britain in the collections of laws that were produced in the Byzantine period. In the fifth century the *Codex Theodosianus* was compiled from a variety of earlier laws and enactments; for an English version and commentary see Pharr, C. (trans.) 1952. *The Theodosian Code and Novels and the Sirmondian Constitution*. New York: Greenwood Press. In the first half of the sixth century, *Digest of Justinian* was issued covering a very broad range of subjects, and collating not just laws but also legal opinions with a bearing upon the application of the laws: Watson, A. (ed.) 1998. *The Digest of Justinian*. University of Pennsylvania Press. Rev.ed. 4 vols.

The material in these compilations was by no means restricted to the later Roman period, since there are several sections of the codes which date from the first and second centuries, particularly in the *Digest of Justinian*, where the useful habit was adopted of attributing the legal opinions to their original author, so that the chronological context and their long-term relevance can be evaluated. Sometimes the rescripts of the Emperors were included. These are the replies to governors and officials who had enquired about particular points of law, one being addressed to an official in Britain.

A compilation of laws with direct value for the study of the Roman army is the book attributed to Sextus Ruffus (or Rufius) Festus, who was a provincial governor under the Emperor Valentinian II, who reigned from AD 371 to 392 (C. E. Brand, *Roman Military Law*, Univ. Texas Press, 1968). If this is so, then Ruffus could have written from direct experience of the army, gained while he was in office; he may have started out as a soldier himself.

Most of the laws refer to purely military matters but some of them show that there was some consideration for civilians too. Any misdemeanours that threatened the safety of colleagues or could influence the outcome of a battle were usually dealt with by execution, flogging or mutilation. Running away from a battle, striking or wounding an officer, open insubordination and inciting men to mutiny, all fell within the category of capital punishment. For a rapist, it was recommended that the nose of the offender should be detached. Punishments were harsh in Roman times, but due consideration was given to length of service, conduct, and war record. It was recommended that when a soldier who had gone AWOL eventually returned to his unit, there should be an enquiry as to why he had done so, in case he faced personal or family problems. The military laws demonstrate that the high officers and administrators of the Roman army, not generally noted for their kind humanitarian principles, understood the ancient equivalent of battle fatigue and shell shock.

MAPS AND ITINERARIES

Knowledge of Roman surveying is fairly extensive, but the study of maps is limited to the surviving examples, of which there are very few. These are discussed in Dilke, O.A.W. 1985. *Greek and Roman Maps*. London: Thames & Hudson. The discovery of fragments of the marble plan of the city of Rome, the *Forma Urbis Romae*, demonstrates that the Romans could produce accurate and detailed plans of their cities and individual buildings. The larger view is demonstrated by Ptolemy's *Geography*, produced in the AD 140s, during the reign of Antoninus Pius. This is a brilliant work for its time, using a variety of sources to produce co-ordinates for all the places of the known world, stretching as far as India. Ptolemy's full name was Claudius Ptolemaeus. He was a mathematician and astronomer from Alexandria, and he admits that he used the work of Marinus of Tyre, who is otherwise unknown to modern scholars. Ptolemy's work was produced in eight books. His text includes lists of place names with longitude and latitude, and he gives other information describing the topography of the areas around the places.

The co-ordinates for the map of Britain were probably compiled from information gathered during Agricola's governorship of the province and his campaigns in Scotland, where he was accompanied by a Greek scholar and teacher, Demetrius of Tarsus. The author Plutarch met Demetrius in *c*.84 and heard from him about the British expedition. In Ptolemy's work there are several place names in Scotland, most of them probably relating to forts that the Romans established under Agricola or his successor, but the known forts cannot necessarily be equated with Ptolemy's place names.

There is a distortion in the mapping of Scotland in Ptolemy's work, since he turns the northern half towards the east, and there are some strange omissions. Ptolemy has information on the situation in Britain after the reign of Hadrian, and he correctly places XX Valeria Victrix at Chester, and VI Victrix, brought to Britain by Hadrian, in York. He places II Augusta at Exeter instead of Caerleon, but this mistake arises from the similarity of the names, Isca Dumnoniorum for Exeter, and Isca for Caerleon. However, though Ptolemy uses post-Hadrianic information, there is no mention of either Hadrian's Wall or the Antonine Wall.

It is thought that Ptolemy intended to give the co-ordinates for his readers to make their own maps, and though there are some maps attached to late copies of his work it is thought that these must be original Byzantine versions and not copies of his own work. The

Romans probably did produce illustrated maps, as demonstrated by a thirteenth-century copy of a world map, the original version of which possibly dates to the second century AD. This is the so-called Peutinger Table, a Roman map showing most of the inhabited world ranging from the far west, including Britain and Spain, to the furthest known eastern parts, reaching as far as India. The routes and the places named on them are accurately depicted, though there is no attempt to draw the whole map at the same scale. For the study of Roman history, the map shows that the military high command and governors of provinces had access to information about major routes, rivers, mountains and other geographical features across the whole Empire.

Rather than drawing maps as we know them, the Romans drew up lists of routes, noting the forts, towns, settlements and posting stations along them and the distances between the various named features. One of these lists, probably military in origin, is the *Itinerarium Provinciarum Antonini Augusti*, better known as the Antonine Itinerary. It is doubted whether it is an official document at all, but some authors think that it was originally made for Caracalla's journeys at the beginning of the third century. However, there are some later place names dating from the Tetrarchy in the fourth century, so the information is clearly not of one single period.

For the study of Roman Britain the Antonine Itinerary can be used in combination with other sources which also provide the names of certain cities, towns and military features. The itinerary greatly assists archaeologists and historians in establishing routes and tracing Roman roads. Occasionally it has been possible to speculate as to the likely locations of the towns named on specific routes, but hitherto unknown in the archaeological record. The itinerary is described and discussed in Rivet, A.L.F. and Smith, C. *The Place Names of Roman Britain*. London, 1979.

LITERARY SOURCES
There is a considerable quantity of ancient literature giving information about Roman Britain, covering a very long time span from the pre-

Roman Iron Age to the fifth century AD. The written sources range from very detailed accounts to garbled, cursory and tantalising notices about Britain in Latin and Greek works, sometimes just one sentence, and sometimes of dubious authenticity, but it is not feasible to dismiss the so-called evidence out of hand. Some of the literature is worth its weight in gold, while other literary sources must be used with extreme caution. Some ancient writers had axes to grind just as much as modern authors do, and some of them were necessarily biased, either because of the restrictive political climate in which they worked, or simply because of their natural predisposition. Some ancient writers researched their subjects properly, delving into the archives, using official documents and carefully checking their facts, while others reported that they had not been able to verify the source for their tales, but then included the narrative anyway, for what it was worth.

One of the most misleading facets of ancient literature concerns the anachronisms that have crept in, possibly arising from a lack of understanding of authors who wrote at a much later date than the sources that they were using. Greek and Roman historians were perhaps not aware of how much things had changed over the years, and therefore sometimes judged by the contemporary practices of their own times. This has led to the occasional unwitting misuse of specialist terms, especially military ones. It is always useful to ascertain the background to ancient literature, to find out who the author was, under which Roman Emperor or political system he worked, why he wrote, how did the work survive, who copied it, and how old is the most authentic copy. All these factors can help us to evaluate the accuracy and worth of an ancient source.

First Contact 55 BC to AD 43

JULIUS CAESAR AND HIS COLLEAGUES

When Gaius Julius Caesar, the Roman governor of Gaul, invaded Britain in the late summer of 55 BC, his colleagues Marcus Licinius Crassus and Gnaeus Pompeius Magnus, more conventionally known as Pompey the Great, were consuls for that year in Rome. During the previous year Caesar had held meetings with Pompey and Crassus, and the three of them had arranged the political world to their mutual satisfaction. Between them they had enough disposable wealth to buy the whole of Rome, so they foresaw no difficulty in persuading the Roman electorate to vote for Pompey and Crassus as consuls, which would give them the opportunity to put into effect their political programme during their term of office. Equally important, they could secure for themselves appointments or commands to be taken up after their consulships, and Caesar could look forward to an extension of the command that he already held in Gaul.

Modern scholars label this alliance between Pompey, Crassus and Caesar the first triumvirate, because of its superficial similarity to the so-called second triumvirate formed by Mark Antony, Octavian and Aemilius Lepidus some months after the assassination of Caesar. The difference between the two alliances was that the first was a purely private agreement, while the second was a legal arrangement officially sanctioned by the Senate, though the senators were more or less coerced at the points of several swords. 'Triumvirate' is an invention of modern historians, with only insecure links to the Latin title *Tresviri* applied to Antony, Octavian and Lepidus, but not to Caesar and co. The Romans of Caesar's day were somewhat less respectful. Recognising the immense power and potential danger of the unofficial alliance, they dubbed it the Three Headed Monster.

Acting on behalf of Caesar, Pompey and Crassus had passed a law to extend his command in Gaul, so he was secure in his appointment until the terminal date of 1 March 50 BC. This date is much discussed by modern scholars, but from Caesar's point of view, the main consideration, in 55 BC, was that he had been granted enough time to plan for rather more grandiose achievements than simply overrunning some of the tribes of his province of Gaul. He would think about the terminal date much later, when it was imminent; these things could always be manipulated.

Pompey the Great already had a glorious track record as a successful general, having rounded up the pirates from the whole of the Mediterranean in far less time than he had been given for the task, and then gone on to take over and win the campaign against Mithradates, king of Pontus, who had been a thorn in Rome's side for several years. After these spectacular successes, Pompey was the foremost military man in Rome, but his political skills in his own city did not match his considerable administrative abilities in organising the territories he had fought over. He was thwarted by the Senate at every turn, because the senators debated at length each and every minor detail of the political arrangements that he had made in the eastern territories, interminably delaying the necessary ratification for them. By the same means he was prevented from settling his veteran soldiers on the land. Frustrated by the Senate, Pompey gained the support of Caesar, who was consul in 59 BC. In one tumultuous year, Caesar had sorted out Pompey's problems and a few more besides, and had obtained for himself the post of governor of Gaul for five years from 58 BC, not just the territory on the Italian side of the Alps, but the whole of Gaul from there to the Atlantic coast.

Marcus Licinius Crassus was a better politician than Pompey but his military reputation was not so glamorous. He had the dubious distinction of having put an end to the rebellion of the slaves under Spartacus. It had been a necessary but not a noble task, since slaves were not considered a worthy enemy, however dangerous they had become, and even there Pompey had claimed the victory because he had been on his way home from his campaigns in Spain when he met the remnants of Spartacus's army, and crushed them. To redress the balance Crassus had formed grandiose plans for true military glory. As his consulship ended he proposed to lead an expedition against the Parthians, Rome's most formidable enemy in the east.

By 55 BC, Caesar was definitely a force to be reckoned with in Roman politics, but he had not yet equalled Pompey in achievements and prestige. Since his appointment as governor of Gaul in 58 BC he had subdued some tribes and made diplomatic agreements with others, but he was nowhere near the completion of his task, and would in fact need another seven years to conquer, subdue and begin to pacify the whole of Gaul. As the summer of 55 BC progressed, it would be only a matter of months before Crassus would set off for the Parthian campaign, and if he was successful against such a vast and organised Empire his stock would rise to unprecedented heights in Rome, eclipsing the fame of the current proconsular governor of Gaul. If Caesar could achieve something spectacular, not hitherto attempted by any Roman general, it would enhance his reputation and keep him in the Roman political limelight. The Romans soon forgot their heroes unless they were constantly reminded of them. The expedition to Britain, remote, mysterious, even romantic, would be something that they had never seen before.

BRITAIN BEFORE CAESAR

Britain and the European continent were not entirely unknown to each other in the first century BC. For at least two centuries before Caesar, the Greeks were aware of the existence of the island, which they called Albion. This name was also applied to Spain, but at some point before

Caesar's day, the island acquired its name Bretannia, converted by the Romans into Britannia. The use of a generic name for the country might give the impression that the island was inhabited by people who called themselves Britons, conscious of a common identity, using the same language, and sharing the same culture, religion, and way of life. On the contrary, there was never any such unity or uniformity, even during the Roman period. For one thing, the differences in terrain, landscape and soils, especially between the north and south, precluded any close similarity in agriculture and animal husbandry across the whole country, and successive gradual infiltration of tribes from Gaul into the south-eastern areas of Britain introduced cultural divergences and created shifts in the balance of power. Some tribes from Gaul perhaps came at first for booty, and then later to settle, but they retained their original tribal names, so that there were, for instance, groups of Atrebates in both Britain and Gaul. Caesar himself noted that the small farms in south-eastern Britain were very similar to those in Gaul:

> The inland part of Britain is inhabited by tribes who, according to their traditions, are native to those areas, and the coastal areas are occupied by tribes who came from Belgium [*ex Belgio*] for plunder by invading the land. Almost all these tribes are still called by the names that they had when they went to Britain. After they invaded they stayed and began to farm the land. The population is innumerable. The farm buildings cluster together like those of the Gauls, and there are great numbers of cattle. (Caesar *Gallic War* 4.12)

Archaeologists identify a discernible cultural development among British tribes, attributed to Belgic influence spreading from the south-east. Like many other terms, the use of this one is disputed. Although Caesar was writing about events and people he had seen for himself, it is not certain what he meant to convey by the term 'Belgium'. It is a subtle distinction to make, but it referred to a people rather than a territory, and was probably not interpreted in terms of a country. In any case, it should not be considered as exactly coterminous with the nineteenth-century creation that is now called by the same name.

As in Gaul and Germany, the tribes of Britain did not exist in close harmony with each other. According to the Greek geographer Strabo the Romans obtained slaves from Britain, implying that they probably left it to aggressive tribes to raid other tribes and round up their captives to be shipped out by dealers. Struggles for supremacy resulted in the absorption by powerful tribes of smaller and less powerful tribes, with a corresponding fluctuation of territorial boundaries. In his commentaries, Caesar mentions tribes such as the Cenimagni, Segontiaci and Cassi, who disappear from the record after the first century BC, perhaps because they had been obliterated by their more aggressive neighbours, or had combined with other tribes more peacefully and adopted new names. Tribal names are not necessarily immutable, nor do they always signify common ethnic origins, a factor which can be demonstrated by the case of the Alamanni, who appeared in Germany and Gaul in the third century AD. This tribe was probably an amalgamation of tribesmen of different origins, regardless of race, since the name simply means 'All Men'.

The Iron Age tribes of Britain that Caesar encountered were not yet fully developed, and were certainly not static. British society was in transition, in a process that was still going on when the Emperor Claudius ordered the invasion and occupation almost a century later in AD 43. During the long period that separated the tribal communities of Caesar's day from those of the first century AD, many developments and changes no doubt took place, not all of which can be discerned.

The tribes of Britain in the mid-first century BC are mostly anonymous, and their territorial boundaries cannot be established. There is much more information regarding these topics by the time of the Roman conquest of AD 43, when tribes can be named and their territories roughly defined, so it is possible to make some tentative generalisations about the possible social and political set up in Caesar's day. In Wales and the south-west, hill forts predominate over other kinds of settlement, but nothing has been discovered up to now that suggests a powerful central base for a tribe or group of tribes. It seems most likely that these tribes were not united under a single ruler, but were divided into smaller groups who probably fought each other from time to time. This is implied by the number of hill forts, indicating that people lived in great insecurity, but it is not certain that all of them would be occupied at the same time, or whether they were permanent settlements or acted as places of refuge in times of warfare. The same could be said of the inhabitants of Cheshire, Shropshire and Staffordshire, where hill forts are known but no central place has been identified. By contrast, in the Pennine areas, known in the first century AD as the territory of the Brigantes, there is an abundance of fortifiable hills, but the hill fort culture did not develop, possibly because the tribes were more primitive than their southern neighbours, or perhaps endemic strife among the tribesmen was non-existent or even successfully controlled. On the other hand there seems to have been no tribal centre in the mid-first century BC where a single Brigantian ruler could exercise power, and though two large settlements are known, one at Almondbury near Huddersfield and another at Stanwick further north, these perhaps date from the period of the Roman invasion and early conquest. Caesar had been informed that the northern tribes differed from the southern ones, and that they lived on milk and meat, which suggests a pastoral rather than an agricultural society.

In his two expeditions, Caesar encountered only the tribes of the south-east, whose names we do not know. Only one ruler is named in Caesar's account, when during the second expedition the Britons agreed to give the overall command to Cassivellaunus, but there is no mention of his tribe or his main settlement area, except that his territory lay north of the Thames, so it is assumed that he was chief of the Catuvellauni. Cassivellaunus was emerging as a powerful ruler with designs on the lands of other tribes, and his descendants seem to have fostered the same ambitions. By the time of the Claudian invasion, the tribes of south Britain had established centralised settlements, known to the Romans as *oppida*, the most important one being at Colchester, with other settlements at Verulamium (St Albans), and Silchester. The inhabitants of these settlements established mints and issued their own coins, based on Greek examples. Such a process implies that there was some form of hierarchical structure with centralised control to co-ordinate this corporate effort. The use of coins probably altered the balance of power, not just because of the obvious display of wealth, but because the land where the precious metals were to be found would become supremely important. If you were not already in control of such land, then it would become necessary to obtain control of it and then defend it in case other tribes developed the same aims. The British coinage of the first century AD can yield information about the rulers of the tribes, since they began to put their names on their coins, but the distribution of coinage does not necessarily imply that the persons named on the coins ruled the territory where they were found. It can only be said that such rulers had obtained precious metals and established mints, which implies centralised control and probably a hierarchical society, with all members of that society answerable to the ruler, whose influence extended beyond his boundaries.

The organisation of trade probably stemmed from the same sort of centralised control, or enhanced the ability of certain chieftains to rise to supremacy and remain there. Trading ventures across the Channel had a long history before Caesar embarked on his ten-year conquest of Gaul. The well-known pre-Roman port of Hengistbury Head in Dorset was not just a convenient landing place but a fully developed fortified trading centre, where cattle were brought for sale and metal workers set up shops, and probably an array of secondary supporting businesses were established to provide equipment, food and accommodation, storage and transport. Goods inwards included many amphorae, most probably containing wine, but they were also used for oil and other goods. Pottery from Brittany was in plentiful supply as well. These are the items which leave definite archaeological traces. For other more perishable items, supporting evidence is derived from literature. Writing at a later time, shortly after the death of Augustus in AD 14, the Greek geographer Strabo lists the goods imported by the Britons as jewellery and fine wares, and the goods outwards as grain, cattle, precious metals, hunting dogs and slaves. This information is most likely anachronistic as regards the trading that went on at Hengistbury Head, which declined as a port probably about the same time as Caesar reached the northern parts of Gaul. One reason for this may have been that Caesar defeated the Veneti, the coastal-dwelling tribe whose ships probably carried the goods into and out of Britain:

> The Veneti have the most extensive control over the sea coast and they possess numerous ships, which they use to sail to Britain, and they excel everyone else as navigators. (Caesar *Gallic War* 3.8)

As the depot at Hengistbury Head declined, trade between the Continent and Britain did not cease, but relocated, and also developed and expanded. There is evidence that traders operated at Poole in Dorset, perhaps on a smaller scale than at Hengistbury, but there were also ports or harbours in the south-east. In his description of Britain at the time of his two invasions, Caesar says that most of the traders from Gaul usually landed in the south-east, where the population was more advanced than the rest of Britain.

> The most civilised of the Britons are the people of Kent [Cantium], a coastal region. Their way of life hardly differs from that of the Gauls. (Caesar *Gallic War* 4.14)

It is not clear how this trade with Britain was organised, whether it operated as simple exchange arrangements between small trading firms, or even individuals, or whether there was some larger corporate enterprise. There may have been a combination of all types of trading ventures. Some of the goods may have been paid for in coinage, others may have been bartered. The distribution of coins is not a reliable guide to trading ventures, since coins can arrive at sites via gift exchange, or via theft, and an accrual of coinage may simply mean that someone such as a tribal chief wished to impress his neighbours without actually using the coins to purchase anything. With that in mind it is still clear that even in Claudius's day in the first century AD, the tribes of the south and south-east of Britain were more highly developed than those further inland.

THE FIRST EXPEDITION 55 BC

Most of the information about the tribal organisation of Britain in the first century BC is derived from archaeology, with little or no support from Greek or Latin literature. Conversely, information about Caesar's invasions derives wholly from his own account, amounting to a few paragraphs in his commentaries on the Gallic War, and archaeology scarcely enters the picture. Even if it could be discovered for certain where Caesar's army landed and made camp, such brief visits to the island will have left hardly any traces. Caesar gives no clear information about places in his commentaries, except for his mention of the River Tamesis, or the Thames. His commentaries are written in the third person and mostly in the present tense, and they were designed to be read out loud, or perhaps more accurately they would have been almost 'performed'. His audience would be interested only in his own exploits and those of the army. Names of places in the distant island would not have meant much to them.

It has been suggested that Caesar probably planned to invade Britain in 56 BC, but was forced to wait until the following year. In 57 BC he discovered the close connections between some of the tribes of Britain and Gaul during his second year of office, when the tribal leaders of the Bellovaci had fled to Britain and taken refuge there. Then in 56 BC he discovered that the Britons had sent help to the tribes of Armorica (Brittany) when they broke out in fierce rebellion. If he had planned an expedition to Britain in that same year, any intended invasion was thwarted by the outbreak of hostilities with the Veneti, a tribe dwelling on the coast of Gaul. They were expert seamen, and in the process of fighting them the Romans had to build ships and become expert seamen themselves, finally discovering a way of bringing down the masts of the enemy ships and disabling them. At this juncture, Caesar may have entertained thoughts of invading Britain, but it is perhaps more likely that he would put any plans on hold, until he had come to an arrangement with Pompey and Crassus, and then waiting until they had been elected consuls and had passed a law to extend his command for a number of years. This would legalise his future actions, and also give him the opportunity to mount an expedition to Britain, with ample time to repair the damage if things went wrong.

In 55 BC Caesar was delayed once again, this time by the aggressive activities of the German tribes, who were fighting each other and also threatening the peoples of Gaul on the other side of the Rhine. Such a situation could not be left unresolved while Caesar sailed off to Britain. If they were not checked the Germans could undo everything he had achieved in Gaul. The root of the problem was the constant aggression from the Germanic Suebi, who terrorised their neighbours until they succumbed to Suebic domination, or fled. The tribes who became subservient, paying tribute and doing as they were told, potentially swelled the Suebic coffers or the numbers of the Suebic warriors. The tribes who moved away caused further disruption as they sought lands on which to settle. Caesar found a justifiable excuse to intervene when the Ubii of the right bank of the Rhine appealed for Roman assistance as the Suebi approached their territory. He set off in early spring, intending to cross the Rhine, a daring plan that would doubtless be reported in Rome with great aplomb. The Ubii offered to supply boats to ferry the Roman soldiers across the river, but Caesar considered this too dangerous and slow, and more importantly it would not be sufficiently dignified for the Roman army. Caesar needed to make an indelible impression. Instead of using boats he built a bridge, which he describes in some detail in his account of the Gallic War, in a passage which tantalises archaeologists and engineers who have tried with only partial success to reconstruct the bridge on paper via diagrams, or in reality across a river. The Roman army could muster enormous manpower, so it took them only ten days to complete the structure, cutting the first timbers, bringing them to the chosen site and then constructing the bridge. Caesar crossed the Rhine and spent eighteen days in Germany, burning villages and destroying crops to undermine the ability of the Suebi to make war. The tribes melted away, overawed by the speed and ruthlessness of the expedition. When the troops had been withdrawn, Caesar destroyed the bridge, leaving no ready-made access for the Germans to cross into Gaul. Even without the laconic hyperbole of Caesar's commentaries, it still remains an impressive demonstration of strength.

The British expedition can be regarded in the same light, as a similar demonstration of strength, as well as a reconnaissance exercise. Caesar knew that he had left it too late to embark on an invasion of the island, but characteristically he was determined to risk it. The summer was well advanced, so there would hardly be enough time for decisive campaigning, much less occupation of the island, but Caesar thought it would be sufficient achievement to make a landing, and study the inhabitants, the terrain, and the coast, finding where the best landing places were.

There has been considerable speculation about Caesar's motives and what he wanted to achieve in his two expeditions to Britain. Technically the island was outside his province, and according to the law a governor was not allowed to cross his provincial boundaries. He had already done so by crossing the Rhine, and now he proposed to cross the Channel. In both cases he could argue that the tribes of these two areas outside his province threatened its security. His official reason for the British expedition was that British tribesmen had been sent to help the Gauls.

[In preparing for war] the Veneti brought help from Britain, which lies opposite their territory. (Caesar *Gallic War* 3.9)

Caesar was intent upon setting off for Britain. He knew that in nearly all the campaigns in Gaul, help had come for the enemy from there. (Caesar *Gallic War* 4.20)

These observations converted his dash to Britain in 55 BC, and his longer expedition in the following year, from somewhat dubious adventures into justifiable actions. The Romans insisted that they never waged war without just cause, or so they always maintained. Modern scholars suggest that the mineral and agricultural wealth of Britain would be very attractive. Sources of grain were always important, and according to Strabo grain was one of the main exports from Britain.

It certainly seems that the Romans hoped to find precious metals. In one of his letters, Cicero lamented the fact that there was no silver in Britain, an assumption that turned out to be untrue, and within a very short time after the Claudian conquest the Romans were mining for it. Cicero also said that there was hardly anything except slaves to be gained from Britain, and he sneered that such slaves would hardly be versed in literature and the arts. The biographer Suetonius offers a less tenable reason for Caesar's invasion, which he attributes to Caesar's inordinate love of pearls, which were to be found in quantity in Britain. The British expedition may have been profitable in this respect, since Caesar decorated his famous statue of Venus Genetrix in Rome with pearls. But a more compelling reason for invading Britain, as suggested above, was glorification of Gaius Julius Caesar, to enhance his reputation and ensure a successful political and military career in the future.

Before he embarked for Britain, Caesar tried to discover pertinent facts about the island. Although the Romans called it an island, which they thought was shaped like a triangle, they knew very little about the northern areas, and were not entirely sure that it really was an island until the Roman fleet sailed all the way round it after Agricola's campaigns, about AD 83 or 84.

The shape of the island is triangular, with one side lying opposite Gaul. On this side one angle in Kent [Cantium] faces east and the other faces south. This side stretches about 500 miles. The second side inclines towards Spain and the west, where Ireland [Hibernia] lies, about half the size of Britain, the sea passage being about the same as that from Britain to Gaul. In mid-channel here, there is an island called Man [Mona]. Several smaller islands are said to lie near the mainland, concerning which some writers have said that the night lasts for thirty days in midwinter. We could find out nothing about this from inquiries, but by measurements made with a water clock we observed that the nights were shorter than on the Continent. The length of this side, the natives believe is seven hundred miles. The third side bears northwards and has no land confronting it, though the angle of this side faces towards Germany, and is supposed to be eight hundred miles long. (Caesar *Gallic War* 5.14)

Livy and Fabius Rusticus compare the shape of Britain to an elongated shoulder blade, or an axe head … [When Agricola was governor] it was then for the first time that a Roman fleet sailed all the way round the coast and verified that Britain was an island. (Tacitus *Agricola* 10)

As Caesar says in his commentaries on the Gallic War, no one went to Britain without good reason, so nobody knew much about the country:

No one except traders travel [to Britain] without good cause, and even traders know only the south coast and the areas adjacent to Gaul. Even though Caesar summoned traders from all parts of Gaul to his headquarters, he could not discover the size of the island, the number and strength of the peoples who lived there, their methods of warfare, or the landing places suitable for large ships. (Caesar *Gallic War* 4.20)

The traders probably genuinely knew nothing more than was necessary to enable them to navigate to their destinations, land there, unload goods, pick up outgoing cargo, and sail back to Gaul. If they did know more, it is quite possible that they were reluctant to give Caesar all the information that he needed. A summons to Roman headquarters may not have been a comfortable experience, and the loyalties of many traders may have lain elsewhere than with the Roman governor, who had only recently arrived and was currently blazing through Gaul as a conqueror, upsetting more than just trade. After being interviewed by Caesar, several traders went off to Britain and informed the tribes of the forthcoming Roman invasion.

In admitting that he did not learn much about the size of the island, the number and nature of the tribes, their strengths and weaknesses, or their military organisation and how they fought, Caesar emphasised the difficulty of his planned invasion, which in turn made his successes all the greater. He sent off two men to try to find out more. One was Commius, a Gallic tribal chief who had been installed with Roman backing as leader of the Atrebates in Gaul. A branch of the Atrebates were also settled in Britain, so the choice of Commius to act as ambassador to the British tribes might seem a good one, except that the British Atrebates were not settled close to the tribes that Commius was instructed to visit, and loyalties between tribes were far from reliable in negotiations. Why should proud tribesmen of southern Britain listen to a Roman-backed chief of the Gallic Atrebates, and agree to accept Caesar as overlord without a struggle? The unofficial embassy was not a success, and Commius was held captive, only released when Caesar had fought a few battles on British soil.

While Commius endeavoured to win over the Britons, a Roman officer, Gaius Volusenus, who had done good service against the Veneti, was sent off in a warship to spy out the land and discover the best landing places. He was away for five days on this task, but did not risk making a landing, because he would hardly be a welcome visitor, coming from a Roman war galley. He does not appear to have discovered Richborough, where some of the Romans of Claudius's army landed, nor did he find the Wantsum channel which at that time separated the north-eastern tip of Kent from the mainland. The modern so-called Isle of Thanet really was an island then.

Meanwhile Caesar assembled his troops in the territory of the Morini, at a place called Portus Itius, not certainly identified, but generally accepted as Boulogne, which was renamed some time later as Gesoriacum. Having heard from traders that a Roman invasion was planned, representatives from some British tribes came to him in Gaul to submit to him and offer hostages. Caesar accepted their submission:

> [Caesar's] intentions had been reported to the Britons by traders, and delegates came from several tribes, promising to give hostages and to accept the empire of the Roman people. He listened to them, made generous promises, encouraged them to keep their word and sent them back home. (Caesar *Gallic War* 4.21)

The Romans had built some ships for the invasion, and acquired several more from the Veneti. In total Caesar says that he had eighty ships to transport two legions, and eighteen more to transport the cavalry, who were to assemble at a place which he does not name but describes as 'the further port' which may have been Ambleteuse. Arrangements were made to keep order in the areas of Gaul which he had recently subdued, and to protect the main port for the return of the fleet. At the first sign of fair weather, Caesar embarked his two legions, travelling without baggage or vast food supplies. The cavalry was to follow, but their transports were blown off course, some of the ships spending a horrendous night on a stormy sea, and then sailing back to port.

The point where Caesar's fleet approached Britain is not named, but he described it as a place with cliffs, where the British tribes were drawn up on the heights, and able to hurl missiles down onto the Roman ships. Caesar ordered the fleet to sail on for another seven miles until a more hospitable, flatter part of the coast offered better landing facilities, perhaps in the area between Deal and Sandwich, but this is only informed speculation. Caesar summoned the officers to a meeting to explain that when they were ordered to disembark, they should do everything very rapidly because of the danger of the shifting seas, where they would have to fight in the water in order to gain a foothold on shore. The Britons followed the progress of the fleet along the coast, and were ready for the Romans when the ships came to shore. Since the ships were too big to beach them properly, the soldiers had to jump into deep water and struggle to remain upright while the Britons on shore had the advantage and could hurl weapons at them. There was great disorder, so much so that the soldiers could only form up around whatever standard they could see, not necessarily their own. While they fought, Caesar ordered the crews of some of his oared ships to row up towards the beach to threaten the flank of the British tribesmen, and then the famous standard bearer of the Tenth legion, who is unfortunately not named for posterity, jumped down and started forward, encouraging the troops to follow him. By degrees the Romans managed to gain a foothold on the beach, and the Britons withdrew. There could be no pursuit because the cavalry had not arrived, so Caesar made camp, at an unknown site.

Delegations from some of the British tribes approached Caesar making overtures for peace, with offers to give hostages. Commius was returned intact to the Romans. Some of the tribes settled down near the camp, so it seemed as though the uneasy peace might be an enduring one. But Caesar had noted that among the warriors who had opposed him on the beaches, there were some from the tribes which had supposedly submitted to him while he was still in Gaul:

> Caesar complained that although [the tribesmen] had voluntarily sent delegates to the Continent [Gaul] to arrange a peace, they had now begun to make war on him without cause; but he said he would forgive them for their ignorance, and demanded hostages. (Caesar *Gallic War* 4.27)

It was certain that at the first sign of Roman weakness, the peace overtures would be withdrawn. The tenuous hold of the Romans was exposed quite unexpectedly. It was the time of the full moon, and its effect on the tides was not properly understood. Since the ships could not be beached out of reach of the waves, some of them were wrecked in the high tides. Caesar describes the event quite candidly, but then he could hardly have glossed over the disaster when it had been witnessed by two legions, and in describing adversity and then how it was surmounted, he could only enhance his reputation. He sent to Gaul for replacement tackle, tools and equipment, and cannibalised the ships to create seaworthy ones, losing about twelve in total.

The Britons observed all this without actively making too much of it, but in small numbers they started to melt away from the camp. They left several of their men quietly working in the fields to avoid suspicion, while they covertly collected an army and planned how to defeat the Romans. It is not known who led them at this time, but the way in which they calmly and stealthily withdrew and then reassembled suggests that one chieftain had the authority to adopt a plan and keep the warriors in check.

The Romans had not brought food supplies with them, so foraging parties had to be sent out to gather crops. In a part of the field where the foragers habitually worked, the crops had been left standing, alerting the Britons to the exact area where the legionaries would aim for next, so the tribesmen waited, hidden in woods, while a group of soldiers from the Seventh legion set out to bring in the grain. These were ambushed, and might have been annihilated if the men in the outposts that Caesar had established had been less vigilant. The fighting had stirred up large dust clouds, alerting the men of these outposts and then Caesar, so he set off and finally rescued the foragers, who had been surrounded.

In a much quoted, but pertinent passage, Caesar describes with admiration the way in which the Britons used their war chariots, manned by a driver and a warrior:

> They fight from their chariots in the following manner. First they career in all directions and throw their weapons, and by inspiring terror with the horse teams and the noise of the chariot wheels, they create confusion and panic among the enemy. They work their way into the ranks of the cavalry and the warriors jump down from the chariots and fight on foot, while the drivers move off in the chariots and place them so that the warriors have a means of escape if they are hard-pressed by the enemy. In this way they combine the mobility of cavalry with the stability of infantry, and by daily use and constant practice they become so skilful that they can gallop their horses down the steepest slopes without losing control, swiftly stop and turn them, and the warriors can run along the chariot pole, and stand on the yoke, then dash back into the chariot. (Caesar *Gallic War* 4.33)

A late Roman source insists that the Britons attached scythes to their chariot wheels, and the statue of the British Queen Boudicca on the Thames embankment depicts her in such a vehicle, but the use of scythed wheels is generally discounted by modern historians. Not the least problem would be how to avoid scything down the warriors as well as the enemy, or injuring the horses drawing the other chariots.

Chariot fighting had died out in Gaul, so this was a novelty to the Romans, who were at first thrown into panic. In this instance, Caesar restored calm among the foraging party, but withdrew without trying to fight a pitched battle. He admired the charioteers and the warriors, respecting their skill, and he had to acknowledge that his army was unable to combat this kind of fighting. But by his second expedition he had worked out how to do it.

Clearly a more serious battle was looming, and since the Roman cavalry had failed to arrive, Caesar was hampered in fighting and totally unable to pursue even if he prevailed, because the Britons could get away very quickly in their chariots. When the inevitable battle was joined, he had only thirty horsemen that Commius had brought with him. Caesar describes how he formed up his legions, and won the battle, without elaborating on the details. The Britons came once again suing for peace, so he demanded twice as many hostages as he had asked for previously, and ordered them to be delivered to him in Gaul, where he had always intended to spend the winter. Since the equinox was approaching, with the possibility of storms, he did not want to risk sailing across the Channel with a depleted fleet, and set off back to Gaul as soon as the sea and the weather were calm. When his reports reached Rome, the Senate voted twenty days of thanksgiving for his victory. It all served to keep the distant governor of Gaul in the Roman limelight.

THE SECOND EXPEDITION 54 BC

In planning for his second expedition, Caesar applied the lesson that he had learned from the first. During the winter he had the fleet repaired and had many new ships built, this time to a different design, lower than usual to facilitate loading and disembarking, and making the ships easier to beach. They were also broader than usual, in order to accommodate draught animals. He also wanted sails as well as oars to make the ships more manoeuvrable. In total he had 600 new ships and twenty-eight war galleys, though sixty of these ships were blown off course and never made it to the assembly point, which was once again Portus Itius.

There were delays before Caesar could embark. First he set off to deal with the Treveri, who eventually gave their name to Trier in Germany (the French name for this city being Treves). This tribe ignored Caesar's summons to a council, and Caesar could not be seen to condone such behaviour. Then he summoned chiefs from all the Gallic states, and held some as hostages, also levying 4,000 cavalry from them. Gaul was not quite as peaceful as he had hoped, and he had to take some chieftains with him to Britain to keep an eye on them, and to ensure the good behaviour of their tribesmen. One of the most restive chiefs was Dumnorix of the Aedui, who refused to submit to such treatment, and was held as a captive while preparations were made to set sail. After nearly a whole month of bad weather, at last there was a fair wind, and the fleet was prepared. At this point Dumnorix left the camp, probably thinking that Caesar was too preoccupied to chase after him. But the preparations for embarkation were halted, and some cavalry were sent to bring Dumnorix back, with instructions to kill him if he would not come. He died shouting that he was a free man. Fortunately his tribe remained loyal to the Romans.

Once this bloody episode was over, Caesar put Titus Labienus in command of Gaul, with instructions to guard the ports, and the expedition set sail at sunset, with five legions instead of two this time, and probably 2,000 cavalry, but Caesar only says 'an equal number to those left behind on the continent'. He had given Labienus 2,000 horsemen, so it is likely that he took an equivalent number to Britain.

The ships were blown off course at first, but managed to sail to the landing place that Caesar had used in the previous year, which was, as suggested above, possibly between Deal and Sandwich. The transport ships had to row hard to keep up with the warships, but arrived with the main fleet. Caesar mentions that there were many privately owned ships with his fleet, making about 800 in total, the sight of which convinced the Britons, who had assembled to meet them, that discretion was the better part of valour. They moved away rather than fight on the beaches against such an enormous number of men. Caesar heard of this from some prisoners that he captured. This meant that he would have to go in search of the British warriors, so he made camp, put a guard on the ships, and set off on a night march. He came to a river, probably the Stour, where he found that the Britons had fortified a place nearby, which he says was protected by nature and human engineering, so it sounds like a small hill fort, which archaeologists have suggested may have been at Bigbury, not far from the Stour.

Caesar made another camp, left a guard there, and took the legions to assault the fortifications. Some of the soldiers of the Seventh legion put their shields over their heads and along their sides to form a tortoise (*testudo*) and successfully stormed the place. The Britons fled but Caesar did not pursue them, because he was unsure of the terrain, and had not fortified his own camp properly.

It must have seemed like déjà vu when a message arrived to inform Caesar that the ships had been wrecked once again. Forty of them had been lost. Caesar arrived back at the coast, selected craftsmen from the legions, sent messages to Labienus in Gaul to send tools and equipment, and to build as many ships as he could, as fast as he could. Then the remaining ships were all brought up on shore. If the figures given by Caesar are correct this meant hauling about 760 vessels onto the beach, which would have been an immense task, involving large numbers of men and occupying a very long stretch of the coast. Caesar does not elaborate about the private vessels, how many had been lost, or who was responsible for them. Some of them may have been owned by keen military officers, and others by hangers-on who had come for goods or slaves or other get-rich-quick trading opportunities.

This delay gave the Britons a welcome opportunity to plan what to do next. They sank their differences, collected an army and gave Cassivellaunus the overall command of it. This is the first named individual of the inhabitants of Britain:

> The Britons assembled from all directions, and by common consent they had given the supreme command of the war to Cassivellaunus, whose lands are divided from the coastal zones by the River Thames, about eighty miles from the sea. Before this, there had been continual warfare between this chieftain and the other tribes, but the Britons had been persuaded by our arrival to give him the command for the whole war. (Caesar *Gallic War* 5.11)

Caesar does not provide further information about him, except to say that the British ruler's territory came down to the Thames, which probably means that Cassivellaunus was chief of the Catuvellauni, the tribe that was settled there at a later time, when the Romans began to record lands and tribes.

Cassivellaunus did not seek a major battle with the Romans, but resorted to guerrilla warfare, harassing the cavalry then withdrawing, a ruse which worked well when the Romans pursued too far and found themselves trapped. The Britons used their terrain to good advantage too, hiding in the woods near the place where the Romans were building their camp, and then dashing out to attack. Caesar planted outposts, which received the same treatment. The way in which the Britons fought still perplexed the Romans. They were light armed, nimble and fast moving, and they left groups of warriors all around to form a reserve. These men could preserve their energy and then relieve the fighters as they became exhausted. On one occasion Caesar records how the Britons managed to break through the Roman lines when two legionary cohorts had formed up with a small gap between them, which the Britons exploited. It required infantry and cavalry working together to combat the Britons.

Avoidance of pitched battles was a sensible tactic for Cassivellaunus to adopt, but when three of the Roman legions and all the cavalry went on a foraging expedition, the urge to attack was too strong. Fortunately for the Romans the legions stood their ground and gained the upper hand, repulsed the British tribesmen and the cavalry pursued them as they withdrew. Cassivellaunus never tried to attack the Romans en masse again.

As Caesar advanced towards the River Thames, heading for the one place where it was fordable, the Britons fortified the north bank, placing sharp stakes in the water and along the banks. Nonetheless the legions crossed the river, despite the high water, which was at times up to their necks. They circumvented the man-made obstacles, and drove the Britons off. It is not certain where this confrontation took place, but a case has been made for the area where London was later founded.

On his home territory now, Cassivellaunus pruned his warrior band to reduce the number of mouths to feed, keeping 4,000 charioteers, providing mobility and striking power against the Romans wherever they went. He drove off cattle, moved the people away, and scorched the earth to deny the Romans food and fodder. Rather than risking a battle he continued to restrict his attacks to hit and run raids. Caesar responded by keeping his army close together and burning crops and villages.

The tables began to turn when the Trinovantes approached Caesar, offering hostages as a sign of goodwill, and more important, food supplies for the Roman troops. They were no friends of Cassivellaunus, whose expansionist tendencies had made enemies of his neighbours. He had killed the chief of the Trinovantes, as Caesar probably already knew, since the chief's son Mandubracius had come to him in Gaul. With this in mind, it is possible that Caesar had gathered intelligence about the current feelings of the Trinovantes with regard to the Catuvellauni, and had instigated their actions by suggestion, or perhaps something rather less subtle. The tribe asked Caesar to install Mandrubracius as their new chief. In return for their co-operation the Trinovantes were guaranteed protection, not only against other British tribes but against the potential ravages of the Roman troops. There may have been a formal treaty, where the Trinovantes became friends and allies of the Roman people, a political device that bound states or tribes to Rome, but this is to go further than the evidence allows.

Whether or not the Trinovantes entered into a formal agreement, the example spurred other tribes to submit to Caesar, probably because the prospect of prolonged wars and ruined crops was worse than submitting to the Roman leader. Cassivellaunus's days were numbered now that other tribes had gone over to the Romans. Caesar found out where the main British stronghold was situated, and marched there, finding a fortified settlement in woodland, protected by a bank and ditch, with fences constructed from felled trees. It is postulated that this defended site may have been at Wheathampstead. It was probably not a permanent settlement. Strabo describes the fortifications of the Britons:

The forests are their cities, for they fortify a large circular enclosure with felled trees and build huts and pen their cattle, though not for a long stay. (Strabo *Geography* 4.5.3)

Caesar says that his troops attacked this fortification from two sides, compelling the Britons to leave rapidly from another side. Cassivellaunus was not yet ready to give up without a fight. He sent word to the four chieftains who ruled in Kent, to ask them to attack the Roman fleet as it lay on the shore, no doubt covering an enormous area that the Romans would probably find difficult to defend. The chieftains responded to Cassivellaunus and attacked, but the legions guarding the ships stood firm and drove the Britons off. After this attack failed, Cassivellaunus probably had no further resources to fall back on.

It was time to come to terms. Commius, the Atrebate chief, acted as intermediary for Cassivellaunus. The terms were light enough, since Caesar was anxious to return to Gaul, as Cassivellaunus probably knew. He had to give hostages, agree to pay an annual tribute to Rome, and make a promise not to harm the Trinovantes, whose lands lay temptingly on his borders. The British chief may have struggled to keep his face straight as he acceded to Caesar's demands, knowing that all he had to do was to wait until Caesar had returned to Gaul, and watch for an opportunity to expand his territory while the Romans were not looking.

BETWEEN CAESAR AND CLAUDIUS

An unanswerable question concerns Caesar's ultimate intentions for Britain. He may have considered a full scale conquest, converting the whole island into another province when he had subdued the whole of Gaul. It has been pointed out that the language that he uses in describing his arrangements with the chiefs is diplomatic and official, as though he thought of his expeditions as more than just exploratory adventures designed to glorify his name, and may have intended to utilise the agreements he had made as the first stages in annexation. On the other hand it is likely that he did not consider splitting hairs over terminology, using words that the Romans would understand, and at the same time leaving his options open. Nothing came of any designs he may have had on Britain. The historian Tacitus says that Caesar revealed Britain to the Romans, but did not bequeath it. After the conquest of Gaul, Caesar had no time to turn to Britain. He became immediately involved in civil war with his erstwhile ally, Pompey the Great, and shortly after the final victory against the Pompeians in Africa and Spain, he was assassinated in 44 BC. For the next fourteen years the Romans fought each other, until in 30 BC Octavian emerged victorious over Antony and Cleopatra, his last rivals for sole power.

It is not known whether the tribute that Caesar had asked for was ever paid. There are hints in the work of Strabo that it had ceased, but the Romans were more than compensated by customs dues, without the bother and fuss of conquering, annexing, garrisoning and administering the island:

> At the moment more revenue is gained from customs duties than tribute could bring in, if you deduct the cost of the forces that would be needed to garrison the country and collect the tribute. (Strabo *Geography* 5.8)

Tribesmen were generally more comfortable making an agreement with a leader or ruler, as opposed to a state, and the agreement was often considered still valid for the leader's heirs, so for a while the Britons perhaps did pay their annual tribute to Rome, especially when Octavian/Augustus became the heir of Caesar. The general assumption, however, is that the tribute levied by Julius Caesar ceased at some point. In Rome there seems to have been no public outcry against the Britons for defaulting on their agreement, which would have made a reasonable excuse for another expedition to reinforce the demands. This may be what lies behind Dio's statements indicating that on three occasions in 34, 27 and 26 BC, Augustus did prepare for war against the Britons. On the first occasion, no motive is listed, but for the second and third abortive campaigns, a reason for concern is given, albeit somewhat vague. Augustus reached Gaul in 27 BC, but stayed there because there was considerable unrest in the province, and in any case it seemed that the Britons were suddenly willing to come to terms. These terms are unfortunately not outlined, nor is there any further enlightenment when Dio says that in the following year Augustus was anxious for war in Britain because the people would not come to terms, which implies that demands had been made in 27 BC, and the Britons had prolonged the discussions, then finally refused to meet the demands, which may well have been made for the payment of tribute as agreed with Caesar. Perhaps this problem was put on the back burner until a suitable opportunity presented itself. In the literature of the Augustan age, the eventual conquest of the island was taken for granted, at least in the early part of Augustus's reign.

Although he may have planned to invade Britain if opportunity arose, Augustus never did so. As mentioned above there were three separate occasions when a campaign might have been mounted, but nothing came of them. Augustus was presented with further excuses to invade when two British chiefs came to him to ask for help in fighting off their enemies, but although he records the events in his account of his achievements during his reign, the *Res Gestae*, or literally 'things done', he never rose to the bait. The full name of one of these British rulers is lost, surviving only as Tin..., previously restored as Tincommius, supposedly a son or a descendant of Commius of the Atrebates. More recently coins have been discovered in Atrebate territory in Hampshire, with the name Tincomarus, which is the most likely restoration of the name in the *Res Gestae*. The other chief was Dubnovellaunus, ruler of the Trinovantes.

The arrival of these two British chiefs is not dated in Augustus's memoir of his achievements. They may not have arrived both at the same time, and it can only be surmised that they came, individually or in tandem, sometime after 30 BC when Antony and Cleopatra were defeated, and Octavian became sole ruler of the whole Roman world, though he did not publicise his achievements in such a blatant way. It is thought that the *Res Gestae* was composed at some point before AD 7, so somewhere between these two dates of 30 BC and AD 7, the

British tribal chiefs were clearly having trouble keeping their lands and rule intact. It may be that Dio's account of abortive preparations for a British campaign in 27 and 26 BC are contemporary with the flight of the two British chiefs, but there is no proof. It seems that there had been some sort of dialogue with the Britons at that time, which may have concerned the tribute that Caesar had levied, and/or an attempt to force the Catuvellauni to honour their promise not to harass the Trinovantes.

The Trinovantes and the Atrebates were neighbours of the Catuvellauni, now one of the most powerful tribes in Britain, with the most aggressive expansionist policies. Catuvellaunian rule extended from the Thames into Northamptonshire, and they seemed keen to gather more lands. By 15 BC a chieftain called Tasciovanus had succeeded Cassivellaunus, whose date of death is not known. Tasciovanus may have been his grandson. More crucial than his precise family relationship to the previous rulers was the fact that Tasciovanus had started to issue coins, and some of them have been found in Essex. The appearance of coins may mean nothing more than gift exchange or trade, but some of Tasciovanus's Catuvellaunian coins have mint marks from Colchester, so it would seem that at an unknown date he had taken over the capital of the Trinovantes. He was succeeded by Cunobelinus, perhaps the most famous British tribal ruler, known to the Elizabethans and Shakespeare as Cymbeline. Coins of Cunobelinus bear the Latin legend TASC.FIL, or in its expanded form *Tasciovani filius*, son of Tasciovanus, indicating that although Cunobelinus may not have been a natural son, he was designated heir and successor of Tasciovanus. He was a worthy choice, if strong rule and an appetite for expansion were required, and he seems to have exercised this appetite without opposition from Rome, despite the fact that Tasciovanus and then he himself had breached the agreement with Caesar to leave the Trinovantes in peace.

After Caesar's invasions, several tribes were still in contact with Rome, according to Strabo:

Some of the chiefs of the Britons have secured the friendship of Caesar Augustus through their embassies and by paying court to him. They have made votive offerings on the Capitol Hill and have almost made the whole island Roman property. (Strabo *Geography* 4.5.3)

The Trinovantes were among those who retained their allegiance to Rome. Remains of Italian wine amphorae are regularly found in their territory, most especially in their tombs. Their contact with Rome may have been limited to trading activities, but it was enough to ensure that they remembered the Romans and knew where to turn for help. Similarly the Atrebates retained contact with Rome. They issued coins from their capital at Silchester, with Latin words and Roman forms, probably produced by Roman die cutters and mint workers, which suggests that close diplomatic contacts had been formed between the tribal leaders and Rome. After about 16 BC Roman imports began to pour into Atrebate territory.

It is suggested that the Atrebate leader Tincomarus may have been eventually ousted by his brother Epillus, who was succeeded after only a short time by another brother, Verica. These last two Atrebate rulers issued coins on which they called themselves *Rex*, Latin for king. This may simply mean that they had adopted Roman terminology to describe their ruling status, but some authors have seen this as confirmation that they were officially recognised as 'friends of the Roman people' or client kings as modern historians label them. It was a system that the Romans regularly adopted, where the native ruling elite were offered protection in return for keeping their own people under control, and sometimes they were obliged to contribute men for the Roman army. Gifts from the Romans, and trading rights with Rome were often part of the package, usually sealed by an official arrangement or treaty. This may be to read far too much into the use of the title *Rex* on British coins, which perhaps held no connotations whatsoever of a Roman alliance. Whatever the true relationship of the Atrebates to Rome, their growing imports of luxury goods may have attracted the Catuvellauni. Coins of Cunobelinus have been found at the Atrebate settlement at Silchester.

Around the same time Cunobelinus started to mint coins at Verulamium. Control of trading ventures may have been one of the foremost reasons for extending Catuvellaunian dominance over neighbouring lands and people.

Once they had installed themselves in Colchester, the Catuvellauni provided their settlement with defensive rectilinear ditches, surrounding the site known to archaeologists as Sheepen Farm. It is thought the earlier capital of the Trinovantes lay some short distance away at Gosbeck's Farm, where curvilinear ditches have been found. The finds at the Sheepen site show that the Catuvellauni developed an almost insatiable desire for Roman goods. Amphorae carrying oil and wine are abundant, and good Roman pottery and metalwork are found in quantity, possibly arriving with shiploads of more perishable luxuries which have not survived. Most of the items were brought from Italy, but some hailed from Gaul, or Spain.

The potential power that control of trade would bring may have been what brought the Cautvellauni to the Trinovantian capital in the first place, rather than a desire for territorial conquest which just happened to give them a lucrative spin-off by way of imports. By the first century AD they were importing a broader range of goods, and the spread of these items widened, covering a larger area. It may be that the Catuvellauni were entrepreneurs in trade themselves, since the Dobunni, further to the west, clearly liked the pottery that they made, but these tribesmen also began to import other commodities that may have come through the hands of enterprising Catuvellaunian traders. Colchester would be an excellent centre to bring in goods for home use, or for redistribution.

The obvious importance of trade with the Britons of the south and south-east, which seems to have operated on a large scale, raises the question of how it was organised. Once the goods had arrived at a tribal centre, the native leaders themselves could have arranged for the redistribution for profit or for gift exchange, but the sheer quantity of goods inwards suggests that somewhere on the coasts and river estuaries there were regular dealers and shippers who brought cargoes of Roman goods in and shipped a return cargo of British goods out. There is evidence of a trading depot at Poole harbour, which perhaps came into being as the port at Hengistbury Head declined, but it is postulated that other sites further to the east may have been established, especially along the Thames, where Roman dealers, not necessarily from the city of Rome, perhaps set up trading centres. These may one day come to light via archaeological research.

Strabo's assertion that the British willingly paid their customs dues on imports implies that there was an organised collection process, perhaps with Roman officials at the points of delivery and disembarkation. How did the Britons pay their tribute, or their customs dues? In Caesar's day, before the British rulers had started to mint coins on a regular basis, tribute may have been levied in kind, probably in the form of grain, or slaves. Customs dues may have been paid by the same methods, rather than in coin, though by the early first century AD the Romans had found out that there were deposits of silver in the island, and they were mining for it within a very short time after the conquest under Claudius in AD 43. If the pre-conquest system of collection of customs dues embraced payment in kind, there would be a need for Roman officials to assess the amounts to be levied, to ensure that they equalled the relevant percentage of the value of goods inwards.

When Caesar entered his province of Gaul in 58 BC, the future connection between Britain and Rome was assured. Even if he had never set foot in the island, the Romanisation of the whole province of Gaul, only a few short miles away from Britain over the Channel, would have affected the tribes of the south and south-east in some way, if only on the basis of increased trade and a knowledge of the powerful state of Rome, where assistance could be obtained in cases of internal warfare of external threat. As it was, Caesar's expeditions had served to highlight these factors, and also to show that despite contrary winds and Channel tides it was possible to land an army there. As early as Augustus's reign, ejected British rulers tried to persuade the Romans to help reinstate them, just as rulers of tribes all around the Empire knew where to turn for assistance. Probably in AD 39, Adminius, the son of

Cunobelin, turned up at the court of Caligula, because he had been exiled from the kingdom, and at best he hoped for Roman intervention, or at worst, sanctuary for himself. Caligula may have considered mounting an expedition to Britain. He appeared in Gaul with troops, as though to prepare for an invasion, but there was an incursion of the Germans across the Rhine, and the only achievement with slight regard to Britain was the building of a lighthouse at Boulogne.

In the following year, or at least before AD 43, it is thought that Cunobelin died, succeeded by his sons Caratacus and Togodumnus. Under their rule the Catuvellauni probably took advantage of internal squabbles among the Atrebates to infiltrate their territory. According to Dio, a British chief called Bericus arrived at Claudius's court in AD 43. His name is usually given as Verica, who may have been overthrown by the Catuvellauni, though opinion is divided on the reason why he fled to Rome. When he did so, he perhaps did not anticipate that the response to his request for help would result in the Roman occupation of Britain for nearly four hundred years.

2

Invasion & Conquest AD 43 to 60

CLAUDIUS BECOMES EMPEROR

Immediately after the assassination of the infamous Emperor Caligula in AD 41, his uncle Claudius, hitherto considered an unimportant member of the Julio-Claudian family because of his lameness and his speech impediment, was found hiding behind a curtain by the German Imperial bodyguard, who proclaimed him the next Emperor. Claudius was reluctant to take on the government of the Empire, but was given little choice in the matter except to accede to the wishes of the bodyguard, or perhaps be run through with a couple of swords while the soldiers went off to search for someone else to proclaim, thus ensuring that in having someone to guard they still had jobs and pay packets.

Claudius had grown up through the reigns of the first three Emperors. As a child he had witnessed the later years of Augustus's reign, and had lived through the whole reigns of Tiberius and Caligula. He was related to them all by blood or by marriage. His father was Nero Claudius Drusus Germanicus, the second son of Livia by her first husband, before she married the rising politician Octavian/Augustus. Livia's family connections were helpful to Octavian, who also attempted to manipulate the political future of the Roman Republic by arranging a marriage between his sister Octavia and Mark Antony. Claudius's mother was their younger daughter, Antonia.

Born in 10 BC at Lugdunum (modern Lyon), Claudius was scarcely one year old when his father, campaigning against the Germans, had a serious fall from his horse, damaging his leg. He lived long enough to say farewell to his elder brother, the future Emperor Tiberius, who travelled from Rome to the German frontier in record time to see him. The military achievements of these two brothers, Tiberius and Nero Drusus, were legendary, and though Claudius had little chance to witness their exploits for himself, he would be aware of their joint reputation, which contrasted sharply with his own lack of experience. Barred from many aspects of political life, except for holding token appointments under Augustus and Caligula, and totally excluded from any hope of army command, Claudius had become a scholarly recluse, but his years of study were of great use to him as Emperor.

The expansion of the Roman Empire stagnated after the disaster in Germany in AD 9, when three Roman legions under the governor Quinctilius Varus were wiped out by the supposedly pacified German tribes. Augustus died five years later, advising his successor Tiberius to leave the boundaries as they were, and not to try to gain territory beyond them. Tiberius had spent most of his life at the head of armies, fighting battles on behalf of his stepfather Augustus on the northern frontiers, and was only too happy to give up warfare and attend to government and administration. His relationship with the Senate and people of Rome was not a happy one, and despite his efforts to improve this relationship he soon withdrew from public life as much as possible, eventually retiring to the island of Capri. Tiberius left many of the provincial governors in their posts for several years, so that the paths to promotion became somewhat clogged. No one was going anywhere, except the notorious Praetorian Prefect Lucius Aelius Sejanus, to whom Tiberius delegated most of the affairs of state. Sejanus quickly took advantage of the freedom that he was allowed, and instituted a reign of terror in Tiberius's name. His lust for power was limitless. He even tried to ally himself to the Imperial family by marriage, but was rebuffed. Only one person, Claudius's mother Antonia, had the courage to denounce Sejanus and explain to Tiberius that the Praetorian Prefect was all powerful in Rome. Tiberius arranged for the execution of Sejanus by the other Praetorian Prefect, Sutorius Macro.

Tiberius died aged seventy-eight in AD 37, succeeded by his great nephew Gaius, more popularly known as Caligula. His reign was disastrous but mercifully short, ending with his assassination in AD 41, when Claudius, nephew of Tiberius and uncle of Caligula, became Emperor against his will. He took his role seriously, expressing perhaps too much interest in the finicky details of government, legal affairs, and the welfare of the people, not just with regard to the Romans or Italians, but also the provincials of the growing Empire. He had undoubted ability, but he lacked military experience, and wished to share in the glory that conquest of new areas could bring him and the Romans. The project of Britain had been one of the main literary themes of the early years of Augustus's reign, and Claudius would have read the works of the poets and historians who constantly kept the theme alive. In Tiberius's reign the projected conquest of Britain may have sunk into the background, but under Caligula it had revived, briefly, when the British chief Adminius appeared at the Imperial court, having been exiled by his father Cunobelinus. Then, barely two years after Claudius had become Emperor, Verica, ruler of the Atrebates, arrived from Britain, seeking help to regain power in his kingdom.

THE MATTER OF BRITAIN

Claudius's desire for military glory is often quoted as the reason for his invasion of Britain, but other considerations may have influenced his decision to conquer the island. Although Strabo said that the cost of garrisoning Britain would probably outweigh the potential profits, nearly one hundred years of trading with the tribes of the south and south-east had revealed what might be possible if the area of trading activities could be extended. Britain yielded metals, tin and copper in the south-west, iron ore in the Weald and the Forest of Dean, lead and potentially silver in the Mendips and the Pennines, and in Wales there was gold. Strabo list the principal exports from Britain:

[The island] produces grain, cattle, gold, silver and iron, which are exported along with hides, slaves and dogs specifically bred for hunting. (Strabo *Geography* 4.5.2)

From the sea there was a reliable crop of oysters and their pearls, though Tacitus scoffs at their low quality. In the north, the natives raised cattle, which would be a source not only of meat but hides, as listed by Strabo. Hides were always of supreme importance to the Roman army, so much so that the taxes levied from the Friesian tribes consisted mostly of leather. All these economic factors will have been considered by the Emperor Claudius, but in the absence of a written treatise from the Emperor himself, setting out his thoughts on Britain, speculation is the only tool with which to judge the motives for his enterprise.

Time and manpower were available for this new project. Gaius had created two extra legions and placed them on the Rhine. By this time, the German tribes were slightly less hostile, and their warrior skills had been turned to the benefit of the Empire as the tribesmen were recruited for the Roman army. The potential threat to the provinces bordering on the Rhine and Danube had diminished, so there were now large numbers of soldiers who could be considered superfluous to the defence of the areas where they were stationed. Julius Caesar had shown that an invasion across the Channel from Gaul was feasible, though if he had ever intended to annex Britain he had not been granted the time, and had therefore revealed only a small part of the island in the south and south-east.

Uncertainty about what they might encounter in the rest of Britain may be the reason why the troops that Claudius assembled in Gaul initially refused to embark. Knowledge of the tribes beyond the Catuvellauni was probably sparse, and though the Romans called Britain an island, it was not yet known for certain what happened in the furthest northern parts of it. There was probably a suspicion among the troops that anyone venturing that far would fall off the edge of the world. Another consideration is that the legionaries who took part in Julius Caesar's expedition knew they were to go back to Gaul for the winter, but the soldiers of Claudius's army were to be permanently uprooted and sent into what they probably regarded as exile. So they decided that they were not going.

Among Claudius's intimate staff was his secretary, Narcissus, an ex-slave but now undoubtedly powerful within the Imperial household and a good man to know if you wanted to get on in life. Narcissus was sent to speak to the troops. According to Dio he was not allowed to utter a word, but one of the soldiers, copied by others, shouted '*Io Saturnalia*', referring to the winter festival of role-reversal, when the slaves of a household were given a meal served by their masters. The legions and auxiliaries embarked.

The commander of the British expedition was Aulus Plautius, whose family had been allies of the Claudians for some time. Claudius's first wife, Urgulanilla, was a member of the family of the Plautii, and though it was not a successful match, the two families remained allies. Aulus Plautius had been consul in AD 29, but as suffect consul for only a few months, rather than one of the *consules ordinarii*, who gave their name to the year. The system of appointing a pair of suffect consuls, or several pairs, who took over government as the preceding pair stepped down, enabled a greater number of senators to gain some experience of government, and the appointment then qualified them for other civil posts, or for military commands. By AD 42, Plautius was the governor of Pannonia, where the IX Hispana legion was based. He brought it with him for the British expedition.

The other legions known to have formed the invasion force were II Augusta from Strasbourg, XIV Gemina from Mainz, and the XX legion from Neuss. These last two legions did not yet have their respective titles Martia Victrix and Valeria Victrix, which were awarded after the suppression of the rebellion under Boudicca in AD 60 or 61. Although it is known which legions took part in the conquest of Britain, the exact numbers of men in Claudius's invasion army cannot be established beyond a rough estimate. If each legion contained 5,000 men, this would give a paper-strength of 20,000 soldiers, but it is not known whether some men may have been left behind in the original bases until the troops of the Rhine and Danube were reshuffled. Similarly it is not know how many auxiliary troops accompanied the legions. Despite the unknown and probably unanswerable questions about the numbers of men, it is usually estimated that the invasion force for Britain totalled about 40,000 troops. This is assuming that there were only four legions in the invasion force. On very slender evidence, it is suggested that there may have been another legion, or at least a detachment (vexillation) from it, VIII Augusta from Strasbourg. This assumption derives from an inscription from Turin naming the patron of the town, the veteran soldier Gaius Gavius Silanus, *primus pilus*, literally 'first spear' or chief centurion, of VIII Augusta. The inscription says that he was highly decorated by Claudius in the British war, receiving torques, armbands, and *phalerae* (metal discs to be displayed over the armour on the chest), and the supreme honour of the *corona aurea*, or golden crown. Unfortunately the inscription does not give any details about Gaius Gavius's exploits in Britain. One inscription cannot be taken as proof that the whole of the legion named on it was in Britain during the invasion, and it is notable that the text mentions only the higher ranking posts that Gavius held, starting with his appointment as *primus pilus* in VIII Augusta, and then as tribune of three units in Rome, first the *Vigiles*, then the Urban Cohorts, and finally the Praetorian Guard. This could indicate that Gavius had served in other legions in a lesser capacity, perhaps as centurion, and that it was his brave deeds in Britain, possibly while he served in one of the four legions there, that helped to gain promotion for him in other units.

THE IMPERIAL ROMAN ARMY

The Roman legions were all given numbers, but the system can be confusing. Some legions were allocated their numbers during the Republic, but although there was an army in the field on an almost permanent basis, there was no standing army and troops could be disbanded after a campaign ended. There was never a logical numbering procedure whereby successive numbers were allocated to each legion as it was formed. At the end of the civil wars, Augustus drastically pruned the number of legions that he inherited, and out of the remainder, about twenty-eight legions, he created the standing army. Numbering did not start afresh from I to XXVIII, since the older legions, formed under Caesar or Mark Antony or Augustus himself, retained their original numbers. This entailed some duplication, so that there were, eventually, no less than six legions with the number I, six more with the number II, five numbered III, and so on. Their descriptive names, such as Augusta, Hispana, Alaudae and Ferrata, serve to distinguish them from each other. However, there seems to have been only one XX legion, and after the Claudian conquest it spent its life in Britain.

Only Roman citizens could serve in the legions, but this does not mean that all the men came from Rome, since Roman citizenship had been awarded to Italians, and then to some provincials. The smallest unit within a legion was the century, commanded by a centurion and his second-in-command, the *optio*. The terminology implies that there were a hundred men in a century but the full complement was eighty men, based on the tent group (*contubernium*) of eight men. Six centuries of eighty men and their officers were grouped together to make one cohort, but there is no evidence to suggest that there was a cohort commander, so responsibility for routine organisation and discipline in peacetime, and action in battle, rested with the centurions. Ten cohorts made up one legion, though in some legions, if not all of them, the first century was of double strength. These figures allow historians to work out an approximation of how many men there would be in a legion, somewhere between five and six thousand. This is all that can be said, since no contemporary Roman or Greek source outlines the number of men in a legion, and it is not known if the legions were all of a standard size.

The men who commanded the legions were senators who had experience of both military operations and of civilian government. The Roman career path, or *cursus honorum*, embraced all kinds of appointments, mixing administrative posts with army ones. The legionary legates (*legati legionis*) of the Empire were appointed by the Emperor, and often stayed in post for about three years. They could look forward to further appointments, for example as governors of a civil province which contained no troops, then perhaps election to the consulship.

Second-in-command of the legion was the *tribunus laticlavius* or 'broad stripe' tribune. The broad stripe on the toga indicated senatorial status, but the young men who were appointed as *tribuni laticlavii* had not yet become senators, although they were drawn from the senatorial class. After one year or more of military service these young officers customarily embarked on a series of administrative posts in Rome or the provinces. It was usual for young men to enter the Senate after an appointment as quaestor, and after serving in a variety of several civilian and military posts some of them could look forward to an appointment as legionary legate.

The camp prefect (*praefectus castrorum*) was third-in-command of the legion. He was usually a career soldier who had served as a centurion, working his way up to the post of senior centurion (*primus pilus*, or 'first spear') of the first cohort, which as mentioned above was usually if not always of double strength. The camp prefects were not from the senatorial class, but from the middle classes, or equestrians, who ranked below the senators. Lack of senatorial status did not stultify their careers, however, since there were always good prospects for promotion for men who had been camp prefects. A fortunate few could be promoted to the Praetorian Guard, or occasionally as procurators looking after financial affairs in the provinces.

Other officers in the legion included the *tribuni angusticlavii* or 'narrow stripe' tribunes, indicating that they were not senators but equestrians. These young men were usually at the beginning of their careers. There were five of these tribunes in each legion, with varied duties which could include taking command of detachments of legionaries. Since there were no military academies or staff colleges where such men could be taught the business of command, they presumably relied upon knowledge gained from military manuals, of which some survive, and from advice from family, friends and fellow officers. The centurions were the men who really counted, to both the senior officers and to the serving soldiers. Since they could make life for the ordinary soldiers either miserable or bearable, as they wished, they had to be appeased and often bribed, for instance when a soldier applied for leave. Centurions were of mixed origin, some being career soldiers, while others may have been appointed simply by asking influential friends for a posting. Military experience was not a necessary attribute for officers and commanders. Nevertheless the Roman army generally functioned reasonably well.

In addition to the legions the Romans recruited units of *auxilia*, literally 'help troops'. The auxiliary soldiers were not Roman citizens, and in Claudius's day these units were still undergoing the final stages of their development. Under the older Republican arrangements, native warriors were engaged to fight alongside the legions, usually under their own native commanders, for the duration of the war. Under the Empire, the auxiliary units were converted into regular formations of the Roman army, comprising non-citizen soldiers commanded by Roman officers. On completion of twenty-five years service the auxiliaries were rewarded with Roman citizenship, which at first extended to their children, but the privilege of enfranchisement for all the soldier's offspring was withdrawn by the Emperor Antoninus Pius, and granted only to the children born after the soldier received his citizenship.

The auxiliaries were organised as cavalry units (*alae*), infantry units (*cohortes*) or mixed cavalry and infantry (*cohortes equitatae*). The majority of these cohorts were 500-strong (quingenary), but a proportion of all three types of auxiliary units were 1,000-strong (milliary). The milliary cavalry units were rare, usually restricted to only one in each province. Commanders of auxiliary units were Roman officers, called prefects in the quingenary units, and tribunes in the milliary ones. They were all from the equestrian class, with genuine promotion prospects as they worked their way up through the various units.

DIPLOMAS – TEXT BOX

From the reign of Claudius, soldiers who had served their full term, twenty-five years in the case of auxiliaries, were entitled to honourable discharge (*honesta missio*) and the grant of Roman citizenship. Diplomas were not usually issued to legionaries, except in special circumstances, for instance when some sailors from the Misenum fleet were enlisted in legions I and II Adiutrix, and would normally have received diplomas if they had remained as sailors. Auxiliary soldiers were non-citizens until they reached the end of their service, and the citizenship they were given on discharge carried with it certain privileges at law and in tax status. Soldiers were exempt from direct tax payments and from the reign of Domitian they did not pay the indirect taxes of *portoria* or *vectigalia*. This exemption extended to veterans and to their wives, children, and parents (Tacitus *Annals* 13.35.2). Typical of Roman realism, tax exemptions were declared invalid on the soldiers' illegal transactions (Tacitus *Annals* 13.51.1).

Diplomas were issued to each retiring soldier, though it is possible that it was not an automatic process, and the soldier had to ask for one. The diploma was a two-leaved bronze tablet recording the man's name, with the names of witnesses who attested to the fact that he had served his full term of twenty-five years or more. Only the last unit in which the soldier had served was given on the diploma. The term diploma is a modern description; no one knows what the Latin word was. A diploma was not an actual discharge certificate as such, though it proved that the veteran had served his full term and was now a Roman citizen.

The diplomas contain much useful information for historians. Inscribed on the bronze there is usually the complete text, reproduced in abbreviated form on another leaf. The text usually begins with the name of the Emperor, his victory titles and his number of years with tribunician power. Then the names of the consuls are given, and the precise date of discharge. The governor of the province is listed, sometimes with the previous governor if the new governor had not been long in post. Sometimes this information can be used to fill gaps in knowledge, where no other source attests the governor's name. It would seem that the authorities waited until several units of the province were ready to discharge soldiers, so that the ceremonial – if there was any such arrangement – and the office work could be conducted all at once instead of in piecemeal fashion. The text goes on to enumerate the last units in which the retiring cavalry and infantry men (*equites et pedites*) had served, but it must not be supposed that this provides a complete list of units of the auxiliary garrison of the province, since not all of them would be discharging soldiers at exactly the same time. It is a useful source of information for some of the units in the province, but the diplomas do not mention the forts where these units were stationed.

The text goes on to say that the soldiers had served twenty-five years or more, which shows that some men probably did serve for a longer period than specified. In some cases it is stated that citizenship was given to those who did not already possess it, so it is likely that a few auxiliaries were already citizens, and as time went on the distinctions between citizen legionaries and non-citizen auxiliaries was blurred. The subsequent text of the diplomas reveals how the Romans condoned behaviour that was supposed to be illegal. Marriage was forbidden to Roman soldiers but it was recognised that they formed attachments to local women wherever they were stationed, and the formula granting citizenship to the soldier himself also grants the same privilege to the woman who had been associated with him during his service. The woman was now raised from illegal companion to the status of legal wife, with Roman citizenship, which was also granted to any woman that the soldier married after discharge. Citizenship was also granted to the children of the union between soldier and his 'wife' before discharge, though from the reign of Antoninus

Pius onwards only the children born after discharge were given citizenship, so that the non-citizen sons of auxiliaries could be recruited into auxiliary units.

Though the texts of diplomas all followed the same pattern there was no standard formula. Sometimes there were only infantry men to be discharged, sometimes the soldier's woman was called *uxor* (wife) and sometimes *mulier* (woman). At the end of each diploma it is stated that a copy of the text was to be placed behind the temple of Augustus in Rome, next to the statue of Minerva. The majority of extant diplomas have been found in different provinces of the Roman Empire, but some have been found in Britain, one in a fragmentary state at Vindolanda, another dating from the Antonine period at Chesters fort, but the most complete version was found in Malpas in Cheshire. Most of the soldiers would probably settle down in the *vicus* outside their forts and raise their families, perhaps engaging in some trade or other, which some enterprising soldiers began while still serving in the army, though this evidence derives from papyrus records, concerning the provinces of the east. At least one case is known of a soldier who was recruited in Pannonia, served in Britain, and after discharge went home to the Danube.

THE INVASION

The main sources of information about the course of the invasion and the first years of the Roman conquest derive from Dio. The historian Tacitus did cover the subject, but the relevant parts of his work have been lost, a great misfortune, since he wrote at the end of the first century, and was consequently writing about comparatively recent history – and he could check his facts with people who remembered the events. He also had the great advantage of inside knowledge about Britain, having married the daughter of Gnaeus Julius Agricola, who served as tribune in one of the legions of Britain during the rebellion of

Boudicca, subsequently commanded the XX legion as legate sometime later, and went on to become governor of the island from *c*.AD 77 to *c*.AD 84.

In the absence of Tacitus's account, historians have to rely on Cassius Dio, whose Roman history was written in the early third century. It is judged by many scholars to be fairly reliable, since Dio seems to have used equally reliable sources, including official records. Apart from the rhetoric that he invents, like all ancient authors, for the speeches delivered by his main characters, the events that he relates are probably not too far from the truth. Unfortunately, his wording does not always guarantee clarity, especially at a remove of nearly twenty centuries. For instance, when Dio says that Plautius invaded Britain in three waves, so as to avoid the potential opposition that a single force may have encountered, it is not certain whether he means that there were three successive sailings and landings in the same location, or whether there were three simultaneous landings at three different places. If there was only one location for disembarking, this was almost certainly at Richborough. From there, the Romans could access the Thames easily, and buildings of Claudian date have been detected on the site. Furthermore Richborough was later used as one of the main entry points to Britain, and a huge arch was built, foursquare, massive and designed to impress. If there were other landing places, only guesswork can tentatively identify them. Dover and Lympne have been suggested, and also possibly Fishbourne, because it lay in the friendly territory of the Atrebates. One day, archaeological finds may prove where the Roman forces landed and made their first camps.

The first possibility, of three waves landing in succession, implies that one third of the force would have to gain a foothold to allow the others to come up safely, and the alternative interpretation, of three different groups using separate landing places suggests that the whole army would have to join up somewhere, and run the risk of being defeated piecemeal before it had done so. In the end, though, none of this applied, because there were no Britons to fight. It was said that they did not believe that the Romans would arrive. Dio's Britons are not like Caesar's. They keep on being taken by surprise, though Dio does mention marshes and woods, which the Britons relied upon for their version of guerrilla warfare.

Plautius went to look for the Britons, and defeated the Catuvellaunian leaders, Caratacus and Togodumnus, separately. There is a frustrating lack of detail in Dio's laconic account, with no indication of where these battles were fought. As a result of these victories, Plautius received the submission of a tribe that Dio calls the Bodunni, usually (but not universally) taken to be the Dobunni, who had been subject to the Catuvellauni.

The next scene takes place at a river crossing, where the Britons camped on the opposite bank, secure in their conviction that the Romans would not be able to cross, but they had reckoned without the Celtic warriors among the army, who were trained to swim across such obstacles in full armour. Dio gives no tribal name or military unit for these so-called Celts, so it is tempting, if rash, to link them with the Batavian units who swam across the River Po near Placentia some years later, during the civil wars of AD 69, but it is not known if any such units were in Britain as early as AD 43.

The Britons were surprised by these aquatic warriors, whoever they were, and they were even more disturbed when the Celts used their arrows to bring down the horses of the chariots, removing the possibility of a quick getaway. Even so, the British warriors gave as good as they got, and Plautius sent over more troops under Titus Flavius Vespasianus and his brother Sabinus. The legionary commander Vespasianus became more familiarly known, twenty-seven years in the future, as the Emperor Vespasian.

The action broke off for the night, but it was not yet a victory, because the Britons attacked again next day, surrounding and nearly capturing an officer called Gnaeus Hosidius Geta, but under his direction the Romans rallied and drove the Britons off. Geta was awarded *ornamenta triumphalia*, the highest distinction for Roman officers, the insignia of a triumph for military exploits. In Republican times he would have been awarded a real triumph in Rome, to parade through the streets and dedicate the spoils of war to Jupiter in the temple on the Capitoline Hill. During the later Republic the state had been disrupted by generals whose successes in warfare, and concomitant command of soldiers who were loyal to them rather than to the government, had led some of them to make a bid for supremacy. Augustus himself had risen to power in this way, but in order to retain his position as head of state he could not allow any of his generals to rise too high, so he put a stop to any overt display of power. The triumph was the most overt display of all, and so it was restricted to immediate members of the Imperial family. In the place of an actual triumph, the *ornamenta triumphalia* conferred the supreme distinction on successful generals, without the pomp and ceremony or the potential for inflaming the populace.

After their defeat in this second battle, the Britons drew off to the Thames, which Dio actually names. The Britons, knowing their terrain, chose a place near the point where the river flows into the sea, where a lake was formed at high tide. It is suggested that this may have been at London. Once again the Celts crossed the river, and some troops used a bridge further upstream, which does not seem to have been defended. In the ensuing battle the Britons fled, but they knew their way across the marshes, and the pursuing Romans did not, so the Britons got away and the Romans were bogged down, with many losses. The subsequent fate of the Britons is unknown. Caratacus fled westwards, turning up sometime later as a leader of the Silures and Ordovices in Wales. For unexplained reasons, his brother Togodumnus died, or was killed. The Catuvellauni were now without a leader, and there is no information to suggest whether they appointed one. The Romans were poised for the final attack on the tribal headquarters at Camulodunum, modern Colchester. And at this point, Plautius called a halt. It was said that he had been instructed to send for Claudius if he met with difficulty, so that the Emperor could sweep into Britain and then be seen to be the fearless leader of the Roman army. It is more likely that he and Plautius had agreed that the Imperial household should be summoned when the fruit was ripe for picking, so to speak.

It is not known what Plautius did in the interval between calling a halt and the arrival of Claudius. Presumably he made camps, consolidated what he had gained so far, put out feelers to the other tribes to test their reactions, possibly forming alliances to be ratified by Claudius himself. As soon as the Emperor received the news, he placed his fellow consul Lucius Vitellius in command during his absence, and set out with all haste from Rome. He sailed down the Tiber to Ostia, took ship for Marseilles, crossed Gaul by land and water transport, and embarked for Britain. He had already made preparations for this part of the expedition. In order to impress the Britons, he had even assembled some elephants, which was perhaps not something that could be arranged on a whim at short notice.

Once he had joined the army, Claudius made straight for the Catuvellaunian capital, going for the jugular, as it were. The battle was a resounding success. Claudius was hailed by the troops as Imperator several times, a most unusual circumstance for a single short campaign. The spontaneous acclamation of the soldiers for a successful general had its roots in Republican times, and the Emperors zealously collected these honours, numbering them on inscriptions in abbreviated form, as IMP I or IMP II and so on. Claudius was already IMP III at the beginning of 43, and had collected another twelve salutations by 47 when Plautius was succeeded as governor by Ostorius Scapula. Claudius's final total was twenty-seven Imperial salutations, an unprecedented number, especially for a man who had little or no experience of military service until late in life.

A fortunate result of the Emperor's success in Britain was the voluntary submission of eleven tribes under their various rulers. This achievement was evidently very important to Claudius. According to the biographer Suetonius, the Emperor put on displays in the Campus Martius in Rome, recreating the storming of a town, with actors playing the parts of the British kings who submitted to the Emperor, in a Roman parallel to the drama-documentaries that are frequently broadcast to modern audiences on television. The event is also recorded on a fragmentary inscription found in Rome, from the triumphal arch that Claudius set up, probably dating to AD 51 or 52. The text specifically mentions REGES BRIT, and a fragment records the number XI, eleven

British kings. As one scholar famously remarked, it has never been more difficult to choose a British first eleven. Only a few of the tribes are identifiable. King Prasutagus of the Iceni, who were neighbours of the Catuvellauni in what was to become East Anglia, was no doubt one of these allied rulers, since the Iceni were described as such under the next governor, Ostorius Scapula. The Brigantes of the north, ruled by Queen Cartimandua, are also presumed to have made an alliance with the Romans. It is to be expected that the Atrebates were counted among the allies, though nothing is known of what happened to their ruler Verica, who had sought Claudius's help. Verica disappears from the record without trace, just as his probable successor Tiberius Claudius Togidubnus enters it, fully fledged with no known past history.

Togidubnus is the most famous of the allies who submitted to Claudius. His name is sometimes rendered as Togidumnus, or Togodumnus, or even Cogidubnus, or Cogidumnus, all of these versions being forms of the Latin construction of a British name, where the sounds for 'b' and 'm' were interchangeable. Connection with Caratacus's brother of similar name is unlikely and cannot be demonstrated. Togidubnus's full Romanised name indicates that Claudius had bestowed Roman citizenship on him, and in accordance with usual practice, Togidubnus took the names of the man who had enfranchised him. This was a signal honour for a British ruler so early in the conquest, but unfortunately we do not know the circumstances of the grant of citizenship, nor is it possible to say where Togidubnus had come from.

According to Tacitus, several *civitates*, states or tribes, were grouped together by the Romans and installed under the rule of Togidubnus, though it is not known which tribes were incorporated into his new kingdom. They were eventually merged to become a single tribe called the Regnenses, the people of the *Regnum* or kingdom of Togidubnus. Tacitus says that the king remained loyal to the Romans up to recent times that he himself could remember.

Togidubnus is named in full on an inscription found in the early eighteenth century at Chichester. The inscription is damaged, and for several years the text was interpreted as R[EX] LEG. AUG. IN

B[RITANNIA]. This would mean that Togidubnus was king and also a *legatus Augusti*, a legate of the Emperor in Britain. Cultivation of the elite was normal, but elevating them to such high rank and bestowing office on them was not. More recently, another much closer look at the stone and its damaged text has resulted in a more acceptable interpretation of Togidubnus as REX MAGNUS, or great king, which was a formula used for those client kings who allied with Rome and ruled over more than one area or tribe. This fits the bill much more easily, corroborated by Tacitus's statement that Togidubnus was ruler of several *civitates*. It has been suggested that Togidubnus was the occupant of the first buildings on the site of what would become the truly lavish palace at Fishbourne, though this remains a theory. Someone of tremendous importance obviously lived in this early villa, not yet a palace, but it is not certain whether this may have been a Roman official. In his rule over different tribes, whoever they were, Togidubnus perhaps used more than one centre, in the territory of each of his subject peoples. Presumably while he remained loyal to the Romans, so did the tribesmen, but this is not necessarily the case.

It is not known under what terms the British kings submitted to Claudius. There may not have been an entirely standard formula for all the tribes, but perhaps the arrangements were tailored to circumstances. There would be legal agreements about obligations to be observed, territorial boundaries to be established, all of which would probably be more favourable to the Romans than the natives. In theory, the Romans were the protectors of the tribes who had submitted. Modern historians refer to the rulers of such allied states as client kings.

CLIENT KINGS

'Client king' is a modern term invented by historians to describe the relationship between Rome and those rulers who had chosen to enter into the formal arrangement which recognised them as friends and allies of the Roman people. The precise formula was *rex sociusque et amicus*, king and ally and friend, each term outlining their status, king in their own territory, and an ally and friend of the Romans, which meant that they must have the same friends and enemies as the Romans, and could not ally with any other power unless the agreement was sanctioned by Rome. Client kings were not entirely free after coming to an arrangement with Rome.

There was some formality in granting client status to a king and his people, often accompanied by grand ceremonial after the Senate had decreed formal acceptance. The initiative for seeking such acceptance usually came from the ruler and his tribe or state, rather than through Roman compulsion. Cleopatra, for instance, was determined to achieve such recognition after the death of her father, Ptolemy Auletes, because it meant that she would receive Roman protection for herself and her regime, and by such means she could perhaps forestall Roman schemes for the outright annexation of Egypt, at least for her lifetime if not for her heirs.

Trading rights were probably an important part of most of the agreements made between allied rulers and the Romans, and in most cases the tribe or state was obliged to contribute troops for the army, or more precisely, in Republican times at least, they contributed troops to fight alongside the Roman army, rather than as part of it.

The arrangements which the Romans made with client kings were theoretically tailored to the mutual needs of Rome and the particular kingdom. In Rome itself, the term *clientes* was used to describe the adherents of the upper-class senators, whose social and political standing was judged in part by the number of clients who accompanied them into the Forum or to meetings. The *clientes* rendered services to the great man, and in return received his assistance and protection. They would turn up in the mornings at the house of their patron, perhaps report on previous activities, perhaps receive money, or instructions about particular tasks, or perhaps not be noticed at all. It was a mutually satisfying way of life for both parties. Theoretically that was how it was supposed to work for the kings and allies and friends of the Roman people. The scheme had at first been applied to the Italian states and kingdoms when Rome was steadily expanding her influence over the peninsula. When the Empire began to grow, the system was used for the kingdoms bordering Roman territory. The support of the Romans often shored up the rule of the king, or sometimes queen, in his or her own lands, and help could be summoned if necessary, especially if there was an external threat that was too strong for the ruler to resist. In return for this protection, the client king was expected to furnish men, money and supplies for the Roman army whenever they were demanded, usually but not always for campaigns conducted near the king's territory.

The client kings remained attached to the Roman government of the Republic and the Empire, but until their kingdoms were annexed, as they usually were, the population was not subject to taxation as the inhabitants of the provinces were. Sometimes, however, the demands for assistance for Rome's wars could become burdensome. The security of Rome was of paramount importance to the Senate during the Republic, and to the Emperors during the Empire, so intereference in the client king's affairs was taken for granted if there was disorder in the kingdom, or external threat. On slender evidence, it is postulated that there was probably a Roman official stationed within the client king's territory to keep an eye on social and political developments. There seems to have been such an official in Thrace before Claudius annexed it as a province, but this may not have been the norm for all client kingdoms. Nothing is known of such arrangements in Britain.

Acceptance as a friend and ally of the Roman people did not exclude a Roman presence of some kind within the territory of the king, although it was not necessarily a military presence. In the Danubian lands of king Maroboduus, who actively sought an alliance with Rome, there were resident Roman traders in the first century AD, who were given the right to conduct business in the kingdom by means of the treaty of alliance, which incorporated the legal right to trade, *ius commercii*. Even before the conquest, Roman traders probably gained a foothold in southern Britain. In some of the client kingdoms Roman troops may have been sent to protect the trading communities and also the ruler, all in the interests of Rome, of course, rather than for the security of the ruler himself, in case of external attack or internal revolt which might upset the neighbouring Roman provinces. It is suggested that there may have been some Roman soldiers in Britain before the invasion under Claudius, protecting the Catuvellaunian Cunobelinus. This king is not known to have been a client of Rome, but if the suggestion that troops were present is correct, it reveals how the Romans infiltrated areas outside their provinces, and they certainly would not hesitate to do so in the case of their allies.

Since the Romans were nearly always in the ascendancy, the interests of the client kings were sometimes overruled. In Britain, after quelling some disorder, the governor Ostorius Scapula decided to disarm the Britons who had been allowed to keep their arms after the initial conquest. This order embraced the Iceni, who had voluntarily entered into alliance with Rome, and his action caused justifiable resentment. Protests were quickly suppressed, but resentment remained under the surface, re-emerging to fuel the later rebellion under Boudicca.

Client kingship was not normally hereditary, so when a king died, even if there were heirs, the kingdom was often annexed. Where there were no heirs, the kingdom was at risk from attempted usurpation, so in the best interests of the populace, the king could bequeath his kingdom to Rome, in the hope that at least there would be internal peace and protection under Roman rule. King Attalus of Pergamum took this course during the Roman Republic. Much of his wealth was siphoned off to line Rome's coffers, but this may have been a better alternative than civil war or fragmentation of the kingdom as enemies encroached upon it. For the Iceni, this arrangement did not work so well. The king Prasutagus had no male heirs, so he tried to protect the kingdom by bequeathing half of it to the Emperor, but the result was appropriation of all his wealth and lands, and gross mistreatment of his wife Boudicca and their two daughters. Then in quick succession came the subsequent revolt, total defeat, and annexation.

Other client kings in Britain were more fortunate. Togidubnus, the ruler of several *civitates* in the south of Britain, was granted Roman citizenship and seems to have enjoyed a long life under Roman protection for himself and his people. There is no evidence that the privilege of citizenship was granted to Cartimandua, but she may have received gifts of money or goods. Gifts of money and sometimes food supplies often flowed from Rome into the territory of the client king, in part to enable the ruler to maintain his position, and to reward and stabilise his warriors. Roman goods are found in the north, especially at Stanwick, which was probably fortified when Cartimandua's husband Venutius rebelled, but Roman products are even more in evidence in the territories ruled by Togidubnus. For Cartimandua, military support for her regime may have been even more important than gifts with which to control her warriors. On more than one occasion, her political struggles with her husband were sorted out by Roman troops. This is interpreted as proof of an alliance with Rome, the terms of which obliged the governors to intervene and protect the queen. If there had been no such agreement, the governors could have chosen to ignore the discord, unless Brigantian warriors erupted into the province itself. In the end, the queen herself had to be rescued and physically removed into Roman protective custody. It was not entirely unusual for client kings to end their reigns in this way. The dissidents who expelled their ruler were usually suppressed, after which the kingdom would be annexed, though in the case of the Brigantes there was a slight hiatus before this occurred.

CLAUDIUS RETURNS TO ROME
Claudius was absent from Rome for six months, and spent only sixteen days in Britain, a lightning campaign if ever there was one. The Senate voted the title Britannicus to Claudius, awarded him a triumph, ratified all the arrangements that he had made with the tribes, and authorised the building of two triumphal arches, one in Gaul at the point of departure and one in Rome. The triumph was splendid, shows and displays were put on celebrating the conquest of the Britons, and coins celebrating Roman victories in Britain were issued in AD 46 and 49. Claudius did not jealously guard all the honours for himself, but was also quite lavish with rewards for his governors of Britain.

Before returning to Rome, Claudius disarmed the Britons, which directive probably concerned the Catuvellauni and their hangers-on, or those who had been the immediate enemy in the fighting. It was not applied universally to all tribes, since the next governor, Ostorius Scapula, made further demands for disarmament. The Claudian victory was not as complete as it was portrayed, since Caratacus had escaped, but he could not now return to the Catuvellauni, who were crushed. When Claudius left, overall command was handed back to Plautius:

> Claudius disarmed the Britons and handed them over to Plautius, authorising him to subjugate the remaining areas. (Dio 60.21)

This is the only hint as to Claudius's Imperial policy. Eventually Britain was made a province, but Tacitus says this only happened bit by bit, a process that seemed to be an ongoing development under the first two governors. After all, as Tacitus says, the Romans had merely conquered the part nearest to the Continent. This constituted, at best, a foothold rather than a province. There was still a lot to do, but it is not known how far Imperial policy intended to go, whether the Emperor Claudius considered drawing a line somewhere, retaining and administering only the parts that were profitable to the Romans, or whether he intended to conquer the whole island.

THE TERM *PROVINCIA* – TEXT BOX

The term *provincia* did not originally define a territory, but denoted a specific task allocated to a magistrate. With the acquisition of a growing empire and the consequent need for a regular supply of governors to administer the new lands, the word *provincia* began to be applied to a territory as well as to any other duty, thus acquiring the territorial sense in which the word is used today. The *provinciae* or individual tasks could be quite flexible, routine or novel, short- or long-term, and could involve such things as repairing roads, managing the forests, attending to the grain supply, or any other assignment that the

Senate decided upon, some of which could have military duties attached, and some of which were administrative. In the early and middle years of the Republic the serving magistrates took up their *provinciae* whilst in their year of office. The consuls and sometimes the praetors commanded the armies if there was a war, and in times of peace all magistrates attended to the tasks they had been allocated. Later on, when the increase in administrative duties necessitated the employment of more personnel, the promagistracy was established, which conferred on the magistrate the relevant powers of a consul or a praetor, without the necessity of actually holding the administrative post of consul or praetor. It became more normal for magistrates to attend to duties in Rome whilst in office, and then take up the various *provinciae* at the end of the year, when they became proconsuls and propraetors. The Senate decided on the tasks that were necessary, and also which were to be given to praetors and which to consuls. By various means, mostly bribery, certain politicians could insinuate themselves into lucrative or prestigious *provinciae*, and to counteract this development the tribune Gaius Sempronius Gracchus passed a law in 123 BC to ensure that the Senate decided upon which *provinciae* were to be allocated to the consuls before the elections were held, which was intended to remove the scramble for lucrative appointments that might yield sufficient profit to pay the debts incurred in election campaigns. This did not always work. When Julius Caesar made it clear that he intended to stand for election as consul for 59 BC, the Senate tried to block his rise to power by allocating the mundane duty of caring for the woodlands and paths as the *provinciae* for the retiring consuls of that year – the last thing that anti-Caesarians wanted was Julius Caesar in a *provincia* that gave him a territory and command of troops. The ploy failed miserably. Caesar's consular colleague Calpurnius Bibulus was no match for him in popularity, audacity, or ruthlessness, and instead of labelling the year as the consulship of Caesar and Bibulus, the people of Rome dubbed the year 59 BC as the consulship of Julius and Caesar. It was with little difficulty that Caesar changed the allocation of the *provinciae* for 58 BC and arranged that he should be allocated Gaul as a territorial province, with himself as proconsul in command of several legions. He held this post for the next ten years.

The Romans did not attempt to impose a rigid uniformity in the government of the provinces, but varied their approach according to local circumstances. When territory was annexed after military conquest, there was much work to do in organising the province, establishing the legal framework and the taxation system (which was often based on existing arrangements), drawing up the constitutions of the various towns and cities, and fixing the boundaries. This work was summed up in the *Lex Provinciae*, which was ratified at Rome by the Senate and the people, and formed the basis of government of the province from then onwards. Unfortunately there is no evidence from Britain to suggest that this formal procedure was adopted when the province was created.

Since it is not known how much territory Claudius, or even his successors, intended to take in at first, some scholars have argued that the road known as the Fosse Way, established some short time after the conquest, was a frontier, marking the point where the Roman advance was to cease, even if only temporarily. This road runs from the south-west to the north-east, linking the coast of Devon to Leicester and Lincoln, and then beyond to the Humber, and at first sight it looks similar to the boundaries that were established much later in Germany and eventually in Britain itself when Hadrian's Wall was built. This interpretation was based on the assumption that the road was laid out with deliberate intent, all at once, with forts strung along it for the protection of what lay behind the road. More recent examination has shown that this was not the case. It is more probable that different parts of the route were established at different times, and as more forts and military posts have been discovered lying behind the route, and also in advance of the road, it is clear that it does not qualify for the description of frontier, either as a linear barrier or a wide frontier zone, which is in any case an anachronistic concept for the early Empire. It is perhaps unlikely that Claudius had any intention of calling a halt, preferring to leave his options open, so that he and his governors could deal with situations as they arose.

EXPANSION AFTER CLAUDIUS'S VISIT

The ensuing campaigns in Britain while Plautius was still in command cannot be reconstructed in detail. The whereabouts of the legions can be suggested by extrapolating backwards from the points where they created their first, more permanent legionary fortresses, and sometimes it is possible to suggest their intermediate stopping points from the remains of camps, but the overall picture is considered to be much more fluid and complicated than the archaeology is able to illustrate. The legions would not move everywhere as complete bodies, but troops would be split up and used as detachments, called vexillations, or in even smaller groups, perhaps in combinations with other parts of legions or auxiliary units, to guard the previously conquered territory, to protect routes and convoys, to find and transport supplies, to build camps and temporary forts, to explore new terrain and gather intelligence. Sometimes legionaries and auxiliary soldiers would be camped together, and then moved on, perhaps in different combinations.

The most detailed information, still sparse at that, concerns the exploits of the future Emperor Vespasian. The biographer Suetonius credits him with thirty battles, the conquest of twenty towns (*oppida*) and two tribes. Unfortunately it is not stated which tribes or which towns were concerned. The one fixed point is that Vespasian conquered the Isle of Wight, specifically named by Suetonius, so it is assumed that the main areas of Vespasian's operations were in the south-west, and extrapolating from this it is conjectured that the Dumnonii and the Durotriges were the tribes that he conquered, but this is not corroborated in any of the ancient sources. The supposition is based on the geographical location of these tribes and the probable direction of Vespasian's campaign, and though it is a feasible conclusion it remains an informed guess. Vespasian's legion, II Augusta, eventually arrived at Exeter as its longer-term base, but archaeological evidence suggests that this base was not established until *c.*55. By then Vespasian had long since returned to Rome and been appointed to the consulship. If he was not responsible for actually placing the legion at Exeter, Vespasian perhaps moved towards the area, and his troops are probably the ones who besieged and stormed the hill fort at Maiden Castle in Dorset, and built Roman forts in the British strongholds of Hod Hill (also in Dorset) and Ham Hill in Somerset.

Before Plautius was recalled, the other legions advanced further into Britain. IX Hispana struck out northwards, leaving traces of temporary camps in its wake, but none of these sites are securely dated, and need not indicate a steady progress to its eventual fortress at Lincoln, which was founded, like Exeter, *c.*55. The camp at Longthorpe is the most famous of the stopping points which might belong to IX Hispana, but it is only large enough to accommodate half of the legion. Other smaller camps may have held vexillations, since the legions did not always keep together, marching as one body. Moving towards the north-west, XIV Gemina may have been camped at Leicester, and is attested at Wroxeter by a couple of undated tombstones of legionaries who had served in this legion. These tombstones may be of a relatively early date, since the legion is not listed with its Martia Victrix title, which was awarded after the rebellion of Boudicca, but the absence of such titles may simply mean that the sculptor omitted them. It does not provide definite proof of dating.

The XX legion, or part of it, was at Colchester for a few years, where its role in keeping the peace and controlling the natives would be of prime importance at this early stage in the conquest. It is not certain precisely where the fort for the XX legion was located. On the site of the British settlement at Colchester, probably on the spot where Cunobelinus had placed his own dwellings, a Roman fort has been found, but it may not be the earliest on the site. Since it is not securely dated it could just as well belong to the period after the revolt of Boudicca in 60. However, it would make an unequivocal statement to build a fort directly over the place where the king of the Catuvellauni had held court, so on balance this is perhaps the first thing the Romans built, and maybe some of the XX legion occupied it for a while.

The So-called Temple of Claudius and the Imperial Cult

Underlining the supremacy of Rome and the Emperor, a great temple was founded in the town of Colchester. It would be a constant reminder of the conquest and subjugation of the Catuvellauni and the other tribes who were defeated with them, but whether the temple was actually dedicated to the divine Claudius during his lifetime, as is often supposed, remains unclear. Some scholars have argued that it could not have been built and dedicated to him while he still lived, because it was not customary in Rome to represent the Emperors as living gods, and in Claudius's case it would have been contrary to his stated wishes. He refused the honour when some provincials tried to dedicate places of worship to him. Others reply that in the provinces, representation of the Emperor as a living god was not frowned upon. Nevertheless, a very large Roman temple eventually appeared in the centre of Colchester, some short time after the invasion, and its podium is preserved as the foundation for William the Conqueror's equally massive castle.

It is possible that the temple was dedicated to Claudius after his death in 54, though some scholars argue that even in 60 the temple was not finished and had perhaps not been dedicated at all. However, worship of the Emperors after death, when they had become divine by means of a decree of the Senate, was perfectly acceptable to Romans in Rome and in the provinces. After Augustus was deified, it became normal practice to deify the Emperors when they died. Only a handful of Emperors were not deified, such as Nero and Domitian, who had not endeared themselves to the Senate, nor indeed to many other groups of society. Other Emperors went to their deaths in full expectation of being deified. When the Emperor Vespasian was dying, he retained his sense of humour to the very end. 'Oh dear,' he said, 'I seem to be turning into a god.'

The Imperial cult is distinct from the worship of deceased and deified Emperors. The cult was established in the provinces during the reign of Augustus. While the worship of an individual while still living was not a Roman custom, it had long been common enough in the provinces of the east, where the god-king was a well-established tradition. The Greeks were eager to render divine honours to the Roman general Quinctius Flamininus in 191 BC, after he had defeated their enemies and declared the Greeks to be free. The first Roman to be deified was Julius Caesar, in 42 BC, two years after his assassination. A convenient comet appeared in the sky at the time, which his great-nephew Octavian exploited to the full, as a sign that Caesar had indeed been taken up into the heavens and become a god. It was convenient for Octavian, as the heir of Caesar, to declare himself the son of a god, the closest he came to actual divinity in his lifetime. Caesar himself had claimed descent from the goddess Venus, but this was veiled in the mysteries of the remote past, whereas Octavian could claim a much closer relationship to a deity. When he was declared Augustus by the Senate, there were plenty of people in the Empire who were willing to worship him, but he would not allow it. As a compromise he sanctioned worship of his *genius*, or spirit, combined with worship of Rome itself in the guise of the goddess Roma. The Romans believed that people and places had a spirit, and sometimes dedicated altars to the *genius loci* or spirit of the place. From there, it was a short step to assimilating local gods, whose worship was not usually suppressed anywhere in the Roman Empire, unless it represented a threat to state security.

As a means of unification and of generating loyalty, the worship of Rome and Augustus was sanctioned throughout the Empire. In 12 BC in Lyon (Lugdunum) an altar was set up at the confluence of the rivers Rhone and Saone. The Council of the Three Gauls would meet there every year, to renew their oath of loyalty to Rome. The army also observed the cult, each individual unit swearing their loyalty in what was probably an annual ceremony.

A college of priests served the cult, called *seviri Augustales*, the majority of whom were freedmen, though the most famous example from Britain is the Roman citizen Marcus Aurelius Lunaris, who may have been a merchant, perhaps dealing in wines. He set up an altar in Boulogne in 237, declaring himself a *sevir* of the colonies of Lincoln and York. His family had probably been enfranchised in 212 when the Emperor Caracalla declared all freeborn people citizens of Rome. It was said that the Emperor's ulterior motive was to make everyone liable to pay the taxes that were levied from citizens. It may also be Caracalla who elevated the civil town at York to colonial status, since it was described as a *municipium*, or a town of lower status, when his father, the Emperor Severus, died there in 211.

The appointment as *sevir Augustalis* was an honourable one, but it was probably expensive. Tacitus says that the priests who had been chosen to officiate in the Imperial cult in Britain, just after the conquest, had to disburse large sums from their own fortunes to administer the proceedings, but in the early days there were perhaps very few of them, so the expenses would fall on only a small number of men. There was no Imperial compulsion to adopt the worship of the Emperor, so the altars that were set up in the provinces were presumably a result of local zeal, and the priests were local men who adopted the practice. The ritual centred round an altar, not necessarily accompanied by a temple building. At Lyon there was no temple. In Britain, it is likely that the altar in the courtyard of the so-called temple of Claudius in Colchester was the focal point of the Imperial cult, worshipping Rome and Augustus. By this time Augustus was a title, signifying the ruling Emperor, not the original Augustus.

The establishment of the Imperial cult in Colchester, no matter to whom the temple was dedicated, would have been particularly galling for the Britons, especially for those who had submitted voluntarily and then found out that the Roman peace actually entailed exploitation and abuse. Those men who participated in the cult would probably have been immediate targets for the rebels under Boudicca. Perhaps if the Britons had been dealt with more leniently and given time to adapt, they would have adopted Emperor-worship readily enough, but as it was, the focal point of the cult was assiduously destroyed along with the rest of the town in AD 60.

CAMPAIGNS IN WALES: OSTORIUS SCAPULA AD 47 TO 52

The state of play in Britain when Aulus Plautius returned to Rome to receive high honours from Claudius is not known. He probably left in the late autumn of AD 47, perhaps remaining in the province to hand over in person to Publius Ostorius Scapula, who arrived just before winter. The only source for this is Tacitus, so the chronology depends on his work, though for one short period he admits that he has conflated the events under two governors for ease of description. The first task for Ostorius was to contain the eruption of hostile tribes into the territories of those who were allied to Rome, but it is not certain which tribes were involved. The restive Britons allegedly thought that the new governor, who did not know the troops or the terrain, would probably not retaliate, especially as winter was setting in, but he did so, using the auxiliary troops, or the light-armed soldiers as Tacitus calls them.

All may have been well if the Roman action had ended there, with the identification and punishment of the ring-leaders, but Ostorius decided to pre-empt further trouble by disarming the tribes he suspected of hostility. Among them were the Iceni, who had voluntarily become allies of Rome. Finding now that Roman promises were like pie crusts, easily broken, the Iceni justifiably resented this treatment, and raised revolt, influencing their neighbours to do likewise. The Britons prepared a fortified place, surrounded by a rampart of earth, with a very narrow entrance to prevent access by the Roman cavalry. Undeterred, Ostorius attacked, ordering his cavalry to dismount and fight on foot. The subsequent defeat of the rebels quietened the other tribes, at least for the time being. Ostorius then turned his attention to Wales, attacking a tribe labelled by Tacitus as the Decangi – perhaps an error in later copies of his work, and usually taken to mean the Deceangli. Then there was some disturbance among the Brigantes of the north, which seems to have been dealt with rapidly, and peace was restored.

After this, according to Tacitus, Ostorius prepared for a campaign against the Silures of south Wales. He brought the XX legion out of Colchester, and put in its place a colony of veteran soldiers. These may have been taken from more than one legion. The Romans had planted colonies of soldier-settlers in Italy during the early Republic as a method of finding lands for time-served veterans and also employing them for the protection and control of newly won terrain, so this early colony in Roman Britain followed this pattern. According to Tacitus's timescale the colony was established in 49.

The campaign against the Silures was a difficult one. Tacitus says that a legionary base was required to keep them in order, which may mean that the XX legion from Colchester was placed in the legionary fortress at Kingsholm, near Gloucester. This site was not occupied for long. Some scholars have argued that it was founded in 48, others that it belongs to the year 49. Perhaps as early as 55 the legion moved on to the fortress at Usk, but even though it is possible to supply approximate foundation dates for the fortress sites, it is not certain which legions or parts of legions occupied them.

During Ostorius's campaign in south Wales, the Catuvellaunian king Caratacus emerged once again, as leader if not ruler of the Silures, who placed their trust in him. But he was defeated, and moved on to rally another tribe, the Ordovices in central Wales. His final battle was at a fortified site, with steep slopes on most sides. Where the ground was flatter the Britons built ramparts. There was also the added defence of a river, which may have been the Severn. In crossing this river, Scapula's soldiers suffered casualties, and while they approached the British fortifications, they were at the mercy of the missiles thrown by the Britons inside. But then they locked their shields, forming the *testudo* or tortoise with shields over their heads and at their sides, and thus protected they were able to storm the camp. Once again Caratacus was forced to run for his life, this time leaving his wife and his daughter to be captured by the Romans. He went north, to the Brigantes.

This tribe had allied with Rome on a voluntary basis, like the Iceni. By doing so, the Brigantes secured for themselves a peaceful interlude while the Romans left them alone, and though the tribal elders may have been able to foresee that this independence might one day come to an end, it was best not to provoke the Romans by harbouring a fugitive. Queen Cartimandua decided to hand over Caratacus to her allies, the Romans, an act which may be construed as treachery of the basest sort, or political common sense, depending on one's point of view. Britain was not a united country at the time, and the tribes remained very distinct from each other, concerned with their own affairs. They protected their own boundaries, and though they were usually quite ready to profit by seizing lands belonging to others, they were not always ready to throw in their lot with a disadvantaged tribe, and thereby risk the loss of what they had gained. Cartimandua was presented with a moral dilemma. There were no Romans thundering down on her borders at the moment, but if she helped Caratacus in any way, by sheltering him or giving him access to her warriors, some of whom were probably champing at the bit to go and fight the Romans, there would soon be legions not only arriving on her doorstep but breaking and entering. Caratacus may have been a brilliant and inspiring warrior leader, but his track record so far was not representative of his supposed skills. He had run away after his defeat at Colchester, and then he had joined the Silures, where he was defeated again, fled to the Ordovices, ditto, and now he wanted to rouse the Brigantes. More than likely he would bring defeat and disaster down on them too, probably while he himself fled once more to another tribe. It probably did not take Cartimandua more than a day or two to come to her decision.

Caratacus was taken prisoner and despatched to the Emperor Claudius in Rome. Tacitus devotes considerable verbiage to the spectacle of the British ruler in the capital city. He invents noble speeches for him, or perhaps in this case he adapts memories of the speeches that really were made. There is no doubt that Caratacus made an impression on the Romans. Unlike other prisoners, the Gallic leader Vercingetorix for instance, who spent six years in prison and was then executed after appearing in Caesar's triumph, Caratacus was spared. He was allowed to live freely in Rome, in a sort of gilded cage for his retirement.

Back in Britain, Ostorius Scapula found that the Silures of south Wales were far from beaten. They used guerrilla tactics against the Romans, descending on a party of legionaries when they were building a camp, and killing the camp prefect, eight centurions and many soldiers. Then they attacked a foraging party and put up a stiff fight when Ostorius came to the rescue with some auxiliary troops. He was forced to send in his legionaries, and then the tables were turned. This battle was won but the war was destined to go on interminably. The Silures had heard that Ostorius was determined to exterminate them, and so they had nothing to lose by fighting him. Spurred on by the determination of the Silures to keep on fighting, and exasperated by the insensitive treatment meted out by the Romans, other tribes were also becoming restless. Then in 52, before he could conclude his campaigns, Ostorius died, totally worn out according to Tacitus. It is unlikely that sympathetic gestures were made by the Silures.

TROUBLE IN THE NORTH: AULUS DIDIUS GALLUS AD 52 TO 57

There was a hiatus while the province was without a governor. Claudius lost no time in choosing and sending out a fresh governor, Aulus Didius Gallus, but the time taken to deliver a message from Britain, and for the new governor to travel to the province inevitably entailed considerable delay. In the meantime, a legion commanded by Manlius Valens suffered a severe defeat. It is not known where or when this occurred. Shortly afterwards there was trouble once again in the north with the warlike elements of the Brigantes, involving an internal squabble between Cartimandua and her husband Venutius. Some auxiliary troops were sent to restore order, followed by a legion, probably the IX Hispana under its commander Caesius Nasica.

Tacitus had little or no regard for Didius Gallus, and says that the difficulties that he encountered were exaggerated, so that the victories would seem correspondingly great. He accuses Didius, who was getting on in years, of letting his subordinates do the work for him and sitting back, content to keep the Britons at arm's length. This means he made no efforts to extend Roman rule into new territories, which was always the mark of a keen general for the Romans, who thought of the Empire as without end, in both the territorial and temporal sense. Probably all that really happened under Didius was consolidation, and pacification of the tribes who had been defeated, by diplomatic means combined with demonstrations of strength where necessary. Didius had been successful as governor of Moesia on the Danube, where pacification and stabilisation were the order of the day, though he committed his troops to battle readily enough when it was necessary, and he was rewarded by Claudius. In Britain, he may have moved the legions into positions where they could keep a watch on the Welsh tribes, the XX legion to Usk, XIV Gemina to Wroxeter, and II Augusta to Gloucester. Rather than make a spectacular advance himself, he may have prepared the way for his successors.

Some scholars have seen this period as the context for the statement in Suetonius's biography of Nero that at one time the Emperor considered giving up the province of Britain. Suetonius does not supply dates or any other details, but if it is a true story, Nero may have been influenced by the fact that there was no forward movement, and it was still costing lives and precious time just to keep hold of the areas that had already been gained. The accusation against Nero may have been true, but it is worth bearing in mind that Suetonius wrote his Imperial biographies under the Emperor Hadrian, and at some point during the work, he and the Emperor seriously fell out with each other. Nero had such a bad reputation that any story told against him would probably be believed, and there was no danger of being accused of defamation of character. The wording of his accusation against Nero is perhaps significant:

> He [Nero] was never moved by any desire or hope of increasing the Empire. He even considered withdrawing from Britain, and only refrained from doing so out of deference, so that he would not appear to belittle his father's glory [meaning Claudius and the original conquest]. (Suetonius *Nero* 18)

It did not really matter if Suetonius claimed that Britain was nearly lost due to an Imperial decision some seventy years earlier, because it had patently remained Roman. What did matter, when Suetonius was writing, was what Hadrian had done. He had reversed the policy of Imperial expansion and had started to enclose the Empire within fixed boundaries. What was even more shocking was that he had deliberately given up territory that had been conquered by his glorious predecessor Trajan, known as *Optimus Princeps*, the best ruler. Trajan was technically Hadrian's 'father', just as Claudius, the conqueror of Britain, was Nero's 'father', whose glory he was unwilling to diminish. The parallel is striking. Lack of expansion always rankled with the Romans, military commanders and merchants alike, who saw potential glory and profit disappearing down the drain. Hadrian therefore, by implication, was worse than Nero. Perhaps this was merely Suetonius's scarcely veiled revenge on Hadrian, reviling him by proxy.

THE BRITONS BECOME PROVINCIALS

There is very little evidence to elucidate Imperial plans for Britain. Writing nearly six decades after the conquest, Tacitus says that under the first two governors, the part of Britain nearest the Continent was made into a province. All that can be said is that the new province comprised an unknown extent of territory, and that other areas were added to it as further advances were made.

During the Republic, when a province was added to the Empire, a formal arrangement was drawn up, embodied in the *Lex Provinciae*, the law of the province. While there were certain standard requirements applicable to all provinces, this law was usually designed to encompass the individual customs and circumstances of the province and the mutual obligations of the provincials and the Romans. There is no evidence to prove whether or not this happened in Britain. The new province of Britannia, whenever and however it was formed, was an Imperial one, as opposed to a senatorial province. This distinction dates from the reign of Augustus, when he attended a meeting of the Senate, ostensibly to hand back government of the Empire to the senators, and was promptly rewarded with numerous honours and, conveniently, the control of the provinces containing armies. From then on, the provinces were governed either by the Emperor via his legates, or directly by the Senate. In certain circumstances, provinces could be reassigned, senatorial ones being taken under the Emperor's wing, or Imperial ones being sufficiently pacified to have troops withdrawn and to be reallocated to the Senate.

As government of the provinces evolved, a career structure (*cursus honorum*) for senators was established, based on Republican custom which was adapted to meet new circumstances. Before they held any of the important magistracies, aspiring young men of the senatorial class usually gained experience in minor administrative offices, and most but not all of them usually served in a legion as the senior tribune, called *tribunus laticlavius*, or broad stripe tribune, which distinguished them from the other five military tribunes, *tribuni angusticlavii*, who were drawn from the equestrian class, ranking next in line after the senatorial class. After gaining this military and administrative experience, the next post was usually as quaestor. From the late Republic, by decree of the Dictator Lucius Cornelius Sulla, the office of quaestor automatically conferred entry to the Senate. In the early Empire there were twenty quaestors, elected annually, which provided twenty new senators each year. The quaestors were responsible for various tasks, often dealing with finance, either in Rome, or as financial assistant to a governor of a senatorial province. After another five years, when they could hold further offices such as tribune of the plebs, aspiring senators could become one of the twelve annually appointed praetors, which opened up several further senior posts, including command of a legion, or government of a province. The supreme office, attainable only in a senator's more mature years, was the consulship. There were always two consuls, elected each year, eligible to command armies and responsible for all aspects of government, and during the Republic they were answerable to the Senate alone. During the Empire, consuls were recommended by the Emperor, and in reality, though the Senate's functions were retained, and elections were still held, the consuls were answerable to the Emperor.

Under the Imperial system, in general, the unarmed provinces were governed by senators who were sent out for one year, with the title of proconsul, assisted by one of the quaestors to administer financial affairs. The governors of Imperial provinces commanded troops, but since all the Imperial provinces were technically governed by the Emperor himself, the governors acted as deputies, or legates, of the Emperor. Their titles were listed on inscriptions in abbreviated form as LEG. AUG. PR. PR., standing for the full title *legatus Augusti pro praetore*, indicated that they acted on behalf of the Emperor, as legates with praetorian rank. Although the governors of provinces with more than one legion were usually ex-consuls, who outranked the praetors, they still governed *pro praetore*. The governors of Roman Britain were usually the most senior men of their day, only equalled by the governors of Syria, the province bordering the Parthian Empire. Usually these governors had some experience of commanding troops, as *tribunus laticlavius* as young men, and then after further appointments in civilian posts, as legionary legate. They had often governed other provinces, sometimes fighting in various wars, before they arrived in Britain.

The governors of the Imperial provinces were not assisted by quaestors to look after finances. Instead a procurator was appointed, from the equestrian class, assisted by a staff of freedmen. The main tasks for the procurators of Britain were to collect taxes, and distribute pay to the troops. There was sometimes a conflict of interests in this system, since the procurator was answerable directly to the Emperor, so he could go above the governor's head, but he was presumably limited to those matters that had a bearing on finances. Not many of the procurators who served in Britain are known. The two men who were appointed before and after the rebellion of Boudicca are respectively the most infamous, and the most famous, of the handful of procurators who are attested. They were diametrically opposed in attitude, actions and reputation. The villain of the piece is Decianus Catus, whose rapacity was one of the immediate causes of the rebellion, and the hero is Julius Classicianus, who tried to make reparation for abuses that had triggered the rebellion, urging the recall of the allegedly vengeful governor, Suetonius Paullinus.

Roman society was hierarchical. Wealth was the most important attribute for any class of society, and there were rules about status. No one could become a senator without a demonstrable fortune of 1 million *sestertii*. The qualification for the middle classes of Rome, the equites or equestrians, was set at 400,000 *sestertii*. Upward mobility was not impossible, and became more common as time went on, but in all cases of advancement, aspiring equestrians and senators really needed to be noticed by the Emperor. There was tremendous snobbery among the Romans all over the Empire. When Claudius enfranchised the Gauls, making it possible for the wealthy elite groups to become senators, not many of them did so, and the attitude of the Romans to newly enfranchised provincials who became senators is epitomised by a snide remark circulated in Rome, that no one would show the new senators the way to the Senate House. Provincials did eventually penetrate into the higher ranks of Roman life, especially those from the eastern cities, where Greek culture had been established long before Romans arrived on the scene. It was the spread of Roman citizenship that enabled men from the provinces to rise high. Without it, there was no access to the senior government appointments or military commands. Many administrative posts were open to freedmen, some of whom were even wealthier than senators, but no matter how much wealth they had accumulated, in the early Empire ex-slaves could never be regarded as the equals of the equestrians or senators.

In the western provinces, where town life as the Greeks and Romans knew it had not developed, various different tribes pursued their own particular way of life, squabbled over boundaries, sometimes allying with each other and sometimes making war on each other. Their culture and religion was not necessarily primitive, and their customs were not necessarily always obliterated by the Romans, provided that the Romans could establish and maintain control. One of the customary methods of doing so in such a province was the cultivation of the local elite, in a similar fashion to the way in which the client kings were treated, but these client kings were usually situated on the borders of the province. Within the province, the most promising local rulers or families were encouraged to co-operate with the Romans. If this was successful, when the time came to devolve responsibility for local government onto the local populace, the elite groups could step in as leaders of the community.

One of the most wide-ranging and deeply felt effects of the Roman occupation would be the immediate obliteration of tribal ambitions for territorial conquest and annexation. From now onwards, that was the prerogative of the Romans. Internal strife and external boundary disputes were policed by the Romans, so any autonomy that the Britons may have hoped to retain in these respects was annihilated. They lived where the Romans said they should live, obeying new rules, and they would keep the peace with each other, or else! For most of the Britons, who were not among the favoured elite, this so-called *Pax Romana* just after the conquest did not bring peace and prosperity. The natives of a province, non-Romans, were lumped together under the heading of *peregrini*, which strictly means foreigners, somewhat galling for people living in their own land. For the first years, the Britons were under military rule as the occupation proceeded, and for many tribesmen exploitation and abuse were the only things they received from the Roman soldiers, sometimes with the connivance of the administrators.

Just as the Britons belonged to different tribes, the Romans were also ethnically diverse. The soldiers of the legions, with Roman names and citizenship, came from Italy, Gaul and Germany, and many of the auxiliary soldiers had a tribal background not unlike the Britons themselves. The administrators, and especially the traders, probably hailed from all over the Empire, perhaps speaking Greek or other languages, and using Latin for official business, and buying and selling. But however culturally diverse the occupying forces were, what united them was the concept of *Romanitas*, in which the Britons did not share. The Britons were a conquered people, and could be treated as subhuman. Tacitus records how arrogant veterans forced the British farmers off their lands, abusing them in several other ways.

It would be some time before the Romans realised that the initial treatment of the Britons was not the way to win hearts and minds; in fact it was counter-productive. The tribes who were being exploited would eventually rebel, and the tribes who were as yet unconquered would hear of the effects of Roman rule and resist more vigorously because there was nothing to lose. The way forward was to integrate, to find ways for the Romans to work with those Britons who were willing to compromise, and for the Britons to become not just allies of Rome, but to become Romans themselves. In this way, the foundations were eventually laid for the process of integration, but total Romanisation was never uniformly developed across the whole island.

THE CONQUEST OF WALES: QUINTUS VERANIUS AND SUETONIUS PAULLINUS AD 57 TO 60

The province was reasonably peaceful when Didius Gallus was replaced by Quintus Veranius, who had been consul in 49, and had been governor of Lycia. He started by ravaging the territory of the Silures once again, perhaps without provocation. Then he died. In his will he said that he could have conquered the province in two years. Perhaps he did not mean the whole island, but it was a boast that Tacitus, who had heard about the British campaigns of his father-in-law Agricola and his predecessors, would have found amusing.

The next governor was Suetonius Paullinus, a veteran of campaigns in the Atlas mountains in Mauretania. He was said to have been the first to cross the Atlas range, so by the time he arrived in Britain he had already earned a sound military reputation. According to Dio he was an ex-praetor when he commanded in Mauretania, so at some time after this, perhaps as a reward for his exploits, he was presumably appointed to the consulship. The date is not known, but if he was suffect consul instead of *consul ordinarius* his name would not be recorded as one of the consuls of the year. Nothing is known of his whereabouts or his appointments until he arrived in Britain, probably in 58.

Tacitus says that Suetonius had two successful years as governor of Britain, but there are no firm details as to where he operated. Wales is the most likely venue, especially as the Roman troops reached the island of Anglesey at the latter end of these two years. The fact that Suetonius Paullinus was experienced in mountain warfare, and his troops went on to campaign in north Wales, suggests that there was some element of forward planning in his appointment, as opposed to a rapid and convenient choice of any qualified candidate to replace the governor who had unexpectedly died in the middle of a campaign. It may simply be coincidence, but if the Emperor Nero had taken advice about the next most likely theatre of action in Britain, it is possible that the name of the man who had already campaigned successfully in mountainous territory would spring to mind.

It is customary to view this campaign into north Wales and Anglesey as an effort to eradicate the Druids, whose headquarters were located in the island, but it can also be regarded as a means of rounding off the conquest of Wales. To leave the island unconquered would be a threat to security, and Tacitus says that many fugitives gathered there. There were certainly Druids as well, but the campaign may not have been mounted with specific reference to them.

If Suetonius himself did not leave reports or memoirs about this episode, Tacitus was in a fortunate position as the son-in-law of Gnaeus Julius Agricola, who was *tribunus laticlavius* at this time, but the legion to which Agricola was appointed is not known. Tacitus explains that Agricola was selected to assist Suetonius on his staff, which may mean that he was attached to headquarters, but this is perhaps to read too much into the statement. The graphic description of the Britons awaiting the Romans on the shore of Anglesey may be a fanciful reconstruction on Tacitus's part, but it sounds as though it comes from personal memory, something that impressed the young Agricola.

The water separating Anglesey from the mainland was shallow, and the sands shifted with the tides, so the Roman infantry troops were ferried across the straits in flat-bottomed boats, while the cavalry waded or swam across next to their horses. The British warriors were encouraged by the Druids, earnestly praying to their gods and cursing the Romans. There were some women there as well, swathed in black clothes and waving torches. Momentarily stalled, the Romans were urged on by Suetonius, and managed to repulse the Britons. A few lines in Tacitus's account describe the savagery of their fighting. Everyone was cut down, warriors, women and Druids alike, and the religious sanctuaries among the groves of trees were torn up and burned. Then a garrison was installed; both Tacitus and Dio agree that the campaign was properly finished. It must have been a triumphant moment for Suetonius. That is, until a messenger or messengers arrived with the news that the south was in uproar. The British tribes had combined, and they were killing and burning and destroying towns, led by a woman.

3

Rebellion & Reconstruction AD 60 to 69

REBELLION

The rebellion of Boudicca and its suppression occupied at most several months, in reality a very short period in the history of Roman Britain, but one that has attracted a disproportionate amount of interest. It is a tale worthy of playwrights and novelists, for its epic tragic qualities, with two protagonists both fighting in desperate circumstances. The fact that one of them was a woman only intensifies the interest. It has been suggested that the role of Boudicca has been over-emphasised by the Roman authors, in order to discredit the Emperor Nero, an idea to which Tacitus may have subscribed, but which is the more readily apparent in the account written by Dio, who invents a speech for Boudicca, or Boudouika as he names her in Greek. Haranguing her troops before leading them to destroy the hated Roman towns, she reviles the Emperor, who has the title of a man but is really more like a woman, painting his face, and spending his time singing and playing the lyre. After nearly two centuries, historians such as Dio could still make good copy out of reviling Nero. This speech that Dio invents serves to present his own views, just as other ancient authors put words into the mouths of their heroes and villains, to expound the opposing points of view, and also to provide a sort of plot exposition to explain how the events had begun. The Britons would have been well aware of Nero, but it stretches credulity somewhat when, according to Dio, Boudicca compares and contrasts herself with other women, Nicotris ruler of Egypt, and Semiramis of Assyria – 'these things we learned from the Romans' she adds, as though Dio himself wished to pre-empt the question of how did a British queen know of these things.

Even if Boudicca was merely a figurehead, and the British tribes were led by some unnamed warriors, the story is too deeply embedded in the national heritage to eradicate the Queen of the Iceni as the overall commander of the rebels. She ranks with Cleopatra and Zenobia as the most powerful female enemies of Rome. Though all three of these women rulers lived at different times in very different locations, their aims were very similar, namely the preservation of their kingdoms and people. Boudicca also shares with them another feature, in that their fame obscures the fact that there is precious little information about them. At least Cleopatra and Zenobia are known by their real names, whereas Boudicca has suffered from various spellings, most famously Boadicea, which is most likely a copyist's error in the ancient sources. The more recent version of her name varies between Boudicca and Boudica – the one with the double 'c' being sanctioned by the computer spell-checker, not that this is the best authority. The version with only one 'c' is now favoured by some modern writers. The most important point is that Boudicca, however it should be spelled, may not even be the queen's real name. It may be a title, signifying Victory. In a way, she is the first Queen Victoria.

Tacitus, in the *Annals*, places the rebellion in Britain in the consulship of Caesennius Paetus and Petronius Turpilianus, the two *consules ordinarii* who gave their names to the year, which is indubitably AD 61 according to modern reckoning. Traditionally, the rebellion started in AD 60, but there is nothing apart from Tacitus's statement to throw any light on precisely when the events unfolded. The main problem is to fit everything that happened into the year 61.

BRITAIN IN AD 60–61

The rebellion seems to have taken the Romans by surprise. It probably seemed to them that the population in the areas that had been overrun were starting to settle down. Some of the local elite were adopting a Roman lifestyle, or were at least not unfriendly to the Roman government. It seemed that the military units left in the various forts, mentioned by Tacitus, could keep control while the bulk of the army went on campaign elsewhere. Three somewhat rudimentary towns had been established at Colchester, London and Verulamium. The town of Colchester was of the highest status, as a colony where veteran soldiers were settled. The status and development of London and Verulamium is not certain. Tacitus, writing towards the end of the first century, says that London was not a colony at the time of the rebellion, but he adds that it was an important centre for trade, which indicates that trading ventures were already flourishing, probably organised by Romans or Romanised provincials rather than native Britons. There would probably be a large number of culturally diverse personnel, as in any port. Although in the very early days of the conquest, the Romans administered the province from Colchester, perhaps before the rebellion of Boudicca, or a few years afterwards, London quickly became the headquarters of the governor. Since Decianus Catus fled there after the assault on the Iceni, it is assumed that London was already the procurator's administrative centre. Verulamium, which eventually became a *municipium*, or chartered town second in rank to a *colonia*, was possibly the slowest to develop, or at least archaeological investigations have revealed that although a grid pattern of streets had been established, and some shops had been built, there were few significant Roman buildings in the town at this time of the rebellion. Nonetheless it was a Roman town in spirit, most likely with Roman inhabitants and pro-Roman Britons, and it would seem to the Romans that all was set fair for peaceful development as the south and south-east started to look like a settled Roman province.

Just over fifty years earlier, the Romans had made a similar mistake. Archaeological evidence shows that in Germany in AD 9 some of the military installations were being given up for civilian development, so the newly conquered territory was poised at the point of transition between military occupation and civil administration. The governor who had been appointed was Quinctilius Varus, now almost a synonym for disaster. He had experience of Roman provincial rule in the east, where he was governor of Syria from 6 to 4 BC, and had to arbitrate between two rival contenders for the throne of Judaea, finally using armed force to quell riots. In AD 7 he was appointed governor of Germany, where he tried to hasten the formation of the province, together with the imposition of Roman law, and most importantly the levying of taxes. The Germans under their leader Arminius made it clear that they were not ready to accept Roman domination, and destroyed three legions. The Emperor Augustus used to wander about the Imperial palace shouting 'Give me back my three legions', and expansion into Germany ceased.

Both Tacitus and Dio acknowledge the abuses that had been visited on the conquered Britons. Most of the tribes may initially have been glad to be rid of the aggressive Catuvellauni, but soon found that they had jumped out of the frying pan into the fire. When the governor Ostorius Scapula put down some troublesome elements and then decided to disarm the Britons, the Iceni were the first to protest. They had allied with the Romans voluntarily and now they were being treated as the enemy. The Trinovantes too had grievances, having exchanged Catuvellaunian domination for an infinitely worse Roman version. The veterans at Colchester had been given lands to farm, which probably came from the territory confiscated from Cunobelinus's lands, but in the way of any people who feel that they are in a position to dominate and exploit, they had probably started to encroach on Trinovantian estates. Taxation had probably also begun to bite somewhat more rigorously, to the point where it was unendurable. It seems that the Romans had become too greedy, and were not supervised sufficiently well. There were many ways in which provincials could be exploited, and the Romans had centuries of practice at it. Intimidation and the extraction of protection money is not a modern invention.

How the Soldiers Supplemented their Pay and
Exploited the Provincials – Text Box

As supplements to their regular pay, issued three times per year, soldiers could look forward to extra cash from a variety of sources, such as Imperial donatives, from booty, and from their own financial activities such as money lending, and property transactions, and not least little scams, protection rackets, and extortion. Augustus bequeathed certain sums to all the armed forces, including 125 *denarii* to each Praetorian Guardsman and 75 *denarii* to each legionary. Succeeding Emperors generally paid out sums to the army whenever an important victory had been won, except that Marcus Aurelius refused to do so when his finances were strained. Other Emperors paid unexpected donatives on special occasions; for example it was said that Hadrian paid a total of 70 million *denarii* to the soldiers during his reign, to mark his accession and then the adoption of his intended heir, Aelius Caesar. When his daughter married, Antoninus Pius paid out cash to the soldiers, and after the reigns of Severus and Caracalla, donatives were paid to the army more regularly.

The value of booty taken in wars is harder to assess, but it was always a possible means of increasing income. Tacitus (*Histories* 3.19.6) says that the spoils from a city taken by storm were awarded to the soldiers. Some idea of the amount of booty brought home from foreign wars can be ascertained from the monuments in the Forum in Rome, specifically the reliefs on the Arch of Titus celebrating the conquest of Judaea, and on the Arch of Severus showing the spoils from the Parthian capital.

Military men could run businesses while they were still serving, and many of them probably did so without hindrance or breaking the law, but most of the evidence for soldiers as businessmen and property owners derives from the law codes, concerning cases where there were disputes. A soldier called Cattianus serving in one of the eastern provinces sought justice because a dealer had illegally sold his slaves, and another complained that his brother had sold his share in a vineyard without asking his permission, in order to settle a debt. There is not much evidence for soldiers in business in Britain, but once the army had stopped campaigning on a regular basis and settled more permanently in forts, some enterprising men may have set up businesses, probably run by their slaves. Lending money would be one of the easiest ways to earn a profit while doing not very much except keeping an eye on the accounts and using the backing of military power to extract the repayments.

Extortion in all its forms was another means of supplementing military pay. This is securely attested in the eastern provinces, where records are better preserved than in Britain, but presumably the soldiers were no better behaved in the western provinces. The number of times that the Prefect of Egypt issued edicts to try to curb the behaviour of the soldiers only serves to illustrate that the authorities were powerless to eradicate the problem. A papyrus dating to the second century AD records the accounts of a civilian businessman who regularly entered certain sums paid to soldiers, and openly describes this process as extortion, for which he uses the Greek word *diaseismos*. This may have been a sort of protection racket, perhaps only one example among many, operated by one or two unscrupulous soldiers, or organised groups.

One of the scams outlined by Tacitus, in describing how Agricola rooted out abuses of the Britons, concerned the requisitioning of grain as part of the tax payments. The soldiers would direct the British farmers to take their grain to impossibly distant places, and then perhaps accept payments for relaxing their directives, while still accepting the grain, so the food supply was assured, the soldiers got rich, and the Britons paid twice. The serving soldiers had several methods of browbeating the natives, but once they had retired they were no better behaved. At Colchester the veterans settled in the colony forced the Britons off their lands and farmed it themselves, and probably had ways of extracting money payments or food supplies to which the military and civilian authorities turned a blind eye.

TAXATION AND TRIBUTE

From ancient times it has been recognised that there are only two certainties in life, death and taxes. If government and administration is to function properly, money or goods are required to oil the wheels and pay for services, amenities and buildings. Armies require pay and supplies. The provincials were expected to make their contribution to these governmental functions, and both Strabo and Tacitus note that the Britons did not generally object to paying taxes. In addition to the provincial taxes, local taxes were levied to support the various communities. Not many self-governing towns had been established before the rebellion of Boudicca, and those that were just beginning to develop were not necessarily an expression of native ambitions, but were mostly Roman foundations, satisfying the needs of officials or traders. The *civitas* capitals, where a tribe or local community set up a central place where local government could be organised and administered, were not fully developed in the first years after the conquest. When they were established, their governing councils were made responsible for collecting both the local and the provincial taxes, supervised by the Imperial procurator and his staff, who administered the finances of the province, and were responsible for the supply and pay of the army.

There are several staple commodities that can be taxed to raise revenues: people, under the heading of the poll tax, which Boudicca complained about, according to Dio; land, based on acreage and produce; the produce itself; property; trade and commerce; and movement of goods into and out of harbours, across internal and external boundaries, and along major routes. The Romans levied taxes by all these methods. During the Republic, Roman citizens were liable for the *tributum*, an extraordinary tax that was not levied in Italy after 167 BC, when

Roman coffers were beginning to swell as booty flowed in from foreign campaigns and conquests, so the acquisition of provinces paid for the running of the Empire.

Citizens were also subject to an inheritance tax of 5 per cent (*vicesima hereditarum*), levied if substantial sums were left to non-relatives. The proceeds of this tax were paid into the *aerarium militare*, the military treasury that was set up by Augustus in AD 6, in order to provide pensions for discharged veterans from the Roman army. Augustus had created the standing army from the massive numbers of soldiers still under arms in 30 BC at the end of the civil wars. Until the creation of the *aerarium militare* there was no regular scheme to pay off veterans, except for the sporadic allotment of land, which did not serve the purpose because by the time of the early Empire, soldiers were not usually accustomed to farming. Cash pension schemes were preferable by far to having lots of ex-soldiers, all superbly trained in the use of weapons, wandering over the Empire without financial support.

There were also taxes on the sale of slaves, set at 4 per cent, and on their manumission, when owners paid 5 per cent of their market value. Indirect taxes were grouped under the heading of *vectigalia*, the most important being *portoria*, the tax on goods into and out of ports and harbours and across boundaries. This tax was levied in Britain before the Claudian conquest, and the Britons were so eager to obtain Roman goods that they paid it without hesitation.

As for tax payments, they can be collected in cash or in kind. The Friesians paid in leather hides, the Britons probably in grain. All methods of collection are subject to abuses, and the Roman system did not exclude this. The most famous of the scams employed by the Romans in Britain is related by Tacitus, when Agricola tried to put an end to exploitation. When the Britons brought their grain they were ordered to take it to a collection point miles away, so they would pay to avoid the journey, or on occasion they would be forced to buy grain to meet their quotas. The quotas themselves may have been falsely measured. A bronze corn measure, dating from the reign of Domitian was found at Carvoran in Northumberland. It bears an inscription on its side stating that it holds seventeen and a half *sextarii*. It actually holds more than that. It is possible that it has nothing to do with collection of grain as payment of tax. Perhaps it was the kind of measure used by the troops when collecting their rations from the granaries inside the forts, used just like modern beer glasses where the line marking the capacity is not at the very top. But as a method of cheating the natives it would have worked wonderfully well. The British farmers were hardly in a position to protest, since it is highly likely that the military was involved in tax collection in the north of England. Instead of arguing, it would be more prudent to accept the judgement that there was not enough grain in the measure and then deliver some more, or buy it to meet the demand.

Before any tax on people and land could be levied and collected, it was necessary to assess its value, based on a survey, so when a new province was created, it was customary to take a census. Just as William the Conqueror needed to know who held which lands and what these lands were worth, the Romans needed to know the same things, how many people there were and what they produced. William waited twenty years to carry out his survey, and it did not include much beyond the River Mersey or the borders of Yorkshire. The Romans would probably not delay for an entire decade, and would not stop short of the borders of what they had overrun, since agreements with allied tribes who were not yet absorbed into the province could include the payment of tribute. The census was usually taken every five years, but not much is known about how it operated in Britain, whether a census of newly won territory would be carried out immediately every time a bit more was added, or whether the five-year cycle would apply. Only two censors are attested in the province. One was appointed to take the census of the Anavionenses in the second century. No one knows where this particular tribe lived, perhaps somewhere in north-west England, or in Scotland. In the third century, Aurelius Bassus conducted a census in Colchester.

Though the collection of taxes was supervised by the Imperial procurator, there were lower-ranking officials called *publicani* who oversaw the business at a local or regional level. During the Republic the *publicani* were notorious for corruption, and were reviled accordingly. They would bid for the privilege of collecting taxes and then set about gathering more than was supposed to be levied in order to line their own pockets. During the Republic in Julius Caesar's day, some of the *publicani* bid too much and found that they could not even meet the targets, much less get rich themselves. They had to be rescued and bailed out by the government, which has an oddly familiar sound to modern audiences of the early twenty-first century. Not much has changed in two thousand years. When the *conductores* replaced the *publicani* in the second century they were unable to resist the same temptations to feather their own nests.

For local towns of all sizes the most important revenues derived from lands, forest, mines and salt works. The money raised from these and other taxes went towards the upkeep of buildings and roads, and whatever else the local council wished to do. Councillors were also expected to embellish their towns and finance public works out of their own pockets – it was matter of honour. Sometimes local communities overreached themselves and got into trouble, either by borrowing or speculating too wildly, or by being unable to finish their grandiose projects. A local community in North Africa started to build a tunnel which went wrong, and the project had to be rescued by a military engineer. The younger Pliny encountered similar concerns when he went to govern Bithynia-Pontus; his letters to the Emperor Trajan reveal the way in which local communities could get themselves into debt or difficulties in seeing projects through. Early in the second century, investigation into such matters became more common. Town councils were theoretically autonomous, but Imperial interference was sometimes necessary when financial ignorance or incompetence threatened to result in disaster. Officials called *correctores* or *curatores rei publicae* were sent to sort out the problems.

Towards the end of the third century, taxation became more burdensome, chiefly to pay for the army. Revenues declined while expenditure rose, and external threats increased. For a while, tax was collected in kind, to supply the army, and the soldiers were paid not in cash but in rations. The Emperor Diocletian made local councillors personally responsible for the taxes, so if insufficient amounts were collected the unfortunate councillors had to make up the difference. It was not a successful scheme, resulting in great reluctance to serve in what was once an honourable position, and the wealthy classes who could afford to do so moved into the country left the towns to their fates.

The Iceni and Rome

In this climate of Roman taxation and corrupt administration, it is not surprising that Prasutagus, the ruler of the Iceni, had made provision in his will for sharing his kingdom between his family and the Roman Emperor, hoping to protect his people from the greed of the provincial officials. It is not certain how this would work, perhaps entailing outright gift of some territory so that an Imperial estate could be set up, or possibly some part of the revenues were to be earmarked for the Emperor. As an insurance policy to try to ensure that the kingdom retained at least some autonomy, it failed. Prasutagus may have died in AD 59, or perhaps early in 60, leaving his widow Boudicca and their two daughters as his co-heirs with the Emperor Nero. What happened next does not redound to Roman credit. The official in charge of financial affairs, the procurator Decianus Catus, descended on the Iceni, backed up by a few Roman troops, to claim the inheritance for Nero. He probably had another agenda as well. Now that the king of the Iceni was dead it was time to call in any loans that had been made to him by wealthy Romans, or by the Emperor. It seems that Claudius had given generous gifts to some of the British tribes, which may have been interpreted by the Romans as loans and perhaps misunderstood by the Britons, who never envisioned having to pay it back. Rich men like Seneca were known to have lent money as well. It is possible that instructions had come from the Emperor Nero to foreclose on whatever had been lent to the Iceni, or perhaps Catus had made the decision himself. No one knows what exactly happened between the Roman procurator and the queen of the Iceni.

BOUDICCA REBELS

It seems that Catus and his soldiers were somewhat overzealous in carrying out his duties, whatever he thought they were, provoking an immediate protest from the Iceni. The result was that the queen was flogged, and her daughters were raped. This showed how dismally a tribe supposedly allied to Rome could be treated, in what had started out as an exercise to collect an inheritance and the associated taxes. If the procurator had not actually ordered the flogging of the queen, he clearly was not in control of his soldiers.

Catus fled, presumably returning to London, where it is thought that his administrative headquarters were located. Even if his depot was at Colchester he could hardly remain so close to the tribesmen now that this enormity had occurred. The news of what had happened would circulate among the Britons. Some of the tribes would decide that they had had enough and wanted to fight back. Others might hesitate to go to war against an army that had won all its wars up to now. Even if the Romans had been defeated in an engagement, they usually kept going and won in the end. The rallying cry for the Britons would be the mistreatment of Boudicca and what it might signify for the rest of the tribes, but behind this one event there were seventeen years of disappointment and exploitation. Normally when operating among a tribal society the Romans could rely upon internecine strife to keep the various tribes apart, making Roman domination of them so much easier. This time, some tribes sank their differences, as they had done under Cassivellaunus to oppose Caesar, and as the tribes of Scotland would do some twenty years later, under a leader called Calgacus, which may be a title, meaning the Swordsman, rather than a name.

The tribes who rose up with the Iceni will have included the Trinovantes, and possibly other tribes of the south of the island, extending as far as south Wales. Some tribes possibly became overtly hostile without necessarily moving to join Boudicca and her army. Tacitus says that when Suetonius marched from Anglesey he did so through the midst of the enemy. It is presumed that the tribes ruled by Tiberius Claudius Togidubnus refrained from rebellion, nor did the Brigantes of the north join the rebels, though it is not known if individual warriors left their tribes in order to fight the Romans on their own account.

The chronology of the rebellion cannot be established with certainty, especially as certain events would occur simultaneously. Suetonius assembled some troops and left Anglesey as soon as he could, and marched towards the south-east, making for London, the bulk of the legionaries following after. A stream of orders will have gone out to other troops to bring them together while this march took place. There were forts in the south and south-east, perhaps manned by auxiliary troops, and the legions may have been split up, some of the soldiers having gone with Suetonius to Wales and the remainder guarding their bases. II Augusta was at Exeter in the south-west, and IX Hispana was probably at Lincoln. The legionaries from the Anglesey campaign, XIV and XX, joined Suetonius for the final battle.

In the meantime Boudicca had either already sacked Colchester or was aiming for the town. There were many veterans there but the colony had no defences for them to man, and there may have been no time to erect any barriers that might have slowed the Britons. Possibly the veterans were overconfident. They sent to Catus the procurator for help, which supports the theory that he was not in Colchester and that his headquarters lay at London. He sent 200 men, apparently not very well armed. Even if they had been armed to the teeth, the whole enterprise was useless. The Britons swept into the town, forcing the veterans and soldiers to retreat into the great temple, possibly dedicated to Claudius and possibly not even completed yet, but the building was sufficient for them to barricade themselves in. They held out for two days. The slaughter was total, including civilians.

The legate of IX Hispana, Petillius Cerialis, dashed southwards to attempt to stop the Britons, but was badly cut up and had to retreat, having lost many of his legionaries. With difficulty he managed to withdraw the cavalry and get away. It is not known whether Cerialis had brought some mounted auxiliary soldiers with him. The legionary cavalry usually amounted to only 120 men. Cerialis retired to his camp, where he had presumably left a substantial number of men, and remained there behind his defences, according to Tacitus, who was not over-lavish with admiration for Cerialis. If it is supposed that the encounter between Cerialis's troops and the Britons took place in the environs of Colchester, or somewhere in East Anglia, the distance from Lincoln seems too great for a swift dash to the rescue, so it was once suggested that the half-size legionary camp at Longthorpe may have been the base which Cerialis came from and returned to. No one knows where IX Hispana met the Britons, who could have marched some distance north themselves. Currently it is thought more likely that the camp mentioned by Tacitus, but unfortunately not named, really was the legionary fortress at Lincoln, which had been founded c.AD 55.

After the disaster at Colchester the procurator Catus decamped once again, this time out of harm's way to Gaul, leaving Britain to its fate. Tacitus puts the blame for causing the rebellion firmly on Catus's shoulders. The procurator's rapacity was not the only grievance that the Britons suffered, but if he had not descended on the Iceni and the terrible events there had not occurred, it is possible that an outright rebellion could have been avoided, while resentment simmered but did not boil over.

SUETONIUS ABANDONS LONDON

Suetonius finally arrived at London and decided that he could not defend the town. He gave the order to abandon the area, allowing anyone who could keep up with the army to accompany him. It was the correct decision from the military point of view, since there were no defences surrounding the town, and even if there had been a bank and ditch or a palisade, his army would have been worse than useless if he allowed it to be surrounded and possibly trapped in defence of only one town. It would be better to meet the Britons in the open, when he could expect to have more men. The legionaries and auxiliaries that he had summoned ought to have been on the march to join him by now. On his way out from London he brought the troops from the forts in the immediate area, and he was finally joined by the XIV and XX legions. He had about 10,000 men, and would have had more if only II Augusta had marched, but its commander, the camp prefect Poenius Postumus, refused to move. Various suggestions have been made to explain why he did not lead his troops out. He was only third in command, apparently without the legionary legate or the senior tribune, who had perhaps accompanied Suetonius to Anglesey with a detachment. Postumus may have been overcautious in the absence of more senior officers. He may have commanded a reduced garrison, and there may have been restless tribes all around him who made it dangerous for him to leave his post. But no one really knows why he did not march.

London was quickly overrun by the Britons. All remaining inhabitants were killed, and the buildings put to the torch. Excavations in London around the Cornhill area have turned up burnt layers nearly one foot thick, so this may be where the main concentration of buildings lay and where the Britons concentrated their attack. Next it was the turn of Verulamium, where there was a defensive bank of earth and a surrounding ditch but seemingly no one to man the defences. Tacitus says that the Britons avoided the hard work of attacking forts and went for the places where there was no defending force, and rich booty was to be found. About 70,000 people were killed, according to Tacitus, whose description of atrocities is quite restrained, limited to hanging, burning and crucifying. He perhaps knew more, since his father-in-law Agricola was there as a young man, in his post as *tribunus laticlavius*, the senior tribune of a legion, and perhaps with Suetonius's army at the time. It is Dio who provides the lurid details. He describes women with their breasts cut off and stitched into their mouths, and people impaled on stakes. His source material is not known. There may have been official records, or he may have drawn on folk memory. It may all be true. By the twenty-first century no one should be surprised at what human beings, especially those with a grudge, are capable of doing to other human beings.

The Battle
With fewer men than he had hoped for, Suetonius chose his own battleground to meet the Britons. It is not known where this was, but is generally agreed to be somewhere in the Midlands, possibly at Mancetter

where a case has been made for it by comparing the geography of the area with what Tacitus says about the battle site. Suetonius placed his troops with a wood at their backs, facing an open plain which afforded no opportunity for the enemy to mount an ambush. The approach to this site was narrow, which would force the Britons to bunch up. The formation of the battle line was classic. The legionaries were placed in the centre, flanked by the light-armed auxiliary troops, with the cavalry units on both wings, called *alae*, the traditional place for the mounted units, which were called *alae* themselves. The British warriors were accompanied by their families, who drew up behind them in their carts and wagons, like many other tribal war bands.

This is where Tacitus invents speeches for Boudicca and Suetonius to set the scene. Rather than trying to quote her words in direct speech, Tacitus summarises what the queen was supposed to have said, using reported speech to paint a picture of Boudicca and her two daughters riding around in her chariot to harangue each of the tribes. She reminded them of what had occurred at the hands of the Romans, and what might happen if there was no resistance. She said that a legion had been destroyed, which refers to Cerialis and IX Hispana. She pointed out that some of the Romans were hiding in camps, while the rest would not be able to withstand the numbers of warriors that she had brought to this battle. The numbers of tribesmen that were mustered were probably formidable. Tacitus gives the vague description *quanta non alias multitudo*, numbers not seen before, but Dio's estimate of 230,000 warriors at the final battle sounds dubious.

Suetonius's speech, in Tacitus's version, was short. The general pointed out that enemy was numerous but not well armed and they would not stand up to soldiers who had always been victorious. He urged the men to keep close together, and after they had thrown their javelins, to fell the Britons with their shields and swords, without stopping to gather booty. Then he gave the signal for battle.

Dio really goes to town with his speeches, presenting two opposing points of view, in direct speech, almost a theatre piece which would sound so much better when his account was read out loud to an

audience. Putting words into Boudicca's mouth, he emph\
enslavement of the Britons and the injustices heaped upon them. He describes the weakness of the Romans as opposed to the way the Britons live. Whereas the Romans need shelter and defences, and they expire if they cannot have their bread, wine and oil, the Britons are tougher, living on whatever they can find. Since this was written in the third century, Dio probably resorted to rhetorical platitudes about the barbarians, as the Romans called most people who were not Roman. He also includes an anecdote, whereby Boudicca, in order to divine the future, released a wild hare from her tunic, which ran away into the area that the Britons considered lucky. This omen gave great encouragement to the tribesmen. For Suetonius's speech, Dio imagines the governor going the rounds of each division of the army, encouraging them to show how superior they were to the natives, and emphasising the need for revenge, and ending with the 'conquer or die' theme.

The reality was no doubt quite different. The legionaries threw their javelins and then charged in wedge formation, cutting through the British tribesmen, and the auxiliaries and the cavalry using their lances. When the Britons tried to flee they were hampered by the wagons behind them, and about 80,000 of them – according to Tacitus – were killed, for a cost of 400 Roman dead. No one knows what happened to Boudicca and her daughters. She may have been killed in battle, or as Dio says, she may have fallen ill and died a short time later.

Aftermath

The war was over except for the mopping up, but this was a momentous task, with three towns that had been developing along Romans lines utterly destroyed, and an immediate need for replacement troops. Tacitus says that 2,000 infantry, 8 auxiliary cohorts and 1,000 cavalry were despatched from Germany. It seems that the greatest losses had been sustained by IX Hispana, since Tacitus immediately adds, after giving the totals, that this legion was brought up to strength. He may not have been exaggerating, presumably having obtained these figures from his father-in-law Agricola, or even from some reports of Suetonius Paullinus himself.

The story that Nero once considered abandoning Britain, as reported by the biographer Suetonius Tranquillus, has already been mentioned in the previous chapter, but if it is true, then surely it belongs to this episode, when the losses were totalled up and reported back to Rome. If the auxiliary cohorts are reckoned in round figures at about 500 men in each, then the total numbers of replacements that were required in order to bring the British garrison back to functional strength exceeds one complete legion. Tribesmen were not supposed to have the organisational skills or the capability of wiping out Roman troops, so it was a double disaster: a severe loss of manpower, and a blow to Roman pride. Even if this did not lead to thoughts of abandonment, the news would have been very disturbing in Rome. Nero would lose face, and at this moment he still had some face to lose, since he had not yet become the monster that he turned into later. But a quick talk by the statesman Seneca and others may have dispelled any such ideas of abandonment from the young Emperor's mind. Most likely it was pointed out to him that there would be a considerable loss of revenues if Britain were to be evacuated.

The condition of the Britons was desperate. Suetonius placed his cohorts and cavalry in new winter quarters, and sent them out to harass the tribesmen, and as Ostorius Scapula had done some years before, Suetonius probably included tribes merely considered dangerous as well as those who had joined the rebellion. There was no food, because the Britons had relied on the capture of Roman supplies, and had not bothered to plant crops before they set out. It is unlikely that Suetonius and his soldiers cared about any of the Britons, even those who had kept the peace. Revenge as well as mopping up resistance seemed to have been the order of the day. Suetonius and the soldiers had seen for themselves what the rebels had done.

The new procurator, on the other hand, had not. Julius Classicianus, who was sent to Britain to replace the disgraced Catus, was a Gallic noble with Roman citizenship, and was sympathetic to the plight of the Britons. He probably saw more clearly than the governor Suetonius that harsh treatment of the natives, who were resentful and now hungry, could only be detrimental. Retribution is never designed to win hearts and minds, and in Roman Britain it would interfere with government, administration, the production of grain, the promotion of trade, and the collection of taxes, the latter being Classicianus's main responsibility. From the beginning, he and Suetonius seem to have clashed, and Classicianus allegedly told the Britons who complained to wait for the appointment of a new governor. He perhaps sent reports to Rome to reiterate this, recommending that Suetonius should be recalled.

Something of the sort prompted Nero to send his freedman secretary Polyclitus to Britain to try to reconcile the governor and the procurator, and no doubt he was ordered to bring back a report on the state of affairs in the island. Trailing an enormous entourage through Gaul, Polyclitus arrived and assessed the situation, to the astonishment of the Britons, who did not understand how or why an ex-slave should be able to wield such power. The report to Nero was possibly reassuring, or if the true situation was revealed it was decided to allow Suetonius to remain as governor for the time being. Then he apparently lost some ships and their crews, which is usually described as a valid reason to recall him, but one wonders whether Nero, who was able to give orders to the great general Domitius Corbulo to fall on his sword, needed any valid reason to replace a governor. Nero and his advisers were probably waiting for a suitable opportunity, in order to save Roman sensibilities, seizing upon the loss of ships as the official excuse to have Suetonius recalled. It would not be advisable to give the Britons the satisfaction of seeing the governor removed solely because of his harsh treatment of them.

A Change of Policy

The new governor Petronius Turpilianus was consul in 61, and as his office came to an end, perhaps after only a few months, he set out for Britain. Tacitus says that he was lenient, and willing to listen to the Britons. The activities of the two years that he spent in Britain are virtually unknown. The rebuilding of the shattered towns was no doubt the most important of his priorities, but there are only vague hints of what he may have achieved, for instance the first phase of the Forum in London may have been started under Turpilianus. There was no military activity to speak of, not unusual in the circumstances perhaps, but Tacitus, ever the advocate of expansionism, accuses Turpilianus of idleness. It was a peaceful province that was handed over to Marcus Trebellius Maximus in 63. Some of the credit for promoting the peace must go to Classicianus, whose work after the removal of Suetonius is not recorded. He probably worked closely with Turpilianus and then Trebellius, but he died in office, perhaps *c*.63 or 64. His wife set up a funerary monument for him in London, which can still be seen in the British Museum.

The origins and background of Trebellius Maximus are obscure. His term of office in Britain was a long one, but although it began well, it ended badly when the civil war erupted after the death of Nero. There was no military action under the new governor, and in the absence of forward campaigns, four legions were somewhat superfluous. In 66 or 67, one of them, XIV, now with the title Martia Victrix for its part in the defeat of Boudicca, was withdrawn by Nero, along with eight auxiliary cohorts of Batavians. They were destined for a campaign in the Caucasus. For a short time the legionary complement of Britain comprised II Augusta, IX Hispana, and XX Valeria Victrix, the title bestowed on it for its part in suppressing Boudicca.

Trebellius may have been responsible for moving the XX legion out of Usk to resettle in Gloucester, a somewhat retrograde movement since it had moved from Kingsholm near Gloucester only a few years before. Alternatively, some scholars think that it may have gone to Wroxeter when XIV was recalled by Nero, but for XX that move probably occurred some years later. II Augusta and IX Hispana remained respectively at Exeter and Lincoln. The soldiers were no doubt kept busy on patrols, carrying out police work, securing supplies, perhaps even helping to rebuild the towns, but they were not given the opportunity for military action. Inactivity for prolonged periods was not good for army morale, and boredom and discontent set in. The XX legion perhaps had more cause for complaint than the others, because it had been moved around much more frequently from one base to another. The legionary legate, Roscius Coelius, took it upon himself to be the spokesman for his own XX and the other legions, and rapidly became the leader of the restless troops. He accused Trebellius of impoverishing the legions, which might mean that pay was in arrears and Trebellius had done nothing to remedy the situation, but it could also imply that without profitable campaigns, the soldiers were deprived of a means to collect booty and get rich quick. Trebellius may also have tried to put a stop to the various schemes that soldiers could set up to exploit the natives, given that he had possibly been ordered to placate the population and keep the peace so recently won.

HARD TIMES

The period after the rebellion of Boudicca is a dark age, singularly devoid of sources, either literary or epigraphic, and as far as can be discerned from archaeology, recovery in the devastated towns and countryside ranged from slow to non-existent. It was probably just as much a period of stasis in the civilian and administrative spheres as it was in military circles, so perhaps the reason why it is not possible to elucidate what was happening is because not much was actually happening. After the rebellion was crushed, the people of Britain were in dire straits, probably for some considerable time. In the year after the rebellion, many farms presumably still stood empty in the lands of the Iceni and Trinovantes. Even if the numbers of tribesmen killed in the battles are exaggerated in the ancient sources, there would be very many who never returned to their lands. Some of those who did return may have been rooted out and executed, or sold as slaves while Suetonius exacted his revenge. Defeated tribesmen would probably be declared *dediticii*, a title reserved for people who had surrendered, and were deprived of all rights. If this was the case, then some of them may have been recruited into the Roman army and sent away from the province. It was usual practice to remove potential troublemakers in this way, especially after the conclusion of a war. During the civil war of 69, Tacitus says that the Roman general Caecina commanded a motley collection of Gauls, Lusitanians and Britons. The status of these Britons is unknown. They may have been volunteers, but they could just as easily have been defeated tribesmen removed from their homes after the rebellion of Boudicca.

The Iceni were not exterminated, as demonstrated by the later foundation of their capital at Caistor-by-Norwich, named Venta Icenorum for the tribe. But it is significant that it was not properly established until the reign of Hadrian, and remained smaller than other tribal capitals. Despite its location in a fertile area, near enough to the coast, Caistor-by-Norwich did not develop as did, for instance, the capital of the Dobunni at Cirencester (Corinium Dobunnorum), which flourished and became the second largest town in Roman Britain.

The possible scenario of the later AD 60s is demonstrated by the archaeological excavation of one Roman villa, at Gorhambury, near Verulamium. It had started out probably as a British farm, or a collection of a few huts, but just before AD 60 a Roman-style villa was built. Then after the rebellion the inhabitants on the site, either the existing ones or new farmers, reverted to living in huts. Sometime later, the residents tried again, and a new villa was built. Verulamium itself did not recover rapidly after the destruction and burning, as though there was no one to invest in new buildings, or the momentum had run down.

One place where reconstruction seems to have begun quite soon after the rebellion is London. If it was the administrative headquarters of the procurator and probably also the governor by this time, the impetus for recovery most likely came from the Imperial administration. A new Forum was laid out at this time. It would be another decade before the structure identified as the governor's palace was planned and built, though this need not mean that the governor himself and his administrative staff were located in some other town. Since London was also an important trading centre, the merchants and traders would have a vested interest in setting the town on its feet once again. They were in a better position than the native Britons to make profits, so they may even have contributed the money to kick-start the proceedings. Usually town building was funded by the local community, but in this case the government may have helped, and the army may have done some of the building work, though this is not proven. Building materials were used bearing government stamps, but it is not known if the inhabitants of London paid for them.

THE CIVIL WAR IN ROME

In AD 69, when British civic and commercial life may have been reviving, the Roman world lurched into a home-made crisis, and everything was put on hold. There was hardly anyone left who had a good word for Nero, but the unifying influence of opposition failed to produce any consensus of what to do about the situation. The Roman world was divided into factions who were prepared to fight each other. In 68, the governor of Gallia Lugdunensis, Julius Vindex, sounded out other governors to try to persuade them to join him in a revolt against Nero, who had lost the support of every class of society. Eventually he was forced to commit suicide in June 68, allegedly proclaiming 'What an artist dies in me!' The legions of Upper Germany suppressed Vindex, but then tried to appoint their governor Verginius Rufus as Emperor. He refused politely, which was a courageous act in the presence of thousands of men armed with swords. In Spain, the troops promoted their own governor, Galba, as the next Emperor. He marched to Rome where he received the support of the Praetorian Guard and became Nero's successor. But then after seven months the Praetorians changed their minds, killed Galba, and chose Otho in his place, in January 69.

Only a few days before the elevation of Otho, the troops in Germany proclaimed Vitellius, so there were now two Emperors. The three legions in Britain supported Vitellius, who summoned a total of 8,000 men from the British garrison to join him. It may have been at this moment that the governor Trebellius Maximus was forced to leave Britain by the machinations of Roscius Coelius, legate of XX Valeria Victrix. Trebellius supported Vitellius and perhaps went with the 8,000 legionaries to join him.

While two rival claimants for the Empire fought it out, chaos reigned in Gaul and Italy. There was no official governor in Britain, except the self-appointed Roscius who took charge of affairs for a short time. It is significant that the legions did not rush headlong to Vitellius even though they sided with him, and neither did the Britons of the south take advantage of the situation to rebel once more. They may have been too thoroughly suppressed to try, but they may also have begun to settle down, beguiled by the trappings of Roman civilisation, which Tacitus sneers at, saying that it marked their enslavement. Some of them had become accustomed to a life of leisure and luxury, Roman style.

The Vitellian troops defeated Otho in April 69, so Vitellius was now sole Emperor. He appointed a governor to Britain, Marcus Vettius Bolanus, who had been consul in 66. Vitellius decided to remove XIV legion from Italy, where the soldiers were becoming unruly. He ordered it to march back to Britain. They set fire to a part of Turin as they were leaving. The legion and the governor may have arrived in Britain together, and XIV may have gone to Wroxeter, only to be withdrawn and stationed on the Rhine a short time later. Tacitus dismisses the new governor Bolanus as ineffective, because he was unable or unwilling to impose discipline on the fractious troops.

When the Brigantes started to fight among themselves, Bolanus had to intervene and restore order. It was the usual story of a ruler being ejected and appealing to Rome for assistance. In this case it was Queen Cartimandua who had fallen out once again with her husband Venutius, who had already caused similar trouble for the governor Didus Gallus. The queen had divorced Venutius and married his armour bearer Vellocatus, so her ex-husband and the anti-Roman groups retaliated and fought against the queen. Venutius was no doubt fully aware of the power struggles going on in Rome, and of the surly mood of the legionaries in the south of Britain, so he probably reckoned that there would never be a better chance to seize power. The unrest among the legions may be the reason why Bolanus sent some auxiliary units northwards to Brigantia, without legionary back-up. There were some skirmishes, perhaps, but in the end the Romans had no choice but to extricate Cartimandua and leave Venutius in power. Then, as Tacitus says, the kingdom was left to Venutius and the Romans were left with the war. But it was not fought for another year or two, under a different governor. It is easy to blame the governor Bolanus for his apparent lack of enterprise in not marching in to gain control of the territory and pursue Venutius, but it was a very large area, with mountainous terrain that the Britons knew well. Apart from the fact that the Roman troops may not have been reliable, such a campaign in the north needed more detailed planning and the assembly of battle groups and of supplies, for which Bolanus may not have been ready. He may have considered that the southern parts of Britain, especially south Wales, were not sufficiently pacified for troops to be withdrawn for a campaign in the north. On the other hand, a poem by Statius addressed to Bolanus's son suggests more than just passive acceptance of the status quo in the north, referring to the building of forts, and in a cryptic remark he suggests that Bolanus won a breastplate from an unnamed British king, so there may have been more military action than is discernible in the pages of Tacitus.

The forts referred to in Statius's poem may have been built to contain the Brigantes without encroaching on their territory. There were already a few forts on the southern border of Brigantia, a small one at Templeborough and larger forts at Rossington Bridge, Broxtowe and Osmanthorpe, which had been established by previous governors, either by Ostorius Scapula or perhaps Didius Gallus, who had been obliged to assist Cartimandua some years earlier. It has been suggested that Bolanus placed forts in the territory of the Parisi, a tribe living to the east of the Brigantes, particularly at Malton, where a large fort was built, capable of housing part of a legion, or more than one auxiliary unit. It remained in occupation even after the legionary fortress of York was built. At best, from the archaeological evidence, it can be said that Bolanus contained the situation, but was unable to embark on full conquest of the north, while the whole Roman world held its breath, waiting to find out who would finally emerge as Emperor.

In Rome Vitellius tried to unite the shattered Roman world by sparing the men who had opposed him, and issuing coins proclaiming the unity of the army. But in the eastern provinces, two men were watching and waiting. Titus Flavius Vespasianus had been appointed governor of Judaea, in the latter half of 66, to quell the revolt that had broken out there. It was said that Vespasian had committed the unforgiveable error of dozing off, probably bored out of his mind, while Nero was reciting poems on his literary tour of Greece. The Judaean appointment was Vespasian's reward for this transgression. At about the same time, Vespasian's colleague

Gaius Licinius Mucianus was appointed governor of Syria. They had been corresponding for some time, through the medium of Vespasian's son Titus. When they heard that Galba had been proclaimed Emperor, Titus set off to congratulate him, but he had travelled only as far as Corinth in January 69, when he heard that the Praetorians had killed Galba and proclaimed Otho, and at about the same time, the Rhine legions proclaimed Vitellius. Titus turned back. If Vespasian and Mucianus had not already discussed the possibility of making a bid for the Empire, they probably started now. Tacitus says that the instigation came from Titus, but it was Vespasian who was spontaneously proclaimed Emperor by the two legions in Egypt on 1 July 69, followed by his own troops in Judaea two days later, and then by Mucianus's soldiers shortly afterwards. The alleged spontaneity had probably taken several months to organise. The rallying cry was then, and forever afterwards, the illegitimate rule of Vitellius and the chaos he had brought to Italy. Vespasian was to be the saviour of the state, not just an adventurer who fancied a taste of supreme power. The Jewish historian Josephus and the immediate court circle faithfully propagated the image. Vespasian himself did not march on Rome immediately, remaining in Judaea until he could safely hand over the command to his son Titus. In Vespasian's place, Mucianus set off overland to Italy in August 69, and fortunately the Flavians had an ally in Antonius Primus who was in Pannonia and therefore much closer to Italy. He was the commander who faced the Vitellian troops at the battle of Cremona and won. He had done more than anyone to win the Empire for the Flavians, but his big mistake was to allow his soldiers to sack Cremona, a blot on Vespasian's rule that had to be eradicated, so Primus was sacrificed. It was given out that he had disobeyed Vespasian's orders, so the new regime could distance itself from the carnage.

In Britain, a new era was about to start. Gnaeus Julius Agricola was appointed legionary legate of XX Valeria Victrix in 70, replacing the troublesome Roscius Coelius. The governor Vettius Bolanus was left in post until 71, when he too was replaced by Petillius Cerialis. After some years of stasis, the advance was to begin again.

4

Almost the Whole Island AD 69 to 96

FLAVIAN EXPANSION

The term 'Flavian' derives from the family name of the three Emperors who reigned from AD 69 to 96: Titus Flavius Vespasianus, who was proclaimed in 69, and his two sons who became successively the Emperors Titus (79 to 81) and Domitian (81 to 96). In Britain throughout this period there were major advances in both the military and civilian spheres. The three known governors who were appointed by the Flavians conquered the rest of the island, and during their tenure of office there were considerable developments in the towns and cities, perhaps encouraged by the governors whenever the natives expressed an interest in adopting Roman forms and fashions. The process of Romanisation was once construed as an active policy on the part of the Emperors, carried out through their governors and the Roman armies, but now it is seen as a piecemeal development more dependent on example and native initiative than on Roman prompting.

The three known Flavian governors are Petillius Cerialis, Julius Frontinus and Julius Agricola. From about 84 there is little information about the governors of Britain, until c. 118. Compared to the brief notices that have survived about the first two, Cerialis and Frontinus, there is a disproportionate amount of information about the third, Julius Agricola, because the historian Tacitus married Agricola's daughter, and wrote a biography of his father-in-law. The major problem is to match the archaeological information with what the sources tell us about the activities of these governors, particularly those of Agricola, seemingly so well described but with a frustrating lack of identifiable place names.

Conquest of the Brigantes: Petillius Cerialis AD 71 to 73/74

Quintus Petillius Cerialis Caesius Rufus was the legate of IX Hispana at the time of the revolt of Boudicca. Unfortunately he did nothing to enhance his reputation by dashing to the rescue and being soundly beaten by the Britons, but later he chose to take the side of the Flavians apparently from the very beginning. It has been suggested that after the rebellion of Boudicca was crushed, the troops sent as replacements from Germany were accompanied by Vespasian's son Titus, who was a military tribune in Britain at some unspecified time. It seems that the majority of the legionary soldiers were needed to fill the ranks of IX Hispana, so it is just possible that Cerialis met Titus at this time. At any rate Cerialis joined the Flavians in December 69, before Vespasian arrived in Rome, and he appears to have married Vespasian's daughter, Flavia, perhaps as his second wife.

As a trusted member of Vespasian's circle, in 70 Cerialis was chosen, with Annius Gallus, to suppress the revolt of Civilis and the Batavians on the Rhine. This rebellion had been prompted by Antonius Primus, the general who defeated the Vitellian troops at Cremona. He incited the revolt as a short-term means of keeping the Vitellian troops of Germany too busy to intervene in Rome, but the rebellion had spiralled out of control, and it required an army to put it down. To assist in this endeavour, XIV legion was brought back from Britain. The legionaries had probably not yet had time to unpack properly since Vitellius returned them to Britain because they were causing trouble in Italy. This was the final removal; the legion never returned to Britain. Cerialis may have been rewarded with the consulship for his exploits in suppressing the rebellion. According to the Jewish historian Flavius Josephus, who had joined Vespasian in Judaea, Cerialis was consul in 70, most likely as suffect consul, since his name is not quoted as one of the eponymous consuls of that year.

His next appointment was as governor of Britain, in 71. There had been little or no advance in the province since the rebellion of Boudicca, though there had been some trouble with the Brigantes which the previous governor Bolanus had merely contained, since it was not the most auspicious time to embark on a northern campaign. The situation that Cerialis inherited was somewhat threatening, since the Brigantes were no longer ruled by the pro-Roman Queen Cartimandua. Her husband Venutius had been left in charge when the queen was rescued, and there was probably no shortage of anti-Roman warriors who would rally around Venutius if he decided to go to war.

There were a few early Roman forts, built of turf and timber, on the edge of Brigantian territory, at Templeborough and Rossington Bridge, Broxtowe and Osmanthorpe. These forts may have been in existence since the days of Didius Gallus, or even earlier. Bolanus may have built the large fort at Malton in the lands of the more peaceful Parisi, to guard the east flank of the Brigantes. There are probably more turf and timber forts awaiting discovery. The known forts on the southern borders and flank of Brigantia would hardly be enough for control of the whole territory, which covered most of northern Britain, up to the River Tyne and the Solway. With Cerialis's arrival, Roman policy changed from one of containment to active invasion. There were now only three legions in Britain, and only a short time earlier Vitellius had taken a contingent of 8,000 men from the province to shore up his army in his bid for power. In manpower terms this approximates to one and a half legions. To make up the numbers Cerialis brought with him II Adiutrix from Germany. It may have gone to the fortress at Lincoln, which was occupied by troops until *c*.77 or 78, while IX Hispana, Cerialis's old legion, probably went to York, where the fortress was founded *c*.71. Very little of the speculation about which legions were based in which fortresses is proven by incontrovertible evidence, so these suppositions may one day be overturned if new evidence comes to light. Troop dispositions were in any case quite fluid as the wars were fought, and vexillations and sometimes whole units moved from place to place in quick succession, splitting up and recombining as they progressed through the country.

In describing Cerialis's former exploits, Tacitus has little respect for him, insisting that in the suppression of the Batavian revolt Cerialis's success was due to good luck rather than good management. In Britain, the general is represented in a more favourable light:

> Petillius Cerialis at once struck the Britons with terror by attacking the state [*civitas*] of the Brigantes, said to be the most populous in the province, and in many battles, some of them bloody, he conquered a great part of Brigantia ... Indeed Cerialis would have overshadowed the exploits and reputation of any other governor, but Julius Frontinus, a great man, sustained the burden. (Tacitus *Agricola* 17)

The troops that Cerialis took with him on campaign are not known. Out of loyalty to IX Hispana he probably gave this legion the chief role in the campaign, advancing into the eastern parts of Brigantia, and it has been suggested that he allowed the legate of XX Valeria Victrix, Gnaeus Julius Agricola, to command in the west, to effect a pincer movement on the tribesmen. Agricola was certainly given independent commands, according to Tacitus:

> At the beginning Cerialis only shared with Agricola the hard work and the danger, but eventually he shared the glory as well. Frequently he tested him with command of part of the army, and sometimes, judging by results, he gave him control of larger forces. (Tacitus *Agricola* 8)

It is suggested that Cerialis reached Carlisle, and probably penetrated into southern Scotland. The first known fort at Carlisle has yielded early Flavian pottery and coins, and the timbers of a gateway were shown by dendrochronological analysis to have been felled in 72 or 73. In the east it is not clear where the Romans campaigned, but perhaps they arrived at the Tyne as well as the Solway. Somehow the fort at Castleford in

Yorkshire and the half-legion base at Malton have to be fitted into the picture, and it is not certain how much was achieved by Bolanus when he contained the Brigantian revolt. Marching camps over the Stainmore pass across the Pennines, and a series of camps around Carlisle, have been attributed to Cerialis, as part of his pursuit of the Brigantian king Venutius. Temporary camps are notoriously difficult to date, and a line of marching camps gives no information about which troops were using them, or in which direction they were marching. Nonetheless it seems that Tacitus was correct to say that Cerialis had overrun nearly all of the territory of the Brigantes. Unfortunately he does not outline the next stage, of garrisoning the area and dealing with the natives.

Conquest of the Silures: Julius Frontinus AD 73/73 to c.77

Sextus Julius Frontinus is better known as an author than as a governor of Britain. He was placed in charge of the aqueducts and water supply of Rome, and wrote a manual on the subject, called *De aquae ductu urbis Romae*. He may have accompanied the Emperor Domitian to Germany in his campaigns against the Chatti, or at least he prudently mentioned a few of Domitian's activities in his book called *Strategemata* on military stratagems. Frontinus is a sterling example of the versatility of Roman high officials; he commanded armies, governed provinces, investigated engineering, improved the water supply, studied military history and wrote books. He will certainly have had experience of civil administration as well, but not much is known about his career, except that in 70 he was urban praetor in Rome. This was an important post, in which he would act as chief magistrate when the consuls were absent. He may have commanded an army group formed from vexillations in the suppression of the revolt of Civilis. Before he was appointed governor of Britain he must have been consul, but it is not known in which year.

The only information that has come down to us about Frontinus's term of office in Britain derives from Tacitus, namely a bald statement that the new governor conquered the Silures of south Wales. This leaves open to interpretation what else he may have achieved. Some scholars argue that he did nothing in the north of Britain, while others suggest that he could not have left the whole area unattended. There may have been unrecorded Roman activity under the direction of one of Frontinus's officers, even if this activity entailed merely consolidation of what Cerialis had achieved. Frontinus probably operated in north Wales as well as the south. He is credited with the foundation of the legionary fortress at Chester, which was still being built when Agricola took over, and besides the legionary base it is highly likely that Frontinus established some auxiliary forts in north Wales. A cavalry unit stationed in Ordivician territory was badly cut up just before Agricola arrived, and it is probably safe to assume that this unit was not there in complete isolation.

The campaign against the Silures was hard fought, but ultimately successful. It may have been Frontinus who founded the *civitas* capital of the Silures at Caerwent (Venta Silurum). If this seems a little too precipitate, coming directly after the war, there is a parallel from the German provinces, when Gnaeus Domitius Corbulo campaigned against the Friesians, or Frisii, in the reign of Claudius. This tribe had hitherto been quite loyal to the Romans, but had erupted in protest when their taxes were increased. They did not pay in cash, but in hides, and all went well until a somewhat insensitive Roman official decided to increase the standard size of the hides to that of the aurochs, a truly enormous beast which has been extinct since the seventeenth century. It was too huge and powerful for the Frisii to rear on farms or to capture and skin on a regular basis, and their own beasts did not even begin to approach it in size. The result of this impossible request was a rebellion, which Corbulo suppressed, and then according to Tacitus, the defeated Friesians gave hostages, and settled in the area that he marked out for them, imposing on them a senate, magistracies and laws.

CONQUEST OF THE NORTH: GNAEUS JULIUS AGRICOLA AD 77/78 TO 83/84 THE FIRST TO THE THIRD CAMPAIGNING SEASONS AD 77 TO 79

The conquest of the Silures, the foundation of the legionary fortress of Chester, and perhaps the establishment of the *civitas* capital at Caerwent is the sum total of what is known or broadly surmised about the governorship of Sextus Julius Frontinus, unlike his successor Gnaeus Julius Agricola whose biography by his son-in-law Tacitus is a thinly disguised eulogy. Without Tacitus's work, however, precious little would be known about Agricola. A fragmentary inscription from Verulamium records the building of the Forum in the town. Part of a name survives, the main element being IULIO ...GRIC, which is easily restored as Julius Agricola. His name is accompanied by the title PR.PR, indicating that he was pro-praetorian governor. Dating evidence derives from the fact that the Emperor Titus is described as the son of the divine Vespasian, so the inscription was set up after the death of Vespasian, which occurred in 79. This may be the actual year of the inscription, since the other vital piece of evidence concerns the number of years that Titus had held tribunician power, restored by archaeologists as VIIII (this number was not always written as IX), which makes the year of the Forum dedication 79, though an alternative reading has been suggested which would date it to 81. On lead pipes from the fortress at Chester, where the water supply was being installed, Agricola is named in full. These too are dated to 79, but Vespasian is still named as Emperor, so the pipes were laid down just before his death, which occurred on 24 June 79. Dating evidence doesn't get much closer than that.

If the inscription and the lead pipes were the only evidence for a governor named Gnaeus Julius Agricola, it would never be supposed that this man had already served in Britain twice, as tribune of a legion under Suetonius Paullinus, and as legate of XX legion under Cerialis. It would never be suggested that he held office for nearly seven years, since most governors served for about three years and then went on to other posts. It would be discerned from archaeological excavations that the Romans had reached Scotland and built some forts under the Flavian Emperors, but it would probably be assumed that there was more than one governor spanning this period. Agricola broke all the rules. It was not usual to carry out successive military appointments in the same province, and it was not usual to remain in post for such a long period. The most unusual factor is that a biography should have been compiled, and that it should have survived.

There is a wealth of information in Tacitus's work, but it does not contain all that historians and archaeologists need to know. There are no firm dates, so that there has been a perennial debate about when Agricola arrived and when he left. Tacitus writes of summer and winter seasons, alternating his accounts of military activity in the campaigning seasons with descriptions of civilian affairs in the winters. He gives few place names, only some of which are firmly identified, so that the task of marrying the archaeological discoveries to the text is fraught with difficulty. If the relevant sections of his *Histories* had survived, it may have been possible to corroborate and augment what is stated in the *Agricola*, but the books are lost. Nevertheless, the *Agricola* is invaluable. It is all we have, apart from Dio's few statements that are derived from Tacitus, and it must be remembered that Tacitus was not writing for an audience of archaeologists two thousand years in the future.

The dating controversy arises from the lack of knowledge as to when Agricola held the consulship. It would be a suffect consulship, taken up after the eponymous consuls stepped down, so the consular records do not record Agricola. Tacitus says Agricola entered his post as governor of Britain immediately after holding the consulship, so if he held it in 76, he would probably arrive in 77, and if he was consul in 77 then he would arrive in 78. This in turn affects the date when he left. In the end, it is probably an insoluble problem unless some startling piece of evidence turns up to settle the matter once and for all.

As soon as he arrived Agricola gathered the troops and set off for Wales, where the Ordovices had almost annihilated a cavalry unit. Tacitus says that it was late in the summer and the army was beginning to think about winter quarters, but this only emphasises Agricola's zeal and energy. After dealing with the Ordovices, he went on to Anglesey, where Suetonius had put in a garrison but was forced to leave when the rebellion of Boudicca broke out. The island had become a refuge for fugitives according to Tacitus, and in any case the conquest of Wales was not completed without a firm hold on Anglesey. It seems to have been a sudden decision to attack. The Britons were expecting ships to appear to ferry the soldiers across, but:

As usual with decisions taken at short notice, there were no ships available. The determination and energy of the general got the troops across [the straits]. He selected special auxiliaries who knew the fords, and whose native practice was to swim while carrying weapons and leading their horses. He told them to leave their equipment, and then threw them into the attack so suddenly that the enemy were astonished. They had been expecting an attack by sea, but now they saw that nothing was insuperable for men who waged war in this way. (Tacitus *Agricola* 18)

This passage sets the heroic tone for the rest of the governor's achievements. During the winter after the Welsh campaign, Agricola set about weeding out the various abuses that were inflicted on the Britons. Having served twice before in the province he presumably knew exactly what went on.

The second campaigning season was the first full one. Agricola gathered his army, as Tacitus says, which raises the question of where the troops came from. The legions were dispersed in the fortresses at Caerleon, Chester and York, which remained as legionary bases almost until the end of Roman Britain, and there may still have been a legion at Wroxeter. Several suggestions have been made as to which legions occupied these bases, but there is no absolute proof for any of the permutations. It is almost certain that II Augusta was at Caerleon, and IX Hispana was at York, but it is assumed that XX Valeria Victrix was at Wroxeter and II Adiutrix at Chester.

It is much more difficult to detect the location of the various auxiliary units, and to provide secure dates for the few forts that are known in the south. In order to assemble sufficient manpower for Cerialis's and Agricola's northern campaigns, it is suggested that some of the military posts in the south were given up, if not under Cerialis and Frontinus, then possibly now, as Agricola moved further north and established new forts. It is reasonable to suppose that some units were brought out of the garrisons of the south, and the process began of turning the evacuated forts into civilian developments. Likely candidates are Exeter, Cirencester, and Dorchester-on-Thames, but archaeological investigations suggest that civilian development in these places generally did not begin until about 80. The lack of buildings does not preclude a brief period of settlement inside the evacuated forts, but this is to go further than the evidence will allow. All that can be said is that Agricola founded a lot of forts in new areas, and he presumably drew the necessary soldiers from the south, which in turn implies that military government ceased in those areas and civilian government was established, but the details are lacking.

It is not clear where exactly Agricola aimed for in his second season. Tacitus says that Agricola was everywhere on the march and personally chose all the sites for pitching camp, dismissed as *topoi* by some modern authors, the usual sort of praise for an active general who harassed the enemy continually, raiding and attacking without let up. There is no hint as to where Agricola did all this. A more useful passage describes how the Romans entered new areas:

> As a result [of the campaigns] several states [*civitates*] which until then were used to acting independently gave up violence and sent hostages. They were surrounded by forts with such skill and thoroughness that no new part of Britain was won with so little damage. (Tacitus *Agricola* 20)

The reference to new areas suggests that Agricola was in southern Scotland, beyond the Brigantian territory that Cerialis had overrun. If Cerialis was the founder of the fort at Carlisle, then the forts that were so skilfully sited by Agricola ought to have been founded to the north of the Tyne–Solway line. Alternatively, it is possible that there was a need for consolidation in the hill country of the western Pennine area, which may not have been thoroughly pacified by Cerialis or Frontinus. This suggestion derives from the reference to forests and estuaries in Tacitus's description of the campaigns, but mention of forests and estuaries could easily apply to the west coast of southern Scotland, too, so it has to be said that no one knows the location of the 'new places' of Tacitus's description.

For the following year, the third campaigning season, which belongs to 79 if the early dating for Agricola's campaigns applies, there is an identifiable place name, or rather a river name, the Tay. Agricola marched *'usque ad Taum (aestuaria nomen est)'* says Tacitus, 'up to the Tay, which is the name of the estuary'. The Romans encountered new peoples (*novas gentes*), and Agricola built forts, which were occupied during the winter, distressing the natives who were used to fighting in summer and recouping their strengths in winter, but the new governor gave them no rest. Agricola needed to find a way to control groups of tribesmen who had no vested interest in risking a set battle, but could disperse and use their terrain for guerrilla warfare. He probably did it in the time-honoured brutal but effective way of preventing movement, attacking and burning crops and food stores in winter, and generally harassing the people:

> No fort established by Agricola was ever taken by storm or given up in surrender or retreat. The soldiers could make frequent raids and were secure even if besieged because they had supplies to last for a whole year. The winter held no fears for them because they were self-sufficient, whereas the enemies were in despair because they were accustomed to recoup the losses of the summer by successes in the winter, but now they were given no rest in summer or winter. (Tacitus *Agricola* 22)

It was probably after these campaigns to conquer new peoples that the Emperor Titus was hailed as Imperator for the fifteenth time, in 79. Dio records this event after giving a short synopsis of Agricola's activities in Britain, not in chronological order but amalgamating different events without regard to their sequence. Dio specifically states that it was in connection with Agricola's achievements in Britain that Titus received the acclamation, but unfortunately he does not unequivocally relate the advance to the River Tay to the honours for the Emperor, which leaves considerable leeway for archaeologists to interpret the passage according to whichever dating is adopted for Agricola's arrival and departure. According to the later dating hypothesis, Titus's Imperial acclamation would belong to the fourth season, which was not one of campaigning and expanding the Empire, but one of consolidation, which seems a less likely achievement for Titus to celebrate, as opposed to the forward thrust of the previous year. The problem remains open to debate.

CONSOLIDATION: THE FOURTH SEASON AD 80

By his fourth season Agricola had overrun a large amount of new territory, and as Tacitus says, it was important to secure the recent conquests. Agricola spent the whole year on this task, before setting off on further expeditions. The consolidation probably extended from northern England to the 'new peoples' of Scotland that Agricola encountered in his third season. Tacitus says that in the fourth season, if only the glory of the army and the Roman name had allowed it, Agricola could have found an ideal place to call a halt (Tacitus calls it a *terminus*), between the estuaries of the Clyde and Forth, which he secured by planting garrisons (*praesidia*).

It is reasonable to assume that in consolidating his hold on the territory he had won, Agricola built forts up to this line, if not beyond it as far as the Tay. The problem is to identify where they were. In the past it was customary to assign to Agricola all the forts from Lancashire and Yorkshire up into Scotland, but as one scholar expressed it, this cannot be true, otherwise Agricola would have arrived at his final battle accompanied only by his batman. It is possible that Cerialis, Frontinus, and Agricola himself bypassed the Lake District, which seems to have been occupied at a later time, but the routes through and across the Pennines would require protection, so some forts were built to secure communications and supplies, as well as to keep control of the tribesmen. Forts which are definitely Agricolan in date are Lancaster, Ribchester and Brough–under-Stainmore. A map of Roman Britain with all known fort sites marked on it gives the impression that northern England was very closely guarded, but the forts were not all occupied at the same time, and without precise dating evidence, it cannot be said that Agricola built the entire network of forts in these areas.

Roman Fortresses and Forts – Text Box

A typical Roman fort of the Imperial period was shaped like a modern playing card, with two short sides and two long sides, and rounded corners. This is the evolved version of a Roman fort, since the earlier fortified camps of the early Empire were not so regularly shaped and were not generally designed as permanent bases for troops. Some of them had oval defences, or were laid out to suit the terrain. Typically, early Roman forts were built of earth and turf ramparts (called *murus caespiticus*), topped by a timber breastwork, with access by timber-built gateways with towers on either side. There were usually interval towers ranged along the walls and at each corner. Forts were usually surrounded by one or more ditches, with sloping sides, and an aptly labelled 'ankle-breaker' drainage channel at the bottom. The Romans usually took this drainage feature seriously, judging by the number of excavations that show that the ditch had been cleaned out and squared off, sometimes more than once. In the second century from the reign of Trajan onwards, when the majority of forts had become permanent bases, rather than semi-permanent ones occupied for varying periods while the provinces were pacified and Romanised, forts and fortresses were generally, but not universally, built of stone. In some cases this meant re-fronting existing forts by cutting back the turf rampart, and in others building in stone from the outset.

Depending upon the type of unit stationed in them, forts varied in size from 0.6 hectares for the small *numerus* forts in Germany and Dacia, to 20 hectares for a legion. There were a few double legionary fortresses such as Vetera (modern Xanten) and Mogontiacum (modern Mainz) until after the failed revolt of Saturninus in AD 89, who gathered the combined savings of his legionaries to attempt a coup against the Emperor Domitian. After this, Domitian decreed that no two legions were to be housed together.

The internal arrangements of fortresses and forts were on the whole standardised, but with regional or local variations. The centre range usually housed the headquarters building (*principia*), flanked by the commander's house (*praetorium*) and the granaries (*horreae*). There were four main streets within the fort, and its orientation was taken from the direction that the headquarters faced. The road running across the fort in front of the headquarters was the *via principalis*, with its two gates labelled for the right and left sides (*porta principalis dextra* and *porta principalis sinistra*). The road that connected the *principia* to the front gate (*porta praetoria*) was the *via praetoria*, and behind the headquarters another road, the *via decumana*, ran to the rear gate (*porta decumana*).

In several forts archaeological evidence shows that there were other communal buildings, for example the workshop (*fabrica*) where metalworking, woodworking and repair of equipment and weapons would take place. There was usually a hospital (*valetudinarium*). It should be acknowledged that from the ground plans alone, the workshops and the hospitals might have been confused, each consisting of small rooms ranged round a central courtyard, but in a few cases medical instruments have been found, which strongly supports the label 'hospital'. The forts on Hadrian's Wall at Wallsend and Housesteads, and the fortresses on the Conetinent at Vetera (modern Xanten) and Novaesium (modern Neuss) are among examples where hospitals have been found.

The majority of the buildings inside the fort would be the barrack blocks. For the infantry in legionary fortresses and auxiliary forts, barracks were normally laid out with ten rooms subdivided into two parts, one for sleeping and eating and one for storage, each room accommodating eight men, and therefore housing one complete century of eighty men. A veranda ran the full length of the ten rooms, and at the end of the barrack block there was usually a suite of rooms for the centurion. The centurion's quarters were probably very comfortable, and some evidence has been found for wall paintings in centurion's barracks. Cavalry barracks were different, reflecting the organisation of the *turma*. From the evidence at the fort at Dormagen on the Rhine, and Wallsend on Hadrian's Wall, it seems that the men and their horses were housed together. In at least three of the Dormagen stable blocks, there were double cubicles, with soak-away pits in those along one side, and hearths in those on the other, indicating that men and mounts lived in the same block.

One of the prime considerations in establishing Roman forts was the protection of routes. The forts at Carlisle in the west and Corbridge in the east almost certainly belong to Agricola's advance into Scotland though it is thought that Carlisle may already have been occupied under Cerialis a few years before. These forts would protect communication routes and provide supply bases for the northern advance. At Corbridge the Agricolan fort was not built on the site of the remains exhibited today on the edge of the modern town, but at the Red House site some short distance away. This fort was discovered when the modern A69 was being constructed, to take traffic away from the town. It has been interpreted as a supply base on account of the open-ended shed-like structures found there. Nothing similar has been found at Carlisle, where the fort identified as Agricolan is too small to suggest that it functioned in the same way.

From Northumberland and Cumbria into Scotland there were two main routes, Dere Street in the east leading up to the Forth, and in the west the road ran through Annandale to the Clyde. Forts were built to protect these routes, though on the principle that Roman forts were usually situated at intervals of about one day's march, it seems that not all of them have been discovered. On the west side the fort at Dalswinton was the largest and most important. There are two successive forts on this site, each with two phases of occupation. One of the two-phase forts is definitely dated to the Flavian period, while the other is not dated but it is situated in a less well chosen position, which probably indicates that this fort was built first, and then a better site close by was chosen for a second fort. Since it seems unlikely that Agricola was responsible for all four phases of occupation, either his predecessors Cerialis or Frontinus were there before him, or his unknown successor occupied the area after him. The fort at Loudoun Hill also has four phases of occupation, which could perhaps be explained in the same way. It is tempting to link the supposedly earlier phases with Cerialis's drive to the north during his campaign in Brigantia, but up to now there is no firm evidence to support the theory.

On the eastern side of the country, the fort at Newstead was built in close proximity to the three Eildon Hills, from which it takes its Roman name of Trimontium. The three hills have to be viewed from a particular angle to see that there are indeed three peaks, one of which looks as though it is struggling to get away from the other two. On Eildon Hill North, a Roman watchtower was built, in the middle of what is considered to be the tribal capital of the Selgovae. This implies that the tribe was hostile and required close supervision. It is usually considered that the neighbouring tribe of the Novantae were also hostile. By contrast, the Votadini of the eastern coastal strip seem to have been friendly to the Romans. This tribe occupied their stronghold of Traprain Law through the Roman occupation, and few forts have come to light in the territory of the Votadini, implying that there was no need to guard it closely.

Tacitus's statement that in the fourth season Agricola had found an ideal *terminus* for his conquests is exact enough to locate it on a small-scale map, running across the country between the Forth and Clyde, but on the larger scale it proves to be very irritating, because up to now there is very little indication of where the *praesidia* were established between the Forth and Clyde. Like all the forts in Britain at this time, these *praesidia* would be built of turf and timber, and so traces of them may have been superseded or obliterated by later buildings, or perhaps were not recognised during nineteenth-century excavations, but even so it seems that Agricola's forts were not all built on exactly the same sites as the those of the Antonine Wall, which also connected the two estuaries in the second century. The only indication that Agricola may have chosen some of the sites that were occupied in the Antonine period derives not from archaeological traces of fort walls or buildings, but from the artefacts of Flavian date found at Cadder, Castlecary and Mumrills.

The forts of Flavian date at Mollins and Camelon, and more recent discovery of a Flavian fort at Doune, suggest that Agricola's potential *terminus* was never intended to run along the same line as the Antonine Wall. His criteria would be slightly different. Although one of the prime considerations would be the control of movement, he was not looking for suitable geographical terrain on which to build a running barrier, like the Antonine turf wall with forts strung out along it. Frontiers of this solid kind were not the fashion in Agricola's day, but the Flavian system for guarding the borders of Germany consisted of a road with watch towers, and though there is no absolutely precise dating evidence for this system, it was perhaps contemporary with Agricola. He would site his forts in places where the garrisons could keep watch over the surrounding area, send out patrols, guard communications and supplies, and control movement up and down the north–south routes to his rear, as well as east to west.

In the west, the fort at Barochan Hill was probably part of the Agricolan *terminus*, watching over the estuary of the Clyde, while Elginhaugh fulfilled the same purpose on the eastern side. The fort at Elginhaugh yielded high-quality Flavian finds, suggesting that it may have been Agricola's headquarters. It may not be wholly by accident that in the seventeenth century, when General Monck administered Scotland under Cromwell, he set up his headquarters at Dalkeith, not far from Elginhaugh.

One of the major problems of matching the known military installations to Tacitus's narrative is the date of the forts at Ardoch and Strageath and the road and watchtowers running along the Gask Ridge around the western edge of Fife. Since dating evidence is not sufficiently precise to pinpoint the foundation dates with any certainty, these forts and towers could belong to any of Agricola's campaigning seasons from the fourth to the seventh, or indeed to the period after he had been recalled. However, Tacitus is unequivocal in his description of the third season, when he says that Agricola reached the Tay. The towers of the Gask Ridge ran from Ardoch to the fort at Bertha on the Tay. It is permissible to speculate that there may have been more towers, not yet discovered, on the road south of Ardoch as far as Camelon, which would join the towers and forts of the Gask Ridge to the *praesidia* of the *terminus*. In that case it is possible that the forts at Ardoch, Strageath and Bertha and the postulated intervening towers were built to guard the route to the north as part of the consolidation process of the fourth season, when Agricola would have time and manpower because he and his army were not engaged in major campaigns. This suggestion is unorthodox, since a later date is usually favoured for these forts and towers.

THE FIFTH TO THE SEVENTH SEASONS AD 81 TO 83

If the fifth season occupied the summer of 81, as it does according to the earlier dating for Agricola's tenure of Britain, then the order, or the permission, to resume the advance after the fourth season's halt came from the Emperor Titus. In September 81 Titus died, so according to the scenario of the later dating, the halt on the Forth–Clyde line and the building of forts was carried out in the final months of Titus's reign. In this case the fifth season and the advance beyond the Forth–Clyde line began in 82, so the order to resume the conquest would emanate from the Emperor Domitian, Titus's brother.

At the opening of the fifth season's campaigns, Agricola may have concentrated on western Scotland. Tacitus describes how the general 'crossed in the first ship', in other words leading from the front in a combined ops manoeuvre with the fleet and the army. The problem is that there is no mention of what he crossed. The only clue is that the army arrived at the point where Scotland faces Ireland, which places him firmly in the west, and it has been argued that since Tacitus mentions the Forth and the Clyde in the previous season, it ought to be the River

Clyde that Agricola crossed. The part of Scotland which faces Ireland is taken to mean the Mull of Kintyre, but it has also been argued that in his fifth season Agricola was indeed operating in the west, but much further south in Galloway. On the grounds that the Romans marched past the Lake District and garrisoned it later, it is suggested that this area had been ignored in the initial advance into Scotland, and Agricola needed to consolidate before he marched further north.

There is hardly any detail in Tacitus's work about the events of the fifth season. Great attention is paid to Ireland instead of Scotland, starting with the Irish king who arrived at Agricola's headquarters after being thrown out of his kingdom in a family squabble. Agricola gave some thought to the conquest of Ireland, which he thought would require one legion and some auxiliaries. Anyone from the time of Henry II in the twelfth century to the Earl of Essex in the sixteenth would be able to point out that the Irish tribes might be primitive, but it would prove very difficult to pin then down and defeat them. For the Romans, of course, it remained a passing fancy, and Agricola turned back to Scotland.

For the final two seasons, leading up to the great Battle of Mons Graupius, Tacitus devotes many more words and provides more detail than he does for the previous seasons. It makes no difference now whether the early or late dating for Agricola's governorship is used, since in either case the final two-year run-up to the Battle of Mons Graupius took place under Domitian. After so many seasons in Britain, Agricola may have anticipated that he would be recalled, but it seems that Domitian was satisfied with what had been achieved so far and authorised Agricola to continue along the same lines. So the sixth season was spent north of the Forth, concentrating on the eastern side of the country, and working in co-operation with the fleet, reconnoitring the harbours. The fleet was also used to make sudden raids from the coast, to spread terror and perhaps inspire the Britons to fight. In northern Scotland, the natives did not need to risk a battle, but could retreat into the mountains and wait until invaders went away, so in the sixth season Agricola failed to bring about the final conflict. Tacitus describes how the tribesmen retaliated:

The people of Caledonia started to arm themselves. They made great preparations, which were exaggerated by rumour. They caused alarm by attacking some forts, as though they were provoking [the Romans]. There were some cowardly men [in Agricola's army] who advised that it would be safer to retreat behind the Forth rather than be driven back. In the interim, Agricola found out that the enemy was about to attack in large numbers, so to avoid being surrounded by forces who outnumbered his own and knew the terrain, he split his army into three groups and advanced. (Tacitus *Agricola* 25)

One of these three army groups was attacked and nearly defeated. The tribesmen (Caledonians, but Tacitus does not call them by this name, preferring to use the phrase 'the people of Caledonia') knew that the IX legion was understrength and was therefore the weakest of the three groups. The lack of manpower may have arisen because a vexillation had been sent to Germany, where Domitian was preparing for a war against the fierce Chatti. Alternatively, there may have been a need for a number of legionaries from IX to remain at their base at York to keep a watch on northern England. Whatever the reason, the knowledge that IX legion was weak implies good intelligence on the part of the Britons, who launched a night attack, creeping up to the Roman camp, where they quickly despatched the sentries and burst in, slaughtering as they went. Agricola had posted scouts who informed him that the Britons were on the move, heading for the camp of the IX legion. Agricola seems to have been on the march even before the Britons reached their destination and began their assault, but by the time he and the Roman troops arrived, the IX legion was in tremendous difficulties. But now the Britons were caught between two armies, one in the camp and one coming to its relief. The tribesmen were thrown out, but there was no pursuit, and the Britons disappeared into the forests and marshes. Tacitus says that if the tribesmen had not been aided by their terrain which covered their escape, the war could have been concluded.

This Roman victory spurred on the soldiers, who were impressed with their own achievements and now clamoured to be led to the furthest parts of the country. Even the ones who had advised retreat were all fired up and eager to march. One wonders who these sudden fire-eating converts were, and if Agricola reminisced to his son-in-law about them through clenched teeth. Somehow, the enthusiasm of the troops had to be maintained over the winter, since the advance to the north did not begin immediately.

There was an interesting event at the end of the sixth season, when the recently recruited tribesmen of the Germanic Usipi, who had been forcibly enlisted and sent to join the Roman army in Britain, decided that they no longer wanted to be Roman soldiers, and they resolved to set off for home. They killed their officers, stole some ships and set sail, but the winds and the tides took them all the way around the island, and they ended up on the same side of Britain where they had started. Their fate was worse than serving as soldiers, since many of them starved to death and the ones who survived were sold as slaves when they fetched up on the coast near the territory of the Frisii. Their exploits had important consequences for the Romans. For the first time, there was proof that Britain was an island, officially confirmed later on when Agricola's fleet circumnavigated the whole country and the participants were able to report what the northern seas were like. The sailors observed that in the late summer the sun did not set in the most northerly parts, but simply skirted the horizon for a short time and then started to rise again.

The final push to conquer Scotland began in Agricola's seventh and last season. His family was with him in Britain, and at the beginning of the summer, his infant son died, but Tacitus says that he bore the loss well, and the coming campaign provided a distraction for him. The tribes had been making preparations to meet the threat that they knew was coming, and had at last formed alliances and chosen a leader, just as the Britons of the south chose Cassivellanus to co-ordinate the campaigns against Julius Caesar. The leader of the Caledonian tribes was Calgacus, renowned for his bravery and nobility, as his name, or rather his title attests: he was 'the Swordsman'. He assembled 30,000 warriors, which seems a high figure for a sparsely populated area, but it is not known where the limits of his recruiting grounds lay.

Apart from the report that the fleet was used for plundering raids and attacks from the coast, Tacitus does not provide much detail about how the Romans arrived at Mons Graupius, where the final battle occurred. The description of the battle itself, and the speeches of the Roman general and the Caledonian leader before it took place, occupy a large proportion of the whole work. Hints as to what the Roman army did on the way to the battle and where they were when it was fought have to be gleaned from the words that Tacitus invents for these speeches.

THE SEARCH FOR MONS GRAUPIUS

The puzzle of Mons Graupius will probably never be solved. It has to be located near a mountain, which for Scotland does not narrow the choice very much. There is a consistent mindset among some scholars that casts doubt on the ability of Agricola and his army to get very far into Scotland, so it is suggested that this final battle must have been fought on the flank of the Highlands, certainly not in the interior of the mountain zone, and probably not much further north than Aberdeen. One of the more recent suggestions for the battle site is at Bennachie, where there is a very large Roman marching camp at Durno that could have held Agricola's forces as he assembled them for battle. But until more evidence comes to light, it is not certain that this suggestion is any more valid than any other mountain location.

Any suggestion that the battle may have been fought in the Highlands is dismissed with a snort of derision. The main problem is that no traces of Roman camps and forts have been found further north than the Great Glen, and those that have been found are all located on the edge of the Highlands, guarding the routes through the glens into and out of the mountains, so it is considered inconceivable that the Romans ever set foot in the Highlands, at least before the main battle was fought, and probably not even after the Romans had won it. The forts at the mouths of the glens are considered to be springboards for further attacks into the mountains to round up the tribesmen after the great Battle of Mons Graupius.

It is worth pointing out that other armies which conquered Scotland found it necessary to go into the Highlands to persuade the natives to fight, and to remain there to stop them from gathering. It has been said that in Scotland it is the invaders who starve while the natives take to the mountains and wait. In the seventeenth century, General Monck led his troops all over the mountain passes, on routes which even the natives said their forefathers never used. Nearly a century later the Hanoverians placed garrisons in the mountains. Scotland is not conquered unless the Highlands are controlled, and while it could be argued that Agricola or his successor had achieved this by establishing forts at the glen mouths, the important point is that it is a considerable achievement to persuade the Britons to fight a pitched battle, risking everything on a single chance to win. It suggests that Agricola had gone into the Highlands to flush the tribesmen out, making it impossible for them to find refuge there, burning and destroying settlements and food supplies, and so ensuring that the Britons had nothing left to lose by fighting him. When compared and contrasted with the campaigns of the Emperors Septimius Severus and Caracalla at the beginning of the third century, Agricola's achievement in bringing about a major battle is of supreme importance. Although Severus planned very thoroughly for his campaigns, ensuring supplies for the troops and combining land operations with the fleet, he did not bring about a decisive battle. Dio says that Severus never fought a battle and never saw the enemy drawn up in battle lines, and Herodian emphasises how easy it was for the tribesmen to run off and hide. After the campaigns of Severus and Caracalla, there was peace for some years, but the country was not occupied and held down as it was under Agricola and the succeeding Flavian governors.

Apart from scepticism that Agricola conducted any military operations in the Highlands, similarly the idea that Agricola, or indeed Severus, could have reached the ultimate northern coast is also dismissed. But if Agricola stopped short of the extreme end of the island he had not conquered the whole of it, and the fact that he had not reached the ultimate shore would be clear to all the soldiers who took part, not to mention any observers who were with the army, like the Greek scholar Demetrius of Tarsus, who sailed with the fleet to some of the islands that surround Britain. Demetrius may be the same man as Scribonius Demetrius, who made two dedications at York, one to the gods of the governor's headquarters, and one to Ocean and Tethys, both of them quite appropriate if he was attached to Agricola's entourage and went on sea voyages with the fleet.

Despite the belief that Agricola never reached the ultimate northern coast, a case has been made by one or two scholars for locating the final Battle of Mons Graupius in the northernmost part of Scotland. It was late in the season when it was fought, which suggests that there had been a long march to arrive there, corroborated by Tacitus's version of Agricola's speech to the troops, which in turn indicates that the long march had not taken the Romans around in circles but had brought the troops directly to the far north. More important, the speech that Tacitus invents for the leader Calgacus implies that there was nowhere else to go:

> There is no land beyond us, and even the sea provides no refuge because we are threatened by the fleet … we are the last people on earth, the last free men, we live in a remote land known only by rumour, and this has protected us until today. The farthest point of Britain is open … there are no people beyond us, only sea and rock. (Tacitus *Agricola* 30)

The debate about the location of Mons Graupius will be a perennial one, but at least it can generate enthusiasm and scholarship, possibly more so than if Tacitus had been able to give a complete modern grid reference to the site. Archaeological finds may one day reveal the place, just as the site of the *Varusschlacht* has been found in Germany, where the Roman legions of Quinctilius Varus were wiped out by Arminius in AD 9.

The description of the preliminaries to the battle and the combat itself occupy several pages in Tacitus's account. The fighting took place on the slope of a hill, where Calgacus's warriors formed up. Agricola put his legions in reserve and fought the entire battle employing only his auxiliaries. The cavalry attended to the British chariots while the

Batavians and Tungrians attacked the main force, but the Britons began to move down the hill in an attempt to get round the Roman rear. Agricola had kept some cavalry in reserve, so he threw them into the fighting. They managed to break through the ranks of the tribesmen and then come round to attack them from behind. This trapped the warriors between the horsemen and the Roman infantry units, so there was great slaughter, amounting to 10,000 Britons according to Tacitus. Only 360 Romans were killed.

Next day there were no Britons to be found, which suggests that they had gone to ground in the mountains and valleys. Technically it was not such a complete victory as Tacitus claims on behalf of his father -in-law, since a large number of tribesmen were still alive and free, and the task of extracting them from the mountains would be labour-intensive. It was late in the season, and Agricola did not try to pursue and round up the warriors. It is not known if he made any treaty arrangements with the tribes, although he did take some hostages, suggesting that there may have been some sort of dialogue. He marched slowly back towards the south, to impress the Britons by his nonchalant progress. The fleet was ordered to sail round the island, allocating some troops to the prefect in command of the ships. Then he put the army into winter quarters.

AFTER AGRICOLA

Agricola was probably recalled in 84, perhaps using the winter following the battle to begin the process of consolidation of the Roman hold on the north. Tacitus says that Agricola handed over a peaceful province to his successor, who may have been Sallustius Lucullus. He is attested as governor at some unknown time, but it is not clear when he arrived in the province. Very little is known about events in Britain after Agricola's departure. The man who had completed the conquest of Britain could look forward to honours and further important appointments, but instead he was ignored, a point which Tacitus emphasises on behalf of his father-in-law. He suggests that the lack of promotion was due to Domitian's suspicion and jealousy. There may be some partial truth in the accusation, but no one knows why Agricola, the British specialist, was not called upon to carry out any further tasks. He had hoped to be made governor of Syria, but the offer never came, and he died, probably in 93, a disappointed man. Three years later, Domitian was assassinated, and a short time after that, when everyone could breathe freely again, Tacitus started work on his biographical tribute to his father-in-law. If he had not done so, the mystery of Flavian Scotland would hinge on a jumble of forts and camps around the Highland fringe, and on the routes to and from northern England.

THE CAMPS AND FORTS OF AGRICOLA'S CAMPAIGNS

Attempts have been made to trace the movements of Agricola's army on campaign by assigning the known temporary camps to individual seasons. On the march, the Roman troops traditionally built a camp every time they halted for the night, by digging a ditch and throwing the earth inside the perimeter to create a rampart. On top of this they often placed wooden stakes to form a palisade. Such temporary camps are notoriously difficult to date, though a line of camps, evenly spaced and more or less the same size can indicate the route that an army followed, but that is about all. Questions as to the direction of the march, whose army they belonged to and when they were built, can very rarely be answered. There were at least four major campaigns in Scotland under different governors or Emperors. Agricola campaigned in the first century, and in the mid-second century the governor Lollius Urbicus fought battles in the north in the reign of Antoninus Pius. At the beginning of the third century Roman armies campaigned probably up to the far north under the personal direction of the Emperor Severus. Another foray into Scotland took place under Constantius at the beginning of the fourth century, but even less is known about his achievements than about the other campaigns. Without secure dating evidence, the various series of camps that have been found could belong to any of these campaign armies.

There are only a few camps that can definitely be assigned to Agricola. There are two very large square camps at Dunning and Abernethy that could have held a campaign force on the march, and these are usually assigned to Agricola's army. The so-called Stracathro camps, named after the place where the first example was discovered, can be attributed to Agricola with more certainty. These camps have very distinctive gateways, with a curving bank and ditch projecting outwards around one half of the gate. This is called a *clavicula*, and examples are known from other provinces. The aim was to force anyone entering the camp to turn his unshielded side towards the defenders. The Stracathro camps are quite distinct because in addition to the curving bank and ditch they also display a second projecting arm, emerging from the opposite side of the gate, running straight towards the end of the curve, leaving a narrow gap between the two. No such camps have been found in Britain except in the Flavian period, and they are not found at all in other provinces. It suggests that Agricola himself had a hand in designing them.

There are six known Stracathro type camps, all near forts that were presumably built a short time later. They vary in size. Only the two on the east of the Highlands at Auchinhove and Ythan Wells are large enough to hold a substantial force. The others are at the mouths of some of the glens leading out of the Highlands to the southern lowlands. As such, they probably do not mark a line of march round the southern edge of the Highlands, but they most likely represent a temporary arrangement to watch the glens and the traffic into and out of them, while Agricola finally rounded up the Britons and brought them to battle. The main objection is that such an arrangement would reduce his available manpower when it came to the final battle, but on the other hand if he penetrated to the far north, he may have thought it more important to ensure that the tribes did not take to the mountains, march through the glens, and come down behind him.

As for the permanent forts in Scotland beyond the Forth–Clyde line, these may have been planned, or even founded by Agricola himself, but it is possible that he did not have enough time to complete them all, and that it was his unknown successor as governor who finished what Agricola had begun. Like the forts further south, most of these installations would be built of turf and timber. A fort was planted at the mouth of each of the Highland glens, with the legionary fortress of Inchtuthil guarding the most important route through the valley of the River Tay. From west to east, the other forts are Barochan on the Clyde, Drumquhassle, Menteith, Bochastle, Dalginross, Fendoch, Cargill (which lies south-east of the legionary fortress), the two larger forts at Cardean and Stracathro, with a small fortlet at Inverquharity guarding a minor route between these two. There may be more forts awaiting discovery, but despite efforts to identify Agricolan installations continuing around the eastern edge of the Highlands and up to the Moray Firth, nothing has yet been confirmed. One of the difficulties is the short time that any such forts would have been in occupation, and another is that some of the rivers in Scotland can change course in severe floods, so it is possible that vital evidence has been washed away.

The occupants of the legionary fortress at Inchtuthil are not attested. It is suggested that it was XX Valeria Victrix, while II Adiutrix was at Chester. The other forts would be most likely manned by auxiliary units, but possibly not in a neat arrangement with one discrete unit allocated to each fort. Mixed garrisons may have been stationed in the forts, combining cavalry and infantry, as was the case later on at Newstead and possibly Dalswinton. It is not known for certain how the glen-blocking forts worked, but it is reasonable to suppose that the troops patrolled the glens to the north and the lowland areas to the south, more along the lines of police work than military operations. It is usually considered that the forts were springboards for the penetration and pacification of the Highlands, but there is no evidence that the Romans adopted these measures. However they functioned, the units of the Highland line, and the garrisons of the forts on the roads to the south, were not given more than a few years to practise their technique before they were withdrawn.

SCOTLAND IMMEDIATELY LET GO

Tacitus's famous phrase, *perdomita Britannia, statim missa* (Britain was conquered and immediately let go) is a bitter indictment of the

Emperor Domitian, on behalf of Agricola. It could be questioned whether Britannia was really *perdomita*, but it seems that *statim missa* is not quite the exaggeration that it was once thought. Tacitus was accused of exaggerating, because the older theories regarding the abandonment of Scotland were based on the probability of a gradual phased withdrawal, but it now seems that the first-century occupation of Scotland was indeed very short. It appears that around 87, the glen-blocking forts and the legionary fortress at Inchtuthil were abandoned. The evidence for the date derives from coins. Excavations at Stracathro and Inchtuthil produced bronze *asses* of 86, but nothing later than this date. These bronze coins were the small change used to pay the soldiers, whose cash wages were reduced to a small sum after the deductions had been made for food and clothing, any lost or damaged equipment, compulsory savings, the burial club, and other items. The fact that the bronze *asses* of 86 were all in mint condition means that they had not been in circulation for very long. No coins of a later date have turned up at any of glen forts, even though bronze coins of 87 and later dates reached forts further south in quantity.

The coin evidence, taken together with the fact that the forts at Fendoch and Mollins – and the legionary fortress of Inchtuthil – were deliberately and tidily demolished, suggests that the Romans left the whole area precipitately, and that all units were withdrawn at the same time. The legionary fortress had not even been completed, and the Romans buried over a million nails there, in preference to packing them up and transporting them, and definitely in preference to allowing the natives access to so much iron.

The reason for the withdrawal was the war on the Danube. The Dacians had erupted into the Roman province of Moesia, defeated the Roman troops and killed the governor. The Emperor Domitian assembled another army under the Praetorian Prefect Fuscus. The Dacians defeated this army as well. The Danube provinces were much closer to Rome than Britain was, and therefore much more of a threat, so when Domitian prepared for a third war, the soldiers from Britain would provide some of the necessary manpower. The Emperor spent much of the year 87 in preparation for the new campaign, so this ties in well with the postulated date of 87 for the withdrawal of troops from Scotland. II Adiutrix may have been removed at the same time, though it is not attested in Moesia until 92. If the legion left Chester as XX Valeria Victrix was marching from Inchtuthil, there would have been a smooth evacuation and reoccupation of the Chester fortress. If there was any delay, the Wroxeter fortress may have been used to house the extra troops. But it is more plausible that Domitian ordered II Adiutrix to leave Britain in 87, rather than shuffling them about unnecessarily.

Probably at the same time that Inchtuthil and the glen forts were abandoned, the forts at Newstead and Dalswinton were enlarged to take more troops. A mint coin of 86 was found at Newstead in the ditch of the first fort, which had been filled in as the new fort was built. The new garrison was probably mixed, consisting of legionaries and auxiliary cavalry, and at Dalswinton there may have been two cavalry units. It has been suggested that the forts at Ardoch and Strageath, and the Gask towers belong to the withdrawal phase rather than the period when the Romans were advancing, but it seems needlessly laborious and time-consuming to build forts simply to organise protection of the area during a phased withdrawal, which is in any case discredited by the coin evidence of a rapid and complete evacuation, leaving nothing beyond the Forth–Clyde line. It is certain that nothing north of this line was occupied after 90, but the finer details of which forts were still in use between the Forth–Clyde line and Newstead and Dalswinton are more difficult to discern.

The years between 90 and the assassination of the Emperor Domitian in 96 are very dark in more ways than one. In Britain, these are dark years because there is hardly a glimmer of information to illuminate what happened in the final decade of the first century. Only one governor is known for certain, Sallustius Lucullus, who may have been Agricola's successor. He did not survive for long. The official story was that he had had the temerity to invent a new spear and name it the Lucullan, after himself, so he was executed on Domitian's orders. There may be more to the story. He may have been involved somehow in the revolt of the Rhine legions under the governor Saturninus in 89, or perhaps Domitian merely thought he was, and that was enough to warrant his execution.

During the dark years at the end of Domitian's reign everyone in Rome lived in fear of the increasingly paranoid Emperor. After the revolt of Saturninus, Domitian became ever more suspicious of the senators. He feared assassination so much that he had the palace corridors lined with polished slabs of stone so that he could see in their mirror-like surfaces if anyone was coming up behind him. He started to execute people on the merest hint of conspiracy or treason. He may have been suspicious of Agricola, whose achievements in Britain had after all earned his brother the Emperor Titus an Imperial acclamation. Agricola was spared from any accusations of disloyalty by dying before the Emperor. Three years afterwards, Domitian was stabbed to death by his secretary. The senators claimed that they had no complicity in the plot, and appointed one of their own respected members, Cocceius Nerva, as Emperor. He was already of advanced age, and died after only two years, but he had adopted as his successor the successful general Trajan, who became Emperor in 98. His brief dealings with Britain are outlined in the next chapter.

CIVILIAN DEVELOPMENT UNDER THE FLAVIAN GOVERNORS

During the Flavian era in southern Britain, a great surge of building works and town development has been detected wherever archaeological excavations have taken place. No town has yet been shown to possess a Forum and basilica before Flavian times, with the possible exception of Silchester, part of Togidubnus's kingdom, where a timber building dated *c.*50 was found underneath the late first-century Forum, but it is not certain whether this first building should be identified as a predecessor to the Forum. At other towns development of civic buildings is persistently Flavian in date. It might be expected that at Canterbury, where Claudian buildings have been found, there would be an early establishment of a Forum and basilica, but even here, among the most Romanised tribe, the Cantiaci, development is still Flavian. Similarly, in

London, where the administrative headquarters of the procurator and most probably the governor were located, public buildings also seem to be lacking until the Flavian period.

It is all too easy to attribute all this building work to the influence of Agricola, because Tacitus says that this is what he did:

> His [Agricola's] plan was to urge the primitive people who lived in scattered settlements, and were inclined to make war, to become accustomed to peace and quiet and the pleasurable life. For this reason he encouraged individuals and advised communities to build temples, Forums, and houses, by praising the people who were eager and castigating the laggards, and as a result people competed for honours instead of having to be coerced. (Tacitus *Agricola* 21)

Tacitus's statement that Agricola encouraged the Britons to move from their scattered settlements and build Forums and basilicas, temples and houses, is the most unequivocal evidence for persuading, but not actively coercing, the Britons to embrace the Roman way of life, though the passage carefully ignores the achievements of Agricola's predecessors. The theory that Romanisation was deliberately fostered by the government and spread by the army is now discredited. In the southern half of Britain, military occupation was much reduced towards the end of the first century, and yet this was the area where Romanisation rapidly developed after the army withdrew, whereas the military forces occupied the more northerly parts of Britain in great strength and for a long period, but most of the natives continued to live in Iron Age-style roundhouses throughout the Roman era.

TOWN HOUSES – TEXT BOX
In his account of Agricola's activities in Britain, Tacitus says that Agricola encouraged the Britons to build houses. He uses the word *domus* for 'house' and although it is not certain whether he was referring to houses in the new towns, or to country houses, or to

villas and farms, the more usual meaning of the term concerns town houses. Towns in Britain had only just started to develop under Agricola, and the earliest houses were fairly modest. Under the burnt layers at Colchester, Verulamium, and London, usually dated to the Boudiccan rebellion, the first few house sites have been traced, revealing that they were small and utilitarian. This is the case for most towns where excavations have been carried out, and it is assumed that the character of town houses was similar in all towns. In the colonies of Colchester, Gloucester and Lincoln, the first inhabitants were most likely veteran soldiers and their families, and their houses were built within the confines of the military barrack blocks.

Many town houses had shallow stone foundations, probably supporting timber buildings, with wattle and daub infill between the timbers, the daub consisting of clay and dung mixed with horsehair and straw, which often turns out a pale pink colour. Floors were of rammed earth or clay, or occasionally of timber, and roofs were thatched or covered with wooden shingles. Roof tiles are known to have been used but do not often turn up in excavations of the early houses. The occupation of the early towns seems to have been commercial rather than strictly residential, so it is assumed that some of the buildings were probably shops with living accommodation, either at the rear, or perhaps in an upper storey. It cannot be illustrated who lived in these establishments. Possibly they were occupied by Roman or Romanised merchants from other provinces rather than native Britons, and even when houses begin to develop, it has been doubted whether the British town councillors would reside in them, perhaps preferring to make their permanent homes in the villas in the countryside around the towns. On the other hand it has been pointed out that timber buildings are not necessarily primitive. A Roman timber house in London possessed wall paintings and mosaics. Nonetheless, it has been clearly demonstrated that the villas in the countryside, contemporary with the early town houses, are generally much better appointed and more comfortable.

In the second century the quality of houses in towns began to improve. At Cirencester the rows of shops were replaced with stone houses, and at Verulamium after timber buildings were destroyed in a serious fire *c*.AD 155, stone houses were built, spaced further apart, most likely to prevent fire from catching hold and spreading. Towns were divided into square plots called *insulae* and several town houses can be shown to have plenty of land around them in their *insula*, which may have been used for gardens. Houses such as these had plenty of space to expand, so some owners built wings on two sides, or eventually created enclosed courtyards with gardens, as at Silchester, Cirencester and Verulamium. At Cirencester, some houses may have been occupied by farmers who travelled out to their fields; one house had barns attached.

As time went on town houses were repaired, altered and enlarged. Roof tiles became more common, floors were sometimes mortared, internal walls of timber were replaced in mortared stone, and in the best houses wall paintings and mosaic floors started to appear. Different schools of mosaicists have been identified, so there was sufficient work to sustain several workshops, and expert plasterers and artists would be in demand to produce wall paintings. Many houses had underfloor heating installed, but even sophisticated houses do not seem to have been connected to the water supply or to the drainage system of the towns. Some houses were occupied for centuries, for instance a London house built in the second century was repaired and rebuilt continuously, and was still in use in the fifth century, and a house at Dorchester was built in the fourth century, with mosaics in all the rooms, and at least one window was glazed. Such examples may not have been the norm, but provide evidence that it was not all doom and gloom in late Roman Britain.

A more rational view of the Flavian advances in civic life would be to attribute at least some of the work to Cerialis and in particular Frontinus. The establishment of civil settlements at Exeter, Cirencester, and especially at Caerwent, might be his work. Chichester, Winchester and Silchester were probably Romanised initially by Togidubnus, but like other towns they received their public buildings in the late Flavian period, and may be associated with Agricola, or his successor. Only at Verulamium can the building of a Forum be definitely connected to Agricola. The inscription recording the dedication of the Forum complex bears his name, but the original impetus for the building could have started under Frontinus. The date of the inscription is interpreted as either 79 or 81, so if the first alternative is correct, it is questionable whether the building could have been planned and finished wholly in Agricola's tenure of office, since he arrived in the late summer of 77, which allows only two years for the initiation of the building to its completion. The later dating for his appointment as governor places his arrival in 78, which would make the timescale of only one year even more improbable.

The design of the Forum at Verulamium is reminiscent of the headquarters building of a Roman fort, with an open square in the centre, enclosed on three sides by a colonnade, and on the fourth side by the offices, or in the civilian version, the basilica, usually an aisled building with the centre section raised above the aisle or aisles, so that the windows of the higher walls provide light inside the building. The question is, who built the Forum at Verulamium, and at other towns? It is conceivable that military engineers could advise on the projects during the winters, and perhaps some legionaries could have helped with the work, but while the three Flavian governors were constantly engaged in warfare it is doubtful if there would be enough manpower to be able lend some men to supervise building work in the towns. For those towns which developed in the late Flavian period, the military may have assisted, since the far north was abandoned, and even though several auxiliary units and a legion had been removed for Domitian's wars, there may have been enough experienced soldiers with time on their hands.

Apart from administrative buildings, some towns acquired other public establishments in the Flavian period, for entertainment and religious practices. There was a theatre at Colchester before 60, and Canterbury acquired one *c*.80. At Verulamium, it appears that a site was prepared for a theatre in Flavian times but there was no building work until the mid-second century, unless flimsy temporary structures were erected for various performances and then demolished, as was customary in Rome itself, until Pompey the Great built the first permanent theatre in stone in the first century BC. Amphitheatres were built outside several towns, though these are mostly dated to post-Flavian times. Silchester possessed a timber amphitheatre probably as early as 55, and at Cirencester a disused quarry was converted into an amphitheatre. These structures may have been used in all towns for many more diverse events than combat between gladiators and the slaughter of animals. Festivals, processions and religious observances may have taken place in them.

One of the more important establishments in any Roman town was the bath house, and eventually the British towns acquired one or more bath complexes. At least two sets of public baths were built in London at the end of the first century, but Silchester already possessed a bathing establishment in the 50s.

It is unlikely that the Roman government helped to finance the establishment of civic buildings, temples, theatres, amphitheatres and baths, so the cash would have to be raised by the leading Britons. The desultory development of towns in the first decades of the Roman occupation may be explained in part by the impoverishment of many tribes after the suppression of the Boudiccan rebellion. Only a few tribes already used coinage when the Romans invaded, so for the rest the introduction by the Romans of a completely different economic system to their own may have set some British elite groups at a disadvantage.

The encouragement of the Britons to establish towns, enabling the Britons to enjoy the Roman way of life, was not entirely altruistic on the part of the Romans. One of the more pressing reasons was the need to devolve local government onto the British communities to relieve the pressure on the provincial administration. It is possible that the British tribes had already started to govern themselves without the appurtenances of elaborate buildings, but once the Forum and basilica appeared in a town it can be taken as a sure sign that there was also a town council and magistrates to carry out the functions of government, to administer the law and supervise the tax collection within their boundaries. The town officials may have used their native language for day-to-day business, but Latin was the language for dealing with the Romans, for administration, finance and law. Agricola encouraged the spread of Latin and literacy, and took a personal interest in the education of the sons of the British elite. He considered that the Britons possessed a greater natural ability than the Gauls, which suggests that he had talked to some of them and observed them at close quarters. On the whole, what Tacitus says about Agricola's contribution to the development of Britain should not be dismissed merely as eulogistic hyperbole.

Another aspect of civil development is the appointment of *legati iuridici* to Britain. These officials were appointed by the Emperor, and were first introduced by Vespasian. It is suggested that *iuridici* were appointed during periods when the governor was fully occupied on military campaigns. Two are known from the Flavian period: Gaius Salvius Liberalis, who was in Britain from 78 to 81 while Agricola was engaged on his northern campaigns, and Lucius Javolenus Priscus, attested in Britain from 84 to 86. Both these men were of praetorian rank and had commanded legions. Their functions would be primarily the administration of justice, and to handle all aspects of legal work which the governor on campaign could not attend to personally. They may also have been involved in the development of new towns, helping to set up their administrative systems, advising on rights and privileges, and the duties and obligations of the inhabitants and the town councils. For the first generation of town councillors, the proceedings would be something of a culture shock, no matter how much contact they may already have had with Roman goods and the Roman way of life. There would be a period of initiation into a different way of governing their people. Nowadays, when so many systems are changing as computerisation grows ever more important, and one person performs the tasks that three people used to carry out, there are counsellors who can advise workers who have to cope with changes to the way in which they operate. The *legati iuridici* may have been called upon to facilitate the transition from tribal rule to Roman administration.

CIVITAS CAPITALS

The *civitas* (plural *civitates*) is sometimes translated as state, but it does not imply anything as large or sophisticated as the modern version of a state. *Civitas* was the term used by the Romans in less well developed areas to describe the territory of a tribe, implying a unit of local government. The word is related to *civis*, citizen, but this does not automatically indicate Roman citizenship. The *civitates* of Britain were inhabited by non-Romans, and would be called *civitates peregrinae*. Archaeologists invented the term *civitas* capitals to describe the towns of Roman Britain where the headquarters of local administration were centred, though this simple generalisation is subject to much debate.

Evidence for the existence of *civitas* capitals in Britain derives from some inscriptions, which unfortunately do not provide any firm dating evidence, and there is more information in two Roman documents. One of these documents is the *Antonine Itinerary*, a list of roads, naming towns along each of its routes, dating from the end of the second or beginning of the third century AD. The second document is the *Ravenna Cosmography*, a work of the seventh century, but for its British sections, the compilers used information that was well out of date, derived from the second-century situation in Britain. The places listed in these two documents are not precisely the same, but to a large extent they corroborate each other, and the documents also corroborate some of the inscriptions, of which there are eleven that concern *civitas* capitals. Five of these came from Wroxeter, Cirencester, Kenchester, Brougham and Caerwent, and the remaining six were found on Hadrian's Wall, where the *civitates* contributed to rebuilding work, at some unknown date. This was possibly at the beginning of the third century, in the reign of Severus, when the Wall was extensively repaired.

The *civitas* capitals were usually distinguished by a place name attached to a tribal suffix, such as Corinium Dobunnorum, or Corinium of the Dobunni, now called Cirencester, or Venta Silurum, Venta of the Silures, modern Caerwent. In most cases the tribal names have not survived into modern times, in contrast to some places on the Continent. In Gaul, for instance, Lutetia Parisiorum became Paris, not Lutece, which is reserved by modern historians for the ancient Roman version of the city. Only the Cantiaci of Durovernum Cantiacorum are still traceable in Britain, in Canterbury. The other towns usually preserve only the first part of the Roman place name. Winchester, which started out as Venta Belgarum, combines a corrupted version of Venta without the tribal name, but with the addition of the suffix '-chester', derived from the Roman *castra*. The same contraction is represented by Caerwent in south Wales, where the first half of Venta Silurum is combined with the Welsh version of *castra*, Caer, or Gaer. Similarly if you say Coriniumcastra fast enough for long enough with an approximation of an Anglo-Saxon inflection you arrive at 'Cirencester', but not the strictly correct modern pronunciation, rendered phonetically as 'Cissister'.

Civitas capitals were self-governing communities, with a town council whose members and magistrates were responsible for keeping order within their territories, for collecting provincial and local taxes, and for jurisdiction of certain crimes committed within their boundaries. The town council was called the *ordo*, made up of decurions. The decurions of the colonies at Lincoln and York acquired the Roman epigraphic habit and recorded themselves on inscriptions, but unfortunately the members of the councils in the *civitas* capitals are as yet anonymous, either because they did not adopt the custom of recording personal information in this way, and did not set up tombstones, or because such inscriptions have eluded archaeologists. Corporate inscriptions on the other hand do survive. As mentioned above, the most important one is from Caerwent (*RIB* 311), because it sheds light on local government. The inscription is a dedication to Tiberius Claudius Paulinus, who had been legate of II Augusta, in which capacity he would have been based at Caerleon, close to Caerwent, and well known to the inhabitants. He had subsequently been appointed as governor of Gallia

Narbonensis, and then eventually returned to Britain, as governor of the northern half of the island, not long after the Emperor Severus or possibly Caracalla had split Britain into two provinces. The dedication suggests that he was respected in Caerwent, and it was probably set up just before Paulinus returned to Britain. The most important part of the text reads *ex decreto ordinis respubl[ica] civi[atis] Silurum*, 'by decree of the council of the *civitas* of the Silures'. This not only shows the *ordo* making decisions and carrying them out, but reveals that the *civitas* was described as *respublica*, summing up its Roman-style corporate self-government. The term *respublica* did not simply refer to the capital itself, but comprised the whole territory of the tribe, including other satellite towns. The inscription from Kenchester declares the town to be within the *respublica Dobunnorum*, which was governed from Cirencester (Corinium Dobunnorum), and Brougham in Cumbria belonged to the *respublica Carvetiorum*, the Carvetii, whose capital was at Carlisle.

From the body of decurions, magistrates were elected, in pairs called *duoviri*, to carry out the administration of justice, organise tax collection, keep the streets clean and the buildings in good repair, just as in all towns and cities of the Empire, though on a more modest scale. They were also responsible for the territory of the *civitas* or tribe, and for maintaining order among the members of the tribe as well as the inhabitants of the smaller towns within their borders.

The men who formed the government of these *civitas* capitals as members of the *ordo* would require considerable wealth. They were expected to finance building projects and to embellish their towns out of their own pockets. A certain civic pride is detectable in the laconic inscriptions that have survived. The decurions, especially those who were elected as magistrates, would hope to achieve the respect of their communities, but unlike the magistrates of the *municipiae*, the chartered towns, they did not necessarily receive Roman citizenship after holding office, remaining in Roman eyes as *peregrini*, 'foreigners' or non-Romans. Since there is a dearth of personal inscriptions, it cannot be ascertained who these decurions were, or where they lived. It has been suggested that the *ordo* should normally comprise one hundred members, but in most of the *civitas* capitals there are not sufficient houses of the size and scale that would be expected of a council member, so most of the decurions perhaps lived in villas outside the town. Their wealth, like that of all other people of the Roman Empire, would derive mostly from landowning, or perhaps from trade, though nothing can be proved as to where or how the decurions earned a living. Being non-Romans, there was perhaps not the same degree of snobbishness among them about wealth derived from sources other than agriculture. Money from trade was perhaps more acceptable in Britain than it was in Rome, where senators were forbidden to engage in business, or in any kind of work, which was considered sordid. Senators circumvented the law and kept their hands clean by operating businesses at second hand via their middle-class agents, and grew respectably rich on the proceeds.

One of the distinguishing features of a *civitas* capital is considered to be the presence of administrative buildings, such as a Forum and a basilica where meetings could be held and legal processes carried out. This has been challenged, since it is possible to hold meetings without these appurtenances, which may explain why the development of these towns appears to have been rather slow. It was not until the Flavian period that most of these towns received a Forum and basilica, as excavation after excavation has revealed. The main problem is that there is no secure dating evidence for the initial foundation of most of the *civitas* capitals. It has been noted above that the Romans would need to devolve some of the local administration onto the natives as quickly as possible, to relieve their own manpower of these tasks, but apart from Canterbury, where some buildings of Claudius's reign have come to light, and in the realm of Tiberius Claudius Togidubnus, it still seems that the main impetus for civic development occurred in the reigns of the Flavian Emperors.

This leads once again to the debate about Romanisation, whether it was deliberately fostered by the Roman authorities, or simply left to native initiative. Perhaps it was a combination of both. The native towns were frequently built on land that had just been vacated by the military, so apart from the south and south-east, it is perhaps not to be expected that there would be any development until campaigns started in the north of England and southern Scotland, in the early 70s AD, and various forts went out of use as the soldiers moved north. Cerialis, Frontinus, and Agricola would have a vested interest in fostering native self-government to release military and administrative staff and to ensure peace behind them while they campaigned. As mentioned above, it may have been Frontinus who established Caerwent, just after the final conquest of the Silures, but it took some time to flourish, and the town centre was not built up until the reign of Hadrian.

When the first *civitas* capitals were established, it has been suggested that the *iuridici* who were sent to Britain may have rendered assistance and given advice, but it is possible that other Roman officials were normally involved, not least to mark out territorial boundaries. In the undeveloped tribal areas of the Danube, a *praefectus civitatis* is attested in the early period of development, perhaps to oversee the foundation and administration of the first native self-governing communities. There is no hint of evidence for the same kind of officials in Britain, but it remains a possibility that officials did exist who have not found their way into the historical record. If there was never any official Flavian policy to develop *civitas* capitals in Britain, then the almost synchronised development of the towns requires explanation. Perhaps it was not always entirely due to local initiative, and rivalry and a sudden access of civic ambition will not entirely suffice. There was probably more proactive Romanisation than is currently fashionable among historians, and perhaps Tacitus's description of Agricola spending his winters encouraging the Britons should not be discounted.

The main development of *civitas* capitals occurred in the south of the island, except for Caistor-by-Norwich, which was not established until the second century. In the north, there were late additions to the list of such towns, such as the Brigantian capital at Aldborough, called Isurium Brigantum, not founded until after the Romans had overrun their territory. At Wroxeter (Viroconium Cornoviorum) the military forces were in occupation for some time, so that the development of the *civitas* had to wait until the reign of Hadrian, and at Carlisle the capital of the Carvetii is not attested until the middle of the third century.

5

Drawing the Lines AD 96 to 138

When the Emperor Domitian was assassinated in 96, the Romans still held southern Scotland, but nothing north of the Forth–Clyde line. Large forts at Dalswinton in the west and Newstead in the east protected the two main routes northwards, together with a network of other forts such as Glenlochar, Oakwood and High Rochester. It is not certain if there was a clearly marked northern boundary, or if the Romans patrolled far beyond their forts to keep the natives under control. Troop numbers were probably still depleted, after Domitian had taken some auxiliary units and one legion, II Adiutrix, for the major wars on the Danube. There were now only three legions in Britain, based in the turf-and-timber legionary fortresses at Caerleon, Chester and York, where they remained for most of the Roman period. The number of auxiliary units can be only roughly assessed. It is usually considered that it was a shortage of manpower that made it necessary to withdraw from the northern areas of Scotland. No campaign to recover what had been given up seems to have been planned.

The senators of Rome, denying any involvement in the plot to assassinate Domitian, appointed the elderly Cocceius Nerva as Emperor, but his reign was short, only two years, so it is difficult if not impossible to discern any details of his policy for Britain. He was succeeded by Trajan, who was governor of Germany at the time of Nerva's death.

For the next eight decades or so the Emperors were chosen by adoption rather than by bloodline. The system worked well, and though the problems surrounding the succession were not completely eradicated, the Empire was not plagued by numerous attempts at usurpation as it was in the later third century.

The Emperor Trajan was descended from a family of Italian stock who had migrated to Spain and settled in the province several generations earlier. By the mid-first century, as Roman citizenship spread to the elite population of the more Romanised provinces, many of the leading men had become senators, pursuing the normal career combining civil administrative posts with military appointments. Trajan was born in Spain at Italica. His mother was Spanish, and his father, one of the leading citizens of Italica, eventually reached the consulship in Rome and was raised to patrician status by the Emperor Vespasian. Trajan had followed a military career, and had suppressed the revolt of Saturninus against Domitian in 89. As a military commander of some renown, he was acceptable to the Roman armies, so when he was chosen by Nerva as his successor he managed to bridge the gap between the senators and the soldiers. These two groups had fallen out with each other after the assassination of Domitian, who was detested by the senators because he had made them all live in fear for several years, and loved by the army because he had given them their first pay rise for decades.

Trajan was the epitome of the good ruler, in so far as the Romans interpreted the term, earning the title *Optimus Princeps*, the best Emperor. He inherited the Dacian wars from Domitian, who had concluded the first round of hostilities in 88 with the victory at the Battle of Tapae, but he had not eradicated the threat entirely. Since then, Dacian power and ambition had escalated under the leader Decabalus, and in tandem with growing power and ambition, hostility to the Romans had escalated as well. The perceived threat was very great to the Romans, so Trajan embarked on another Dacian war, but it was to require two campaigns before a lasting peace was obtained. The wars were on a large scale, expensive in terms of manpower and war material, so the concomitant factor was stagnation in other provinces, of which Britain was one.

There is a dearth of literary evidence for what was happening in Britain at this time. Most of the information that is available derives from diplomas, the two-leaved bronze tablets that were given to each discharged auxiliary soldier, usually issued when several units had men ready for retirement. One of these, dated to 98, mentions two governors, making it clear that Nepos, perhaps Publius Metilius Nepos, preceded Titus Avidius Quietus, but the dates of each governor's appointment are not known, and there are no details as to what they achieved. Another governor, Lucius Neratius Marcellus, is mentioned in the writing tablets from Vindolanda, and also on another diploma dated to 103. He may have arrived a little earlier than 103, and perhaps remained in the province until 106, when the second Dacian war ended in complete victory for Trajan. If so, Marcellus may have presided over another withdrawal of Roman troops, this time from southern Scotland, and the establishment of a northern boundary line to the province, running along the road called the Stanegate (a name applied in more recent times, meaning Stone Road: Stane means stone, and gate or yate is an old word for road). This route runs through the gap between the River Tyne and the River Solway, more or less the same line that was chosen for Hadrian's Wall.

THE WITHDRAWAL FROM SOUTHERN SCOTLAND

Archaeological excavations can only reveal a certain amount of information about individual sites, and not until enough places have been investigated is it possible to discern a probable pattern of events. From the results of excavation at the forts of southern Scotland it is clear that they were given up, probably before 105, but the circumstances of this latest abandonment are open to discussion. There are signs of burning at Dalswinton, Newstead, Glenlochar, Oakwood and High Rochester. The Romans deliberately destroyed their forts when they abandoned them, dismantling the timbers that may have had some life left in them, and tidying everything up by piling up the unwanted materials and making bonfires, which are usually easily identifiable as such in the archaeological record. The burning at the forts of southern Scotland does not quite satisfy those criteria. At Newstead, other finds have been associated with the destruction, which seem to reinforce the possibility of a severe native uprising so strong that the Roman forts were overwhelmed. In pits near the fort, broken equipment and human heads had been buried, perhaps cleared away by Roman soldiers who came back to salvage whatever they could and remove traces of the destruction. One problem is that the pits are not definitely dated, and the items in them have been used to illustrate more than one period of destruction, in Trajan's reign or in the Antonine period. Furthermore, the grisly finds at Newstead might not be associated with enemy action at all. The remains of human heads may simply mean that the garrison troops pursued the Celtic habit of head hunting and set up their trophies on stakes on the fort walls. Some of the soldiers on Trajan's Column in Rome, depicting the Dacian wars, are shown carrying human heads, and at the forts on the same monument, heads are shown on stakes around the walls. The pits in which these finds and the broken equipment had been buried were perhaps rubbish dumps created when the Romans withdrew peacefully, so the items need not be interpreted as evidence of a tremendous battle that required an expedition to tidy up.

The evidence from Corbridge fort is more puzzling, since the buildings seem to have been set alight where they stood, rather than being demolished and gathered up for a bonfire according to usual Roman practice. This may be a result of a decision not to try to reclaim anything, perhaps because all the timbers and reusable items were too worn to be of use. The major difference between Corbridge and the forts further north is that another fort was built at Corbridge, but the others were not reoccupied. The whole episode is still debated. On the one hand it can be argued that enemy action drove the Romans out, and on the other it can be argued that it was manpower shortages that triggered the withdrawal from southern Scotland and the total obliteration of forts, which was put into effect by the Romans themselves. There was no immediate reoccupation, nor are there any signs that a punitive expedition was mounted. The Romans pulled back to the Tyne–Solway line and remained there.

THE STANEGATE FRONTIER

The northern boundary of the province in the reign of Trajan was marked by the Stanegate, a road with forts strung along it. The road runs from Corbridge through forts at Nether Denton and Chesterholm (Vindolanda) to Carlisle. Smaller forts have been found in between the larger ones, at Haltwhistle Burn and Throp, between Vindolanda and Nether Denton. Pottery from the two fortlets was dated *c.*100 to *c.*120, so they belong to the reign of Trajan. Other fortlets are suggested at Old Church Brampton, where there is some supporting evidence for a fort of some kind, and on grounds of spacing, there may have been forts at Carvoran and Newburgh. It used to be thought that there would be a pattern of alternating large and small forts all along the road, but that idea has been rejected in favour of the theory that the Romans would build forts or fortlets where they considered that it was necessary to guard something or watch routes and river crossings, and the size of the fort and its garrison would be tailored to the perceived threat at each location.

It is not certain whether the road and forts continued to the west of Carlisle or to the east of Corbridge. It may be that the priority for the Romans was to guard the north to south routes through Corbridge and Carlisle, and to keep watch along the road joining them across the Tyne–Solway gap. There may have been no pressing need to continue the defensive line eastwards to the Tyne or westwards to the Solway. But if the road was a frontier, as modern historians describe it, then it might seem that there was every reason to connect the two coasts and watch the whole extent of the country.

Two forts have been suggested as likely candidates for the western end of the Trajanic system, one at Kirkbride on the west coast, and it is possible that the early fort at Burgh by Sands, about one kilometre distant from the Hadrianic fort on the Solway, was built as part of the Stanegate frontier. Burgh by Sands lies about halfway between the fort at Kirkbride and Carlisle, so on grounds of spacing it may have been planned and built in the reign of Trajan, to watch the Solway estuary and the west coast. A timber watchtower was found underneath the later fort at Burgh by Sands, but nothing has been found so far to suggest that there was a line of towers, similar to those on the Gask Ridge in Scotland.

The eastern end of the Stanegate is even less certain. A Roman fort at Washing Well has been identified, but not necessarily accepted as part of the frontier, and the chances of finding a Trajanic fort in the Newcastle conurbation are slender, so it is not possible to say that the Romans definitely watched the east coast and the Tyne before Hadrian's Wall was built.

Watching and guarding would seem to be one of the purposes of the new boundary line, since a watchtower has been found on the hill above Vindolanda, and another at Walltown Crags, both of which may pre-date the Hadrianic frontier, but this has been disputed. If these towers belonged to the Stanegate boundary line, it is to be expected that they did not stand alone, but were accompanied by more watchtowers situated at vantage points all across the Tyne–Solway gap. Unfortunately attempts to identify other structures of the relevant date have not been successful. It can only be said that the Romans were concerned to watch for and prevent any unauthorised movement across or along the road, and that they probably patrolled in advance of the line, and perhaps to the rear as well.

Consolidation of the Hinterland

If there was any intention to advance northwards again in Britain once the Dacian wars were concluded and manpower may have been available, the Emperor Trajan had about twelve years before his death in which to put such plans into operation, but did not do so. He waged war in Arabia instead, so it would seem that for Britain his policy was to keep what the army could control, and to consolidate it. This policy is more evident further south, where the legionary fortresses, built of turf and timber, were refurbished in stone. They had been in occupation for thirty years or so, and the timbers would need to be replaced. The initiative to rebuild in stone may have originated with the governor, perhaps Avidius Quietus, but it was presumably sanctioned by the Emperor. The building work, which continued under the governor Neratius Marcellus and his successor, signifies the end of continual movement of legions around the province, and the beginning of permanent settlement. Caerleon, Chester and York remained the headquarters of the legions for the next two centuries or more, until in the late Roman period everything changed and troops became more mobile. The attested dates of the rebuilding work at the legionary fortresses indicate that it began early in the reign of Trajan. The decision to rebuild the fortresses was probably not related to the withdrawal from southern Scotland, and would have taken place whether or not forts in southern Scotland were occupied. Work at Caerleon started about 100, at Chester in 102, and at York an inscription attests that one of the gates was being rebuilt in stone in 107 to 108. The mention of IX Hispana on this particular inscription is the last time that the legion was seen alive and well in Britain.

WHAT HAPPENED TO THE NINTH LEGION? – TEXT BOX
The romantic version of the fate of IX Hispana, current in the 1950s and immortalised in Rosemary Sutcliff's children's novel *The Eagle of the Ninth*, now made into a film, is that the legion marched off into the Scottish mists and was never seen again. In the novel, an eagle found at Exeter was married up to the story as the lost legionary standard, which was rescued by the hero of the story. It probably isn't true, but it is still a thunderingly good story which should never be allowed to go out of print.

At the fortress of York, there is a hiatus between 108 when IX is last attested and 122 when the Emperor Hadrian's governor, Platorius Nepos, installed VI Victrix in Britain. This legion came from Vetera in Germany. For the IX legion there are hints that it went to Holland, where its legionary tile stamps and mortaria stamps have been found. It has been suggested that this means that the legion or part of it was there for some time, since troops who are just passing through don't stop for long enough to make and stamp their tiles and mortaria. The reason why the legion was at Nijmegen is not known. The Dacian wars were over by 106, two years before the gate at the York fortress was rebuilt and the IX was still there, and the Emperor Trajan had enough troops to garrison the new province that he created after his conquest without summoning legions from other provinces. Besides, there is no evidence that IX Hispana was ever in Dacia. Nor did it accompany Trajan on his Arabian campaign, which ended with his death in 117. The legions who built Hadrian's Wall left several inscriptions attesting their work, but IX Hispana is conspicuously absent. A list of all the legions in all the provinces was drawn up in 170, and IX Hispana is not included.

Various suggestions have been made as to what the ultimate fate of the lost legion may have been. When the Emperor Hadrian succeeded Trajan, the writer of the *Historia Augusta*, a series of biographies of Emperors that picks up where Suetonius Tranquillus leaves off, says that there was serious trouble in Britain. It is possible the IX was badly cut up and was disbanded *c.*117 or 118, though there is not even a whiff of evidence for this in the ancient sources, and in any case this theory is discredited on account of research by Professor Eric Birley into the careers of some of the officers who had served in IX Hispana. The ones who were still alive after 117 were in no way hindered with regard to promotion in other units. If the legion had suffered a disastrous defeat, and was cashiered as a result, this ought to have impacted on its surviving officers, which was clearly not the case.

Another suggestion as to where IX met its end is that it may have been sent from Nijmegen to Judaea *c.*133, with the general Julius Severus, who was governor of Britain until that time. The peace-loving Emperor Hadrian had managed to upset the Jews by his insensitive treatment of them, the memory of which is still a raw subject even today, so that modern Jews still refer to him in scatological terms. As a result of Hadrian's impossible demands, a serious revolt broke out in Judaea in 132. It required great efforts and two years of bitter fighting to eradicate it. There were many Roman casualties, and the IX legion may have been among them. One day, some telling artefacts or an inscription or two may be discovered which will explain what happened to IX Hispana, and where, and possibly why.

THE ACCESSION OF HADRIAN AND TROUBLE IN BRITAIN AD 117

When Trajan died in 117, before he had rounded off his Arabian campaigns, there were some doubts as to the legitimacy of Hadrian's right to be proclaimed Emperor. He was a relative of Trajan, and had been brought up by him, patently groomed for the succession, but his reign began under a cloud. There was a protest, interpreted as treasonable, led by four senators in Rome, who were executed. It was not a good way to start as Emperor, and Hadrian did little to ingratiate himself as his reign continued. He called a halt to any further expansion of the Empire, embarked on a policy of enclosing within running barriers or clearly marked boundaries what he thought the Imperial government could reasonably administer, and set off on a tour of the provinces that occupied most of his reign. As a result of his policies there was peace and prosperity over most of the Empire, and the Romans hated him for it.

Trouble in Britain was a commonplace literary theme at the beginning of most Emperor's reigns, a bit like a mega version of trouble at t'mill in novels about the industrial north. This time, in 117, there is some evidence that it may have been true. The author of the *Historia Augusta* mentions it briefly:

> When he took over the Empire, Hadrian reverted to an earlier policy, devoting his energies to keeping the peace throughout the world. The people subdued by

Trajan had rebelled, the Moors were launching attacks, the Sarmatae making war, and the Britons could not be kept under control. (*Historia Augusta* Hadrian 5.1–2)

So far it sounds like a spot of cattle raiding here and there, but sometime later the writer and scholar Fronto wrote to his former pupil, who was by this time the Emperor Marcus Aurelius, referring to military losses that had just occurred in the east in the war against the Parthians. Fronto tried to console the Emperor by comparing the current losses with other disasters:

When your grandfather Hadrian was Emperor, how many soldiers were killed by the Jews, and how many by the Britons? (Fronto *De Bello Parthico* 2, quoted in A.R. Birley, *The Roman Government of Britain*, Oxford: 2005, p.118)

The casualties in Judaea that Fronto mentioned concern the Jewish revolt that broke out in 132, but there is nothing to suggest that the trouble in Britain occurred at exactly the same time, so this passage about so many deaths caused by the Britons could relate to the beginning of Hadrian's reign. Probably in 118, Hadrian appointed Quintus Pompeius Falco to the command in Britain. Falco was governor of Moesia in 116–118, and Hadrian visited the province at about that time. Though Falco is mentioned in the letters of Pliny and the works of Fronto, and also on inscriptions from various parts of the Roman world, his exploits in Britain are unfortunately not so well documented. It is not certain which of the British tribes could not be kept under control, though it is usually conjectured that the trouble broke out in the north, possibly in southern Scotland, where there had probably been considerable unrest more than a decade earlier. Some scholars have suggested that there was collusion between the Selgovae, Novantae and Brigantes, on more than one occasion, but no source corroborates this theory.

A few other pieces of evidence are usually brought in to support the theory that there was a serious war in Britain in 117 or 118. A commemorative coin was produced in 119 with Britannia personified on the reverse, perhaps to celebrate a victory and the imposition of peace. Further evidence, unfortunately not securely dated, may throw some light on the situation in Britain at this time. Three thousand legionaries were brought to Britain by Titus Pontius Sabinus, whose career inscription states that one thousand men from each of the legions in Spain and Upper Germany were combined under his leadership for an expedition to Britain. No dates are provided so it could be argued that this took place in 122 when Hadrian visited the island, or later in the 130s, but there is nothing to disprove the suggestion that the legionaries arrived in Britain *c.*119, and it is possible that the three thousand men were sent as replacements for the heavy casualties that Fronto wrote about. Added to this is the inscription on the tombstone from Vindolanda of a centurion of *cohors I Tungrorum*, who was 'killed in the war', though which war, and where and when it was fought, is not stated. As a single piece of evidence, this stone does not signify very much, but if this death in a war is contemporary with the influx of three thousand legionaries from Spain and Upper Germany, it suggests that the fighting most probably occurred somewhere in the north, and that it was serious, requiring either supplementary troops to help during the war, or replacements for the legions afterwards.

RECRUITMENT OF BRITONS INTO THE ROMAN ARMY
The causes of the trouble in Britain are not known. One suggestion is that the Romans had been forcibly recruiting young men for the army in southern Scotland, which was technically outside the province, if the Stanegate was the administrative boundary. Alternatively, perhaps groups of men had been conscripted from Brigantia. If this is true, the new recruits would not have been allowed to serve in the Roman army near their homes, but the groups would have been sent abroad, a procedure that was probably neither gentle nor welcome.

Britons did serve in the Roman army, some of them probably as volunteers, and others as conscripts, from the first century onwards. According to Tacitus, for the most part the Britons submitted to recruitment willingly enough. There were Britons in Agricola's army at Mons Graupius, most likely allocated to the existing auxiliary units rather than being formed up into whole cohorts of Britons. Local recruitment gradually became normal practice in most provinces as time went on, so that although the original cohorts or *alae* consisted of Gauls, or Tungrians, or Thracians – the units soon lost their ethnic identity as more and more locals replaced the discharged veterans or casualties of war. The original unit names were retained, even though these names no longer represented the origins of the new soldiers. If Britons serving in the Roman army to fight against other Britons seems like treachery of the basest sort, it must be remembered that there was no sense of overall British nationality, but only tribal identity and loyalty.

In Italy in the civil wars of 69, some Britons served in Aulus Caecina's army along with other ethnic groups, but it is not known in what capacity. They may have been volunteers organised as a unit, or conscripts taken from the island, possibly as defeated tribesmen (*dediticii*) after the suppression of the revolt of Boudicca, in which case Caecina's Britons would have been serving for only about eight years when the civil war began. It was customary to draft into the army tribesmen who had surrendered, and forcible removal from their homeland was one way of avoiding further trouble from groups of resentful men after the end of a war. While Agricola was governor of Britain, some tribesmen of the Usipi from Germany were sent to Britain and famously tried to sail back home, but inadvertently sailed all the way round Britain, proving that it was an island. About a century later, during the Danube wars of Marcus Aurelius, over 5,000 defeated Sarmatae were sent to Britain.

Recruitment from inside a province, where the inhabitants were partially Romanised, was probably started as soon as possible to replace the enormous numbers of men who retired each year, or died in service, or had been killed. Non-citizens would be allotted to the auxiliary units and trained as infantry or cavalry, and although only Roman citizens were allowed to join the legions, on occasion, especially when manpower was short, a slight bending of the rules was ignored and non-citizens were recruited and given Roman names.

Recruitment from outside a province was perhaps less common. In areas where there was already a strong Roman influence, tribes such as the Frisii, before they were incorporated into the Empire, and the Usipi, were forced or persuaded to contribute troops. This implies that the Romans could still recruit from areas of Scotland even though they had withdrawn direct control. Around AD 100, a census official called Titus Haterius Nepos conducted a census of the Brittones Anavionenses, who probably lived in the area around the River Annan. The census may have been linked with the levy of troops for the Roman army. It is possible that these British recruits were sent to Germany, where they were formed into units called *numeri* and stationed in small forts on the German frontier. The first dated evidence for such units is from the Antonine era, so it used to be thought that the Britons must have been removed from southern Scotland when Lollius Urbicus, governor of Britain under Antoninus Pius, was fighting a war, just before the Antonine Wall was built across the Forth–Clyde isthmus. Several inscriptions were found dating to the mid-second century naming *numeri* of Brittones, usually with additional names which were based on the places where they served, such as the Brittones Triputienses, or Brittones Elantienes, the latter being derived from the Roman name for the River Elz.

It now appears that the *numeri* of Brittones were formed some time before the reign of Antonius Pius. Archaeological excavations in the German *numerus* forts have shown that the small units arrived there perhaps under Trajan or Hadrian, which ties in with the census of the Anavionenses, mentioned above. On this basis it is just as tempting to relate the formation of British *numeri* to the hypothetical fighting that may have caused the withdrawal from southern Scotland under Trajan, either as a cause of the trouble, or measures taken after its suppression.

Apart from the possibility that the Britons were aggrieved about recruitment into the army, there may have been other grievances, such as the abuses that were inflicted on the Britons of the south in the early days after the conquest. If IX Hispana had left the province by 117 or 118, the rebels may have taken advantage of the fact that there were only two legions in the province, stationed at Chester and

Caerleon, and the northern boundary was simply a road watched by a series of forts, manned by auxiliary troops. So far there is no evidence of destroyed forts, or of rebuilding at various sites that can be linked to this postulated rebellion. However, when peace was restored, the Emperor Hadrian planned what was probably the greatest building project that the province had ever seen.

HADRIAN'S WALL

In 122 the new governor, Aulus Platorius Nepos, was appointed by Hadrian to begin the monumental task of building the new frontier. Nepos had been governor of Thrace from *c.*117 to 118, and then of Lower Germany. It gradually became the pattern that governors of Britain first served as the governor of the German province, so perhaps the experience of dealing with northern tribesmen in Germany was of help in dealing with the Britons.

Platorius Nepos probably arrived together with the soldiers of VI Victrix, which had been stationed at Vetera in Germany. This legion was eventually stationed in the fortress at York, but it is not attested there until some years after its arrival. The task that Platorius Nepos had been given by Hadrian was completely new. The Romans had plenty of practice in building military installations, but most forts up to the reign of Trajan had been built of turf and timber, whereas this frontier wall, 80 Roman miles long, was to be of stone for its entire length, though in the west it was initially built of turf. The logistics would be on a scale not previously attempted, from quarrying and transporting the stone to supplying the soldiers with food and equipment, building labour camps to house them, ensuring discipline, and protection of the workforce.

The ideology behind the building of the Wall was also something new. For the Romans, although marking out boundaries was quite normal, it had never been suggested before that a Roman province should be enclosed within a solid, permanent, running barrier. In the first century BC Julius Caesar had built a wall, several miles long, to stop the migration of the Helvetii into Gaul, but this was not meant to be a permanent boundary line, and was certainly not the sort of frontier that Hadrian introduced into the Empire. It was a momentous change of policy from the Roman ideal of *imperium sine fine*, power without end, in both the temporal and territorial sense.

It was not just in Britain that Hadrian called a halt to further expansion. The boundaries of the northern provinces on the Continent were the River Rhine in the west and the Danube in the east, save for Trajan's new province of Dacia, which lay north of the Danube. Where the frontier of Lower Germany diverged from the Rhine to take in the north-facing salient of the Taunus and Wetterau regions, Hadrian established the *limes*, or frontier, a running barrier consisting of a timber palisade, guarded by watchtowers set back a little from the frontier line, and small forts, called in German *Kleinkastelle*. The larger forts were some distance away, up to two kilometres distant in some cases. Some parts of this frontier had already been marked out by the Flavian Emperors, especially by Domitian, but there was no palisade, only a road guarded by watchtowers, similar to the Gask Ridge road and towers that Agricola established around the western edge of the Fife peninsula.

In Africa, Hadrian's frontier was not a continuous barrier, but sections of stone wall were built, with the purpose of controlling the transhumance routes, to allow the flocks and herds and their drovers to move along the roads without encroaching onto the fields and crops of the more sedentary peoples. Thus the frontiers were adapted to the needs of the particular province in which they were set up.

The line chosen for the British frontier may have been inspected by Hadrian himself, who visited the province in 122. It is possible that while he toured the northern areas he resided for a short time at the fort at Vindolanda, one of the forts along the Trajanic boundary line of the Stanegate. Some short distance to the north of the Stanegate there lies the geological feature known as the Whin Sill, which runs west to east across the centre section of the land between the River Tyne and the Solway estuary. It is a north-facing outcrop of hard rock, several feet high, which turns northwards when it approaches the east coast. The castle at Bamburgh is founded on an outcrop of the Whin Sill. There is a relatively flat area to the north of the Sill, where the softer rock has been worn away over several millennia. From the top of the cliffs there are good views to the north, and in some places there are equally good views to the south as well. In other words the Whin Sill is a gift from the gods to anyone who wants to create a north-facing frontier in one of the shortest gaps across the country from coast to coast. Hadrian may have walked or ridden along it to assess its suitability for his purpose. The geographical factors outweighed any consideration for tribal boundaries, as it is generally accepted that some of the Brigantes who were settled in the area to the north-west of the Wall were cut off from the main tribe when the frontier was established.

The original plan was to build a stone wall, starting at the Newcastle end on the River Tyne, where Hadrian built a bridge, which gave its name to the fort, Pons Aelii, the bridge of Aelius, Hadrian's family name. The Wall was to be 10 Roman feet thick, and perhaps 15 to 20 feet high, but no one knows how high the Wall was in its original state, nor what it looked like. There may have been a walk along it, and there may have been crenellations, both being features which go together: a wall walk can exist without crenellations, but not the other way round – why crenellate if no one is going to walk along the top of the Wall and look out from it? But the presence of a wall walk is hinted at but not securely attested, and at the top of the stone wall in Africa, better preserved than the British example, there is merely a triangular capstone. Nevertheless, reconstructions of the Wall often show it with both wall walk and crenellations.

Vexillations from the three legions in Britain – II Augusta, VI Victrix and XX Valeria Victrix – did the building work. The solders of each work group, normally a legionary century, set up a roughly carved 'centurial stone' when they had completed their allotted sections of Wall, usually naming the centurion. Legionaries also built the military installations along the Wall. Every Roman mile along Hadrian's Wall there was to be a fortlet, called by modern archaeologists 'milecastles'. For the convenience of modern studies, the milecastles have been numbered, starting from the eastern end. Each milecastle had two gates, one through the Wall itself to the north, and a corresponding one in the south wall of the building. There are at least three slightly different designs for the gateways, which may be representative of each legion's individual building style. In older reconstruction drawings, the milecastles are usually shown with only one tower, on the northern gate, but it was pointed out some time ago that the foundations of both the north and south gates are exactly the same, so there may have been towers on the south gates as well.

Between each milecastle there were to be two watchtowers, which in Hadrian's Wall terminology are called turrets. So far the British and the German frontiers share a similar plan with a running barrier, guarded by small forts and watchtowers, but there are differences in construction. In Germany there was and still is an abundance of trees, and the Roman frontier was marked by a timber palisade, whereas in northern Roman Britain trees would have been scarce, a feature that is perhaps disguised nowadays since trees have been planted in modern times by the Forestry Commission. Stone on the other hand was, and is, ubiquitous, so the Wall was built of two skins of dressed stone with a rubble core, and the milecastles and turrets, also in stone, are not free-standing like the German *Kleinkastelle* and towers, but are set into the Wall itself.

The western sector of the Wall was initially built of turf blocks, like the walls of the early forts in Britain. Beyond the River Irthing there is only red sandstone, not as durable as the stone used for the rest of the Wall, so this may be the reason why the Turf Wall was built there, as a stopgap until sufficient stone could be quarried and transported. Another reason is that there may have been a greater threat from the tribes who lived beyond the Wall in the western sectors, and consequently there was a need for speed in establishing the frontier. It may be significant that the outpost forts built to the north of the Wall in Hadrianic times were all in the west, so there may have been a greater need for vigilance in this area.

In front of the Wall on its northern side there was a ditch, except where there was a precipice which made it unnecessary to dig a defensive work to prevent anyone from getting too close. The original plan for the northern ditch, the Wall, milecastles and turrets was soon changed, while Platorius Nepos was still governor. The 10-foot Wall was reduced to a width of 8 feet, probably to reduce the amounts of stone to be brought from the quarries, and thereby hasten the building work. In some places, however, the legionary gangs whose task was to build the foundations had already laid a 10-foot base, so there are some parts of Hadrian's Wall where a 2-foot section of the broad foundation protrudes to the south, with the narrower 8-foot Wall on top of it. In some places the original broad foundation was not used, as at Great Chesters, for example, where there are two sets of remains; the broad foundation with no Wall on top of it runs parallel to the narrow Wall on a narrow base, and then the two join up a little further on. It may be that the builders decided that a much more substantial and deeper foundation was needed at this point, so they abandoned the broad one that had already been laid and built another one, 8 feet wide like the Wall itself, then met up with the original broad foundation and built the narrow Wall on top of that.

The most important change was the so-called fort decision. Some short time after building work had begun, it was decided that the Stanegate forts to the south were not suitable for the purpose of guarding the frontier line, and the forts should actually be attached to the Wall all along its length. This required the legionary builders to demolish parts of the Wall, and in some cases the turrets and milecastles that they had already built or started to build, and then lay out the forts on top of them. At Chesters fort, a turret was destroyed and the fort built over it, and at Housesteads, not only a turret but part of the original frontier Wall were both taken down, and the fort laid out on top, but with its northern wall projecting slightly further over the cliff edge than the frontier line had done. This feature can still be seen today at the northern edge of the fort, where the line of the original Wall and the turret are clearly marked.

Inscriptions from the forts at Halton and Benwell mention the governor Platorius Nepos, so it is clear that the decision to build forts on the Wall was taken quite soon after work had started. The change of plan may have originated with Hadrian himself, or he may have taken advice from Nepos, who had possibly discussed the way in which the frontier was to work with his staff officers and legionary and auxiliary commanders. After all, the frontier was a new concept. Although the Romans had gained experience in controlling the tribes by means of forts placed along routes, they had not had to deal with a system that enclosed the province within a running barrier. Freedom of action would be limited if the troops could cross the Wall only at the milecastles. Although all the milecastles possessed two gates, and access through the Wall was easy enough for small numbers of men, trying to deploy troops through them would not have been convenient. If the larger forts were to be attached to the Wall, then the garrisons could emerge from their own fort gates to patrol the territory to the north, or to operate to the south behind the Wall. Cavalry forts like that at Chesters generally protruded north of the Wall, and had six gates rather than the more usual four, with three of them giving access to the north.

Auxiliary forts on the Wall were built at Newcastle-upon-Tyne, Benwell, Rudchester, Halton Chesters, Chesters, Housesteads, Great Chesters, Birdoswald, Castlesteads, Stanwix, Burgh by Sands and Bowness-on-Solway. The fort at Vindolanda strictly belongs to the Stanegate but is often counted as part of the Wall, even though it lies to the south of it. The fort at Carvoran also belonged to the Stanegate system, and is excluded from the Wall by the ditch known as the Vallum (see below) which makes a detour to the north around it. The fort at Carrawburgh was not part of the original plan to move the forts up to the Wall, but was added later, with its northern defences formed by Hadrian's Wall itself.

The forts varied in size, designed to accommodate auxiliary units of either 1,000 men (milliary) or 500 men (quingenary). Infantry units were stationed in the central sector, while cavalry units (*alae*) or part-mounted units (*cohortes equitatae*) could operate in the less hilly terrain to the east and west. Chesters fort held a quingenary *ala*, and the fort at Stanwix near Carlisle housed a milliary *ala*, the only one in the province. The commanders of these units were very senior officers with long experience of command. The officer at Stanwix would outrank all other auxiliary unit commanders on the Wall, and may have been in charge of the whole frontier system.

Outpost Forts and Coastal Defence

In the west, the frontier system extended northwards beyond the Solway estuary, and down the Cumbrian coast. It has been argued that the western part of Hadrian's Wall and the territory to the north required greater protection, which may be why the Turf Wall was possibly built at speed because of the perceived threat from the tribes to the north of the Brigantes, or even from the Brigantes themselves, some of whom probably lived beyond the frontier on the western side, so it may have been partly for their protection that in this area, forts were built at Bewcastle, Birrens and Netherby. It may be significant that there are no Hadrianic equivalents on the eastern side, though at a later time, forts were built at Risingham and High Rochester.

The outpost forts have been interpreted as advance warning systems to protect the Wall, but it is more likely that they protected routes to and from the north and controlled movement, Bewcastle in particular being well placed to do so. In Severan times, another Roman fort was built here, and much later a medieval castle, which, although it was in bad state of repair, was still garrisoned in the sixteenth century by the Wardens of the March, in order to watch for raiders, because that route was the most common one for the cattle rustlers. In 1528, Lord Dacre wrote to Cardinal Wolsey about the raiders who passed through the Bewcastle area: 'all the misguyded men come thorow Bewcastelldale and retornes for the most part same way agayne'.

Along the Solway estuary and down the west coast, a series of small posts were built, equivalents of the milecastles and turrets, though without the Wall. In Hadrian's Wall terminology these smaller installations are called milefortlets and towers, to distinguish them from the milecastles and turrets on the Wall. Full-sized forts were built at Beckfoot, Maryport and Moresby. There may be more forts that have not been discovered, depending on the extent of the coastline that the Romans wished to keep under close surveillance. It is usually suggested that the whole system stretched as far as St Bees Head, though the evidence is slight. Archaeologists joke about tracing the system down to Liverpool.

At the eastern end, the Wall was eventually continued down to the Tyne, ending at a place appropriately called Wallsend, where a fort was built. It is thought that this was a secondary decision, since the original plan seems to have been to begin the frontier at Newcastle, where the broad 10-foot Wall was built for some distance westwards, whereas the Wall from Newcastle to Wallsend was built to the 8-foot specification. The Wall stretches down to the River Tyne from the south-east corner of the Wallsend fort, and though there are no traces of watchtowers or turrets along the southern bank of the river, it is suggested that there may have been some means of surveillance of the estuary, at least as far as the fort at South Shields.

THE VALLUM

When the forts had been built along the line of the wall, a huge ditch was dug running all along the Wall on its south side. It is known as the Vallum, but this is not the Roman name for the ditch, which would have been called *fossa*, or *fossatum*. Vallum is a term used by the Venerable Bede when he wrote his history of Britain in the seventh century, and it is still a convenient label for modern historians, since it distinguishes the southern ditch from the northern one, but to the Romans it conveyed the whole frontier system. In listing the forts along the Wall, they used the phrase *per lineam valli*, 'along the line of the Wall'.

At points where the Vallum runs close by the forts, it diverts from its straight course to skirt round the south defences, so it was clearly dug after the fort-decision had been made. At Carrawburgh, the Vallum was filled in and the fort was built over the original course, proving that this fort was a later addition, and at Carvoran, the Vallum skirts round the northern defences, cutting it off from the Wall.

The Vallum was at least 10 feet deep, and 20 feet wide at the top with sloping sides, leading down to a flat bottom about 8 feet wide. Sometimes the slope was revetted in stone. Unlike the northern defensive ditch, which was discontinued wherever the higher ground made it unnecessary, or wherever the terrain was difficult, too hard or too wet, the Vallum was continuous, even dug through rock, and carried across streams and marshes all the way from east to west. The course of the Vallum is not rigidly parallel to the Wall, but the distance between the two lines varies. In some places the Vallum lies quite close to the Wall, but in others it diverges quite considerably, enclosing much more land.

The soil from the ditch served to create two mounds, about 20 feet high, one on the north and one on the south, set back some 30 feet from the edge of the ditch. At the western end, the Vallum may have accompanied the forts and milefortlets of the west coast, since it starts to bend sharply to the south as though heading for the line of military installations, but no trace of it yet been found after it makes the detour. In the east it starts to turn towards the River Tyne near Newcastle.

The most puzzling aspect of the Vallum is why it was necessary to erect such a barrier on the south side of the Wall. It is significant that in the early phases of the Wall, it seems that the *vici* or civilian settlements that usually collected around a Roman fort were held at arm's length on the other side of the Vallum and not allowed to encroach on land near the forts. The idea that the Vallum marked out a military zone where civilians were not allowed to settle is attractive, were it not for the fact that a native settlement at Milking Gap, between the Wall and the Vallum, appears to have been inhabited all through the Roman period.

There were causeways across the Vallum at the forts, guarded by a gate that stood halfway across the causeway, so that anyone who wanted to cross the Wall from the north or the south would have to do so under the supervision of the soldiers, but the fact that movement towards the Wall was restricted from the south presumably means that the population of the hinterland was regarded at best as restless and at worst as untrustworthy.

Since it is such an effective barrier, it was once thought that Hadrian's frontier consisted only of the Vallum, separating the Romans from the barbarians, as the *Historia Augusta* puts it. This misconception about what Hadrian actually built arose partly from the testimony of the ancient literature, and partly from archaeological investigations. At the beginning of the third century the Emperor Severus campaigned in Scotland, with the declared intention of conquering the whole island, or so Dio records. The Emperor's object was not achieved, and though he may have reached the far north and defeated the Britons he did not hold the territory. Severus died at York before he could achieve full conquest, and though his son Caracalla may have conducted a final campaign, Scotland was not annexed. Caracalla imposed treaty arrangements on the northern Britons, and returned to Rome.

Severus's most important achievement in Britain, of which he made great play in his reports to Rome, was to repair Hadrian's Wall. Nearly all the later authors from the third century to late antiquity claim that Severus actually built a wall across the island from sea to sea, as though that was the main purpose of his campaigns in Britain. Faced with this corpus of ancient writings all saying the same thing (apart from their tremendous variations in the length of the wall), the archaeologists of the nineteenth century, who found so much evidence of Severan building work, could only agree with the ancient authors that it must have been Severus who established the stone frontier, which they called Severus's Wall. In order to accommodate the statement in the *Historia Augusta* that Hadrian was the first to build a frontier separating the Romans from the barbarians, the archaeologists thought that this first frontier must have been the great ditch which the Venerable Bede had labelled the Vallum. It was only when a building inscription was found naming Aulus Platorius Nepos, who was known to be Hadrian's governor in Britain, that the truth became clear, that the whole frontier system was Hadrianic, and that Severus had repaired the Wall and the forts so extensively that it seemed that the ancient authors must have been correct in saying that he built it. But the original concept that the Vallum was the Hadrianic frontier only confirms its perceived effectiveness in controlling movement.

One of the purposes, if not the main one, of the Vallum would be the protection of the crops grown outside the forts, and the meadows and grazing areas for the animals. Although requisitioning of supplies was one of the ways of feeding the troops, cultivation of the land around Roman forts is well attested. Boundary stones marking the *territorium* of a legion have been found in Spain, and Tacitus refers to 'fields left empty for the use of the soldiers'. At Newstead, sickles were found in the fort. They had been repaired, suggesting long-term use. In addition to growing crops, all units, cavalry and infantry alike, would require horses, for the infantry officers if not for the ordinary soldiers, and draught animals, such as mules and oxen. It was once suggested that the Romans did not eat much meat, but excavations have disproved that theory, since animal bones with butchery marks have been found in the vicinity of some forts. Each unit would keep some sheep and cattle, which were looked after by the *pecuarius* or herdsman, and though the evidence for the *pecuarius* applies to the legions rather than the auxiliary troops, it can be assumed that similar arrangements would be made for all units. The presence of sheep and cattle may have been very tempting to the Brigantes of the north of England, who may have been as adept at raiding as their sixteenth-century descendants were. Cattle raiding was a way of life for the Tudor and Elizabethan Borderers, who performed many of their feats in winter, when the nights were long, the cattle 'in full meat' after the summer grazing, and the bogs were frozen so that if they were chased the raiders could drive their new acquisitions over them quite rapidly. It is not impossible that the Romans faced the same sort of problems and required a way of stopping such raids, which would allow them to carry out their daily tasks without having to detail several men for guard duty over their crops, animals and vehicles. The Vallum would serve such a purpose admirably. It may be possible to drive stolen cattle, horses and sheep over a 20-foot mound, across a flat 30-foot berm, down a steep 10-foot slippery slope, over an 8-foot gap, up another 10-foot steep slope, across another 30 feet of berm, and over another 20-foot mound. But it would take a long time and make a lot of noise.

THE MILITARY WAY

The initial plan for the Wall did not include a service road running all along it. It has been suggested that traffic may have moved along the berm of the Vallum, protected by the earthen mounds on the north and south sides from attack, but there is no proof for this idea, and no traces of metalling have been found, so if marching along the berm was the normal way of getting about it would have been very muddy.

There is no dating evidence for the service road – labelled by archaeologists the Military Way – until the early third century, when the first known milestone was set up, but it is likely that the road was built after the withdrawal from the Antonine Wall, for which the plan seems to have included such a road from the very beginning. The road was founded on a base of large stones, held in place by kerb stones, and topped off with smaller stones and then gravel, cambered for drainage.

In several places the Military Way along Hadrian's Wall is still visible as a raised line under the earth, and in some parts it runs along the top of the north mound of the Vallum, for instance to the east of Chesters fort, where there is only a short gap between the Wall and Vallum. In this restricted area, from the western side of milecastle 23 to the east side of milecastle 26, the road uses the surface of the Vallum mound. The Military Way connects the milecastles and forts, but it does not keep to a standard distance away from the Wall all along its length. If it did so, it would run up and down steep hills just as the Wall does, which would make travel and transport unnecessarily difficult, so instead it aims for the less steep slopes some distance to the south of the Wall. At the turrets, there are usually connecting paths running from the road.

HOW DID THE WALL WORK?

The short and truthful answer to the question of how the Wall functioned is that no one really knows, but speculation based on the sporadic evidence has been assembled to inform several theories. The soldiers who manned the forts were auxiliaries, non-Roman citizens who served for twenty-five years, and were granted citizenship when they were discharged. There are various inscriptions from the Wall that mention legions, or individual legionaries, but there is no evidence that the legions provided the permanent garrison troops.

The soldiers of the central part of the Wall, where the ground is rugged and hilly, were infantrymen, and on the east and west where the terrain was more suitable for horses, cavalry *alae*, or part-mounted *cohortes equitatae*, were stationed. Soldiers from some of the infantry units probably also provided small detachments for the milecastles and the turrets. It may be that cavalry men were detailed to milecastle duty as well, but there does not seems to have been any provision for stabling, and in any case, cavalry troops are better employed on patrolling, scouting and police work rather than watching a stretch of Wall. There was room in the milecastles for a century of eighty men, in the two buildings, each like half a barrack block, situated parallel to the road through the north and south gate. What the soldiers were intended to do in the milecastles, what they actually did, and how they did it, is unknown. Archaeological evidence shows that at a later time the milecastles probably went out of use as purely military posts, but were used for metal working and other similar tasks.

How the turrets were manned is not elucidated. Perhaps men from the forts were detailed for shift work on a rota system. It is suggested that the turrets were used for signalling, and in fact if the men inside them observed something suspicious, day or night, they would have to notify someone, but how they did this is not certain. At one of the towers of the German frontier, a horn was found, so it is possible that alarms could be given by auditory means, but that is about all that can be done, unless there were specific codes for a restricted number of circumstances – one blast for something seen, two for approaching enemies, three for 'they are getting very close', or something of that ilk. On Trajan's Column in Rome, depicting the events of the Dacian wars, timber towers are depicted with burning torches projecting from their top galleries. These may have been used to send signals. A possibility that is not normally considered is that torches were sometimes lit to illuminate what was happening around the tower in the dark. In any case, if signals were sent from the turrets, they would probably not be intended to be relayed laterally for long distances, but would be directed to the nearest fort, where troops could be sent out to investigate the problem. Argument continues among scholars about Roman signalling, which may have been quite sophisticated in both transmission and reception (two different processes, and things can go wrong in both of them), but it is still not known what happened after messages had been received, and how and by whom they were acted upon.

The main duty of the troops would presumably be to watch for unauthorised movement in advance of the Wall, to prevent people from massing, and guard against attacks, but mostly to keep the peace between natives and Romans and probably also between groups of tribesmen. Though the new Wall may have appeared impregnable, no Roman frontier was absolutely impermeable and probably was never intended to be so. Roman frontiers probably relied on psychological effect just as much as armed force, but they were not invincible. Determined and well-planned attacks could overwhelm the frontiers, as demonstrated in the mid-third century when every Roman frontier fell.

The Wall was not intended to be the absolute terminus of the province. The forts all had at least one gate on the north side, and some had three, usually where there were cavalry present, as at Chesters fort. Even the fort at Housesteads had a north exit via a ramp down the steep hillside, though nowadays it would be a rather more hazardous venture to march out via the northern gate. It is presumed that the soldiers went on patrols to the north of the Wall, and stray finds of Roman items, coins and equipment could indicate that some of these patrols continued for a few days and reached distant parts of southern Scotland. All this is speculation, but patrols into the countryside would be a rather more effective way of controlling the natives than simply remaining behind the Wall and watching for any movement. The Wall was not meant to be defended like an elongated castle, which would in any case be hardly feasible, given the number of areas where there is too much dead ground to see what is going on from the Wall itself. The Romans took the longer view, using the open vistas to the north, the object being to stop any hostiles before they could get anywhere near the Wall itself.

With or without a solid frontier line, the Roman army was always responsible for more tasks than military operations in any province. Police work and some of the functions that are carried out by several modern uniformed officials were all part of a Roman soldier's life. On the borders of the Empire and on the boundaries between provinces, the soldiers acted as customs guards, or supported the officials who inspected the goods and collected the taxes. An inscription from a customs post in Africa reveals how the tariffs for all kinds of goods, two-wheeled vehicles, four-wheeled vehicles, and all kinds of animals, were minutely detailed. There is an anecdote about a Greek philosopher who was asked, when he was crossing a provincial boundary, what he was carrying. He replied that he brought nothing except beauty, truth and wisdom, but since these Greek words can also serve as women's names, the soldiers on duty charged him for the relevant number of prostitutes. Since there were crossing points through Hadrian's Wall at the forts, the soldiers probably exercised the same systematic control. The passage through the Wall at the Knag Burn, in the flatter ground east of Housesteads fort, is presumed to have been a customs post and supervised crossing. No doubt some of the soldiers on guard duty took advantage of any opportunities to extract ready cash for themselves as they inspected people and goods passing from north to south and vice versa.

An analogy from Germany in the first century AD illustrates how the rules of the frontier may have operated. The tribesmen of the Ubii, who were friendly to the Romans, complained that they could not cross the boundary between Free Germany and the Roman province until they had divested themselves of their weapons and most of their clothing. It sounds like the Roman equivalent of going through modern airport security checks, minus luggage, drinks, shoes, belts, and anything made of metal.

CIVILIAN LIFE IN THE FIRST HALF OF THE SECOND CENTURY

As the Roman army moved to occupy newly established sites in the north at the end of the first century, the vacated fortress and forts were given over to civilian settlement. Probably in the reign of Domitian, Lincoln was made a colony, where veterans settled and civilian town life could begin. Walls were built almost immediately around the new colony. At Gloucester, after the legion left, the colony was founded probably in the reign of Nerva, and the Forum was begun under Trajan. Veterans seem to have moved into new houses which were built on the same ground plan as the old barracks. The fortress street plan was also preserved, and can still be traced in part on a modern map of Gloucester. Local government would be established as soon as the colony was founded, and most of the early inhabitants would be accustomed to council procedures and Roman law.

In the recently established *civitas* capitals, development had been uneven. Some of them had started to flourish, like Cirencester, while others lagged behind, such as Caistor-by-Norwich, where the after-effects of the Boudiccan rebellion had perhaps retarded development. Just as there is a detectable impetus for civic development under the Flavian Emperors, the Emperor Hadrian also seems to have stimulated communal and private building projects in Britain, and especially the spread of local government in those places where the army had moved on. Wroxeter is an example of a community that had begun to flourish when the troops moved out and the civilians moved in, but it seems to have stagnated. In the Flavian era, a bathhouse had been started but never completed, and then the Forum was built over the site, with an inscription dating it to 129 or 130, some years after Hadrian's visit to the province. It may be that the local community simply could not afford to finish the baths, or there had been too few people to sustain the development of the town at first.

The Forum at Leicester was also built in Hadrian's reign, and the town centres of Caistor-by-Norwich, the capital of the Iceni, and of Caerwent, capital of the Silures, which had both languished since Flavian times, now received a boost under Hadrian. At Caistor-by-Norwich the town centre was at last properly established, and in the Fen country drainage projects were started, attracting more settlers who were chiefly occupied in producing salt. More inhabitants were attracted to the area to engage in such occupations, and brought more prosperity to the town and to the whole area. In several towns better-quality houses replaced the utilitarian ones of the Flavian period, and private enterprise seems to have increased. At Canterbury, and somewhat later at Cirencester, substantial stone houses were built in the first half of the second century, some of them with painted plaster on the walls. During the first century, town houses had usually been built of timber and clay, while villas in the countryside had been much better constructed and appeared to be much more comfortable than the early dwellings in the towns. The improvement in the quality of town houses may mean that landowners had begun to acquire residences in the towns to enable them to attend council meetings, or perhaps the ordinary inhabitants had begun to accumulate more wealth via trade or business. Unfortunately it is not known who owned and lived in the houses, only that living standards began to improve.

SHOPS AND MARKETS – TEXT BOX

The occupation of the early towns in Britain seems to have been mainly commercial rather than residential, and rows of shops have been identified at several towns, usually designated as strip houses, much like a modern street front, though the individual shops were at first of a much more uniform character than modern examples. This may indicate that a landlord financed the buildings and leased out the shops to tenants. At Verulamium shops originally of uniform design started to acquire individual characteristics by the second century, so it is assumed that the original tenants or their families had perhaps bought their places of work from the landlord and begun to embellish them according to personal taste.

Some of the shops may have contained living accommodation, or some of them may have been lock-ups with shutters, like shops in Rome itself on the Via Biberatica of Trajan's market complex, where the grooves for the shutters can still be seen, as well as the pivots where the doors probably folded inwards against the wall. A similar arrangement can still be seen at the long rectangular buildings labelled 'shops' outside Housesteads fort on Hadrian's Wall, where pivot holes and grooves are still in evidence. In the towns of Roman Britain, the rows of shops usually had verandas outside, running along the length of the buildings, a sensible precaution against rain in Britain, and against hot sunshine in warmer climates.

Some workshops have been identified in Britain, where jewellers, smiths and bronze workers produced goods, and at York there were workshops producing ornaments and jewellery made of jet, though it is not certain if the owners of these workshops also operated as retail establishments for customers in the towns.

Evidence for markets is less abundant. At Cirencester, Leicester, Verulamium and Wroxeter additional space was needed around the Forum for markets, so each of these towns built a *macellum*, where local produce from the surrounding farm lands was probably sold, along with pottery and metal goods. At Wroxeter a stall selling samian pottery was overturned in some disaster, and during the clean-up process afterwards the shattered goods were simply left where they landed, in the gutter, thus providing archaeologists with abundant dating materials for other sites. There may have been itinerant sellers bringing their wares to the markets, which would be controlled and regulated by officials appointed by the town councils, who were also probably responsible for keeping the streets clean. In towns where no officially designated area for a market has been found, it is possible that there was just an open space with no buildings for traders to set up their stalls, which would leave very slight trace for archaeologists.

Private enterprise in the towns seems to have flourished from Flavian times, increasing exponentially as the south of Britain was demilitarised. At Verulamium and Cirencester, rows of timber and clay shops lost their uniformity in favour of individual improvements to some of the buildings, which probably indicates private ownership and commercial initiatives. At Wroxeter, where military occupation lasted longer and civilian development occurred later than the other towns, the shops were not built in rows, but were detached buildings, perhaps occupied by the people who had lived in the *canabae*, the civil settlements that grew up around the legionary fortresses. Soldiers were paid regularly and needed to relax and spend money when off duty, so various settlers would be attracted to the military forts and fortresses, ready and willing to take cash for goods and services. When the legionary occupation ceased at Wroxeter, these people would be the most likely to want to move into the town, many of them probably with fully established businesses. In many places the settlers in converted military installations may not have been British natives, but it seems that at least at Godmanchester some of the inhabitants probably were Britons. The settlement had begun as a fort in the Claudian period, with a cluster of civilians living around it, then in the Flavian period the fort was given up and a small town was established, but with some circular houses and some small rectangular ones, not representative of Roman-style buildings. In Hadrian's reign, a *mansio* was built, where official messengers could stay, and a separate bath suite accompanied it. Small workshops and more small dwellings appeared, built of clay and timber, which perhaps represent small commercial enterprises.

Further north, where military occupation had not ceased, civil development as the Romans interpreted it was not very far advanced. It is suggested that the *civitas* capital of the Brigantes at Aldborough (Isurium Brigantum), was established by Hadrian, but this is not proven. In general the northern tribes clung to their traditional way of life, preferring to live in round houses in family groups, as excavation after excavation in the north has shown, although Roman glass bangles, pottery and other artefacts were obviously very welcome in such communities.

The overriding effect of Hadrian's Wall on the local tribes can be seen in the growth of population that has been detected by excavations in Northumberland, and by aerial survey and field work in Cumbria and the west. These discoveries reveal the *Pax Romana* in its best light. The imposition of law and order, the establishment of peace and protection, and uniform corporate government resulted in steady growth. Perhaps for the first time farmers and stock raisers could guarantee the safety of their flocks and herds, and their crops. Generations of people were allowed to live in peace behind the new frontier, and the results are detectable in the archaeological record.

Romanisation, however, never took root in the north. Although new discoveries of Roman-style villas, extending much further north than was once thought, have demonstrated that the north was not a cultural desert, the inhabitants of the more northerly villas may not always have been Romanised Britons, but entrepreneurs of mixed origin who accumulated wealth from their businesses. Cultural diversity between Romans and British natives persisted, and the presence of the army was not a major Romanising influence, as was once suggested. Interaction between Romans and natives is only dimly elucidated, but hopefully it is not wholly epitomised by the derogatory description in one of the documents from Vindolanda, referring to the Britons as Britunculi, wretched little Britons, which does not convey respect and admiration for a subject population.

6

Expansion & Contraction AD 138 to 180

Hadrian died in 138, almost friendless and detested by the Senate. The new Emperor, Antoninus Pius, succeeded him as his adopted son. Antoninus was not Hadrian's first choice. In an effort to secure the Empire against troubles over the succession, two years before his death Hadrian had adopted Lucius Ceionius Commodus, who took the name Lucius Aelius Caesar, but Lucius died unexpectedly, so another choice had to be made. Antoninus was already closely associated with the Emperor, sharing in the government of the Empire, especially during the later years when Hadrian was already ailing. The adoption of Antoninus came on condition that he should himself adopt Lucius Verus, the son of Lucius Aelius, and also the young Marcus Aurelius, Antoninus's nephew through his wife Faustina. Some men thought that the favoured choice was Marcus, but he was very young and would perhaps require assistance if he became Emperor at an early age, especially as Antoninus was not a young man himself.

Antoninus was of provincial stock, like Hadrian and Trajan. His family originated from Gaul. The rise of all three Emperors illustrates how far social mobility had progressed since the early Empire. A century before, when the Gauls were first enfranchised and some of them became senators, it was an enormous advance, but probably no one envisaged that Gallic families would one day furnish Emperors.

Though he was respected by the Senate, Antoninus at first had great difficulty in ratifying Hadrian's legislation, and the senators were definitely averse to deifying Hadrian. The Senate was forced to relent when Antoninus pointed out that if all Hadrian's acts were annulled, then he would not be Emperor. He earned the name Pius for his conduct. He was frugal, careful, just and, according to Pausanias, 'he never willingly involved the Romans in war'. This does not mean that he did not respond to threats. As reported in the *Historia Augusta*, Antoninus waged several wars via his legates, one of them in Britain, under the governor Lollius Urbicus, when according to the same source:

> [Antoninus] defeated the Britons through his legate Lollius Urbicus, and having driven back the barbarians, he built another Wall, of turf. (*Historia Augusta* Antoninus Pius 5.4)

Unfortunately, Pausanias gives no reasons why Antoninus advanced into Scotland. The territory had been abandoned for nearly forty years, and when it was conquered once again Antoninus built a copy of Hadrian's Wall across the narrow neck of land between the Forth and the Clyde.

It was not only in Britain that Antoninus made a forward advance. A few years after his accession he also moved the frontier of Germany a short distance to the east, creating what is now known to archaeologists as the Outer *Limes*, to distinguish it from the first one on the Odenwald, about 25 miles to the west. The new line runs dead straight, aligned more or less north to south, from Miltenberg on the River Main down to Welzheim. The units which had occupied the forts on the old lines for the most part moved across to the new line to occupy the new forts built along it. It was part of a rationalisation of the frontiers, to join the German and Raetian *limites*, and round off a deep inward-facing salient between the two frontiers. There was no war or any discernible sign of trouble to occasion this move.

As for Britain, various reasons have been suggested for Antoninus's decision to move on from Hadrian's Wall, and to build a new frontier further north. He has been compared to the Emperor Claudius, eager for military success, since he was not a soldier. It is also suggested that the generals of Hadrian's day had not been given much opportunity for glory, and were restless, or that the soldiers in Britain had not enough to do and needed to be sent on campaign to sharpen them up and provide active training and experience. Another theory is that the Pennines had by this time been pacified so it was time to regain control of southern Scotland, relinquished while Trajan fought the Dacian wars. Furthermore, the frontier from the Forth to the Clyde would be much shorter and so it would make fewer demands on manpower. These theories have been disputed. If there were military men agitating for a post as governor where they would see some action, the British campaigns would employ only one of them, and it is probably not quite true to say that the soldiers had nothing to keep them busy, especially since the Pennine area was probably not as peaceful as previously thought. If the original intention was to save manpower, the Romans were to be disillusioned, since the subsequent occupation of southern Scotland and the new frontier was more intense than ever before. It seems unlikely that Antoninus would sanction a war in Britain simply to satisfy a demand from his generals, or to provide military success for himself. He showed no aggressive impulses elsewhere, except to respond to threats or rebellions, such as the Moorish revolt in Africa in the 140s. Rather than a thinly disguised excuse for a military exercise it is preferable to interpret the advance into the north of Britain as a similar response to a rebellion. The problem with this theory is that there is no evidence which satisfactorily explains what had happened to trigger this response. It definitely involved a war, but it is not clear why it was fought, or where it started.

When it was thought that the units of Britons on the German frontier were put there by Antoninus, it was suggested that conscription was one of the causes of British unrest. Conscription could still be a cause for protest, but it is probably not related to the units of Britons on the German frontier. The author Pausanias states that the Brigantes in Britain were deprived of some of their territory by Antoninus, because they had invaded the territory of the Genounian district, which he says was part of the Empire. But this garbled information is considered too far-fetched to be true. It sounds as though the Brigantes were outside the Empire, which was not the case for the whole tribe, except perhaps for a small part of it which was isolated when Hadrian's Wall was built. No one knows where the Genounian district might have been in Britain, but it has been pointed out that there was a tribe called the Brigantes in the province of Raetia, and they were neighbours of the Genauni, so the passage probably has no relevance to Britain whatsoever.

The war was conducted by Lollius Urbicus, who was probably appointed as governor of Britain almost as soon as Antoninus became Emperor, since it is known that he was already in Britain by 139. Urbicus fought in the Jewish war under Hadrian and was decorated by the Emperor. He went on to become the governor of Lower Germany, which was becoming a common sequence for governors of Britain.

Two inscriptions from Corbridge, one naming Urbicus as governor, and the other where his name has been restored from a damaged text, show that II Augusta was building a fort there as early as 139 and 140. Building work was also in progress under Urbicus north of Hadrian's Wall at High Rochester where the governor is named on an inscription, and at Risingham, where he is not named but the likelihood is that the two forts were built as part of the same plan. The most likely location for the war is southern Scotland, and the building work at Corbridge, High Rochester and Risingham can be considered as preparation for campaigning beyond Hadrian's Wall. The campaigns of Lollius Urbicus are difficult to trace, but some marching camps have been assigned to him by archaeologists, notably a line of camps of similar size running up the east side of northern England and southern Scotland. This is the best route for an invasion of Scotland because it provides easier marching than the western route, it is more fertile and therefore food supplies can be obtained, and other supplies can be brought by sea. At many of the forts in southern Scotland where Urbicus eventually placed his garrisons, there are usually several camps, but it is difficult to distinguish the Flavian versions from those which may represent the Antonine advance. The camps along the Antonine Wall were mostly work depots for the soldiers building the new frontier, not campaign camps. One very doubtful location for some fighting is the hillfort at Burnswark, a short distance from the Roman fort at Birrens. The hillfort is sandwiched between two Roman siege camps, and inside it there were stone balls and lead sling bullets, presumably projectiles from Roman siege engines. The usual explanation is that the hillfort had been abandoned long before the Romans arrived, and therefore it is thought that siege camps were built for training purposes, so that the soldiers could practise their assaults on the hillfort without endangering lives, aiming at specially marked targets inside it. Not all scholars agree with this interpretation, and some still argue that the evidence from Burnswark is associated with the Antonine advance.

The fighting was all over by 142 when Antoninus took his second Imperial acclamation, attested on two inscriptions and on a coin portraying Britannia. When the fighting came to an end, the building work on the Antonine Wall probably started immediately. Two inscriptions from the fort at Balmuildy show that the building work there was done by II Augusta, under Urbicus, but he was probably recalled shortly after winning the victory, so most of the work would have been carried out by his successor, or successors. Very little is known about subsequent governors, apart from a reference to Papirius Aelianus attested as governor on a diploma of 146, but this does not help to elucidate what was happening in Britain between the governors Lollius Urbicus and Gnaeus Julius Verus, who arrived probably in 158. Archaeology shows that this period was a busy time as forts were built in southern Scotland and along the Forth–Clyde frontier.

THE ANTONINE WALL

Considering that the Antonine Wall was built of blocks of turf, and it has not been repaired for nigh on two thousand years, the wonder is not that only a few stretches of it can still be seen, but that parts of it have survived at all. In some places the ditch that ran to the north of it is better preserved than the mound of the Wall, but there is enough of both Wall and ditch for tourists to enjoy, and even in some of the built-up areas it can still be traced.

The late Roman author Vegetius gives details of how to cut turves for building and gives precise instructions about the dimensions of the turf blocks. Experiments show that much depends on the type of soil and turf, but generally, if the blocks are larger than Vegetius's recommended size, they break up when lifted, and if they are smaller they will not stack so well. The Antonine Wall was built on a stone foundation, in some places with culverts cut through to allow for drainage. All three legions in Britain did the building work, recording the completion of their allotted sectors by very elaborate carved panels, known to modern historians as distance slabs, which are extremely well preserved because they were not open to the weather for a long time, and were buried when the Wall was abandoned. Some of them can be seen in the Hunterian Museum in Glasgow, and one is in the Museum of Scotland in Edinburgh. The stones recording work by VI Victrix and XX Valeria Victrix always mention vexillations from these legions, but the stones of II Augusta only record the legion, suggesting that the whole legion, or most of it, was present. The implications, if this is correct, are that the south-west was pacified and the whole legion could be safely sent north from Caerleon, while the north-west and north-east, guarded by the fortresses at Chester and York, required more control.

The forts along the Antonine Wall were attached to the turf bank, with their northern defences being the Wall itself. It seems that the final number of forts and fortlets was not part of the original plan, which was probably for six main forts at Carriden, Mumrills, Castlecary, Auchendavy, Balmuildy and Old Kilpatrick. These are spaced about 6 to 8 miles apart, and three of them, at Castlecary, Balmuildy and Old Kilpatrick, were built before the Wall. Castlecary and Balmuildy were the only two forts built of stone, and the presence of wing walls at the latter fort could imply that the Wall itself may initially have been planned as a stone structure. The fort at Old Kilpatrick seems to have stood isolated for some time before the Wall builders arrived to join it to the frontier.

As work progressed, plans were changed, and more forts were added, probably after the original six were built, but still within a very short time after the work on the Wall was started. Between Old Kilpatrick and Balmuildy, a fort was built at Castlehill, and Cadder was inserted between Balmuildy and Auchendavy. A fort at Bar Hill was added, but it stood apart from the Wall. These forts could have housed an entire auxiliary unit, whereas the small forts at Rough Castle, Westerwood, Croy Hill, Bearsden and Duntocher were probably designed for detachments.

The Antonine Wall has a ditch to the north, but there is nothing to suggest that anything like the Vallum of Hadrian's Wall was ever contemplated. Seven of the forts of the Antonine Wall have annexes attached to them, surrounded by a rampart and one or more ditches, so it is possible that these additional fortified areas performed the same function on the Antonine Wall as the Vallum did on Hadrian's Wall, although it has to be admitted that modern interpretations of the purpose of the Vallum and the annexes may differ somewhat from Roman intentions. There may have been an annexe at all forts, not yet discovered, since not all the forts have been fully or even partially investigated. The annexes were usually attached to the east side of the forts, perhaps to avoid the effects of the prevailing west wind and gain more benefit from the sunlight, especially in winter. In one or two cases the annexe is even larger than the fort, as at Duntocher, but most commonly the annexes were about half as large as the accompanying fort. At least four of the annexes contain the unit's bath house, which was normally built outside the fort walls, to avoid the risk of fire. The fact that some bath houses were protected by an annexe suggests a modicum of insecurity, or at least a perceived threat. It is not known if the annexes regularly contained buildings, such as animal shelters, workshops, cart sheds and so on. It could be asked why the Romans did not simply build larger forts to contain all that the annexes protected, but perhaps the consequent extension of the perimeters would have strained manpower resources if the fort perimeters had to be defended, though this would have been a last resort, since the Romans usually met their enemies in the open. The close spacing of the forts on the Antonine Wall would surely preclude the possibility of blockade or siege of any one of them, but small raiding parties could do considerable damage. The Romans generally did not think in terms of castles, with an inner and outer bailey, but this is how the Normans might have interpreted forts of the Antonine Wall, and it is reasonable to suggest that if anyone broke into the annexes, they would be vulnerable to missiles from the fort wall, and sallies of the troops. Alternatively, the priority may simply have been to avoid cluttering up the fort with all the animals, stores of fodder, vehicles and other items. On Hadrian's Wall, these things could be left outside protected by a fence, and ultimately the Vallum.

It used to be thought that equivalents of the milecastles and turrets of Hadrian's Wall played no part in the Antonine scheme, but in more recent years, about ten fortlets have been discovered, notably at Duntocher, Kinneil and Wilderness Plantation, which have been excavated, and found to be very similar to the Hadrian's Wall milecastles in plan. They were built of turf, based on stone foundations, most probably with rounded corners, as was seen at Croy Hill fortlet, and at Seabegs. It is probable that they all had a gate in the north and south sides. Investigations at these sites and others have shown that most of them were constructed at the same time as the Wall, or even shortly before it. Apart from the fortlets that have been identified, it is likely that there are similar structures in the vicinity of Rough Castle, Castlehill and Bar Hill, and perhaps even more awaiting discovery along the line of the Wall. Traces of internal buildings are slight but it is probably safe to suggest that the fortlets contained accommodation blocks like the milecastles, though it is not possible to say how they operated.

More recently, small square turf platforms with stone bases have been discovered, attached to the rear of the Wall, labelled 'expansions' by archaeologists. They seem to occur in pairs, two to the west of Croy Hill, and another two to the west of Rough Castle. Between that fort and Watling Lodge fortlet there are two more, but they are widely spaced. It is not known if they were built at regular intervals like the turrets of Hadrian's Wall, and since no post holes suggesting the presence of timber towers have been found, the platforms have not been interpreted as watchtowers. Traces of burning on top of some of them have given rise to the theory that they may have functioned as beacons, or signalling devices, and the apparent pairing of platforms may mean that one platform supported stacks of hay, which were used to transmit smoke signals during the day, while the other platform held logs to provide fire signals at night. Hay stacks and log piles are clearly seen on Trajan's Column in Rome. On the German frontier, just behind the palisade, circular stone platforms have been found with traces of burning, and have been interpreted in the same way, as hay stacks for smoke signals, or just possibly they may have been used to provide illumination at night.

At the eastern end of the Antonine Wall, the Romans used the same sites that Agricola had founded, protecting the road up to the River Tay with forts at Camelon, which lies about a mile north of the Wall, and then via Ardoch, Strageath, and Bertha, which were rebuilt on the Flavian sites. On the south side of the Forth Estuary, Carriden on the Wall protected the approach to the frontier and new forts were built further south at Cramond and Inveresk.

On the west side, the Romans protected both the north and south sides of the Clyde, with a road on the north bank, possibly running as far as Dumbarton. On the south side, the fort at Bishopton guarded the river, possibly aided by fortlets. There may be more installations down the west coast.

North of the Wall, Roman influence would be maintained by patrols and probably small parties sent out for the purpose of gathering intelligence. Contact with the natives was not usually cut off altogether, and cultivation of possibly friendly groups was encouraged. Hadrian had supported some natives beyond the frontiers by means of gifts and subsidies. In this Hadrian was possibly continuing the policy of his predecessor Trajan, but whoever started it, the system worked successfully for many years. The gifts to chieftains helped to back their authority as leaders, and they kept the peace among the tribes. Subsidies sometimes comprised food supplies, on the basis that it was preferable to give sustenance freely rather than have to fight off hungry tribesmen who were searching for food on the other side of the Roman frontier. There is no evidence to suggest that this is how the Hadrianic or Antonine frontiers operated, but it is not out of the question.

THE OCCUPATION OF SOUTHERN SCOTLAND AND NORTHERN ENGLAND

Between the Antonine Wall and the abandoned Hadrian's Wall, southern Scotland was reoccupied more densely than it had been before the withdrawal to the Trajanic Stanegate frontier. The fort at Newstead was the largest, guarding the eastern route to the north, rebuilt at 14 acres (5.95 ha), to house two legionary cohorts from XX Valeria Victrix and also a quingenary *ala*. Two other large forts which could each have housed a milliary unit were built at Castledykes and Glenlochar. The fort at Dalswinton, which had guarded the north–south route in the west during the Flavian occupation, was not rebuilt, but a large fort was established about 3 miles distant at Carzield. Forts at Loudoun Hill and Bothwellhaugh were probably intended for quingenary units, while the fort at Crawford was not large enough for a full quingenary unit, but possessed a large headquarters building, suggesting that parts of the unit may have been outposted in one or more of the smaller forts.

There was a greater number of small forts in southern Scotland than had been established in the Flavian period, which some authors have interpreted as an indication that manpower was stretched. These small fort sites include the old Flavian ones at Cappuck, Chew Green, Lyne and Raeburnfoot, with new additions at Durisdeer, Barburgh Mill, Wandel, Redshaw Brun, Milton, Bankhead and Burnswark. The troops manning the small forts are not known, but it is estimated that there was sufficient space for one century of eighty men. The increased number of smaller posts suggests that there may have been a need for close supervision of routes. There may have been a greater use of mounted troops than in the first century, perhaps for greater mobility in patrolling, or perhaps in pursuit of raiders. The outpost forts north-west of Hadrian's Wall at Bewcastle, Birrens and Netherby were retained, and the route on the north-east side was now reinforced by two new forts on the eastern side, at High Rochester, which was definitely built by Lollius Urbicus, and Risingham, which is not dated but most likely belongs to the same period. The dense pattern of occupation implies that the objective was to pin down the native population.

The soldiers who occupied the new and rebuilt forts of southern Scotland, and the Antonine Wall itself, are presumed to have been withdrawn from Hadrian's Wall, the Pennine area and possibly the Lake District. The forts at Melandra, Brough-on-Noe, Slack, Lancaster, Binchester, Ebchester and Ambleside were probably evacuated, suggesting that the whole area from Derbyshire to Cumbria and Yorkshire was peaceful enough to thin out the garrison. It was once thought that the forts in Wales may also have been reduced in number to provide manpower for the Antonine Wall or associated forts to the south of it, but this has been disputed. It may be significant that in Wales there seems to have been no serious disturbance at the end of the second or third centuries that required a military expedition to quell it, whereas in the north, according to the ancient sources, various troubles occurred with monotonous regularity. Thinning the garrison in the north, if such was the case, was perhaps a little premature.

On Hadrian's Wall the effects of the establishment of the Antonine frontier are more visible. The effectiveness of Hadrian's Wall as a barrier, now that the troops had moved north of it, was more of a hindrance than a help, so mobility was restored, up to a point. The mounds of the Vallum were cut through at regular intervals, and the soil was thrown into the Vallum ditch to provide access across it. In some of the milecastles archaeological investigations showed that the gate pivots were damaged, so it is assumed that all or most of them had their gates removed. What happened at the forts is not so clear. A diploma from Vindolanda dated 146 indicates that at least two forts were occupied at that time, though it is suggested that the soldiers may have been veterans rather than the original units. Housesteads is the only fort for which there is some evidence about its garrison. An altar to Jupiter, Cocidius and the *Genius* of the place was set up by legionaries from II Augusta, who described themselves as *agentes in praesidio*, or as the acting garrison. It was an unusual circumstance, which the soldiers clearly thought required elucidation, and it was perhaps meant to be only a temporary arrangement. There are several inscriptions from other forts mentioning legionaries, but these do not constitute proof that legionaries occupied the Wall during the life of the Antonine frontier. Usually it is considered that the troops in the forts of the older Wall were merely caretaker garrisons, since it is very unlikely that the two frontiers were held simultaneously.

The abandonment of the forts on Hadrian's Wall was not accompanied by a similar abandonment of the Cumberland coastal system, suggesting that it was still considered important to watch the Solway and the estuary, to prevent movement across it and into the Lake District.

THE ABANDONMENT OF THE ANTONINE WALL

Until quite recently it seemed from the archaeological evidence that there had been two or more occupations of the Antonine Wall, separated by short intervals, and a corresponding series of reoccupations, before the final reoccupation of Hadrian's Wall. The alleged marching up and down between one Wall and the other caused innumerable problems for archaeologists who had to try to match what they found on individual sites with the two or more periods on the Antonine Wall, and the subsequent reoccupations of Hadrian's Wall. Following this accepted pattern, historians had to try to find reasons why there should have been such vacillation on the part of the Romans before they settled down on the old line of Hadrian's frontier.

The theory of two, or possibly even three, occupations of the Antonine Wall arose from a variety of pieces of evidence. There was some military disturbance in Britain *c.*155 to 158, which seemed to have been serious enough to demand a complete abandonment of the Antonine Wall, rather than a thinning of the garrison to lend support to the military commander. Then when the disturbance was quelled, whatever and wherever it was, it was suggested that the Antonine Wall was occupied once again, perhaps at the end of the reign of Antoninus, or during the reign of his successor, Marcus Aurelius. Specific dates were not crystal clear from pottery and other evidence, but from the archaeological point of view, it was a reasonable assumption that the whole garrison had left and then returned, but with some troop changes. Some of the Antonine Wall forts were occupied by two different and presumably successive units, and there were also signs of rebuilding or alterations to the internal buildings. At Castlecary, two units are attested, but the fort is not large enough to accommodate both of them at the same time. It is at the fort at Mumrills, the largest on the Antonine Wall, where the evidence for two periods of occupation seemed strongest. The fort was occupied by a 500-strong cavalry unit, *ala I Tungrorum quingenaria*, but there is also epigraphic evidence of a different unit, this time a part-mounted cohort, *cohors II Thracum quingenaria equitata*. The headquarters building started out as quite a large structure, appropriate for an *ala*, but was then reduced in size, more appropriate for a part-mounted cohort, which would not require as much space. It seemed that these two units must represent two distinct periods of occupation, rather than a continuous occupation in which one unit moved out as another moved in. At Bar Hill, the same situation was observed. Two different units were in occupation of the fort, and rebuilding was detected inside it. However, the period between the first build and the rebuilding was extremely short.

Fortunately, matters were clarified when the archaeologist and scholar N. Hodgson looked at the evidence more closely and concluded that the Antonine Wall was occupied only once, for a short period between the start of building in 142 to *c.*158, when it was abandoned altogether and never reoccupied. When the Wall was abandoned, the distance slabs recording work by the legionary builders were all buried, and thereby preserved for posterity.

The main problem now is not the struggle to fit all pieces of evidence in with the alleged Antonine and Hadrian's Wall periods, but to discern why the northern Wall was abandoned in the reign of the same Emperor who built it. The short answer is that nobody knows the reason. The governor of Britain in 158, when the Antonine Wall was probably abandoned, was Julius Verus, who was previously governor of Lower Germany. In Britain, Verus is mentioned on a diploma of February 158, so it is likely that he had been appointed a short time before this, in *c.*157. If there had been some disturbances in the north *c.*155, then presumably peace had been restored by the previous governor, but no evidence is available about what the trouble may have been or who the previous governor was. Some authors have connected the reports of war in Britain in *c.*155 to the passage from Pausanias's work, describing how Antoninus deprived the Brigantes of some of their territory, but this is too garbled to be of use, and in any case it is not dated, and can be brought in for almost any mid-second century trouble. A coin showing Britannia was issued *c.*155, as if commemorating a victory. The figure of Britannia, personified as a woman, is described as subdued. And that is all that is known about this shadowy period.

Under Julius Verus as governor, an undated inscription was set up at Newcastle-upon-Tyne, mentioning vexillations of all three legions of Britain, and the armies of the two provinces of Germany. The trouble is that no one can be certain whether troops were sent *from* the German provinces to reinforce the legions of Britain, or whether the vexillations of II Augusta, VI Victrix and XX Valeria Victrix were contributed *to* the German provinces. In the first scenario, where German legionaries were possibly brought into Britain, it would imply that the disturbances in the island *c.*155 were serious, causing losses that had to be replaced from the Roman armies in Upper and Lower Germany, probably arriving with the new governor Julius Verus. But that leaves a hypothetical gap of nearly three years or so before the losses were made good. In the alternative scenario, where the legions had been sent to Germany and were probably returning to Britain while Verus was governor, it seems that Britain was considered peaceful enough to allow vexillations from all the legions to go to Germany for some unknown purpose. This inscription raises far more questions than it provides answers, and archaeologists would have had an easier life if it had never been discovered.

Whatever the disturbance was in the middle of the 150s, it probably broke out in the north of England, and may have been the trigger for pulling back to the line of Hadrian's Wall, and reoccupying the Pennine forts. The end of the occupation of the Antonine Wall seems to have been peaceful, rather than a result of a military disaster in southern Scotland. Neat and tidy demolition took place at Mumrills, where the timbers and other debris were carted outside the fort and burned, and then the burnt debris was used to fill in the ditch of the annexe. Pits at Crawford were deliberately dug and all waste material placed in them, including some bent nails which could not be salvaged. At Old Kilpatrick the well was filled in, and the same happened at Bar Hill, where the well contained a large amount of old footwear, including leather boots and finely tooled shoes for men, women and children.

Scotland had been overrun and then held over a period of about twenty years, counting from the appointment of Lollius Urbicus, probably in 138 or 139, to the withdrawal in *c.*158. It seems very brief, almost a waste of time, and in archaeological terms it is merely an instant. But when compared with the whole of the Napoleonic era, which lasted from 1796 to 1815, it is a reminder that many significant things can happen in that brief period of two decades.

A tremendous amount of building work was going on in the north of Britain under Julius Verus. He is named on inscriptions from Birrens, Corbridge and Brough-on-Noe. Repairs were made to the curtain wall of Hadrian's Wall itself in 158, though the inscription does not mention the governor's name. It is suggested that the building work from Derbyshire up to the Tyne–Solway line was carried out in advance of the troops coming down from the Antonine Wall, but building seems to have continued under successive governors after the withdrawal from Scotland. It is not known when Verus was recalled, or who succeeded him, but what he had begun was probably continued by the next governor.

North of Hadrian's Wall, the three outposts on the west, at Birrens, where Verus is recorded on a building inscription, and at Bewcastle and Netherby, were retained, as were the two new forts at High Rochester and Risingham. The important fort at Newstead was still occupied, probably together with the small posts on Dere Street at Cappuck and Chew Green. On Hadrian's Wall itself, the milecastle gates were put back, and the causeways over the Vallum were dug out again, though no attempt was made to block up the gaps created in the mounds when the Antonine Wall was built, so that these are still visible in several places. The service road called by its modern name of the Military Way was laid down south of the Wall, and bridges were built or rebuilt, over the North Tyne at Chesters, and over the Tyne at Corbridge. In the west the Turf Wall was replaced in stone, with stone milecastles. In the east, the fort at Newcastle may have been rebuilt at that time, although some authors have disputed the date, preferring to interpret it as part of Severus's rebuilding in the early third century. South Shields fort was rebuilt, and forts were established in the hinterland at Lanchester and Chester-le-Street. The rebuilding was probably intended to be an ongoing and widespread programme, and may have been continued under the next two governors, Pisibanius Lepidus and Marcus Statius Priscus. Apart from their names, little else is known about their terms of office in Britain.

Antoninus Pius died in 161, and was succeeded by his adopted sons Marcus Aurelius and Lucius Verus. In the same year, or possibly in 162, Sextus Calpurnius Agricola was appointed as governor of Britain. He was governor of Upper Germany in 158, and may have been sent straight from there to Britain, where according to the *Historia Augusta* hostilities had broken out again. Calpurnius Agricola is recorded on several inscriptions, in the Lake District at Hardknott, and at Ribchester in Lancashire, where some cavalry had arrived from Upper Germany, probably with the new governor. Building work was carried out by legionary detachments under Calpurnius Agricola at Corbridge. The soldiers of VI Victrix made a dedication to the Unconquered Sun, and XX Valeria Victrix usefully dated their building inscription via the consulships and tribunician years of Marcus Aurelius and his colleague Lucius Verus, proving that Agricola was governor in 163. The prefect of the Hamian archers at Carvoran set up two inscriptions naming the governor, and a fragment from Vindolanda also names him. Although these inscriptions do not necessarily imply that he was present in northern England or on Hadrian's Wall, they show that south of the Wall some forts in the north-west and the Pennines were occupied.

The Pennines and Lake District may have been the scene of the latest troubles mentioned in the *Historia Augusta*, when Calpurnius Agricola was sent against the Britons. There is hardly any archaeological evidence of war, but the frequent disturbances in Britain may have concerned relatively few warriors who were not ready to settle down and succumb to Roman rule, rather than full-scale tribal warfare. In the American West, a handful of highly mobile native Indians could cause widespread destruction and death, to other tribes and to settled farmers alike, and considerable numbers of infantry and cavalry were occupied in pursuit of them. After the Civil War, US Major General George Crook gained his fame by adapting his troops and methods of fighting to solve the problem of Indian raids, but he also tried to assimilate and integrate the Indians, believing that they were entitled to the same justice as anyone else, and full acceptance as human beings. The Romans were presumably just as adept at firm military activity, but were perhaps not interested in actively promoting integration. There seems to have been a firm resistance on the part of the northern Britons, or at least a lack of initiative, to embrace the ideals of assimilation with Rome.

Calpurnius Agricola may have remained in the province until the end of the 160s, but no dates are discernible for his recall. The next known governor was Quintus Antistius Adventus, who was in Britain from about 172 to 174 or 175. He is named on an inscription from Lanchester. Adventus had been governor of Lower Germany until *c*.170. During the 170s the Emperor Marcus Aurelius was fully occupied with the wars on the Danube, and once again the *Historia Augusta* indicates that there was another war threatening in Britain. No traces of this supposed war have been found. It was probably during Adventus's term of office that Marcus Aurelius sent 5,500 Sarmatian cavalry from the Danube to Britain under the terms of a treaty he had arranged with the tribe. It was all done in a hurry because an attempt at usurpation had broken out in Syria, so Marcus concluded the Danube wars for the time being and imposed a peace treaty, whereby the tribesmen were to contribute troops for the Roman army. The Sarmatians delivered 8,000 cavalry in total, of which the majority came to Britain. It is not known where they were housed at first, but it was presumably Adventus's task to distribute them. The Sarmatians are attested at Ribchester at a later time, and some of them may have been sent there as soon as they arrived in the 170s. They were excellent horsemen, wearing their distinctive scale armour, as depicted on a carved relief at Ribchester. Only a short time before, some cavalry from Germany had been sent to the fort at Ribchester, where the low-lying ground near the river would be suitable for horses. It may be that the natives were restless and there was a demand for mobile troops to patrol and keep order in south Lancashire.

After Adventus's recall *c.*174 or 175, a governor called Caerellius replaced him, but nothing is known of his term of office. Probably in 177, Ulpius Marcellus arrived. He is named on three diplomas dated to 178, and on an inscription from Benwell, set up by the prefect of cavalry there, Tineius Longus, who records that he had been raised to senatorial status by the two Emperors. Lucius Verus had died in 169, so the two Emperors of the inscription were most likely Marcus Aurelius and his son Commodus, who was made Caesar in 175, and then colleague and co-Emperor in 177.

Marcus Aurelius himself died in 180, still in the midst of the Danube wars, and Commodus became sole Emperor. As the beneficiary of the long wars waged by his father, Commodus put an end to the fighting with alacrity, and made more treaty arrangements with the tribes, receiving a vast number of warriors for the Roman army all at once instead of an annual contribution. Then he hastened back to Rome. He was probably not as negligent as this description makes him seem, since his treaty arrangements were successful and there was peace in the Danube region for a long time afterwards. As usual, however, on the accession of a new Emperor there was trouble in Britain, and Commodus sent Ulpius Marcellus to deal with it.

Ulpius Marcellus has caused problems for modern historians, or rather it is Dio who complicates matters, because he says that a general was killed in a war with the Britons, and Ulpius Marcellus was sent against them, which makes it sound as though there was a governor in post in Britain at some time before 180 who was killed in the war, and Marcellus was sent to replace the dead man by Commodus, which means that this occurred after his accession in 180. Since Marcellus was clearly in Britain himself in 178 as an appointee of Marcus Aurelius, different solutions to the conundrum were suggested. Some scholars proposed that there were two governors called Ulpius Marcellus, one preceding the general who was killed, and another one succeeding him. Other scholars thought that Marcellus must have served for a short term in Britain, then was recalled and offered other appointments, but when the war broke out and the general was killed, he was sent back to Britain to campaign against the tribesmen. The real alternative seems to be to accept that Marcellus's appointment as governor spanned the joint rule of Marcus Aurelius and Commodus, and the early years of the sole rule of Commodus himself. This would mean that his term of office was very long, though it was no longer than Gnaeus Julius Agricola's in the first century. The probable location of Marcellus's war in Britain, and its course as far as it can be traced, is described in the following chapter.

CIVILIAN DEVELOPMENT IN THE SECOND CENTURY

In the 140s Antoninus Pius made some alterations to the citizenship grants to auxiliary soldiers who had served their full terms in the army and achieved *honesta missio*, or honourable discharge. Previously, the grant of Roman citizenship had embraced the whole of the soldier's family, despite the fact that marriage was supposed to be forbidden by law. The wording of the citizenship grants on military diplomas skirts around this legal impediment by acknowledging the fact that soldiers had formed liaisons with local women. Until the 140s, all the children of each veteran soldier were made citizens when he retired, but Antoninus Pius decided to exclude from the grant of citizenship the children who had been born while their fathers were serving in the army. Any children born after the veteran received citizenship would automatically become citizens themselves. One of the effects of this rationing of citizenship would be that the non-citizen sons of auxiliary soldiers would no longer be eligible to join the legions as citizens, but if they wished to serve as soldiers, they would provide recruits for the auxiliary regiments, which may have been one of the motives for the change.

TOWN AND COUNTRY

Life in Roman Britain flourished in the mid-second century, reaching a peak of development that was never surpassed. Large Roman-style public buildings began to appear in several towns, presumably financed by wealthy inhabitants or members of the town councils. Only very rarely is there any indication of who built these splendid new amenities, but at Brough-on-Humber an inscription states that Marcus Ulpius Januarius, an aedile of the town, built a theatre. This is the only inscription mentioning an aedile in Britain, though these officials were among the lower-ranking ones, and were not generally mentioned on inscriptions. Probably only a few of them would be wealthy enough to build something as grand as a theatre. Unfortunately the building at Brough-on-Humber is known only from the inscription, and no remains have yet been identified.

At Leicester, about AD 150, a large public baths complex was built with a hall next to it, possibly as an exercise area, for sports and leisure pursuits. The baths and exercise hall at Wroxeter were also built in the second century, opposite the Forum, complete with an open-air swimming pool and shopping facilities. A new basilica had to be built at Cirencester because the first one had been placed over the ditch of the old fort, and had started to subside. A new market place was also established near the Forum, possibly replacing an earlier one from the Flavian period.

GOING TO THE BATHS – TEXT BOX

The Romans brought with them to Britain the habit of bathing in establishments that operated like Turkish baths. The bathers covered themselves in oil, which is after all mostly what soap is made of, and then passed through the hot rooms, sweating out the dirt, which was all scraped off with a curved metal instrument called a strigil. The process ended with a cold plunge, which closed the pores of the skin before going outside and, in Britain at least, avoided the risk of catching one's death from the cold. The English diarist John Evelyn escaped the horrors of the Civil War by going abroad, and took a bath in Venice, where the procedure was similar to the Roman one. He was quite surprised by the amount of dirt that came off that he didn't know was clinging to him in the first place.

All baths will have used a huge amount of fuel to heat the water and the hot rooms, and will have required attendants, most likely slaves, to keep the fires burning. The hot water and the hot rooms were heated by fires underneath the floors, which were raised up on columns, the whole system known as a hypocaust, which is a Greek-sounding word invented by the Romans. The underfloor heating was not the only source of warmth. Special tiles called by modern archaeologists 'box tiles', like open-ended rectangular boxes, were set into the walls to carry the heat upwards. One of these tiles is visible in the wall at the baths at Wall (Letocetum) in Staffordshire. The floors and walls of the hot room could become very hot indeed and people probably wore shoes to protect their feet. There are cases on record in other parts of the Roman Empire of people being burnt on direct contact with heated walls or floors, and in one case when irate slaves revolted against their master and tried to kill him, they threw him on the heated floor to see if he was really dead. He was still alive, and gritted his teeth so as not to make a sound, and survived, somewhat burned, to tell the tale. It was probably quite difficult to regulate the heat using fires under the floors and under the boiler for the hot water, which in some instances was scalding.

Bathers would enter the baths via the cold room (*frigidarium*) where there was no heating, and perhaps remove their clothing here, or in the next room, called the warm room (*tepidarium*). Some baths had an additional room where bathers could leave their clothes, hopefully in the charge of a slave who would guard them until the bather returned, but some people probably did not possess this luxury. There is a variety of lead curse tablets from Britain threatening dire consequences to whoever stole cloaks and other items of clothing from the baths, cloaks being the most valuable items.

If the bather had not already been anointed with oil, he or she would do this on entering the hot room (*caldarium*), and sweat out the dirt. There was usually a hot bath available for use after the oil had been scraped off. Then it was back to the cold room and in most cases a cold plunge. There were many variations at bathing establishments, some of them having more facilities than others, though the simple range of three rooms as described here was more or less standard. Usually there was a whole range of amenities for leisure and relaxation outside the baths. Going to the baths was not necessarily just a quick visit to clean up, but a chance to use the libraries, do exercises, meet friends, make new ones, gamble, and do business deals. Some bathing establishments had special opening times for women, others operated mixed bathing. In Rome, there are the remains of several baths to visit. A church occupies part of Diocletian's baths, and the baths of Caracalla, where opera performances are staged in summer, are perhaps the most elaborate, requiring at least half a day to see it all.

Bath houses were built outside Roman forts for the use of the soldiers, and examples are known from the legionary fortresses of Exeter and Caerleon, and at the forts at Chesters on Hadrian's Wall, and Vindolanda, just south of the Wall. A military bath house has been reconstructed at the fort of Wallsend, based on the building at Chesters. In Lancashire there are baths at Lancaster and Ribchester, while in the Lake District military baths have been found at the forts of Hardknott and Ravenglass, and in Scotland at Bearsden and Bothwellhaugh.

In towns, similar establishments started to appear as soon as the inhabitants were able to afford the costs of construction. The baths were often attached to other public buildings, usually the Forum and basilica where official administrative business and legal proceedings were carried out. The largest remains of a town bath complex are those at Wroxeter, where the wall connecting the second century baths to the basilica stands to a considerable height, and the foundations of the rooms of the baths are still visible, together with some of the columns of tiles that supported the floor of the hot rooms, forming the hypocaust where the fires were lit. The so-called Jewry Wall at Leicester is very similar, forming the connecting wall between basilica and baths.

Some private individuals also had baths in their living accommodation. At Chesters fort a bath suite was built in the commander's house. The large palatial villas such as Fishbourne and Lullingstone had elaborate baths, and at the more modest villa at Great Witcombe there were two suites of baths.

As a generalisation, there was more emphasis on marketplaces in several towns, implying that the town dwellers were more prosperous. Shops at Verulamium were arranged in rows at first, and remodelled perhaps by private owners. Then they were replaced with better buildings, with individualistic plans, set at right angles to the street, in the early second century. At Wroxeter stalls displaying wares for sale were probably set up around the Forum. In both these towns there were disastrous fires, at Verulamium in 155, and at Wroxeter in the 160s. Recovery was slow at Verulamium, where an enormous area was obliterated, though the fires are not to be associated with the troubles in northern Britain in 155. When building started again the shops were replaced with larger town houses, surrounded by their own grounds. They were built of flint and mortar, with tiled roofs, which would withstand a fire somewhat better than the timber buildings that had been the norm before 155. It is even possible that the town council had begun to issue fire regulations after so much of the town was destroyed.

The destructive fire at Wroxeter has been associated with a possible uprising of the Welsh tribes. In support of this theory, the rebuilding of some of the forts in Wales suggests that there may have been some trouble with the natives. In contrast to Verulamium, the damage at Wroxeter was cleared up quite quickly. The Forum site was levelled, and with it the debris from a large collection of samian pottery and mortaria, assumed to have been knocked over from a market stall into the gutter. It was left there under the foundations when rebuilding began, thus enhancing Romano-British pottery studies and associated dating evidence.

Second-century town houses such as those at Verulamium generally begin to display mosaic floors and frescoed walls, and a better standard of living. Houses in London and Cirencester had already reached this stage in the later first century, demonstrating their wealth, but now the other towns were beginning to catch up. Mosaic floors were laid at Aldborough, the *civitas* capital of the Brigantes, suggesting the spread of specialist workshops and the acquisition of wealth to pay for such enhancements. It is tempting to associate the larger town houses with the members of the town councils, but some of these houses could also be the dwellings of prosperous merchants whose daily business was in the towns. For those towns where several villas were built in the surrounding area, it is assumed that councillors lived outside the towns and used a town house when meetings were to be held, but this is something that will probably never be proved.

It is not certain how the native Britons shared in the town development. Many of them were probably small farmers, unrepresented in the archaeological record, bringing their produce to market for sale and buying household items while they were there. In the countryside, several examples of Iron Age roundhouses have been discovered underneath Romano-British farms, suggesting that local families profited from the development of the towns and built larger accommodation in the Roman fashion.

TOWN DEFENCES
Defence works are notoriously difficult to date, but it is generally accepted that the main development of town defences seems to have

occurred in the third century, though some towns began to build earthwork defences a little earlier. This was an Imperial matter, since the governing body of a town could not simply decide to build some defences and start work. In the reign of Marcus Aurelius a query about defence works had arisen, and the Emperor's reply, that Imperial permission must be sought before defences could be erected, is preserved in the *Digest*, a sixth-century compilation of laws and Emperor's decisions from the early Empire to late antiquity. The Imperial government could not readily allow any town to build walls which could harbour rebels, any more than a medieval king of England could allow a retainer to build a castle, hence a licence to crenellate had to be obtained for castle building, though some of them were applied for retrospectively, after building had started or even after the castle had been built. In Roman Britain, a request for permission to build walls or earthworks was presumably formulated by the town council, and directed to the governor of the province, who would pass it on to the Emperor for approval.

By the second century, Colchester had flourished and spread beyond its original boundary, but on the line of the old boundary a monumental gateway had been built, marking the entrance to the town from the London road. At some time in the second century, the council decided and presumably received permission to encircle the town within a wall, pulling back from the outlying parts of the town as far as the old boundary, and marrying up the wall to the gateway, the ruins of which can still be seen, now called the Balkerne Gate.

A similar situation can be seen at Verulamium, where the rampart and ditch of the first century were replaced with a new set of earth defences in about 150. Stone gateways were built, but the circuit of earth defences was never completed, possibly because the serious fire of 155 stultified further improvements, and when the recovery began all resources were concentrated on rebuilding the town centre.

Before the third century it is debatable whether the inhabitants of the towns felt the need for defences because of growing insecurity, though there are several coin hoards datable to the reigns of Marcus Aurelius and Commodus that are otherwise unexplained. Economic upheaval could force people to bury their wealth, but there is no evidence for such economic distress, and economics alone cannot explain why the coins were never reclaimed. There was a serious plague during Marcus's reign, which may have decimated populations and led to lawlessness, but such circumstances are not attested in Britain. There may have been no disturbances that occasioned the building of some town walls, and it may be that defences were begun simply for the prestige that a new set of walls and gates would bring to a town.

INDUSTRIES

Manufacturing industries all around the towns are attested, such as local pottery manufacture, and tile making, and it is known that there were timber merchants, and importers of wine and oil, and luxury goods for the markets. No doubt there were many more firms in business than the evidence allows, surrounding most towns and catering for the localised market. It is possible that craftsmen and manufacturers formed guilds, called *collegia*, though only a handful are known, from Chichester, where a guild of smiths is attested in Claudian times, and Silchester, Caerwent, Bath and York, but the relevant inscriptions sometimes only mention the *collegia*, minus any information as to what sort of occupation they were concerned with. Information from Rome and other provinces shows that the guilds provided mutual assistance to their members, and served to regulate production and promote lawful behaviour, providing the Roman government with a ready-made means of control of local industries.

Most industrial processes were established in the countryside rather than in the towns, such as the local mortaria factories, where the industry was dominated at first by Roman citizens, but the number of non-citizens engaged in businesses increased as the second century progressed. The impact of the army would have a great influence on the development of local pottery industries, being the largest consumers with the ability to pay for products. An army contract probably provided the most lucrative means of setting up and maintaining a business. Pottery industries developed in Colchester quite early, and then by the second half of the second century Romano-British pottery manufacture had spread into many other areas. There were factories in East Anglia, and in Oxfordshire and Warwickshire. The Nene Valley factories near Peterborough produced all types of pottery, fine wares and coarse wares, and in Dorset the factories produced the so-called black-burnished wares, mostly supplied to the army. Imports of pottery still arrived in quantity, but there was a decline in samian wares in the second century, a gap in the market which was probably rapidly filled by entrepreneurial Romano-British pottery manufacturers, or alternatively British manufacture was cheaper and caused the decline of imports.

The Romans conducted many mining operations in Britain, for various products, including metals and coal, which was used to heat the bath houses at some of the forts on Hadrian's Wall and the Antonine Wall, and for smelting iron. In some instances coal was used in corn dryers. Coal from Somerset was used at the baths at Bath, the process being described by the third-century author Solinus, who says that it was used in the temple of Minerva, who presided over the baths, equated with the native British deity Sulis. The perpetual fire in her temple was never allowed to go out, and Solinus says that instead of producing white wood-ash, the fire left stony lumps, which were presumably cinders.

Evidence for how the mines were worked has not survived in great detail in Britain, but archaeologists and historians extrapolate from knowledge of mining operations in the province of Spain, for which there is more evidence. Procurators of mines were appointed to oversee all mines, and to arrange how they were worked. Mining contracts were given to individuals or companies, and detailed agreements were drawn up between the lessee and the Imperial government. At Vipasca in Portugal a bronze tablet outlines how the Imperial share of the profits from the iron worked there had to be given to the Emperor before the ore was smelted. As an insurance policy to see that this was done with alacrity, the government offered rewards to informers who told the procurators if anyone was cheating. There were regulations for the safety of the mines, probably drawn up by the procurator. In

Above: The Norman keep at Colchester was built over the remains of the Temple of Claudius, where the legionary veterans gathered at the time of the Boudiccan rebellion, and were slaughtered. By that date, AD 60, Colchester had been raised to the status of a *colonia* for just over a decade. When the Normans built their enormous castle, larger than the Norman Tower of London, they used some Roman tiles, still visible in parts of the walls. The choice of Colchester and London as centres of William I's administration and control echoes the early Roman arrangements for governing the new province of Britannia. Inside the castle keep is the museum, with Roman sculptures and artefacts, and other finds from Colchester.

Left: In its central sector Hadrian's Wall runs along the geological feature known as the Whin Sill, a north-facing cliff that Hadrian probably inspected for himself when he came to Britain in AD 122. This view looks to the east, towards Steel Rigg and Crag Lough. The line of the Wall is marked in the foreground by a modern farm wall, and the northern ditch accompanying the Wall is clearly seen to the right of it. Beyond the trees in the middle distance, the Wall is visible all the way along the cliffs.

Stone foundation of the Antonine Wall at the cemetery of New Kilpatrick. The photo shows the retaining kerb stones at the edges of the rubble core, on top of which the turf Wall was built. Photo James Eden.

Milestone (*RIB* 2290–2292) found about one mile south of Carlisle. The crude inscription indicates that at least in one part of Britannia Inferior Carausius's authority was recognised. The stone was used more than once. The inscribed text in the centre was chiselled out and the broader end was used for the Carausius inscription, then this was superseded by a new inscription mentioning Constantius as Caesar. Photo David Reid.

Above right: The tombstone of Marcus Favonius Facilis from Colchester (*RIB* 200). He was a centurion of the XX legion and he is probably the most famous Roman soldier in Britain. This tombstone appears in many books because it portrays so clearly his clothing, armour and equipment. He wears his sword on his left and a dagger on his right side, and in his right hand he grasps his vine stick, which centurions habitually carried. His boots, greaves, belt and cuirass are clearly shown and the details which could not be rendered so easily in sculpture would be painted, so Facilis in his original state would have appeared far more garish than he does now. The tombstone was found in 1868 in two pieces, and associated with it was a lead cylinder containing bones and a pot dated to the decade AD 50–60. The inscription (not shown) mentions the XX legion without its victory titles of Valeria Victrix, which the legion was awarded for its part in the war against Boudicca *c*.AD 60. This could be taken as evidence that Facilis died before the rebellion, though inscriptions set up later than AD 60 also lack the victory title. The lack of weathering and good state of preservation of the figure does support the theory that the tombstone was probably thrown down during the rebellion and remained buried until the nineteenth century.

Below right: Tombstone of an auxiliary soldier from Colchester (*RIB* 201). Longinus, son of Sdapezematygus, was a *duplicarius* (on double pay) of *Ala I Thracum*, a cavalry unit. He wears scale armour and carries an oval shield, and may have held a weapon in his right hand, since a hole has been drilled as if to support a spear. He rides over a cowering barbarian, a common theme in cavalry tombstones. The father of Longinus was probably a Thracian, but Longinus himself given a Roman name when he enlisted in the army. He served for fifteen years, most likely in the same unit of Thracians, and died aged forty, having reached the rank of *duplicarius*, second in command after the decurion of a *turma*, a division of the Ala, consisting of thirty-two men. The Thracians may have been present in Colchester in the early days, but the presence of one soldier who presumably died there does not necessarily indicate that the whole unit was stationed in the town.

Head of a colossal statue of Constantine in Rome. The troops in Britain proclaimed Constantine Emperor after the death of his father Constantius at York in AD 306. The soldiers called him Augustus, but initially he had to be content with the lesser title of Caesar. It took nearly two decades for Constantine to eliminate all his rivals and emerge as sole supreme ruler of the Roman world.

Early third-century tombstone from South Shields (*RIB* 1064) of Victor, a young Moorish freedman (NATIONE MAURUM). Victor was perhaps born a slave and was only twenty years old when he died. His master Numerianus, a cavalry soldier from *Ala I Asturum* presumably held his freedman in high regard, judging from the fine stone that he set up for him. Victor is shown reclining on a cushioned couch, with a cup in his left hand, perhaps about to be refilled by the boy standing at the side of the couch. The bunch of leaves in Victor's right hand is a feature often found on Palmyrene tombs.

This tombstone (*RIB* 1065) was found to the south-west of the fort at South Shields (Arbeia). The lady is Regina, a British woman of the Catuvellaunian tribe (NATIONE CATVALLAUNA), once a slave but given her freedom, hence the appellation LIBERTA in the top line of the inscription. She was the wife of Barates from Palmyra in Syria, who was wealthy enough to pay for this very elaborate tombstone, in the Palmyrene style, with Palmyrene script on the base. So far only one other native British woman is known from a tombstone, in this case a woman of the Dobunni (*RIB* 621) and another woman from Lincoln may possibly have been a Briton (*RIB* 250). Regina's husband Barates may be the same man who is commemorated on a tombstone from Corbridge (*RIB* 1171), though this stone is worn and only the letters ...RATHES remain. He is described as *vexil[l]a* which ought to mean that he carried the standard (*vexillum*), an embroidered flag suspended on a cross pole, but since no unit is named on the inscription it has been suggested that he was a trader in flags, supplying the army. The connection with Regina is not proven, but the possibility that she was the wife of a Palmyrene trader who dealt in flags is now irretrievably embedded in the history of Roman Britain.

Native Britons entered the auxiliary units of the Roman army either via conscription or on an individual voluntary basis. They were given Roman names when they joined up, so from nomenclature alone it is impossible to discern from tombstones or other inscriptions whether some of the soldiers were native Britons. This stone from the German frontier is more specific, recording in the second line from the top a unit of Brittones Trip[utienses]. The unit was stationed at Schlossau, where the headquarters were situated, but inscriptions mentioning the Brittones Triputienses have been found at watchtowers and other sites, suggesting that the soldiers were split up into smaller groups. Several units of Britons are known in Germany, called *numeri*, which does not denote a unit of specific size of organisation. These Britons may originally have arrived under Trajan or Hadrian, but since they are first attested under Antoninus Pius it used to be thought that they had been recruited by that Emperor when the Antonine Wall was built, as part of a mass recruitment drive to remove troublesome tribesmen. None of the theories about where the Britons came from, or at what date they were recruited, can answer the question of whether they were forcibly drafted or enlisted voluntarily. This stone is a copy of the original, and has been placed on the modern route along the Roman frontier in Germany.

The Roman road known as the Devil's Causeway in Northumberland, north of Hadrian's Wall (No. 87 in I.D. Margary's *Roman Roads*). This view is looking north from East Horton towards Lowick, where the road runs dead straight for six miles, raised on the original line or very close to the Roman road. It can only be heading towards Tweedmouth or Berwick, where there is a superb natural harbour that the Romans cannot have failed to appreciate, but frustratingly there is as yet no evidence of Roman occupation, save for a sherd of third-century pottery from Tweedmouth. One wonders what the Elizabethan builders of the massive fortifications of Berwick may have unearthed. A more splendid example of a Roman road can be seen on the present A68 running northwards from Corbridge, but taking photos on that road is a potentially lethal pastime.

Part of the foundations of the bridge over the North Tyne at Chesters on Hadrian's Wall. This was not the first bridge on the site. The masonry here is probably part of the third-century refit, a much more substantial structure than the earlier bridge. Since no voussoirs have been found to suggest that there were stone arches, and grooves were made in the stone work, probably to receive timbers, it is suggested that there was a wooden superstructure above the piers, of which there were three, with cutwaters facing upstream, and flat backs facing downstream. The river has moved to the west since Roman times, so that the foundations of one of the piers is high and dry, and if the water is low two other piers can be seen. Photo David Reid.

The fortress at York was probably founded in Flavian times, in the last quarter of the first century AD. It was occupied until the fourth century. This photograph shows the late Roman multangular tower, viewed from the outside. It is one of several similar towers built in the late third or early fourth century to enhance the fortress defences. The work is attributed to Constantine, who was in Britain with his father Constantius at the beginning of the fourth century. These towers faced the *colonia* across the river, the civil settlement that was raised to colonial status in the third century. Another separate civil settlement, the *canabae*, clustered around the fortress. When Britain was divided into two provinces, perhaps by Caracalla, York became the provincial capital of Britannia Inferior, and the legate of the legion was also the governor.

Interior view of the multangular tower at York, showing the Roman building work at the lower half of the tower, characterised by the use of a band of tiles, as at Colchester and Burgh castle, where the walls stand to a considerable height.

Part of the northern fortress wall at Chester, running eastwards from the north gate, now marked by a more recent gateway. The original fortress, built of turf and timber, was founded c.AD 75, and its water supply was being installed under the governor Gnaeus Julius Agricola, whose name appears on lead pipes from the fortress. Chester was rebuilt at the end of the first century. For some reason, much debated, the fortress at Chester was larger than those at York or Caerleon. The fortress wall was maintained in medieval times, following the line of the original defences on the north and east sides, but extending to the west and to the River Dee on the south side. The waterway shown in this photograph is the Shropshire Union Canal.

A row of barracks of the legionary fortress at Caerleon (the Welsh version of *castra legionis*). This view is taken in the north-western corner of the fortress, looking south towards the amphitheatre. The foundations of four barrack blocks are laid out here in Prysg Field, but only the first one, on lower ground, is original Roman work. The others are reconstructions made after the excavations, built over the original buildings. Running parallel with the barrack block, the remains of the rampart can be seen as a grassy mound, with a gap where the fortress gate lies.

The rounded corner and foundations of the south-east corner tower at the legionary fortress of Chester.

Remains of ovens at Caerleon fortress, set into the earthen rampart back where the risk of fire would be reduced. The soldiers drew their rations from the granaries, and had to grind their own corn, make their own bread, and cook their other rations in these ovens. Probably one man from each *contubernium*, or 'tent group' of eight men, would be responsible for cooking rations for himself and his seven companions. Stone ovens set into the rampart back have been found at other forts, notably Vindolanda (Chesterholm) south of Hadrian's Wall.

One half of the amphitheatre at Chester, which has been recently re-excavated and displayed. The first amphitheatre was built of turf and timber like the original legionary fortress, and was rebuilt in stone probably in the early second century. The other half of the stone building is still hidden underneath modern buildings, but an estimate can be made of its original large size, in fact this is the largest known amphitheatre in Britain.

The amphitheatre at the western side of the legionary fortress of Caerleon. This is the best preserved amphitheatre in Britain. The fortress was founded c.AD 75, and for fifteen years there was probably no permanent amphitheatre for the entertainment of the troops. It was built around AD 90. The lower circuit was constructed in stone, buttressed all the way round. The stone work was probably never any higher than these remains, so there was most likely a timber superstructure, for which some sockets for beams have been found in the stone foundations. To modern visitors, the amphitheatre appears to be quite isolated in a field, but the site was very cramped in Roman times, since in the fifteen years from the foundation of the fortress, a civilian settlement had grown up. Archaeological excavations have shown that the baths building (not visible now) had to be altered to make room for the amphitheatre. The amphitheatre was an ovoid, with two large entrances at the top and bottom of the oval, and six smaller entrances in the long sides. This photograph shows one of the main entrances looking across to its opposite number. There was seating for about 6,000 people, so the whole legion could be accommodated and perhaps some of the civilians as well.

The Roman auxiliary fort at Tomen-Y-Mur in Wales, later occupied by the Normans who built a motte and bailey castle within the walls. The motte is clearly visible from the modern A470 past Lake Trawsfynydd, demonstrating the good choice of location for both castle and fort, with clear views all around. On the left of the photograph the curve of the Roman rampart can be seen. This fort was in the territory of the Ordovices, on the route from Segontium (modern Caernarvon) to the east. It had several phases, the first probably in timber and earth, and a rebuild in stone in the second century. Later it was reduced in size, and abandoned c.AD 140, when the garrison of Wales was thinned out. The Norman motte occupies the site of the gateway on the south-western side of the reduced fort. To the north-west of the fort there are traces of an oval-shaped amphitheatre made of earth. The only other auxiliary fort where an amphitheatre has been found is Carmarthen.

Modern monument marking the site of the fort at Newstead, with the Eildon Hills in the background. There are three peaks, hence the name Trimontium, but the peaks are not all visible in this photograph. This is a key site in the Roman occupations of Scotland. The first fort belonged to the campaigns of Gnaeus Julius Agricola in the later first century, and was built of earth and timber, but with some unusual features around the gates, where the ramparts were staggered to force attackers to turn left and expose their right sides, undefended by their shields. A larger fort replaced this first installation in the late AD 80s, when Newstead was the main defensive site in the north after the troops were withdrawn from Scotland. This second fort was destroyed, possibly by enemy action, c.AD 90–100. Under Antoninus Pius a new fort was built in stone by the governor Lollius Urbicus, c.AD 140. At the beginning of the third century Severus possibly mustered part of his invasion at this fort, and a line of marching camps leading northwards from it has been discovered which may belong to his campaigns.

The east gate at Birdoswald fort on Hadrian's Wall, looking north-west. It is particularly well preserved, and representative of the gates of most stone built forts of the second century. In general Roman forts were shaped like playing cards, oblong with rounded corners, and four gates, one in each side of the fort. This gate at Birdoswald was built to a common design, with two arches over the dual carriageway into the fort, and a guard house on each side. The springer for the arch can be seen on the portal on the right, and arched window lintels found nearby probably came from the superstructure, though it is not known for certain what the finished gate looked like. The central pier of this gate was strengthened at some time, and the roadway was renewed. In the later Roman period, one portal was blocked, leaving the other single lane in general use. This is usually attributed to the aftermath of the so-called barbarian conspiracy of AD 367, when Count Theodosius restored order. In the fourth century, forts all over the Empire were modified in some way to deal with increased threats.

In the headquarters buildings of each fort there was usually a strongroom, built underground if the terrain permitted. This is the strongroom at Chesters fort on Hadrian's Wall, with its stone vault still in situ, the room being entered down a short flight of steps. Valuables and the pay chest would be kept here, and any cash that was required for day-to-day running of the fort. When this strongroom was discovered in the nineteenth century the wooden doors closing the vault were still in place, but they soon disintegrated on contact with the air. Legend has it that five hundred horsemen ride out of this strongroom on a certain night of the year, roughly the correct number of cavalrymen who were based at this fort.

At each fort there would be a bath house, always built of stone even when the forts themselves were of earth and timber, so as to be fireproof. This photograph shows the entrance hall of the bath house at Chesters, with niches in the back wall which nobody can fully explain, perhaps for statues, or more likely for cupboards to store clothing which was left there while the bather moved through the various warm and hot rooms. The Chesters bath house was so well preserved because it was built on the slope down to the River North Tyne, and so gradually filled up with earth before it became completely ruined. The building serves to illustrate more clearly than any other remains how the bath houses would have looked outside Roman forts.

This is the stoke hole of the bath house at Chesters fort, where the fires would be lit under the stone floors, supported on pillars. This system of underfloor heating was called a hypocaust. The amount of fuel that the Romans required to run one of these bath houses would be staggering, since the rooms had to be heated to produce a healthy sweat, which was scraped off along with the oil rubbed onto the skin, and all the accompanying dirt.

A unique survival: this is the base of a window at the bath house of Chesters fort. This photograph shows the first few courses of stone framing the window, viewed from the inside over the apsidal cold plunge bath. The window may have been glazed, since traces of glass were found nearby. This is a very rare surviving example of what was probably a common feature of Roman buildings in Britain, but for which there is little actual proof. The only other site where glass was known to have been used in a window is a Roman house at Dorchester, but the window itself does not survive.

Hadrian's Wall at Walltown Crags, viewed from the north and looking towards the east. There may have been some unrest in Britain before the visit of the Emperor Hadrian in AD 122, but trouble in Britain was a common theme in the works of the ancient historians, much like trouble at t'mill in nineteenth-century accounts of northern England. Hadrian's policy was to call a halt to expansion all over the Empire, and to consolidate the areas that could be reasonably controlled and administered. He probably surveyed the line of the Wall himself, here running along the western edge of the Whin Sill crags. Except for a short stretch in the west which was initially built of turf, the Wall was built using two lines of squared stones with a rubble core filling. According to the original plan it was to be 10 Roman feet thick, later revised to 8 feet, but not before some of the legionary gangs building it had laid a 10-foot foundation. In places the wide foundation can be seen jutting out to the south of the 8-foot Wall. The width of the Wall and its foundations varies all along its length.

This is the highest section of the Wall at Hare Hill in Cumbria, with sixteen courses of stone. No one knows how high the Wall was, nor what happened at the top. There may have been a wall walk and crenellations facing north, but there is no proof. The two outer skins of squared stones and the rubble core can be clearly seen at Hare Hill.

Every Roman mile along the Wall, a milecastle (a modern term) was built to the south of the Wall, flush with the frontier itself, as shown in this photo of Cawfields milecastle. These small installations probably held a century of eighty men, in barracks on either side of the road through the milecastle. There were two gates, one in the north and one in the south, the foundations of which can be seen here at Cawfields. Most reconstructions show only one tower on the north gate but the foundations were the same in the south so there may have been towers on the south side as well.

Window arch fallen down inside the turret at Walltown Crags, most likely from the upper level.

Between each milecastle on the Wall there were two turrets (another modern term). This shows the foundations of the turret at Caw Gap. It is not known if the turrets had a door in the upper storey to give access to a wall walk, though most reconstructions show this feature. The garrison would be drawn from nearby forts perhaps on a rota basis, but how they functioned can only be guessed.

Stretching away to the east at Cawfields is a fine section of the so-called Vallum, which runs parallel to Hadrian's Wall on the south side. The term Vallum was used by the Venerable Bede to describe what the Romans would have called *fossa*. To the Romans, Vallum indicated the whole frontier system, as expressed in documents *per lineam valli*, along the line of the wall. The Vallum was dug without a break through all kinds of terrain, sometimes close to the Wall and sometimes diverging from it, and to make it easier for the Romans to supervise movement and examine people and goods, crossing points were provided only at specific places. The Vallum ditch was 10 feet deep with sloping sides, and 20 feet wide at the top, with the up-cast from the ditch used to create mounds of earth on the north and south sides.

The medieval castle at Bewcastle in Cumbria was built over the Roman fort on the same site, and was used in the sixteenth century to watch for movements of the reivers through the dales, as attested by a letter sent by Lord Dacre to Cardinal Wolsey in 1528, explaining how the raiders 'come thorow Bewcastelldale and retornes for the most part the same waye agayne'. This is probably the sort of problem that the Romans faced, indicating how the Roman fort was probably employed as one of the outposts to the north of Hadrian's Wall. The first fort here was of standard Roman type, but the Severan version was polygonal and better adapted to the ground, though the buildings inside were of conventional shape and size.

The single-arched west gate of the outpost fort at High Rochester, the arch springing from the moulded stone on the left of the photo. The blocking is modern and the farm wall runs on the top of the Roman fortifications, which can be traced all round the fort, tumbled down in places. The fort was built on Dere Street running to the north from the Tyne–Solway gap, and was probably one of the casualties of c.AD 100–105, when several forts were destroyed or given up. It was unoccupied in the Hadrianic era. When Antoninus Pius ordered the advance into Scotland and built the Antonine Wall, the fort was once more within the administered part of the province and traffic along the road increased. Third-century inscriptions record the building and repair of platforms for artillery, or ballistaria. The fort was destroyed, probably before or during the disaster of AD 367, and not rebuilt.

The Antonine fort at Rough Castle was protected by ditches and by these *lilia*, holes in the ground which contained sharpened stakes. The holes would be covered with branches, so that unsuspecting attackers would think there was firm ground and fall onto the stakes. Photo James Eden.

The Antonine Wall, built of turf, is not so well preserved as Hadrian's Wall, but in some places its course is marked by visible sections of the ditch. This is Watling Lodge, where the immense size of the ditch is still obvious even after centuries of erosion. Photo James Eden.

View of part of the complicated series of ditches surrounding one of the several superimposed fortlets at Chew Green on the Roman road to the north. This road is now called Dere Street, taking its name from its destination, the post-Roman kingdom of Deira. It is followed for some distance by the modern A68, but before climbing up to Chew Green the modern route diverges from the Roman road, and Dere Street traverses the Northumbrian uplands, unencumbered by modern traffic. The road was guarded by forts and fortlets, one of which is this one at Chew Green. The Pennine Way runs across the eastern edge of the site.

The Roman lighthouse inside the castle at Dover. It was one of a pair of lighthouses, situated on the chalk cliffs on either side of the River Dour. This lighthouse is on the eastern side, its companion and the Roman fort being on the west side of the river. On the outside the lighthouse is octagonal, but inside it is rectangular. The upper sections visible here are medieval, and in Roman times there were probably as many as four additional stages on top of these remains, making it a very high building, estimated as 80 feet, so that the light, enhanced by mirrors of burnished copper or silvered bronze, could be seen out to sea. The first fort at Dover, associated with the fleet, the Classis Britannica, was never finished, and was replaced by another larger fort which was occupied, but not continuously, until the beginning to the third century, when the Classis Britannica disappears from view. About AD 270 or 275 the Saxon Shore fort was built. Fortuitously, the earthen rampart back was constructed over a Roman house with painted walls, preserving it for archaeologists who discovered it in 1971. It is preserved as the Painted House, and nearby can be seen the foundations of two towers, one from the Classis Britannica fort, and the other lying close up against the larger tower of the Saxon Shore fort. Photo James Eden.

The south wall and a corner tower of Burgh Castle. The flint-faced walls with tile courses are similar to those at the civitas capital at Caistor-by-Norwich. Only three sides are still visible, the west wall having collapsed, but the remaining walls stand to a considerable height.

View of Richborough from inside the Saxon Shore fort, looking towards the north-west wall. When the Saxon Shore fort was built nothing of the earlier phases would be visible, but in the modern presentation of the site, some of them have been restored. The remains of the monumental arch lie just off the photograph, to the right of the three ditches that surrounded it in the later third century. Photo Jacqui Taylor.

This page: Portchester comprises perhaps the most spectacular Roman building in Britain. The massive walls contain much medieval work, and still give an impression of strength. These two views show the fort from the sea (*top*) and from the land (*bottom*). Photos James Eden.

The remains of the Balkerne Gate at Colchester, viewed from inside, looking west. Before the city walls were built there was a first-century monumental arch over this road, which led to and from London, and when the walls were begun in the second century the arch was incorporated into the plan. There were two rounded towers flanking the gate, and the remains of one tower can be seen in the pub to the right (not shown here). There would have been two smaller arches for pedestrian access, flanking the main roads through the gate.

The Roman city wall at Colchester running southwards from the Balkerne Gate, showing the typical Roman building technique using alternating bands of stone and red tile.

The Newport Arch at Lincoln, the north gate, viewed from inside the area of the legionary fortress, which later became the colonia. This is the only surviving Roman arch still in daily use. The medieval masonry on top of the arch indicates that the road and the gate continued to be used, and both were kept in good repair in the Middle Ages. The road level shown in the photograph is much higher than it would have been in Roman times. The main arch for traffic is flanked by the smaller pedestrian entrance, under repair when this photo was taken. Originally there may have been four arches altogether, two main ones for traffic and two for pedestrians, as at the Balkerne Gate at Colchester. The road is still used for motorised traffic, though there was an accident some years ago when a lorry allegedly carrying fish fingers got stuck and gouged out some pieces of stone. For a while this noble gateway was adorned with tawdry red lights.

This photograph shows the lower west gate at Lincoln, viewed from inside the city. This is the fourth-century version of the gate, with a single archway and two flanking towers on massive foundations. The west wall of the colony can still be traced running under the modern building which was built over it.

The Roman walls of the city of York were kept in repair in the medieval period, and extended. This famous view looks from what would have been the colonia towards the fortress. The headquarters building of the legionary fortress was located on the site of the Minster, and substantial remains can still be seen beneath the ecclesiastical foundations, revealed when the Minster had to be underpinned.

Remains of the south wall of the baths complex at Wroxeter. The town began life as a legionary fortress, converted into the *civitas* capital of the Cornovii when military occupation ceased at the site, probably in the later first century. In the second century the town was enclosed within earth and timber defences. The initial building work on the site of the baths was started in the reign of Hadrian, but then ceased for about three decades, perhaps until the funding was obtained, though no one knows why there was a hiatus in construction. When the baths complex was finally built it became one of the longest-lived buildings in Roman Britain. It was repaired several times as new floors were laid, but by the fifth century it was in decay, and was probably partly destroyed to make way for timber buildings. In the sixth century better constructed and larger timber buildings appeared, which means that people still lived in the town and it was prosperous enough to warrant the expense of erecting substantial buildings.

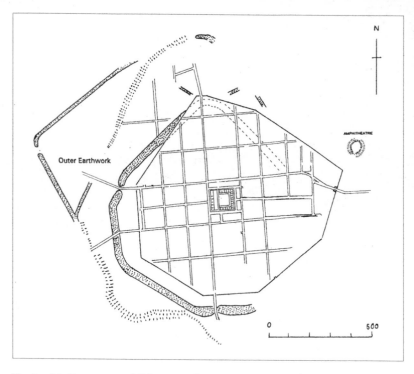

The site of the Roman town of Silchester was first settled by the Atrebates, probably in the late Iron Age, and the town became the civitas capital of the tribe (Calleva Atrebatum). It was part of the domain ruled by the client king Togidubnus, and developed very early, acquiring its timber forum perhaps by the late AD 40s, the baths and the amphitheatre by the late AD 50s or early AD 60s. Defences of earth and timber were erected in the later second century, and about a hundred years afterwards the earth bank was cut away to allow for the construction of a stone wall, parts of which are still visible. The site was excavated at the end of the nineteenth century and a comprehensive plan was produced, though it is likely that some early timber buildings were not recognised. Not much remains to be seen in the interior of the town, which is mostly fields with a farm and a church, but it is still an important site to visit. Drawn by Jacqui Taylor.

Remains of the amphitheatre at Silchester, showing the stone foundations. The first two phases of the amphitheatre were timber constructions, until the stone version was built in the mid-third century. It is thought that audiences would remain standing to watch performances, since there was no sign in the earth banks above the stonework of the timber supports that would be necessary for banks of seats. The amphitheatre lay outside the town to the north-east, and was not included within the defences when the town walls were built. Photo James Eden.

The southern defences of Caerwent, with projecting towers, preserved to a considerable height. The date of construction is disputed. There was probably a circuit of earth and timber walls dating from perhaps the middle of the second century, replaced in stone perhaps in the later second century like other towns in Roman Britain, though archaeologists opt for the early fourth century. The projecting stone towers were added to the north and south walls sometime later, and are not bonded properly with the walls. No towers were built on the eastern and western sides, where the two main gates bisect the walls. There is not much to see of the gates, which probably had two guard towers and two arches over a dual carriageway.

A row of shops at Caerwent in South Wales, one of the most exciting Roman towns to visit, with several areas excavated and displayed and a complete circuit of defensive walls, particularly impressive on the south side. The amenities of this relatively small town included a forum and basilica, temples, a meeting place for the town council, and houses and shops.

Exterior remains of the amphitheatre at Cirencester, the civitas capital of the Dobunni (Corinium Dobunnorum). Not counting London, Corinium was the largest town in the province of Britain. The site was under military occupation until c.AD 70, and thereafter the civilians who had settled outside the fort created their town, soon acquiring a large forum and basilica, possibly a market hall, and a theatre. The amphitheatre shown in this photograph was outside the town on the western side. It was built perhaps in the late first century and remodelled in the second century, in a disused quarry. The sides of the two entrances were reinforced with stone, but a recent study suggests that there is no evidence that there was ever an outer wall of stone to support the earth walls. What survives for modern visitors to see is a circuit of grassy banks standing to a considerable height.

Mosaic floor from Aldborough (Isurium Brigantum) in Yorkshire, the civitas capital of the Brigantes. This is the classic Roman foundation myth, showing the rescue of Romulus and Remus by the she-wolf, rendered in provincial style but demonstrating a high degree of Romanisation. Drawn by Jacqui Taylor.

Mosaic floor from Colchester showing a sophisticated central design, though this is not as elaborate as some of the fine mosaics that have been found in Britain

Small gate at Caerwent, viewed from inside the town. It once gave access through the southern defences, but was later blocked. The left side of the arch can be clearly seen, and the straight join where stone was inserted possibly in the fourth century.

Remains of a Romano-Celtic temple at Caerwent. This temple was built to a common plan developed by the Celtic tribes within the Roman Empire. A rectangular enclosure surrounds the temple, with an entrance in the south side. It is not known which deity was worshipped here. The temple was begun probably about AD 330, and was repaired and altered until the late fourth century. Photo Jacqui Taylor.

Altar to the goddess Brigantia (RIB 1053) found in 1895 south-west of the fort at South Shields. A bird is carved on the back, on the right a patera or dish, and on the left side a jug. The dedicator is Congennicus, a Gallic name attested in Narbonne. Altars to Brigantia have been found at sites in northern Britain, three from Yorkshire, one from Corbridge, and one from Castlesteads. A soldier called Amandus, describing himself as an architectus, dedicated an altar to Brigantia at Birrens in Scotland, which was probably outside the Brigantian kingdom. Amandus was most likely an architectus in the VI legion based at York. Drawn by Jacqui Taylor.

Gilded bronze head of the goddess Sulis Minerva in classical style, from Bath. The Romans regularly equated native gods and goddesses with their own deities. Sulis pre-dates the Romans, and was probably associated with healing, so when the Romans took over the healing springs at Bath they equated the British goddess with Minerva, who also has healing attributes. Several altars dedicated to Sulis Minerva have been found at Bath, along with leaden curse tablets invoking the help of the goddess in recovering stolen goods or exacting revenge. Drawn by Jacqui Taylor.

Model of a so-called Aberdeen terrier, now in the museum at Chesters fort, originally found in Coventina's Well at Carrawburgh on Hadrian's Wall. It is sympathetically sculpted, with a lifelike appearance, and was presumably dedicated to the goddess in fulfilment of a vow. Drawn by Jacqui Taylor.

The Genii Cucullati from the vicus outside the fort at Housesteads on Hadrian's Wall. This carving is paralleled by several other figures from Britain, Gaul and Germany. Another relief carving of three hooded deities from Cirencester shows three very rudimentary schematic figures, but this one is carved in more detail. There may have been a shrine for corporate worship in the vicus but the stone was found in a house, and may have been for private family use.

Modern copy of an altar to Mithras, the god of light, in the temple of Mithras outside the fort at Carrawburgh on Hadrian's Wall. The worship of Mithras originated in Persia and spread to Roman Britain by the early third century. It was an all-male cult, with a strict code of conduct, appealing particularly to soldiers and to merchants. Other Mithraic temples in Britain include the Walbrook, London, and the fort at Housesteads on Hadrian's Wall. This altar was set up by Marcus Simplicius Simplex, prefect of an unnamed unit at Carrawburgh, which may have been *cohors I Batavorum*, since two other altars were found next to this one, dedicated to Mithras by the prefects Aulus Cluentius Habitus and Lucius Antonius Proculus, both of whom were commanders of the Batavians. The altar shown in this photograph must have been very impressive, since the back is hollowed out for a lamp to be placed in the niche, giving Mithras a crown of light through the slots which circled his head, though the damage to the altar has removed those on the right side. The original altar and its two companions are in the Great North Museum in Newcastle-upon-Tyne.

Map showing the principal tribes of Britain at the time of the Roman conquest in AD 43. Tribal names were not static or permanent. Julius Caesar records several tribes of the first century BC whose names do not reappear in the first century AD. Under the Emperors from Claudius onwards there may have been sub-groups of tribes whose names have not been recorded, or smaller groups may have been absorbed by larger federations. In the early third century AD, Dio described the northern tribes, explaining how the Maeatae, not heard of until then, had taken smaller tribes into their federation. Drawn by Jacqui Taylor.

Above: The major towns and the three legionary fortresses of Roman Britain in the second century AD. By this time London was the capital, where the governor's headquarters and probably the financial procurator's staff were situated. The legions, originally four, had been reduced to three, and after occupying various different sites the legionaries were housed in three permanent bases at Caerleon, Chester and York, which remained their headquarters until they disappear from view in the later history of the province. The *civitas* capitals for the tribes were established by the later second century but not all of them had begun to flourish. Drawn by Jacqui Taylor.

Opposite page bottom: Gold *aureus* issued AD 46 celebrating Claudius's conquest of Britain three years earlier. On the obverse Claudius is depicted wearing a laurel wreath, with the legend proclaiming his sixth year of tribunician power and his eleventh salutation as Imperator. He was to receive twenty-seven Imperial salutations in total. The reverse of the coin shows an arch with an equestrian statue on top and the words DE BRITANN on the architrave. Claudius spent sixteen days in Britain, and celebrated his triumph for the conquest in AD 44. A triumphal arch was dedicated in Rome in AD 52. Drawn by Jacqui Taylor.

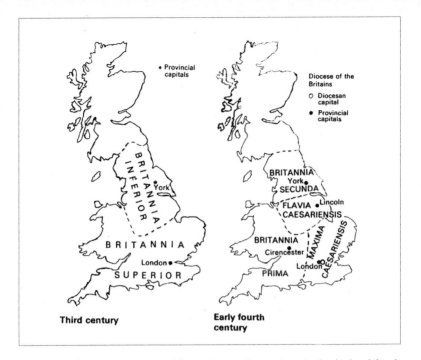

Above: Maps showing the division of Britain into smaller provinces in the third and fourth centuries. At some time in the early third century Britain was divided into two provinces, possibly by Caracalla, *c.*213. The northern province, called Britannia Inferior or Lower Britain, stretched up to and beyond Hadrian's Wall, and was administered from York, where the praetorian governor was also the commander of the legion. Upper Britain, or Britannia Superior, was governed by a man of consular status, whose headquarters remained in London, and he controlled two legions, at Chester and Caerleon. Severus and Caracalla divided other provinces, or adjusted boundaries, so that no governor would have access to more than two legions. At the end of the third century the Emperor Diocletian divided all the provinces into smaller units, grouping them together into Dioceses governed by a *vicarius*, thereby inserting an extra tier of government into the system. The exact locations of the four known provinces are not precisely defined, and the boundaries between them remain a matter for speculation. It is not definitely established beyond doubt that Britannia Prima was governed from Cirencester, but an inscription naming an official of the small province came from there, and it was the largest town in the provinces of Britain, after London. A fifth province called Valentia is attested in the later fourth century, but no one knows when it was created, or if one of the existing provinces was given a new name; consequently it is impossible to place it on a map. Drawn by Jacqui Taylor.

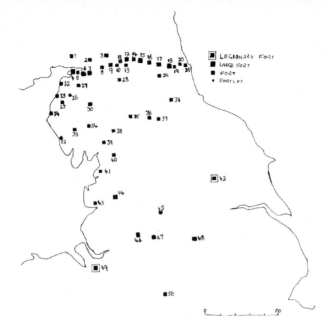

Sketch map of northern Britain under Hadrian, showing Hadrian's Wall and the forts in the hinterland. Even when the stone Wall was fully operational, the Pennines and Lake District remained in occupation. The forts were manned by auxiliary cavalry and infantry units, whose main tasks were probably police work among the tribes, and guarding routes. North of the Wall three outposts at Birrens, Netherby and Bewcastle were established, perhaps to facilitate patrolling and policing, and to give advance warning of impending tribal gatherings. On the eastern side of the Wall, the outposts were not built until after Hadrian's reign. Drawn by Jacqui Taylor. Key to forts: 1 Birrens, 2 Netherby, 3 Bewcastle, 4 Bowness, 5 Drumburgh, 6 Burgh by Sands, 7 Stanwix, 8 Castlesteads, 9 Birdoswald, 10 Carvoran, 11 Great Chesters, 12 Housesteads, 13 Vindolanda, 14 Carrawburgh, 15 Chesters, 16 Halton Chesters, 17 Rudchester, 18 Benwell, 19 Newcastle, 20 Wallsend, 21 South Shields, 22 Beckfoot, 23 Maryport, 24 Moresby, 25 Papcastle, 26 Caermote, 27 Old Carlisle, 28 Whitley Castle, 29 Ebchester, 30 Troutbeck, 31 Binchester, 32 Ravenglass, 33 Hardknott, 34 Ambleside, 35 Brough under Stainmore, 36 Bowes, 37 Greta Bridge, 38 Low Borrow Bridge, 39 Watercrook, 40 Overburrow, 41 Lancaster, 42 York, 43 Kirkham, 44 Ribchester, 45 Slack, 46 Manchester, 47 Melandra Castle, 48 Templebrough, 49 Chester, 50 Rocester.

The reverse of a brass *sestertius* of Hadrian, showing Britannia seated on a rock, holding her right hand to her head, and with a spear in her left hand, and her shield on her left side. As indicated by the initials SC, the coin was issued by decree of the Senate, probably c.AD 136, perhaps commemorating Hadrian's visit to Britain in 122, when he gave orders for a new frontier to be built across the Pennines, linking the River Tyne to the Solway Firth. On the obverse, not shown here, Hadrian wears a laurel wreath and the legend proclaims him consul for the third time. Drawn by Jacqui Taylor.

- - - - - - - - Antonine Wall

Sketch map of northern Britain and southern Scotland under Antoninus Pius. The frontier was advanced into Scotland after the campaigns of Lollius Urbicus, Antoninus Pius's governor, in the AD 140s. The Antonine Wall, built of Turf on a stone foundation, joined the estuaries of the Forth and the Clyde, with a series of large forts in the hinterland, interspersed with smaller installations guarding routes. North of the Wall on the eastern side there were forts at Bertha, Strageath, Ardoch and Camelon, emulating the Agricolan system built in the late first century, when the same line around the western edge of Fife was guarded by forts at the same locations. On Hadrian's Wall the forts were manned by skeleton garrisons or abandoned. Until recently it was thought that there were at least two phases of occupation, if not more, on the Antonine Wall, but after research by Dr N. Hodgson it now seems more likely that it was occupied for only a very short time before being abandoned once and for all. Drawn by Jacqui Taylor. Key to forts: 1 Bertha, 2 Strageath, 3 Ardoch, 4 Stirling, 5 Camelon, 6 Cramond, 7 Inveresk, 8 Bothwellhaugh, 9 Castle Greg, 10 Oxton, 11 Loudoun Hill, 12 Castledykes, 13 Bankhead, 14 Lyne, 15 Newstead, 16 Lamington, 17 Wandel, 18 Crawford, 19 Sanquhar, 20 Redshaw Burn, 21 Durisdeer, 22 Drumlanrig, 23 Milton, 24 Raeburnfoot, 25 Cappuck, 26 Chew Green, 27 High Rochester, 28 Risingham, 29 Barburgh Mill, 30 Carzield, 31 Shieldhill, 32 Burnswark, 33 Birrens, 34 Broomholm, 35 Glenlochar, 36 Lantonside, 37 Netherby, 38 Learchild, 39 Carlisle, 40 Corbridge, 41 Lanchester, 42 Ravenglass, 43 Bowes, 44 Greta Bridge, 45 Brompton on Swale, 46 Lancaster, 47 Ribchester, 48 York, 49 Manchester, 50 Templebrough, 51 Chester, 52 Rocester.

Sestertius of Antoninus Pius, AD 143. On the obverse, not shown here, Antoninus has the title of Imperator II, which he gained for victories in Britain, through the activities of his governor Lollius Urbicus. The supposedly dejected appearance of Britannia on some of the coins of Pius's reign has been used by historians to support the idea that there was some heavy fighting in the province. On the reverse of this coin, however, Britannia is shown in much the same pose as on Hadrian's coins, seated on rocks with a standard and spear, and a shield at her left side. Drawn by Jacqui Taylor.

Medallion of Commodus, c.AD 185. On the obverse Commodus has the victory title BRIT[ANNIA]. The reverse shows Britannia, seated as usual on rocks, with standard and spear, and her left arm resting on her shield. No one really knows what happened in Britain under Commodus, but Dio says that of all the wars that were fought in his reign, the one in Britain was the most serious. Drawn by Jacqui Taylor.

Realising that Diocletian would never recognise him as ruler of Britain, by AD 293 Carausius started to issue coins proclaiming himself as Augustus. This coin was minted at London. Drawn by Trish Boyle.

Very fine and famous gold piece worth ten *aurei* issued in AD 296 from the Trier mint. It commemorates the campaigns of Constantius I to wrest control of Britain from Allectus, the assassin and successor of Carausius. Constantius is shown entering London, where the inhabitants greet him rapturously on bended knee, as though submitting gratefully to his rule. The legend states that he is the restorer of the eternal light, REDDITOR LUCIS AETERNAE. Modesty was not a general characteristic of Roman Emperors. Drawn by Trish Boyle.

Gold *aureus* of AD 194–195 issued by Clodius Albinus, governor of Britain, and at this time supposedly Caesar to Septimius Severus. While he eliminated his rival Pescennius Niger in the east, Severus allowed Albinus to mint coins in Rome, like this one. When it became clear to Albinus that there was no substance to Severus's promises he took troops to Gaul and started to issue coins from the Lyon mint. Drawn by Jacqui Taylor.

Gold *aureus* of Septimius Severus issued in 210, commemorating the victory in Britain against the northern tribes of the Maeatae and Caledonians. The legend on the reverse simply states VICTORIAE BRIT. Drawn by Jacqui Taylor.

Carausius was one of the Emperor Maximianus's generals, fighting against the Gallic bandits called Bagaudae. He fled to Britain when he was suspected of diverting the recaptured booty to his own coffers. He took over the government of Britain, probably including the two British provinces of Superior and Inferior, but he hoped to legitimise his rule and gain recognition from the legitimate Emperors Diocletian and Maximianus. This coin, minted in Britain, proclaims him CARAUSIUS ET FRATRES SUI, Carausius and his brothers. The coin presents him as the colleague and equal of Diocletian and Maximianus, who both took a dim view of Carausius's presumption. Drawn by Trish Boyle.

Above left: Marcus Aurelius Nepos, a centurion of the XX legion who died at Chester, is depicted on this tombstone (*RIB* 491). Great emphasis is placed on Nepos's belt and kilted tunic, and he wears a cloak secured by a fibula brooch on his right shoulder. His vine stick is carried in his right hand. Nepos died aged fifty, having served for an unspecified number of years. Many tombstones include details of length of service, but Nepos's wife, who set up the stone did not include this information. She is also coy about letting us know what her name was, though she is depicted standing slightly behind her husband, in a full-skirted dress, and with her hair arranged in waves close to her head, a style that was common in the early third century. This is the most likely date for the tombstone. Soldiers were forbidden to marry, but they formed liaisons nonetheless, and when the Emperor Severus legalised marriages at the beginning of the third century he was merely recognising the reality of soldiers' lives. Drawn by Jacqui Taylor.

Above right: This stone was discovered damaged and built into the north wall of the legionary fortress at Chester (*RIB* 562). It commemorates Curatia Di[o]nysia, who died aged forty. She reclines on a couch with a mattress and cushions, and she is draped in her finery, with a cup in her right hand. She is plentifully supplied with food and drink on a three-legged table by the side of her couch. There is no mention of a husband, but Dionysia left heirs who set up her tombstone, as indicated by the formula H[ERES] F[ACIENDUM] CURAVIT, her heir set up this [stone]. Drawn by Jacqui Taylor.

Plan of the fort at Hod Hill, an early Roman military installation which probably dates from the first few years after the conquest. It was possibly occupied as part of Vespasian's advance to the south-west. This fortlet was built inside the north-west corner of an older British fort, using two of its sides as the ramparts, so the Romans had only to erect fortifications round the other two sides, in the interior of the hill-fort. The internal layout of the fortlet was more or less regular on the standard Roman pattern with a headquarters building and commander's house, but instead of an individual unit there were probably a number of legionaries and some auxiliaries stationed here together. Drawn by Jacqui Taylor.

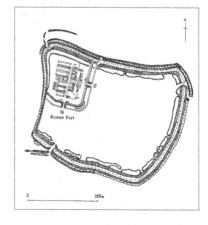

The site of Chew Green has several phases of occupation, relating to the presence of the Romans in Scotland. There were at least three marching camps and also more permanent earth and timber road posts, all more or less superimposed on each other. No firm dates can be provided, but the accepted sequence is that first a large camp was built by Agricola's troops (No. 1 on the plan), then a much smaller road-post was erected at the eastern corner of the camp, followed by a large camp (No. 2 on the plan) on the north side of the earthworks, built probably in the mid-second century. This is thought to have been the temporary construction camp for the smaller camp (No.3 on the plan) completely contained within the first one, this time with clavicular gateways. The last occupation was in a small fortlet surrounded by three ditches, except on its south side. North of the fort there are the slight remains of a Roman watch tower or signal tower. Drawn by Jacqui Taylor.

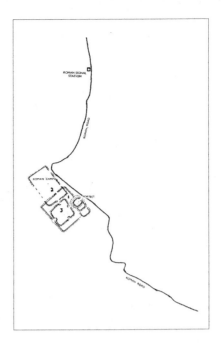

Throughout the Empire the Romans built watch towers along routes and frontiers. These towers differed in style according to their date and purpose, ranging from simple timber towers surrounded by earthen banks, to larger stone structures with more elaborate defences. The plans show (on the left) a typical timber tower and earth bank, built in the late first century by Gnaeus Julius Agricola's troops around the western edge of Fife, along the Gask Ridge, and (on the right) a fourth-century tower of stone with surrounding wall and ditch, one of a series guarding the east coast. Drawn by Jacqui Taylor.

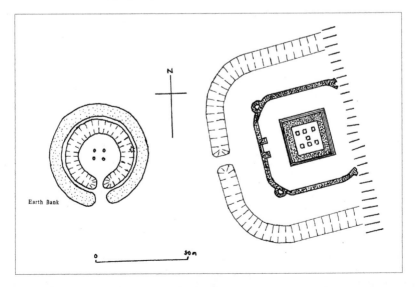

Earth Bank

Map showing the Forts of the Saxon Shore. This label gives the false impression that all the forts were built at the same time according to a coherent plan, and as a response to a single set of circumstances, but this is not the case. The command of the *Comes Litoris Saxonici* is a very late development, not attested until the end of the fourth century. By the time that it was established the forts had already been in existence for a considerable time. The two earliest are Reculver and Brancaster, similar in size and shape, and both of them typical of late second-century forts. They probably belong to the early third century. The other forts were added over a period of perhaps two or more decades, and Portchester and Pevensey perhaps belong to the usurpation of Carausius and Allectus. The title Saxon Shore might refer to the shore defended against the Saxons, or facing the land where they came from, but some authors have argued that it means the shore settled by the Saxons. In the west, forts of similar type to the southern ones were founded at Cardiff, Caernarvon and Lancaster, which guard estuaries or navigable rivers, and may have been established in response to raids from Irish tribes. The command of the *Comes Litoris Saxonici* may have included these forts in north-west Britain. All of these forts in the west and the south and south-east would require naval support, but it is not known how they functioned. Drawn by Jacqui Taylor.

Plan of the Saxon Shore fort at Richborough, a complicated multi-period site. The visible remains in the fort interior now represent parts of several different phases, not all of which are shown on this plan. The first fort was a defended beachhead built in AD 43 at the time if the invasion, then a supply base was built, with several granaries, two of which are marked out where they were excavated inside the later fort. In AD 85 a monumental four-way arch was erected, but now only the cross-shaped concrete remains, marking the four roads through the arch. This arch was converted into a watch tower or signal tower in the middle of the third century, surrounded by an earthen bank and three ditches. All this disappeared when the site was levelled in the late third century and the large fort was built, later incorporated into the Saxon Shore system. Drawn by Jacqui Taylor.

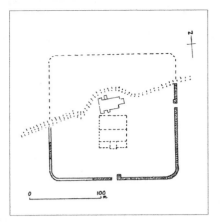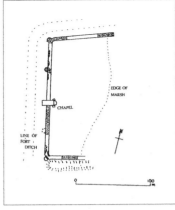

Above left: Plan of the early third-century fort at Reculver, eroded by the sea after the coastline changed. This was a conventional Roman fort of second-century style, built to the standard design, shaped like a playing card, with rounded corners, four gates, and internal buildings of standardised plan. The fort at Brancaster in Norfolk is very similar in size and shape, and is thought to be contemporary with Reculver. The first garrison at Reculver was *cohors I Baetasiorum* from Maryport, which is also a coastal fort. Occupation ended in the second half of the fourth century. Very little is still visible at this site. Drawn by Jacqui Taylor.

Above right: Bradwell was probably built in the decade after AD 275, like the Saxon Shore forts of Burgh Castle, Walton Castle, Dover, Richborough and Lymnpe. It is not quite rectangular, and the seaward side is eroded so its extent and shape are not certain. There may have been a harbour here in Roman times. The Saxon chapel of St Peter was built in the mid-seventh century on the site of the west gate. Drawn by Jacqui Taylor.

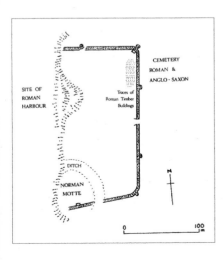

Plan of Burgh Castle, built on a tributary of the River Yare, near Great Yarmouth. The finds suggest that the building of this fort started in the last quarter of the third century, with no previous occupation having been discovered here. Burgh Castle is built in a transitional architectural style, incorporating late third and early fourth-century elements. The lower courses of the towers are not keyed into the walls, but the fact that the upper courses are more successfully bonded suggests that the decision to add projecting towers probably followed very soon after building began. The fort is trapezoidal rather than rectangular, and the south wall on the slope to the river estuary has disappeared. There are signs that there was a harbour here just below the fort. Drawn by Jacqui Taylor.

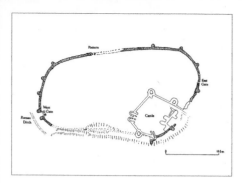

The Saxon Shore fort at Pevensey departed from the rectangular plan of the other forts, adopting an oval shape. It filled the long gap between Portchester and the forts of the south-east coast at Lympne and Dover, and was probably built by either Carausius or his successor Allectus. The results of more recent investigations favour Allectus, some of whose coins were found in debris associated with original construction work, so the foundation date is at some time in the late third century. The fort was occupied until the late fifth century. Drawn by Jacqui Taylor.

Map showing the forts commanded by the *Dux Britanniarum*, the Duke of the Britains (plural) as listed in the fifth-century document known as the *Notitia Dignitatum*. The information is derived from the sections of the *Notitia* dealing with the western provinces (*Occidens*), chapter 40.18–56. The forts in the command of the *Dux*, and the units stationed at each of them, are given, but the date is unknown. The information on Britain probably reflects the situation of the later fourth century. It is not known when the first *Dux* was appointed in Britain. The post was a development of the later Empire, probably already in existence under Constantine, by which time civil and military commands were separated and specialisation in one or the other career had become the norm. The *Dux*, which means 'leader', could be in command of the troops of a single province or more usually of the troops of several provinces all along the frontiers. Drawn by Jacqui Taylor.

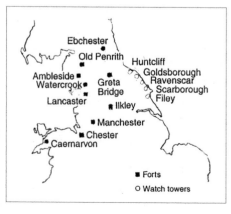

Map showing forts occupied in the fourth century, as attested by archaeological excavations. The problem is that these forts do not appear in the *Notitia Dignitatum*, and for the ones which do appear in the document, occupation cannot always be demonstrated. Another problem relating to this map concerns the command of the watchtowers of the east coast. The towers may belong to the Dux as part of his northern command, or they may be the responsibility of the *Comes Litoris Saxonici*, giving warning of raids from the sea, and supported by naval forces. Drawn by Jacqui Taylor.

Plan of the Saxon Shore fort at Portchester, where the coastline has not changed and the Roman Watergate continued in use into medieval times. The whole circuit of the walls survive because they were kept in repair in medieval times, and nearly all the original towers are visible. The towers were hollow-backed, like many of the towers in the much later medieval castles, a feature which prevented invaders from taking possession of any of them. The main gates were in the west and east sides, recessed so that attackers would come under fire from the flanking walls. The enormous size of this fort is indicated by the Norman castle, dwarfed in the north-west corner. Drawn by Jacqui Taylor.

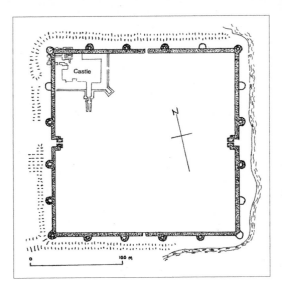

Plan of the colonia of Colchester, and of the Balkerne Gate on the west side of the town. The plan shows the regimented layout of the town, which began as a fort, but was made into a colonia, where veterans from the army were settled, only about six years after the conquest. It was the first colony in Britain, and remained an important town even after its destruction by Boudicca in AD 60. The temple of Claudius was built quite early but perhaps not finished by AD 60, when it was destroyed along with the town. According to the historian Tacitus, the first settlement was not walled, which made it so much easier for the Britons to capture the town and wreak such havoc. The walls were probably built in the second century, by which time the town had recovered and several amenities had been built, such as the theatre. Drawn by Jacqui Taylor.

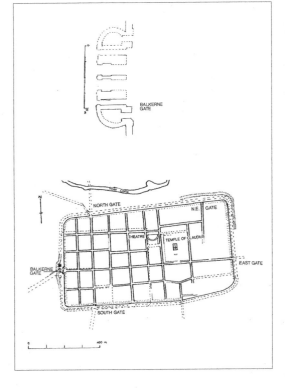

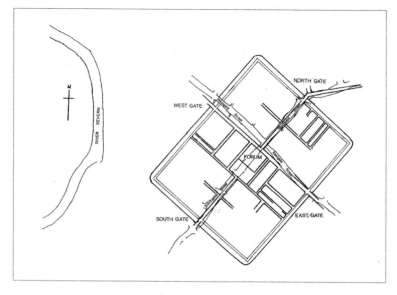

Plan of Gloucester, first a legionary fortress for II Augusta, and then a colonia when the legion relocated. There are few visible remains of the Roman town, as compared to the other colonies at Colchester, Lincoln or York, but the layout and the main Roman streets can be traced in the modern street plan, where the roads are named for the gates, Southgate, Northgate, Westgate and Eastgate Streets. It seems that at first the new colony was occupied mainly or solely by veterans, who lived in houses that conformed to the legionary layout of the barracks. The retired soldiers would provide a back-up force to ensure control of the region when the legion moved out. It seems that the town was slow to attract merchants, traders and other settlers. Drawn by Jacqui Taylor.

Plan of Lincoln, which was raised to the status of a colony after the IX legion moved north to the new fortress at York. The foundation date of the colony is uncertain but was probably in the late AD 80s under the Flavian Emperor Titus or his brother Domitian. The plan shows how the colony spread beyond the fortress, and the whole development was walled quite early. Drawn by Jacqui Taylor.

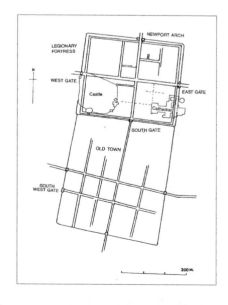

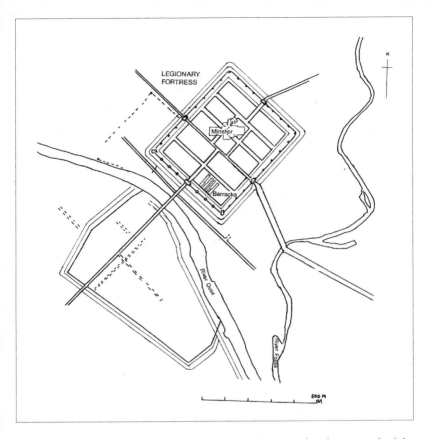

Plan of the fortress and *colonia* of York. The date when the civil settlement, south of the fortress on the River Ouse, was raised to colonial status is not known for certain. It used to be suggested that the Emperor Severus had bestowed this privilege upon the town when he was in Britain at the beginning of the third century, or perhaps it was Caracalla who was responsible for the elevation of the town. Epigraphic evidence shows that York was a colony by AD 237, since at this date Marcus Aurelius Lunaris, possibly a wine merchant, set up an inscription at Bordeaux, naming himself as a priest of the Imperial cult (*sevir Augustalis*) of the colonies of Lincoln and York. Drawn by Jacqui Taylor.

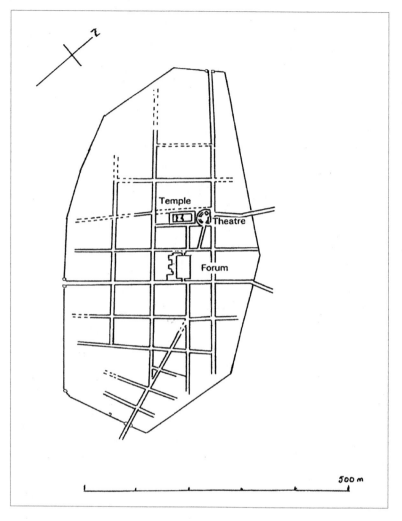

Plan of the Roman municipium of Verulamium, the only town of that status in Roman Britain. A British settlement called Verlamio, west of the later Roman town, was occupied by the Catuvellauni, who had a flourishing coinage before the Roman conquest. The Catuvellaunian king Cunobelinus took over Colchester and made it his capital, but Verlamio did not decline. The Roman town was probably founded quite early, possibly only six or seven years after Claudius's invasion. By the time of the revolt of Boudicca it was a municipium or high-grade town with its own government, but the revolt set back development for at least a decade. Defensive walls may have been built in the early second century, and in the reign of Hadrian the theatre was built. A serious fire destroyed the town c.AD 155, but there was a rapid recovery, and well-appointed stone houses were built, replacing the earlier timber dwellings. Little building work seems to have been done in the third century, but then in the later fourth century at least one splendid house with mosaics appeared, and occupation of the town has been traced into the post Roman period. The modern town of St Albans lies further west, clustered around the abbey built on the site where Albanus was martyred. Drawn by Jacqui Taylor.

many mines collapses were the main danger, and in others it is known that miners could be overcome by fumes. Official control of mines continued into the later Empire, as evidenced by the lists of mines and the officials responsible for them in the fifth-century document the *Notitia Dignitatum*.

Screw pumps, known from the Roman Empire, could drain surplus water from mines, and a sophisticated waterwheel system is known from the Rio Tinto mines in Spain, designed to lift the water in successive stages. This was very labour-intensive, the wheels probably being operated by slaves, since there is no evidence that animals were used, but slaves have to be housed and fed and such a system could not possibly be justified unless the mine was producing a profitable amount of metal.

Water power was used in reverse, to flush out metal ore, and such a system was used at the gold mine at Dolaucothi in south Wales. A reservoir was usually built uphill from the workings, with sluices that could be opened rapidly to release vast quantities of water over the workings and wash away the spoil. If the flow could be regulated to provide less water, it could be used for washing the ore.

A flourishing industry which had been established very early in Roman Britain and continued until the late period was lead mining. The Elder Pliny, writing before AD 79 (he was killed while trying to rescue people from the shore when Vesuvius erupted) says that there was so much lead just under the surface of the ground in Britain that a decree had to be issued limiting its production. This was perhaps to protect the lead mining industry of other provinces. The lead industry served two purposes, to provide waterproof material for piping, water tanks and the like, and for the extraction of silver. When the towns of Roman Britain began to construct civic buildings, especially baths complexes, the demand for lead would increase dramatically. There is evidence that silver was extracted from lead in Britain, for instance in Derbyshire there was a firm calling itself the *Societas Lutudarensium Britannicum ex argentariis*, indicating a silver works at Lutudarum, a Roman place name that is well attested in Derbyshire but has not yet been precisely located. It is not known how much silver was worked from British lead mines, since the ingots that have been found did not necessarily come from British factories.

Stamped ingots of lead have been found which indicate that lead mining was well under way as early as AD 49, only six years after the conquest. The industry was at first under Imperial control, and supervised if not operated by the army, as attested by an ingot stamped by II Augusta, and bearing the names of the consul of the year AD 49. Ingots of II Augusta have been found in Gaul, which may mean that the lead was used in other provinces, or these ingots fell off the Roman equivalent of a lorry on the way to Rome. Mining operations were often leased to contractors who had to give half of their produce to the Imperial treasury, and in Britain civilian contractors soon obtained permission to work the mines, most likely with slave labour. There was a large production centre in Derbyshire, where private manufacturers were active from the late first century, signing the ingots with their names. One of these men, Tiberius Claudius Triferna, operated around Matlock in Derbyshire and also in the lead mines of the Mendips, where his name occurs on stamped ingots. Another contractor was Gaius Nipius Ascanius, whose mines were in the Mendips and in Flintshire. There were also companies working the lead, such as the one mentioned above in Derbyshire, working the lead and extracting silver. Other areas where lead was mined were in Yorkshire and Shropshire, and the north Pennines, where lead was still mined in the nineteenth century.

In Hadrian's reign, Imperial control of some of the lead production seems to have been re-established, perhaps because the main consumers were the military units engaged in building works, the most important being the frontier Wall and a short time later the construction of several forts along it. Later still, some lead mines were controlled by the local communities, as evidenced by the lead ingots that went down with a transport ship off the coast of Brittany, stamped with the tribal names of the Brigantes and the Iceni.

Other metals were mined in Britain, including tin from Cornwall, but this industry does not seem to have been properly established until the third century. It is possible that tin from Spain was imported into Roman Britain for the first two centuries, and then when supplies were nearly exhausted the Romans started to mine for tin in Cornwall. Copper was mined in north Wales on the Great Orme near Llandudno, and in Shropshire, where there was a mine at Llanymynech with three shafts branching off from the cave at the entrance. Tin and copper were required for the manufacture of bronze. There was a bronze smithy at Heronbridge near Chester where some of the original moulds have been found, the patterns suggesting that the factory made ornamented bronze strips for decorating wooden boxes, but this was probably not the main focus of the work done there.

Iron ore was obtained from the Weald of Kent and Sussex, the Forest of Dean, and Somerset. From the distribution of tile stamps of the British fleet, the *Classis Britannica*, the iron industry of some parts of the Weald has been linked with the needs of the fleet, but there would also be a great demand for iron from the army for weapons, equipment and tools. In many cases the army may have been still involved with mining establishments even when they were operated by companies or civilian contractors. The fort at Whitley Castle in the Pennines has been linked with the transport of lead, and it is notable that the fort at Pumpsaint in south Wales lies close to the gold mine at Dolaucothi, and even when the garrison of Wales had been reduced, the Pumpsaint fort, itself reduced in size, was kept in occupation, suggesting a need to protect the mining operations and also perhaps the transport of the gold. If the scenario is converted into a Hollywood western, the need perhaps becomes clearer.

7

Insurrection & Retribution AD 180 to 211

The war in Britain at the beginning of the 180s was said to be the worst of Commodus's reign. According to Dio:

> [Commodus] fought wars with the barbarians beyond Dacia ... but the greatest
> war was in Britain. The people of the island, having crossed the wall which divides
> them from the legions, did a great deal of damage and killed a certain general and
> the soldiers with him. In alarm Commodus sent Ulpius Marcellus against them.
> (Dio 72.8.1–2)

This is the passage that causes confusion, if the Greek word *strategos*, usually translated as 'general', is taken to mean the governor. If this was the case, that a governor was killed, and Commodus sent Marcellus against the Britons, then as outlined in the previous chapter, there is considerable confusion over the dates when all this occurred. Marcellus was already in Britain in 178, when Marcus Aurelius and Commodus were joint Emperors. In 180 Marcus died and Commodus succeeded him, and to take Dio at his word it suggests that Marcellus served for a short time as governor of Britain, left the province to another governor, who was killed, and was now being sent to Britain for a second term. Another suggestion is that there were two governors who took up office within a short time of each other, both called Ulpius Marcellus. (There *was* another Ulpius Marcellus, attested at a later time, but he was most probably the son of the governor under Commodus). The most sensible solution is the one proposed by A.R. Birley, concentrating on what is meant by 'a general was killed', and 'Marcellus was sent against the Britons'. If the general was a legionary legate, it is more likely that Ulpius Marcellus was governor of the province, and being 'sent against the Britons' simply means that he was authorised to make war on them.

Virtually nothing is known about this war in Britain. Even its location is not established, because it is not known which of the two frontier walls the natives crossed. Since the Antonine Wall had probably been abandoned for over two decades before the war of the 180s, the properly functioning wall that divided the Britons from the Roman legions at the time of the invasion would naturally have been Hadrian's. This may be why Dio does not bother to explain which wall was crossed, as it was perhaps taken as read that the Antonine frontier was redundant at the time.

Certain pieces of archaeological evidence have been connected with the war. Excavations at two forts on the Wall not far from the point where Dere Street crosses it, at Halton Chesters and Rudchester, revealed signs of destruction, but none of this was securely dated. There were also signs of destruction at Corbridge, where Dere Street running north–south joins the Stanegate running east–west. Three inscriptions, one from Corbridge and two from Carlisle, have been tentatively associated by A.R. Birley with the fighting during the war. At Corbridge, Quintus Calpurnius Concessinus, a cavalry prefect, gave thanks to a powerful god for the slaughter of a band of Corionototae, an otherwise unattested tribal name rendered into Latin. At Carlisle, a dedication was made to Hercules for the defeat of a group of barbarians, and Lucius Junius Victorinus Flavius Caelianus, the legate of VI Victrix, dedicated an altar for successful actions beyond the Wall. These inscriptions are not dated and may have nothing to do with the war of the 180s, but if one or all of them belong to some other context or contexts, they are indicative of circumstances in northern Britain.

Until more evidence comes to light, nothing else can be said about this war, except that it was all over by 184 when Commodus took his seventh acclamation as Imperator, and the title Britannicus. The successful conclusion of the war failed to bring peace to Britain, since Ulpius Marcellus proved far too demanding for the soldiers. Apart from the comment that Marcellus inflicted tremendous damage on the barbarians, Dio gives no details about the fighting, but devotes several paragraphs to Marcellus's harsh character, one of his traits being his ability to function on very little sleep, or perhaps he suffered from insomnia, and like several people who can't sleep he seemed to resent the fact that anyone else might be having a decent night's slumber. Every evening he wrote out twelve messages on wooden writing tablets, and ordered someone to deliver them to different people at different hours during the night, so that everyone would think that he was always awake. For this reason alone it could be said that Marcellus fully deserved the mutiny that followed the conclusion of the campaigns.

MUTINY OF THE LEGIONS

It is not clear what exactly happened in Britain, but it seems that it was not just Marcellus who had caused resentment because of his harsh treatment. The soldiers tried to set up Priscus, the legate of an unnamed legion, as Emperor, implying that they were also disillusioned with Commodus. If the soldiers merely wanted someone to assume Imperial authority to rid them of Marcellus, they must have realised that Commodus was not likely to view their actions with sympathy. Priscus reputedly declined the offer, dismissing the soldiers with the remark, 'I am no more Emperor than you are soldiers', a very brave, or rash, method of dealing with several hundred men with swords. He seems to have survived long enough to be recalled to Rome with the other legionary legates and was no doubt punished, even though he had not become a usurper.

It is not known when Marcellus was recalled. On returning to Rome he was prosecuted, but not condemned. At about this time, the strange episode occurred when 1,500 soldiers from the army of Britain made their way to Rome, and met Commodus outside the city to air their grievance about the conduct of one of the Praetorian Prefects, Perennis, who had become very powerful, and allegedly had started to appoint equestrian commanders to the legions instead of senators, especially during the British war. During and after the reign of Severus, equestrians were regularly appointed, as military commanders and then also as governors, but it was not usual in Commodus's day. It is permissible to ask why so many soldiers from Britain were outside Rome, and why they resented the appointments made by Perennis, but the answers can only be guessed. The story goes that Commodus was persuaded by his new favourite, Cleander, to give up Perennis to the soldiers, who killed him. This left the route clear for Cleander to establish his dominant influence over Commodus.

There may have been a brief period after Marcellus's recall when there was no actual governor in Britain, and this may be the context in which the *iuridicus* Marcus Antius Crescens Calpurnianus acted as governor himself. An inscription found in Rome detailing his career says that Calpurnianus was *iuridicus* in Britain and also acting governor, but the text lacks a firm date for this appointment. After the mutiny of the British legions, the legates of all three legions were removed from their posts, and when the governor himself was recalled, Calpurnianus would be the only senatorial official left in the province, perhaps until the arrival of Publius Helvius Pertinax, the new governor, *c.*185.

PERTINAX GOVERNS BRITAIN

The family origins of Pertinax were far from auspicious, and if he had been born fifty years earlier he may not have enjoyed such a successful career. His father was a freedman, which might at one time have meant that Pertinax would have had to start his military career in the ranks, but it was an age when ability and patronage could count for more than ancestry. In the Danube wars Marcus Aurelius had appointed several non-senatorial officers to commands for which they had the aptitude and ability, and had then helped some of these men rise to senatorial status. Pertinax joined the Roman army as a cohort commander in Syria, and he served in two posts in Britain, starting as tribune in VI Victrix. He had his ups and downs, reaching the post of prefect of the Rhine fleet, then procurator in Dacia, but was then dismissed in suspicious circumstances. Fortunately, his services were needed when the German tribes invaded northern Italy, and he helped to drive them back. He was now noticed by Marcus Aurelius and was granted senatorial rank, commanded a legion and won a great victory in 172. He was consul in 175, but probably did not go to Rome. Instead he accompanied Marcus Aurelius to the eastern provinces, then he became governor successively of three Danube provinces, and possibly Syria in 180 after the death of the Emperor and the accession of Commodus. Then from about 182 when he returned to Rome he spent some years in unemployment, until he was appointed governor of Britain. It is worth documenting his career in some detail because it illustrates how far social mobility had progressed, and how men of ability and merit could gain a degree of recognition that would probably have been denied to their ancestors, except in special circumstances.

According to the *Historia Augusta*, after Perennis was killed, Commodus appointed Pertinax to Britain by writing him a letter, making amends for the years which Pertinax had recently spent without any appointments, largely because he had made an enemy of Perennis. The legions in Britain were still unruly when Pertinax arrived, because they did not want Commodus as Emperor, as they had already demonstrated by trying to elevate the legionary legate Priscus as their own Emperor. Now they tried again with Pertinax, but he remained loyal to Commodus and squashed the mutiny, probably with great severity. The result was that he was set upon in a riot and left for dead, which meant that when he recovered he was even more severe in punishing the soldiers. In the end he asked to be relieved of his post because of the hostility of the legions, probably leaving the province to his unknown successor in 187.

CLODIUS ALBINUS VERSUS SEPTIMIUS SEVERUS

For a few years after Pertinax left Britain, nothing is known of what was happening in the province. There were cataclysmic events in Rome and another civil war, which relegated Britain to the background for a while. The governor Decimus Clodius Albinus had probably been appointed in 192, and so he played no active part in the plots and assassinations in Rome in the following year. Commodus was assassinated in 193, and Pertinax became Emperor for a short time, which earned him a biographical slot in the *Historia Augusta*. Pertinax did not become Emperor solely because his provincial troops wanted to elevate him, but because he was in Rome when Commodus was assassinated and he was acceptable, at least at first, to the soldiery and the Senate. But the time was not far off when Emperors were made and discarded with monotonous regularity by the armies in the provinces or on campaigns.

The Praetorian Guard soon found that Pertinax was too strict for their tastes, and the Prefect Laetus, who had engineered the murder of Commodus, now had to rid himself of another Emperor. After Pertinax was removed a senator called Didius Julianus tried to bribe the Praetorians and make himself Emperor by means of his wealth, but he soon fell out of favour. There were three men waiting in the wings, backed by their soldiers, to seize the opportunity to take over the state. Septimius Severus, governor of Pannonia, was closer to Rome than the other two candidates, Decimus Clodius Albinus, governor of Britain, and Pescennius Niger, governor of Syria. Severus reached the capital before the others could make a move. He could draw upon sixteen legions from the Rhine and Danube. While marching towards Rome, he issued orders for the deification of Pertinax, the condemnation of his murderers, and of Didius Julianus, and he was obeyed very promptly.

One hundred senators were chosen to go to meet Severus, thus declaring the loyalty of the Senate. Severus accepted the delegation and turned his attention to the Praetorian Guard. He summoned the guardsmen to an assembly outside Rome. They were ordered to wear their parade armour, but they were to leave their weapons behind, which ought to have alerted them to what was to happen next. Some of Severus's soldiers seized the Praetorian camp, and others drew up on the edges of the assembly area. The Praetorian Guardsmen were berated for their disloyalty to Pertinax, and their failure to punish his assassins, and were then discharged and disbanded.

When he attended his first meeting of the Senate, Severus made it clear that he had no intention of arbitrarily eliminating any senators, so when the soldiers outside the meeting house started to clamour for a substantial donative, the Senate was not disposed to argue. Severus beat down the demands to a fraction of what had been asked, possibly as part of a previously rehearsed scenario, where the soldiers reminded the senators of the huge donative that Octavian/Augustus had given his armies in 43 BC. A good method of obtaining a reasonable offer is to name a high price first, so as to be able to display generosity in knocking it down, and then the people who have to pay are usually more content.

Severus was now firmly entrenched as Emperor, with a compliant Senate and no interference from the Praetorians. He had already formed his own bodyguard, and so was protected as far as possible against attacks from would-be assassins, and was later to use this bodyguard to replace the Praetorians. He was free to concentrate on his two main rivals at the extremities of the Empire, opposites in colour as well as location, the black (Niger) in Syria and the white (Albinus) in Britain. Severus decided to deal with Niger first, and therefore, as Dio says, he pacified Albinus, who was nearer to him. He sent him a letter by a trusted friend, putting Albinus on hold by offering him the title of Caesar, which would indicate that he was chosen for the succession, just as Commodus had been made Caesar and then full colleague of Marcus Aurelius. It is disputed by modern scholars whether Severus actually granted Albinus the title, or whether he simply made vague promises, which were interpreted as such. As Herodian puts it:

> Severus desired to win over Albinus by a trick, in case he might harbour designs … on making a bid for power and gain control of Rome, while he [Severus] was fighting in the east. He therefore pretended to honour Albinus, who was foolish and naive and trusted Severus, who sent letters making him several promises on

oath. That is to say, he declared Albinus Caesar, anticipating what the latter hoped for and desired, a share in power. (Herodian 2.15.2–3)

Whatever the impression gained by Albinus and the rest of the Empire, his position seemed more secure when Severus granted him the right to issue coins, and to have statues erected in his honour. Consequently Albinus remained in his province, and made no dash to Rome. He may have believed that he was to become Emperor and remained complacent and inactive, but it is just as likely that he spent the intervening years planning and preparing for a fight which he knew would inevitably arise. While Severus was in the east, making war on Niger, no one could predict the outcome of the war. Though Severus had more troops than Niger, it was not a foregone conclusion that he would be able to defeat the eastern armies and win them over to his cause. While Albinus waited in Britain, he probably reasoned that if Severus won, he would still have to negotiate skilfully to maintain his position, but if he had marched on Rome in the interval and had himself declared Emperor, he would simply have set himself up as an enemy of Severus, so it was better to stay where he was, in the hope that the agreement would be fulfilled. On the other hand, if Niger was the victor, Albinus would have to fight, since as Severus's Caesar he would represent another rival for Niger to overcome.

The outcome of the civil war was that Niger and his troops were defeated in 194, and his adherents were eradicated. This left only Severus and his Caesar Albinus, and for two years there were no hostilities between them. Severus strung Albinus along with promises and did not make the first move, as he had done against Niger, perhaps because he estimated that Albinus was more gullible and less prone to warlike tendencies. The story goes that Albinus only realised that he had been hoodwinked when Severus paid honours to his elder son Antoninus, whose original name was Bassianus, but was changed to Marcus Aurelius Antoninus, better known by his nickname Caracalla, derived from the type of cloak he habitually wore. When he became Emperor, Severus was anxious to associate himself with previous

Emperors, first as the avenger of Pertinax, and then a short time later he declared that he was the son of Marcus Aurelius, thus associating himself with the house of Antoninus Pius. Severus adopted their names in his titles, passing them on to his sons.

The presence of Caracalla and his younger brother Geta ought to have made it plain to Albinus that in the end Severus would favour his sons and make them his heirs, rather than the governor of Britain, but the honours for Caracalla allegedly alerted Albinus and forced him to act. In 196 he declared himself Augustus on his coinage, and gathered his troops to sail to Gaul. He may have been in correspondence with other governors, but in the end he was joined only by the legion from Tarraconensis in Spain, and the urban cohorts from Lyon. The governor of Lower Germany, called Lupus, tried to stop him, but Albinus and his British troops defeated him. Albinus was able to recruit in Gaul before Severus arrived, but was still at a disadvantage, and met his end at the Battle of Lugdunum (Lyon) in 197. His head was sent to Rome. Severus was now sole Emperor and in a position to consolidate his power and tidy up the Empire.

VIRIUS LUPUS, GOVERNOR OF BRITAIN

Immediately after the Battle of Lugdunum, Virius Lupus was appointed governor of Britain. He is no doubt the same Lupus, governor of Lower Germany, who had been defeated by Albinus, but his action in fighting on behalf of Severus would have earned him great credit. The situation facing Lupus when he reached his new province is not known, but probably qualifies for the description chaotic. Albinus may have taken all the troops he could muster in the island, including the garrisons from Hadrian's Wall, so it was generally supposed that there must have been an invasion from the north in 197, judging from the signs of destruction revealed by archaeological excavations at several northern forts, and the amount of repair work that was necessary on the Wall itself.

The troops that Albinus had taken from Britain may well have been relieved of some of their officers when Severus rounded up the defeated army and sent it back to Britain. There would also be casualties to replace from among the soldiery. All this would take some time to organise and complete, and there is no evidence to suggest how it was put into effect. While the province was not as well protected as usual, it seems that the northern tribes had attacked. New confederations had been formed, called the Caledonii and the Maeatae, described by Dio as the two largest groups of people in the north of the island, mostly because they had evidently absorbed other smaller tribes, so that 'the names of the others have so to speak been merged into them'. This is similar to a process that seems to have begun a short time later in Germany and Gaul, when the Alamanni first appeared. The name means 'All Men', representing a merger of tribes in the same way as the Maeatae. The tribal names may not have had any ethnic connotations, so the Caledonii and Maeatae should not be construed as purely racial groupings.

The confederation was possibly a very recent development. Dealing with the events in Britain in the reign of Severus, Dio says that the Maeatae, lived 'next to the wall which divides the island into two'. In an earlier passage describing the British war in the reign of Commodus, he says that the tribesmen had crossed the wall which divides them from the Roman legions, but he does not give them a tribal name. Nor does he give any indication as to which wall he is talking about in either passage, but it is possible that the Maeatae may well be the same as the unnamed tribes who crossed the wall about a decade earlier.

The confederacies of the Maeatae and Caledonii combined the resources and fighting strength of several tribes. Left to themselves the tribes of the north may have contented themselves by fighting each other and seizing lands, crops and cattle. They may have amalgamated as time went on, as tribal society worked towards state formation at its own pace, but it is also possible that the formation of a confederacy may have been a response to the presence of the Romans to the south, a stronger and better organised force which could overcome single tribes more easily and maintain dominance. There is also the possibility that the lands and peoples on the Roman side of the frontier seemed attractive to the northern tribes, for several reasons. When tribesmen broke through the German frontier in the mid-third century, they came via the fertile crop-producing areas of the Taunus and Wetterau, and may have been searching for food as well as portable wealth and adventure. From Hadrian's time onwards subsidies in the form of cash, luxury goods and food had usually been paid to tribesmen near the frontiers to keep them in good order and pacified, though the only evidence from Britain concerns the Votadini in the north-east, whose leaders were clearly receiving Roman luxury goods. There may have been a treaty or some formal agreement between the Romans and the tribal leaders, so that peace in their area and safe passage through it would be assured. The dynamics of Roman dealings with natives are more subtle than simply making war from time to time.

While Albinus was making his bid for power, the Maeatae had probably been causing trouble, taking advantage of the absence of most or all of the troops. On arrival in his province, Virius Lupus was in no position to make war, as Dio reveals:

> Because the Caledonians had not kept their promises and were preparing to assist the Maeatae, and because Severus was attending to the Parthian war, Lupus was forced to buy peace from the Maeatae for a large sum, in return receiving some prisoners. (Dio 75.5.4)

The promises that the Caledonii and perhaps the Maeatae had made and then broken are not elucidated. It is possible that four decades earlier Julius Verus had effected some sort of treaty when he withdrew from the Antonine Wall, but it is perhaps more likely that Ulpius Marcellus had ended his war in 184 with a formal peace treaty in the name of the Emperor Commodus, perhaps exacting tribute and possibly recruits for the army, but more importantly imposing on the elite ruling class an undertaking to keep their people quiet. One of the problems with treaties between tribesmen and the Romans was that the tribesmen thought in terms of loyalty to an individual ruler, and perhaps his descendants, whereas the Romans interpreted the arrangement in terms of the state. When the ruler to whom the tribesmen had sworn allegiance was killed or died, then as far as they were concerned, the treaty was invalidated. Commodus was assassinated, and he left no true heirs, nor had he designated a successor by legal appointment.

The extent of the damage supposedly caused by the new confederacy is not known, but the fact that they had taken prisoners which were then restored to Lupus is taken to mean that they had invaded the province and carried off people and goods. How far they had penetrated is a matter of conjecture. When Dio says that the Maeatae lived next to the wall that divides the island, he may have referred to the abandoned Antonine Wall, which would place them in the Lowlands beyond the Forth and Clyde possibly up to the Highland line, and the Caledonii further north. If so, then they would have to cross southern Scotland to reach the Roman military installations. But not everyone agrees about their location. As already mentioned above, the long-abandoned Antonine Wall was probably discounted by Dio and his contemporaries, so the only Wall worth talking about was Hadrian's. This implies that the Maeatae were located in southern Scotland, and their federation would probably have included the hostile Selgovae and Novantae, known to the Romans of the first century. Wherever the Maeatae lived, and wherever they caused some damage it is presumed that it must have concerned the outpost forts and Hadrian's Wall itself. The problem is that archaeology reveals that there was no repair work on the Wall and outposts until *c*.205, eight years after the supposed invasion and destruction of 197. In the absence of further evidence, this could be interpreted in different ways. Perhaps the Wall was very badly damaged and there were not the resources or the manpower to restore it immediately after Lupus arrived as governor, and this is why he bought off the Maeatae. Perhaps the Wall was not fully garrisoned because the troops taken by Albinus had not yet returned. It is true that the units attested at the end of the second century were not the same as those which garrisoned the forts in the third. The doom and gloom of this scenario paints a picture of the province in a very bad state, with the equivalent of the tumbleweed blowing freely through the creaking gates of the deserted forts of the Wall. Alternatively, the alleged invasion of 197 was probably not as serious as all that, and in any case the delay in effecting repairs need not mean that the frontier was not working properly. In a court of law, the evidence for an invasion in 197 would not stand up to the questioning of a determined lawyer.

Inscriptions and archaeological excavations reveal that there had been some damage at forts much further south in the Pennines, where destruction deposits have been found at Ilkley, Bainbridge and Ravenglass, not necessarily dated to 197. At Ilkley, repairs were recorded by Virius Lupus, who had charge of the work (*curante Virio Lupo leg[ato]eorum pro pr[aetore]*). Building work by VI Victrix was carried out at Corbridge under Lupus. At Bowes the fort baths had been destroyed by fire and were rebuilt by the *ala Vettonum*, under their prefect Valerius Fronto, for *cohors I Thracum*, while Lupus was governor. There may have been more repairs at other forts which have gone unrecorded because the inscriptions have not come to light, but the sum total of repair work under Lupus, if it was indeed caused by restless natives, probably denotes localised uprisings in the Pennines, rather than an invasion from further north. Contrary to previous suggestions, it has now been established that there was no damage at York, Catterick, or at Aldborough at this time. At Bowes, a fire in a bath building need not be a cause for alarm, since any structure where fires have to be lit underneath the floors is surely more at risk from accidents than from hostile action.

The whole episode is puzzling, perhaps inflated by the tendency to try to marry up literary evidence with archaeological findings. There may have been no invasion in 197 at all. When the war in Britain began in the reign of Commodus, Dio says that the tribes had crossed the wall, whichever that was, and done a great deal of damage, and killed a general. When Virius Lupus was governor, Dio merely indicates that war was threatening because the Caledonii were getting ready to help the Maeatae. On this occasion he does not say that the tribesmen had attacked. It is true that his work in both these circumstances survives only as summaries or copied fragments, and the problem may be merely one of semantics, but the difference is worth pointing out. The only hint of hostilities is that the Maeatae returned some prisoners to Lupus when he paid them off, and these could have been soldiers caught off guard while on patrol, rather than men snatched in a raid on a fort. Cash and gifts had been used before to ward off hostilities and would be so used again up to modern times.

Lupus disappears from the record after his term of office as governor, and it is not known when he was recalled. If he was in disgrace because he had used cash to forestall a war rather than risk a battle, it is not recorded, and yet it is precisely the sort of juicy gossip that Herodian might have included in his history. A normal three-year term would mean that Lupus would return to Rome *c*.200, so it is conjectured that an unknown governor, or possibly two successive governors, arrived and did unknown things for an unknown period of time, until *c*.205.

VALERIUS PUDENS AND ALFENUS SENECIO, GOVERNORS C.205 TO C.207 OR 208

The exact sequence of who followed whom as governor between 205 and 208 is not established, but it is likely that Pudens preceded Senecio. While these two men were governors, considerable building programmes were carried out, not necessarily as a result of destruction by tribesmen, since the forts would be showing signs of wear and tear by now. Pudens is known from two, possibly three inscriptions, which attest building work at Bainbridge, where a barrack was constructed, and a dedication to Severus and his sons was set up at Ribchester, naming the governor. Pudens is not named on the inscription recording the repair of an aqueduct at Caernarvon, but the work may have been carried out in his term of office.

Building work continued at Bainbridge under Alfenus Senecio, attested on two different inscriptions, and some further work was done at the fort at Bowes. A granary was built at Birdoswald on Hadrian's Wall, and there was some unspecified building work done at Corbridge. At Risingham a gate that had fallen down through age was repaired. At the last two forts, the work was supervised by the procurator Oclatinius Adventus, who may have been sent to inspect the frontier works, though it was not unknown for procurators to supervise building projects in other provinces. Adventus was eventually to become Praetorian Prefect.

Alfenus Senecio may have remained in post until 207, but this is not proven. Herodian relays a story that the governor of Britain, whom he does not name, wrote to Severus to explain that the natives had revolted and were causing so much damage that there was a need for extra troops, or the presence of the Emperor himself. Perhaps this anonymous governor was Senecio, but although he would have sent reports about the situation in Britain, it is considered unlikely that he also asked for an Imperial expedition to be mounted. Possibly Severus represented the matter to his entourage or even the Senate in this fashion, explaining that he had received a report and he considered it necessary to go to Britain himself. Dio refers to war in Britain, but does not dramatise it, except to say that Severus was annoyed because while wars were being won in Britain by others, he was unable to defeat a large band of outlaws in Italy, led by a man called Bulla. Another reason for going to war in a province far away from Rome, as both Dio and Herodian affirm, was to remove his unruly sons from the temptations of the city. Dio adds that Severus knew from various portents that he would not return alive to Rome. Severus was susceptible to such things. He had married Julia Domna because her horoscope predicted that she would be the wife of an Emperor.

EXPEDITIO FELICISSIMA BRITANNICA

Severus and his family, and a large part of his domestic and Imperial household started the journey to Britain in 208. He would be accompanied by various secretaries and his *comites*, derived from *comes*, which means companion, but the term had assumed an official status when applied to the entourage of the Emperor, and would eventually become a title. A coin of 208 shows the Emperor setting off on horseback. Perhaps he did actually ride a horse for the first leg of the journey, to keep up appearances, but he was now sixty-three years old and suffering from arthritis, and so he was carried in a litter for most of the way, even when he was on campaign.

There were probably extra troops collected on the way to Britain, from the Rhine and Danube armies, and possibly a vexillation was drawn from the new legion, II Parthica, which Severus had raised and controversially stationed near Rome at Albano. It was a safeguard for his rule and also formed a reserve army that could be taken to trouble spots if need arose, though it was not exactly a forerunner of the later mobile armies, which were located much closer to the frontiers.

On arrival in Britain, Severus may have stayed at London for a short while, and according to Herodian he left his younger son Geta in the south, equipped with a team of advisers, to attend to matters of justice and civil government, though this probably gives a false impression that Geta was in total command of the province. Antoninus, or Caracalla, was taken north to go on campaign, so that for the duration of the war he represented no danger to his brother, though Severus knew that he fully intended to despatch Geta if he was given a chance.

Headquarters for the northern campaign were at York, where the remains of a large building on the river frontage have been identified as the Imperial residence. Preparations for the war were already in hand, probably before Severus and his retinue arrived. An altar from Corbridge records an individual, whose full name has not survived, as '*praepositus* in charge of the granaries at the time of the British expedition'. The term *praepositus* did not denote a specific rank, but was a versatile title usually given to an officer in charge of a temporary task or in command of a vexillation, or a group of such detachments. Although there is no dating evidence or anything that associates this inscription with Severus's campaigns, it is generally accepted that the *expeditio* mentioned in the text refers to his campaigns, and that Corbridge would be one of the stores and supply bases for a campaign in the north.

Another supply base was established at South Shields fort, where twenty extra granaries were built to add to the existing two, capable of holding vast quantities of grain and other supplies. Since supplies could be carried up the east coast to be delivered to South Shields and from there to the army on campaign, the fleet was used for transport as well as reconnaissance and perhaps it was even used in the fighting, as Julius Agricola had done over a century earlier. An inscription from Rome concerning an equestrian officer in command of the combined fleets of Britain, the Rhine and the Danube is most likely to be associated with Severus's British expedition.

A fort was built at Cramond on the south shore of the Forth where Agricola had established a fort, and a larger fortress was built at Carpow on the Tay, by VI Victrix. It was perhaps intended as their base, though it was not large enough for the whole legion. These are the only known Severan forts in southern Scotland, emphasising the reliance on the coastal bases, and the fleet, and indicating that the main invasion route lay on the east side of Scotland. So far no coins of Severan date have been found on the Antonine Wall, and nothing has come to light in the forts to the south of it, so it appears that there was no attempt to occupy the area, at least while the campaigns were in progress.

There may not have been time to mount an offensive in 208, which was probably spent in accumulating supplies and perhaps reconnoitring. The campaigns probably occupied 209 and 210. A coin of Caracalla's dated to 209 shows a bridge of boats and the legend *Traiectus*, a crossing, which could indicate the Forth, or more likely a crossing of the Tay estuary. The army seems to have eventually reached the far north. Dio describes how Severus was carried most of the distance in a litter, but was determined to reach the very end of the island, where he observed the movement of the sun and the length of the days and nights.

The literature covering this period has hardly anything useful to say about the course of the war. Even Dio contributes very little, but devotes several passages to a description of the tribesmen. He says that the northern Britons live in the mountains and the marshes, with no towns or agriculture, but they survive on their flocks and herds, ignoring the plentiful fish. They wear no clothes, Dio says, and they go about barefoot, going into battle armed with a spear, a dagger and a shield, but no armour. They hold their women and children in common, living under a democratic system, electing the bravest of their warriors as leaders. Herodian is somewhat more verbose on these themes, and then he more or less dismisses the campaigns as a series of frequent skirmishes, which eventually scattered the barbarians, but he explains how the Britons were able to hide in the marshes, and get away.

The terrain is presented as a somewhat unexpected hazard by Dio, who states that it was Severus's intention to conquer the whole island, but he was presented with tremendous difficulties on the march, through dense forests where the trees had to be cut down, across heights which were levelled, through marshes which were filled up, and rivers which were bridged. The expedition sounds more like an engineering exercise than a campaign in the pages of Dio, and following on from Severus's declaration of intent to conquer the whole island the passage could be construed as an obvious and valid reason why the conquest was not followed by an occupation, though this is not stated in so many words. There is very little infomation about the fighting that may have taken place, since as Dio admits, Severus did not fight a battle and never even saw the Britons drawn up in battle formation. Instead it was a guerrilla war, where the natives used their knowledge of their own ground and could lay an ambush with comparative ease. They put out sheep and cattle to tempt the Romans to keep moving forward and wore them out, then picked off any soldiers who did not keep up with the rest. Wounded men who were unable to walk were killed by the Romans themselves in preference to allowing them to be captured.

Despite the failure to bring the natives to battle, as Agricola had done with spectacular success after two northern campaigns, Severus did manage to impose terms on the tribesmen, and according to Dio they were forced to give up a large part of their territory. It was while Severus and Caracalla were riding to meet the Britons to receive their surrender that a somewhat unbelievable episode took place, when Caracalla drew his sword as though he was about to kill his father. It was not the most auspicious occasion for him to attempt to do so, especially since there had probably been more suitable opportunities while the army was on the march, but this is the tale that Dio tells. Caracalla was restrained and Severus ignored the event until the formalities of the British surrender and the imposition of terms had taken place, then he summoned his son and instructed him to commit the murder there and then if he so wished, or alternatively, since he was Emperor in his own right, to order Papinian, the Praetorian Prefect, to do it. This story merits far more verbiage than the surrender of the Britons, which ought to have been the crowning achievement of the campaigns.

Archaeological evidence for the war is limited to the various lines of marching camps aiming for the north of Scotland, notoriously difficult to date. There are four very large camps, measuring 66 hectares, or 165 acres, running northwards from Newstead fort, where it is possible that a large part of the campaign army assembled for the first campaign. The line of march indicated by these camps, at Newstead, St Leonards, Channelkirk and Pathhead, aims for the Forth, beyond which no camps as large as these have been discovered. The army may have been split up at that point to guard river crossings and communications, though no bases have been found, or some troops may have been ferried northwards by the fleet. From the environs of Ardoch, which was occupied in the first century and again under Antoninus Pius, another line of camps, smaller than those from Newstead, measuring 48 hectares or 120 acres, has been traced skirting the Highlands on the east side, and ending probably at the Moray Firth, though the camps have not been traced quite that far. Then there are two series of even smaller camps, one line skirting the Highlands north-eastwards from Ardoch and another towards Carpow on the Tay. There is nothing to indicate whether these two lines represent two different forces deployed simultaneously, or a single army marching to the north and back again. There is also the factor that the campaigns extended over two years, the first in 209 and another in 210, and it is an impossible task to assign different camps to individual expeditions.

THE ROMAN MILITARY TENT – Text Box
On the march, the Roman army usually built temporary camps at each overnight halt, or sometimes the troops would remain in the camp for a few days, perhaps while some soldiers reconnoitred the surrounding territory, and others rested and prepared food

for the next stage of the march. While in camp the men would live in tents. The eight men of a *contubernium* shared one tent, just as they shared a barrack room in their forts. Different styles of Roman tents are depicted on Trajan's Column in Rome. Some of these are depicted with very low walls, and the sloping cover reaching nearly to the ground, while others are shown with higher walls and looking a little more elaborate. The differences may simply be a result of artistic licence, or it could be that it was intended to show tents for soldiers and officers, perhaps the general or even the Emperor, a question to which no one can provide a definitive answer. The Roman author Hyginus gives the dimensions of military tents, but since no precise date has been established for his work, there can be no certainty as to whether these facts applied to the army at all periods of its existence.

Tents were usually made of leather, and various pieces of leather panels have been discovered from different parts of the Empire, but it was not possible to make anything other than an informed estimate of the structure and size of tents, until the discoveries of full-sized goatskin panels, with evidence of stitching along the edges, at Vindolanda in northern Britain. Carol van Driel Murray, an expert on ancient leather, concluded that at least in Britain, if not in other provinces, the Romans used standard panels of different sizes, the largest 76 cm by 52 cm, smaller ones 52 cm by 38 cm. Miscellaneous narrow strips, and pieces used as reinforcements, and attachments for the guy ropes, were also identified. It was possible, from a study of the stitching and stretching of the leather panels, to reconstruct the tent, working out previously unknown factors such as the height of the walls and the pitch of the roof. One of the problems concerned the use of guy ropes to support the tent. Hyginus says that these extended only one Roman foot from the tent walls, implying that they were pegged in at an extremely sharp angle that would not give as much support as ropes pegged much further apart at a more oblique angle. This led to the conclusion that if Hyginus's figures are correct, the tents were probably framed as well, though it has to be admitted that there is no proof for this. Details such as the arrangements for ventilation of the tent, and how the door flaps were arranged and fastened, remain unclear.

The terms of the surrender were quickly spurned by the tribesmen. When Severus heard that they had broken out in revolt, the Caledonii as well as the Maeatae, he lost patience and gave orders for another invasion, this time with instructions that the soldiers should kill everyone they came across. He was preparing for another campaign when he died at York in February 211. Up to the time of his death he had not renounced his avowed intention of conquering the whole island, so no one can be certain whether he would have brought his intentions to fruition if he had lived longer.

His advice to his sons as he lay dying was allegedly to keep the peace between themselves, to pay the soldiers and to despise everyone else. As a realist, Severus knew that the people of the Empire wanted protection, but they were not too keen on paying for it. But protection could only be had at a price, and the soldiers had not received a pay rise for some considerable time until he granted them an annual increase. This was over and above the donatives that they were paid from time to time, on the accession of new Emperors, or sometimes when there was a special event in the Imperial family.

Apart from granting a pay rise to the armies, Severus also realised that soldiering had to be made more attractive, or the problems of recruiting would be made even worse. The armies of the Roman Empire used up manpower at an alarming rate, even when there were no wars to be fought. Accidents and illness probably accounted for as many casualties as warfare, and desertion was seemingly becoming more common. If it were not for the enlistment of many tribesmen from inside and increasingly from outside the Empire, the armies would have been depleted to dangerous levels. When the Empire was expanding and troops were constantly moved around, the law forbidding soldiers to marry was a perfectly sensible precaution. Emotional attachments and family responsibilities did not make for good soldiers, who were expected to pack up and move on, probably several times during their careers. As the frontiers developed and troops became a little more static, sometimes serving their whole term in the same part of the province or even at the same fort, the men naturally formed lasting attachments to local women. The legal fiction that circumvented the law against marriages is clear from the wording on the diplomas issued to soldiers who had served the full term, when citizenship was granted to the auxiliaries and their children by the women with whom they had formed associations. When a soldier retired, his association was legalised as a proper marriage. Recognising that trying to uphold the law against soldiers' marriages was futile, Severus regularised a process that was already well entrenched by allowing soldiers to marry while still serving in the army. This measure enhanced the tradition of military families, whose sons joined the army after their fathers, and perhaps slightly improved the position of the wives, who had always had to wait for several years before achieving a legalised status for themselves and their children, who had been technically illegitimate.

Severus has been blamed, most virulently by Gibbon, for all the ills that befell the Empire in the third century and later, in part because of the favouritism that he had shown to the army. After his death, it was the soldiers who continually made and disposed of Emperors for the next hundred years, with one or two exceptions when a son succeeded a father or the Senate chose one of their own members to be Emperor. Even then, few Emperors enjoyed a long reign after the Severan dynasty died out, and hardly any of them died peacefully in bed. Being made an Emperor in the third century was an effective death sentence.

Severus's body was cremated at York, and placed in an urn of purple stone that he had thoughtfully provided some time before his death, knowing that all the omens indicated that he would not return alive to Rome. Caracalla and Geta were now joint Emperors, though Caracalla had been made a full colleague of his father much earlier than Geta, who was only made Augustus towards the end of 210. Perhaps Severus thought, or hoped, that this equality would end the bitter rivalry between his sons.

8

The Great Rebuilding AD 211 to 275

The third century in Britain is one of the least documented eras, owing
to the decline in the habit of setting up inscriptions, noticeable in all
parts of the province. This is coupled with an unfortunate dearth
of literary sources for the Empire as a whole. Dio's account ends in
c.229, and Herodian covers the period from Marcus Aurelius to the
reign of Gordian III, ending in 238. Thereafter Britain declined in
importance compared to the major concerns in the rest of the Empire
with pressure on the frontiers from the tribesmen beyond the Rhine
and Danube, and from the newly established Persian Empire which
replaced the less aggressive Parthian regime on the eastern borders of
the Roman Empire. For Roman Britain in the third century there are
only fragments of information, too few and far between to provide a
coherent list of governors and other officials. Dating evidence tails off
as well, especially as the imports of samian wares, the most useful of
dating tools, declined and then ceased in third-century Britain. This
gloomy scenario does not necessarily imply that daily life for Romano-
Britons was similarly gloomy, but we see it through a glass darkly, and
not as a whole but as a series of impressions.

IMPERIAL PEACE
After the death of Severus, it is not known how soon Caracalla and

the Imperial family left Britain. Caracalla may have conducted another campaign in the north, a supposition for which there is no evidence, but the historians Dio and Herodian may well have suppressed any success that he may have enjoyed. One factor that suggests that the Romans did not simply abandon the north when Caracalla became Emperor is that building work was still going on at Carpow until 212. The fortress, not large enough for a full legion, may have been intended to house some of VI Victrix who built it, perhaps to act as an outpost and advance warning system, though it is strange that it seems not to have been supported by forts or road posts to the south.

If he did not organise a campaign, Caracalla perhaps travelled to meet the tribal leaders to arrange terms. Dio says that he made peace with the enemy, withdrew the troops and abandoned the forts, but there is no hint as to what terms he imposed. The usual treaty arrangements would include a demand for recruits for the army, and perhaps subsidies would be given in return for a cessation of hostilities. Some scholars have linked Caracalla's peace terms in Britain with the inscription attesting the presence of *Brittones dediticii* on the German frontier, based at the fort at Walldurn. These *dediticii* were surrendered tribesmen, perhaps commanded by the *Brittones gentiles* who are also attested on the inscription, and somehow distinguished from the *dediticii*. Since Caracalla campaigned in Germany in 213, earning the victory title Germanicus in the autumn of that year, it is quite possible that he took some of the conquered Britons with him to augment the army.

An incontestable result of the peace that was made with the northern Britons is that it lasted for over eight decades. If Severus's orders to the army to kill everyone had actually been carried out, and if many of the young men had been removed to serve in or with the Roman army, the northern lands may have been seriously depopulated. Tacitus invents a speech for the first-century leader Calgacus, who says of the Romans, 'They make a desert and call it peace.' A common pattern for the breakout of revolts against Roman rule is that a victory is followed by a gap of roughly twenty years, and then the next generation thinks of revenge. But in this instance the peace endured.

Caracalla's victory and successful peace terms are a credit to him, but that was soon overshadowed by his first actions in Rome, when he killed his brother Geta, who died clinging to his mother, Julia Domna. Many of the Imperial household were also done to death. Orders went out all over the Empire to remove the name of Geta from all inscriptions, and to destroy his statues and portraits. In Britain, one of the stones where Geta's name was chiselled out was built into the roof of the crypt at Hexham Abbey, and another from the fort at Bowes was preserved inside the adjacent church.

The British governor, Gaius Julius Marcus, together with the legionaries and auxiliaries, may have let it be known that they disapproved of these horrific events, which may explain why there are so many surviving inscriptions declaring loyalty to the Emperor or praying for his welfare. In most of these inscriptions Caracalla is given all his official names and victory titles, and on some of them, like those from Whitley Castle in the Pennines and from Risingham, his fabricated family history is traced through Marcus Aurelius and Antoninus Pius, right back to Trajan and Nerva, emphasising the connections that Severus established to legitimise his new regime. The authors of the Risingham inscription and of others from Netherby, Newcastle and South Shields, remembered to include Caracalla's mother, Julia Domna Augusta, in the dedication. Most of these inscriptions are securely dated to 213 by the number of consular or tribunician years of the Emperor. Not all of them display a clear record of the governor's name, because it was deliberately removed from some stones, just as Geta's was, implying that Gaius Julius Marcus was probably condemned, and that his memory was damned.

The Division of Britain into Two Provinces

At the beginning of the third century, Britain was divided into two provinces, called Britannia Superior and Britannia Inferior – nothing to do with value judgements, since the titles simply mean Upper and Lower Britain, similar to Upper and Lower Germany. According to Dio, whose statement is corroborated by inscriptions, Britannia Superior was administered from London by a consular governor, and included XX Valeria Victrix at Chester and II Augusta at Caerleon. The governor of Britannia Inferior was of praetorian rank, and was also the legionary legate of VI Victrix, administering from York. The main problem is to ascertain the date when this division took place. Herodian says that Severus arranged it immediately after the victory over Clodius Albinus at Lugdunum in 197, but if that is correct then it is puzzling that from 197 onwards until the Severan campaigns in 208 to 211, only a succession of consular governors is attested, with no hint of a praetorian governor based at York. It could be the case that Herodian simply assumed without bothering to check that the division of Britain occurred after the defeat of Albinus, because Severus divided the province of Syria into two smaller provinces in 194 after he had defeated Niger, so it may have seemed to Herodian a very neat and tidy arrangement to treat Britain in the same way, the defeat of the rival Emperor being immediately followed by division of the province he had governed. The two Syrian provinces were not called Superior and Inferior, but in other respects the arrangements paralleled those in Britain: the consular province was called Syria Coele, with two legions, and the praetorian province of Syria Phoenice contained only one legion and the legate was also the governor.

Scholars are mostly in agreement that Herodian was mistaken, but that does not help in discerning the actual date of the division. Gaius Julius Marcus, attested as governor in 213 on several inscriptions, may have governed the whole province, but since the inscriptions all derive from the north, it is not possible to be certain that there was another governor in the south. It is suggested that the province was divided in 216, and until more evidence comes to light, there is nothing to confirm or refute the suggestion. It may be significant that at some point between 212 and 217 Caracalla also made some adjustments to the boundaries of the two provinces of Pannonia, already divided into Upper and Lower provinces, but with an unequal distribution of legions. In the new arrangement the Upper province lost some of its territory and one of its legions to the Lower province, so that they both had two legions. When Severus made his bid for Imperial power he was governor of Upper Pannonia, with access to three legions. His policy for the future, continued by Caracalla, was to ensure that other governors should not be able to emulate him. In splitting up Syria he made sure that future governors would find it more difficult to raise an army than Pescennius Niger had done. Perhaps he had explained to Caracalla his intentions for Britain and Pannonia, or possibly Caracalla learned from experience and made his own mind up that a province with more than two legions constituted a potential danger to himself and his reign.

The boundary between the two provinces in Britain is not definitely known, except that Lower Britain extended to somewhere north of Chester, and somewhere south of Lincoln. It was not an impermeable barrier which could not be crossed by governors of each province. Detachments from the two legions from the Upper province were sent to assist with building works at Netherby, north of Hadrian's Wall, in 219, and officials called *beneficiarii consularis*, most probably from the governor's headquarters in Upper Britain, are attested in the north.

The division would take some time to organise. Even though York had been the administrative headquarters for the duration of the Severan campaigns, it was probably not made ready to function as the permanent headquarters of the Lower province. It is likely that the governor of each province was responsible for collecting taxes and collating census data, so all the administrative machinery for these processes in the north would have to be split off from London and set up at York, with attendant personnel, gradations of clerical staff and a bodyguard for the governor. Accommodation and offices would have to be found, or created. The civil settlement, where Severus occupied a palace, was a *municipium* at the time of his death in 211, but according to an inscription set up in 237 at Boulogne by Marcus Aurelius Lunaris, a merchant from Britain, York was a *colonia*. It was most likely Caracalla who raised the status of the former *municipium*. When the governor of Lower Britain and his staff were established at York, there would be plenty of opportunity for the inhabitants at all levels to make money, by supplying goods and services.

THE ANTONINE ITINERARY – Text Box

The document known as the Antonine Itinerary, or *Itinerarium Provinciarum Antonini Augusti*, covers several routes in Roman Britain and provides evidence for the names of forts and towns. It was probably originally drawn up for Caracalla as he planned journeys across the Empire, but the work is not all of one period, since it contains information that dates to the Tetrarchy of Diocletian and Maximian at the end of the third century. The British sections are included at the very end of the lists of land routes, and are followed by a list of sea routes, called *Imperatoris Antonini Augusti Itinerarium Maritinum*. The fact that Britain is listed in the plural shows that the information dates from after the division of the island into two provinces, which most probably occurred under Caracalla.

It has been pointed out that the Itinerary is not logically organised and may not even be an official document at all, but this does not really affect its usefulness, or its problems, when applying the information in the sections dealing with Britain to the known Roman sites.

The routes listed in the itinerary, 225 in all, are all assigned numbers within the province, as *Iter I*, *Iter II*, and so on, *Iter* meaning 'journey'. For each route the names of the starting places and the ultimate destinations are mentioned first, followed by a list of the places that must be passed through on the way, with the mileages between them. It is not always possible to assign the places names in the list to actual Romano-British sites, and for some of the Roman names there is no other evidence to assist with the identification of the place. The mileages given between places is not always accurate, but this could derive from copying errors, especially as several manuscript versions of the document are known, indicating that many copyists must have been involved with it during its useful lifetime. Another problem is that it is not

---

known if the distances between towns was measured from a point in the town centre or from the boundaries of its territory, and since some towns governed large surrounding areas this could make a difference of a couple of miles.

Some of the places names used are not consistent throughout the whole of the British sections of the Itinerary; for instance, Colchester appears as Colonia in one route and Camulodunum in another. The routes have been listed and mapped in *The Place Names of Roman Britain* by A.L.F. Rivet and C. Smith, London, 1979.

The route (*Iter V*) from London to Carlisle (Luguvallium) runs via Chelmsford and Colchester, and keeps mostly to the eastern side of the country until Catterick, then it branches off westwards through Bowes, Brough, and Brougham across the Pennines. Since progress was on foot or horseback, consideration for the distances between overnight stopping places had to be considered, which could force the traveller to diverge from the more direct routes across country, but it is significant that the route does not attempt to run through the hills of the western side of the Pennines and the Lake District. *Iter II* starts slightly north of Hadrian's Wall on the western side, and runs all the way to Richborough (Portus Rutupiae), expressed as '*a vallo ad Portum Ritupis*' and comes through Brough down to York, and then runs south-west to Chester, again skirting round the Lake District and the western Pennines. It then goes via Northwich to Wroxeter and then to the south. Surely there is material here for a television programme or two?

REBUILDING AND INNOVATIONS

From the early third century onwards for nearly fifty years, evidence from inscriptions and archaeological excavations show that many forts in the Pennines and on the frontier were repaired or parts of them rebuilt. This work, which had already begun under the governors Pudens and Senecio, continued after Caracalla left the province and after it was split into Upper and Lower Britain. Under successive governors, not all of whose names are known, the refurbishment of the forts in northern Britain was undertaken in peace and at a leisurely pace, and the repair work was for the most part to buildings that were not strictly necessary for the defence of the fort. Nor can it be said that hostile actions had caused any damage to necessitate rebuilding. On the whole the north was probably peaceful, otherwise it may not have been possible to spare the troops when Caracalla gathered them for his campaign in Germany in 213.

At the outpost forts north of Hadrian's Wall, some unspecified building was done in 216, and then in 220 and again at some time after 226 at High Rochester, where *ballistaria* or platforms for artillery engines were built and repaired. At Netherby a temple was built, and a cavalry exercise hall, which had been founded some time before, was erected. In the 220s building work was carried out at Chesters fort on Hadrian's Wall, one building having collapsed through age. The theory that 'collapsed through age' is always a euphemism for destruction by the enemy can be discounted, at least in this case. The same reason for repair work was given at Great Chesters, where a granary was restored because it had also fallen down through age. At Vindolanda one of the gates and its towers were rebuilt from the foundations, but the date is not certain. At some time after 226, something was enlarged at Old Penrith, but the inscription sheds no light on what it was. Restoration was done at Whitley Castle, while at Ribchester, Titus Floridius Natalis, legionary centurion and the commander of the unit and also the region, built a temple out of his own funds.

The frontier zone under Caracalla and his successors begins to look very different from the second-century version. The Votadini north of Hadrian's Wall, friendly to the Romans, may have received some of the territory that the Maeatae had been forced to give up. Roman goods still reached the Votadini across the frontier, and the farmers of southern Scotland carried on in the traditional way in Iron Age-style houses, though with less interest in Roman exports than the Votadini. There seems to have been little or no disturbance here, perhaps because frequent patrols from the outpost forts kept the peace.

The new third-century fort at Bewcastle broke the mould. The regular rectangular shape with rounded corners and four gates that had become the norm for most forts in the Roman Empire was abandoned here, and a polygonal fort was built, more suited to the ground upon which it stood. It is not known whose innovation this represented. Perhaps Caracalla or one of the governors surveyed the area and decided that something new was required.

The shape of the new fort was not the only innovation, since the outposts and some of the Wall forts received units of tribesmen, not formed into cohorts or *alae*, called for the most part *exploratores*, or *numeri*. These formations supplemented the auxiliary units. *Cohors I Vangionum milliaria* was based at Risingham, where there was now a *numerus exploratorum* and a unit of *Raeti Gaesati*, allegedly named for the weapon they carried, a spear called the *gaesum*. High Rochetser also received a *numerus exploratorum* in addition to the *cohors I Vardullorum milliaria*. There is no evidence for a unit of *exploratores* besides the *cohors I Aelia Hispanorum milliaria* at Netherby, but the name of the fort, Castra Exploratorum, indicates that such a unit was based there.

On the western end of Hadrian's Wall, the fort at Burgh by Sands contained a *cuneus Frisiorum* in 213. *Cuneus* literally means 'wedge', perhaps referring to a battle formation, but it is also suggested that the term denotes the mounted equivalent of a *numerus*. The unit of Frisii was replaced at Burgh by Sands about 260 by the *numerus Maurorum Aurelianorum*. Two units at Housesteads accompanied the *cohors I Tungrorum milliaria,* called the *numerus Hnaudifridi*, or 'Notfried's Unit', and a *cuneus Frisiorum*. At Great Chesters on the Wall, another group of *Raeti Gaesati* accompanied the *cohors II Asturum*.

The extra units were probably quite small. The *numeri* of the German frontier, where they had been installed probably as early as the reign of Trajan or Hadrian, comprised about one and a half centuries. The forts that they occupied were roughly the same size and shape, and could hold a unit of about 120. In Britain it is not known if these units were the same size as the first-century German *numeri*. If this was the case, then at most about two barrack blocks would be required to house them. If alternating sections of troops were permanently out on patrol, it is possible that less space would be necessary at the headquarters, much like the rota system or double watches of a nineteenth-century ship-of-the-line, where the men coming off duty slept in the spaces which the new watch had just vacated. If the *cunei* were mounted troops, some stabling would be necessary, if only for sick or injured animals, while the rest were perhaps picketed or corralled outside the forts.

At Housesteads and Great Chesters on the Wall, and at High Rochester, where *numeri* are known to have been stationed, the rampart backs were removed at some stage, perhaps to accommodate extra buildings, but it cannot be proved that this had anything to do with housing troops, and the alterations may not be contemporary with the addition of extra units. Various suggestions, all impossible to prove, have been made about how the extra troops were accommodated in forts. It cannot be demonstrated that any special arrangements were made for them in the interior of the forts or that alterations were made to the internal buildings. One suggestion is that the *exploratores* lived outside the forts, and another is that the barracks may have had upper storeys.

The *numeri* appear on several frontiers of the Roman Empire. It has been suggested that they were irregulars, who were with, rather than in, the Roman army; but after the investigations at the fort at Hesselbach in Upper Germany, it was concluded that since this fort and others like it possessed headquarters buildings, the troops were part of the army, presumably paid three times a year just as other troops were, and perhaps discharged after serving for a specified term. Where they were brigaded with another unit, as they were on the third-century British frontier, the headquarters buildings of the forts concerned would have had clerks to deal with the administration of the *numeri*.

Included in the titles of some, but not all, of the *numeri* is their description as *exploratores*, signifying that they acted as scouts, but precisely how is not clear. The soldiers of the cohorts carried out patrols, but it is not known if the two types of unit acted in concert with each other. The main body of the patrol may have been flanked by the *exploratores*, especially when moving in broken country or in hills and mountains. An inscription from Jedburgh, naming the *cohors I Vardullorum* and the Raeti Gaesati together, indicates that this may be the case, except that the *cohors I Vardullorum* was based at High Rochester, with a *numerus exploratorum* but with no mention of the Raeti, which are attested at Risingham. On occasions the *exploratores* perhaps went out on scouting missions by themselves, possibly to the south of Hadrian's Wall as well as to the north of it.

It is not possible to say how the new dual units operated on Hadrian's Wall and in the outpost forts, but it shows that someone had been thinking about how the frontier could be controlled, with more mobile troops, perhaps even with more expendable troops who may have been paid less than the soldiers of the cohorts, but this is to speculate further than the evidence will allow. Other changes on the Wall imply that some thought had been put into its function. Repair work had begun before Severus and Caracalla arrived in Britain for the campaigns, and continued after the war was over. The ancient historians, who wrote at a much later period, make great play of the Wall, as though the establishment of this frontier was the culmination of Severus's plan for the north of Britain. Although he did not build the frontier, he and Caracalla did alter it in several ways. Some of the turrets were given up, and in one or two cases the Wall was repaired and built over the sites of turrets, which were never rebuilt. If the theory about patrols is correct then the turrets as lookout towers would be less useful, since surveillance would be conducted much further afield. Even though this is probably how the units of the Hadrianic system operated, it does seem that there was greater emphasis on reconnaissance and observation than previously. In the milecastles, the northern gates were often narrowed, or completely built up. The Vallum was not put back into commission, perhaps because there was now no need for it, whatever its original purpose had been under Hadrian. From the civilian point of view the decommissioning of the Vallum enabled them to live in new settlements (*vici*) close by the forts themselves, instead of being divorced from the Wall on the south side of the Vallum.

The garrisons in the forts of the hinterland of the Wall also seem to have operated in the same way as the Wall forts, in that units of scouts or additional troops were added, at least at the fort at Lanchester in County Durham, which was built probably in the reign of Gordian III (238 to 244). It held a quingenary cohort of Lingones, and a vexillation of Suebi, from Germany, probably a mounted unit. At Burgh by Sands a unit of Mauri (Moors) arrived to replace the *cuneus Frisiorum*, which was sent to Papcastle. There may have been more of these units, for which evidence has not yet been discovered, or perhaps some of them were never commemorated on inscriptions. The fort at Ribchester, where some of the Sarmatian cavalry was sent in the reign of Marcus Aurelius, seems to have fulfilled a special function, since the commanders of the unit in at least two cases were legionary centurions, who describe themselves as also commanders of the region. Other examples are known from different parts of the Empire where the fort commander was also responsible for the area, one of the most famous, from a later period, being Flavius Abbinaeus, the prefect of the cavalry unit at the fort at Dionysias in Egypt, who was called upon to adjudicate in civilian disputes, and fortunately for historians he left a detailed archive of his correspondence.

CITIZENSHIP FOR ALL

Probably the most far-reaching and most lasting of Caracalla's acts was the *Constitutio Antoniniana*, the extension of Roman citizenship to all freeborn inhabitants of the Empire. The date is sometimes confidently asserted to be 212, but this is disputed and the law could have been passed in 213 after the murder of Geta, perhaps to mollify dissenters, or even in the following year. The ancient authors do not give this measure great coverage, and Dio, who notes it in passing, classifies it among other schemes for fundraising, since on becoming Roman citizens, everyone would be liable to pay the taxes that applied to citizens. The revenues from the tax raised, chiefly on inheritances, went into the *aerarium militare* which Augustus had created in AD 6 to provide pensions for the soldiers. After all, Caracalla had been advised by Severus to pay the soldiers and ignore everyone else, and the pension scheme was just as important as annual military pay, especially if new recruits were to be attracted to serve in the army. Caracalla's attention to the army was assiduous, so his main purpose may well have been to raise more taxes destined for the upkeep of veterans. Severus had already given the soldiers a pay rise, and Caracalla had given them another, so there were probably mutterings through clenched teeth in dark corners about the taxation involved in the grant of citizenship, along the lines of how the soldiers were surely earning enough now to pay for their own pensions instead of having to draw on the military treasury, for which a large proportion of the tax payments were destined.

There were legal advantages in becoming a Roman citizen, so the provincials would derive some benefit from the enfranchisement. For instance no citizen could be condemned to die by crucifixion, but by the early third century many of the former legal privileges had been somewhat eroded. Emphasis was now on rank and wealth rather than citizenship, so the *Constitutio* did not iron out all inequalities. Society was divided into *honestiores* and *humiliores*, the latter being people of low rank who were treated differently at law, and more severe punishments were meted out to them than to *honestiores*. The main advantage of the grant of citizenship was that it promoted unity of the Empire and a shared sense of *Romanitas*, despite the inequalities that still survived.

One feature of the grant that is visible in all provinces is the almost universal adoption of the name Aurelius. Custom dictated that new citizens took the name of the person who had made the grant, so the insistence of Severus and Caracalla on their connection with Marcus Aurelius resulted in a large proportion of Aurelii all over the Empire from the early third century onwards. The family of Marcus Aurelius Lunaris, a merchant with interests in York and Lincoln, and business interests in Boulogne, was certainly one of the beneficiaries of the *Constitutio Antoniniana*.

THE AGE OF THE SOLDIER-EMPERORS

The reign of Caracalla ended with his assassination in 217 by the Praetorian Prefect Marcus Opellius Macrinus, while the Emperor and the army were on campaign in the east, against Parthia. Macrinus was the first non-senator to become Emperor, proclaimed by the army. He was not a soldier himself, but was an administrator and jurist, attributes that were increasingly required of Praetorian Prefects rather than military experience. He did not survive for very long, because he had perhaps reckoned without the women of the extended Severan family, based in Syria, and more than ready to proclaim their own Emperor. Caracalla's mother, Julia Domna, who did not long survive her son, had a sister, Julia Maesa, already equipped with two grandsons, the elder of whom was Marcus Avitus Bassianus. Maesa persuaded the soldiers that Caracalla was his real father, so Bassianus was declared Emperor on 16 May 218, taking the name of Marcus Aurelius Antoninus. He is more infamously known as Elagabalus, whose reign was mercifully short, ending when his teenage cousin, Severus Alexander, replaced him in 222.

Upper and Lower Britain did not feature in the literary sources for the early third century. It was not the important province that it once was, and the focus of the Empire for a while was the eastern frontier, continuously threatened by the Persians. The young Emperor Severus Alexander campaigned against this formidable enemy, not entirely unsuccessfully, from 231 to 232. But then the German tribes from beyond the Rhine broke through the frontier in the Taunus-Wetterau region, causing destruction and mayhem as they poured through into Roman territory. Severus Alexander mounted a campaign from Mainz, but he was not aggressive enough for the soldiers, who killed him in 235 and made a fellow soldier, Maximinus Thrax, the Thracian, Emperor in his place. He had risen from the ranks to become an officer, trusted by the men. The Senate ratified their choice, but not with good grace. The age of the soldier-Emperors had begun, in which the British provinces played little part. After only three years the African provinces declared the proconsul Gordianus as Emperor, and three generations of this family took power. Gordian III was killed during a Parthian campaign in 244. His successor, Philip the Arab, survived until 249. From this time onwards the Romans had to fight on two fronts, sometimes simultaneously. The main troubles came from the new power in the east, where the Sassanian Persians had ousted the Parthian regime and adopted a more aggressive attitude towards Rome. At the same time sporadic raids and invasions were mounted by the tribes pressing on the Rhine and Danube frontiers. Some of the tribes simply wanted to settle inside the Empire, and thousands of them were brought in at various times and given lands to farm, usually on the understanding that they would provide recruits for the army. Other tribes or groups of tribes posed a more serious threat, carrying off booty and captives when they raided Roman territory.

As the invasions across the frontiers became more frequent, civil wars broke out, as would-be usurpers seized power and were then toppled, and not one of the legitimate Emperors, some of whom started out as usurpers, ruled for any significant length of time, or died in his bed. The circumstances were dire. A rapid succession of Emperors, all elevated by the armies in the provinces, was combined with continuing pressure of the Goths on the Danube frontier and German tribes across the Rhine. A lack of confidence in the ability of the legitimate regimes to deal with the various situations facing different provincial governors prompted some of them to seize power in the only way they knew how, by declaring themselves Emperors and taking command of the armies. At a time when all resources were needed to combat threats from the tribes across the Rhine and the Danube, and from the more sophisticated Persians, the Romans were gradually committing corporate suicide by fighting each other. When the troops elevated the Emperor Valerian in 253, he took as colleague his adult son, Publius Licinius Gallienus, and it seemed that there might at last be a chance of restoring order in the whole Empire. Gallienus took charge of the west, and Valerian set off to deal with the war against the Persians in the east.

In 260, disaster struck. All the frontiers fell, and the Persians captured the Emperor Valerian. From 260 Gallienus ruled alone, beset on all sides with seemingly insurmountable troubles. He did not choose a colleague to rule with him, even though he had several relatives who might possibly have filled such a role. Out of purely filial piety he could have prepared a campaign against the Persians to try to rescue his father, but he did not do so. It would have endangered the rest of the Empire to have used up resources for an eastern campaign when the Persians were currently in the ascendancy. The German tribes were poised for invasion, into Germany, Gaul and the Danube provinces, usurpers sprang up overnight like mushrooms, and the eastern and western extremities of the Empire began to split off under their own rulers. The Palmyrene leader Odenathus restored the situation after the Persians invaded Syria and the provinces of the east, and set up a regime that received some recognition from Gallienus, and in the western provinces the troops elevated their own Emperor.

Faced with the disintegration of the Empire, and restricted to the central area and the Danube provinces, Gallienus was forced to make the best use of the resources and troops that he had immediately to hand, and he made adaptations to the army and administration to cope with the difficult circumstances. His prime concern was the army. There was a pressing need for rapid response and increased mobility as various tribes attacked different parts of the Empire, and various usurpers had to be dealt with, so Gallienus collected together all the cavalry that he possessed among the *alae* and *cohortes equitatae*, and welded the troopers into a mobile force with its own commander, perhaps enlisting any soldiers who had mounts and could fight from horseback. He included the legionary cavalry from the various legions or vexillations that were stationed in his shrinking Empire when it began to fragment, and he is said to have increased their numbers. Normally the legions possessed about 120 horsemen, who could fight as cavalry but were more likely used as messengers. Gallienus increased the numbers to over 700. This mounted army has been labelled the forerunner of the later mobile armies, the *comitatenses*, the mobile units that began life under Constantine, but the linkage is not proven since no one knows what happened to the cavalry force after Gallienus was assassinated, and it disappears from the record as a distinct entity.

Gallienus employed the equestrians to a much greater extent than previous Emperors had done. The occasional employment of equestrians in military posts had begun as far back as the reign of Marcus Aurelius, but it was Severus who regularly appointed them to posts in the army and the government that had normally been in the senatorial sphere. In the early Empire, the career path for senators and to a lesser extent for equestrians had combined an alternating succession of civil and military posts, none of which was held for a protracted period. From the second century onwards, there was a tendency towards professionalism and specialisation in either a civil or military career, with men remaining in their posts a little longer. This compensated for the fact that in the early Empire quite high-ranking officers gained appointments to the armies without the need for any military experience. By the third century it was not social position or birth that counted, but military professionalism and permanence, and the equestrians increasingly displayed the necessary criteria. Gallienus took this one step further, and divorced senators from military commands, probably by issuing an edict to this effect. The process cannot have been completed all at once, and there were some senators still in command of troops for a considerable time, until Diocletian gave the final coup de grace to senatorial military careers.

Equestrian provincial governors were not unknown in the early Empire. Augustus had decreed that the governor of Egypt should always be an equestrian prefect, and equestrians had governed some provinces temporarily when the senatorial governor had been killed or had died. Severus had appointed equestrians as provincial governors, usually with the title *praeses*. Gallienus made this a permanent feature, and after the mid-third century the number of senatorial governors declined, but senators do not disappear altogether, since they were still appointed to Imperial consular provinces. It seems that equestrians governed the provinces that were most threatened by external or internal unrest.

THE GALLIC EMPIRE

These reforms of Gallienus did not immediately affect the British provinces, since they were divorced from the Empire until some years after the assassination of Gallienus in 268. Nor did the turmoil in the western half of the Empire from the reign of Caracalla to the formation of the Gallic Empire affect the British provinces directly. The Lower province, governed by a legionary commander of praetorian rank was not one of the foremost places where promotions could be gained, nor was the Upper province much better for aspiring consular governors. As far as is known, no British governor was declared Emperor by the troops, but the governor of Lower Germany, Marcus Cassianus Latinius Postumus, was chosen by the army of the Rhine, and became the first Emperor of the *Imperium Galliarum*, the Gallic Empire.

This was not a nationalist movement to bring the Gallic provinces back to their original tribal organisation, but was a thoroughly Roman administrative system, ruled by Roman laws, with a Senate and two consuls elected annually, and a Praetorian Guard for the protection of the Emperor. Postumus was chosen by the Rhine army to rule because neither the soldiers nor the population had any confidence in the legitimate Emperor Gallienus to protect them from invasion, not necessarily because he was incompetent, though that accusation was levelled against him later, but because the problems of merely staying afloat at this time were overwhelming.

All of Gaul, with the possible exception of Narbonensis, declared for Postumus, and he was joined by the two German provinces, and then Spain, and then the two British provinces. Inscriptions show that he also commanded much of Raetia, which gave him access to the Alpine passes. Even though he could have invaded Italy if he had felt so inclined and was willing to risk a battle with Gallienus, Postumus ruled his western Empire without making any attempt to usurp power at Rome. He was more interested in the protection of his own area than in outright usurpation, a feature which possibly applies to many so-called rebellions in various parts of the Empire from the third century onwards. It was unfortunate that the only way to achieve self-help and protection in a Roman province or group of provinces was to claim Imperial power, which enabled the chosen or self-proclaimed leader to command armies and organise the civilians for the purpose of defence which the central regime could not provide, for any number of reasons. Postumus launched himself vigorously into the task of protecting his frontiers and driving back the tribesmen who threatened provincial security. His task was no sinecure, since even if he could achieve a lasting peace, he would have to rebuild shattered communities and military installations. Archaeological evidence reveals a desolate picture of abandoned frontier forts, and destruction of civilian dwellings. Gallic towns were not walled, even though there had been serious disruption in the 230s when tribes broke through into the German provinces and reached Gaul.

Gallienus never officially recognised Postumus as ruler of the Gallic Empire, unlike his treatment of the eastern secessionist state, governed by the Palmyrene nobleman Odenathus, whose rule was tolerated if not properly sanctioned. There may have been two attempts to regain the west in 261 and again in 265 or 266, but Gallienus never succeeded in winning back his lost territory. Almost another decade passed before the Roman Empire was reunited. After the assassination of Gallienus in 268, the Gallic Empire itself began to fragment. Attempted usurpations blossomed and shrivelled in quick succession in a single year. In 269 Laelianus rebelled against Postumus, who defeated him but then faced another usurper called Marius. In the fighting against Marius, Postumus refused to allow his troops to sack Mainz, and so the disappointed soldiers killed him. The story demonstrates the extent to which the troops had become dissociated from provincial concerns, and how easily a Roman army would sack a Roman city.

The next Gallic Emperor, Victorinus, was proclaimed in 269, by which time the Emperor Gallienus had been killed and a new Emperor, Claudius Gothicus, had replaced him. Claudius sent a general against Victorinus, and though this expedition achieved nothing, Victorinus was quickly assassinated and replaced by the last Gallic Emperor, Esuvius Tetricus. When the end came it was by no momentous upheaval, but more of a damp squib. Claudius Gothicus died in January 270, and after a few skirmishes with potential rivals, Aurelian succeeded him.

The Emperor Aurelian was nicknamed 'hand on hilt' and was a determined individual with a proper sense of his own importance, perhaps derived from the knowledge that self-advertisement was one way of making people believe in him. He declared himself a god on earth, taking the ideology of the divine house of the Emperors one stage further and paving the way for Diocletian's divine rule. In a short reign Aurelian achieved a great deal. He turned his attention first to the Palmyrene Empire, welded together under Odenathus and then his wife Zenobia. By 273 the east was back in the Roman fold. Between fighting various tribesmen such as the Alamanni and Juthungi, Aurelian turned to the west, and began to move against the Gallic Empire. The sources are confused about whether or not there was a battle, but it seems certain that there must have been some fighting, but not a cataclysmic war. It was all over quite quickly. Tetricus was captured but not executed. He was put on display in Aurelian's triumph in Rome, but then he was given a post in Italy and kept his fortune and lands intact.

BRITAIN UNDER THE GALLIC EMPERORS

There is very little evidence from Britain as to how the two provinces fared under the rule of the Gallic Emperors. When Postumus was declared Emperor, the fate of the governors and officials who were already in the island is unknown, but there is no record of wholesale slaughter on the part of Postumus or attempted rebellion on the part of officials in Britain. There was no real choice except to join the Gallic Empire, to contribute taxes, and carry on as before. Revenues would be important to pay the armies of the west, but it is not known how the financial administration was organised in Britain, or whether Postumus siphoned off resources to manage the defence of his provinces.

He governed as a Roman Emperor and presumably made appointments to fill the administrative and military posts in Britain. He may have appointed the *praeses* Octavius Sabinus, attested on an inscription as commander of the troops at Lancaster, at some time between 262 and 266. Since Sabinus was of senatorial status, it seems that either Postumus ignored Gallienus's policy of divorcing senators from military commands and replacing them with equestrians, or as has been suggested, there may have been a shortage of equestrian officers to fill military posts in the Gallic Empire. Postumus would have to utilise all the manpower he could find to command the troops and govern the provinces, just as Gallienus made innovations to the army and the administration in the parts of the Empire left to him.

In the north-west of Britain the first evidence for the *civitas Carvetiorum* at Carlisle dates from the reign of Postumus, so it is suggested that he may have authorised its establishment, though there is no support for this theory. The earliest inscription attesting the existence of the town is dated to about 259. This inscription was recorded in the sixteenth century but the stone is now lost. Part of the text was interpreted as *C[ivitas] Carvetiorum*, but since it is a tombstone and not a building inscription, it does not help to establish the date of foundation of the *civitas* capital. On balance the *civitas* was probably established somewhat earlier that the reign of Postumus, but perhaps developed under the Gallic Emperors.

Sources for the third-century history of the British provinces are in short supply, but archaeological evidence from the fort at Reculver, on the north coast of Kent, once suggested that it was built in the early second century, probably to watch the Thames estuary. Pottery from the fort was dated to *c.*220. More recent scrutiny of the evidence has challenged this early third-century date, placing the fort at Reculver to a period at least thirty to forty years later than originally thought, in the mid-third century, and in its early years it was contemporary with the Gallic Empire.

A fort of similar style and shape at Brancaster on the Norfolk coast is considered to be contemporary with Reculver, and is perhaps also to be dated to about the 250s or the 260s. It watched over the entrance to the Wash. These two forts are built on the standard pattern of first- and second-century forts, with a playing-card shape with rounded corners, but Reculver is too large for the unit that was brought there from Maryport on the Cumbrian coast, *cohors I Baetasiorum*. It has been suggested that other units like the *numeri* of Hadrian's Wall and the outpost forts were stationed with this auxiliary cohort, or that part of the fleet, the *Classis Britannica*, was seconded to these bases, since a coastal fort can deal only with advance warning of the approach of pirates or other hostiles, or the garrisons can mount an attack on land once forces have come ashore. In order to operate more efficiently the forts required support by naval squadrons to help ward off invasions or pirates.

There is no record of the British fleet as an entity after the mid-second century, and the naval base at Dover and its companion across the Channel at Boulogne seem to have been given up by the 270s, though a fort at Dover was still occupied. However, tile stamps from the fleet indicate that some other coastal bases were used, for instance at Lympne and at the site of the later fort at Portchester in the mid-third century. At some time between 270 and 290, more forts were built at Burgh Castle near Yarmouth, Bradwell, maybe Walton Castle, Richborough, Dover and Lymnpe, but the dating evidence can provide nothing more precise than this window of two decades.

These individual pieces of evidence, not necessarily exactly contemporary or even related, could possibly suggest that a new threat had developed around the coasts of the south and south-east, perhaps from the Frankish and Saxon pirates who first appeared in strength *c*.250, and were such a menace towards the end of the third century, when special measures had to be taken, by appointing Carausius to eradicate them. The forts listed here, including the earlier ones at Reculver and Brancaster, were later incorporated into the Saxon Shore, but this label derives from the late fourth century and should not be applied at this early period. There may be more coastal forts from the early third century that have disappeared or not yet been discovered, and it is postulated that a series of watchtowers guarded the banks of the Thames at the approach to London, but this is based on only one example at Shadwell, on the reasonable assumption that it could not have functioned very well in isolation.

It simply is not known how much direct influence the Gallic Emperors were able to bring to bear in Britain. The British provinces recognised Victorinus, as attested by the appearance of his name on milestones, and an inscription also records Tetricus. When Aurelian reunited the Empire, the British governors readily acknowledged him in the same fashion. There was perhaps no rabid witch-hunt to eradicate supporters of Postumus and his successors, but there would be replacements of officials and military commanders who had sympathised with the Gallic Emperors. Unfortunately there is not enough evidence to shed any light on how this was done. When Severus defeated Albinus he seems to have confiscated villas and lands of his supporters in Britain, but before and after Aurelian's activity in Gaul, far from showing signs of stunted growth, Britain had started to reveal an increased prosperity, at least in the private sphere, which provided the foundation for the even greater prosperity of the fourth century.

PRIVATE AND CORPORATE ENTERPRISE

Much thought has been given to the question why the towns in Britain, which were not affected by the invasions across the Rhine like the towns of Gaul, erected defences. This is in contrast to Gaul, where the town dwellers did not begin to think of walls until relatively late, after they had experienced destruction and disaster. It is suggested that in Romano-British towns most of the members of the *ordo* possessed houses inside the towns, whereas the Gallic town councillors lived outside in their villas, and therefore took less interest in corporate than in private matters.

As has already been mentioned, town councils were not allowed to erect defences without permission from the Emperor. One reason for Imperial concern and caution over such requests for defences was that potential usurpers could utilise defended towns to defy the government, and another reason was that in several cases the councils in different provinces overreached themselves financially when they started building works, and had to be rescued. In Britain, the *coloniae* were probably in a better position to provide themselves with walls, as at Lincoln and

Gloucester. These colonies were created in the old legionary fortresses where there were already substantial earth ramparts, to which stone fronts were added in the late first and early second centuries. The walls at Colchester were built in stone from the first, joining the monumental free-standing arches built to mark the entrances into the town. Arches like the Colchester examples preceded the walls of other towns, and were converted into proper gateways.

Until the later third century it may be that the earth defences that had been started around some towns (not all of which were completed) were once thought to be adequate, but subsequent generations considered that stone walls were required for security, or possibly for prestige. There would be considerable expense involved in building a stone circuit, but this is what several town councils achieved in the later third century. From a historical point of view there seems to have been no threat which could have occasioned such a series of building projects in Britain, and in some cases it was a leisurely process, as though there was no urgency, which is why it is suggested that it was done for prestige rather than actual defence.

However, the absence or otherwise of actual threat cannot be properly assessed at a remove of nearly two thousand years. What motivates people is sometimes not actuality, but perception, and perceived threat may have been the reason why so many British towns provided themselves with defences in the later third century. The available evidence does not allow for more than speculation about the threats that may have been perceived, but although it is not recorded, there may have been low-level threat from roaming bands of lawless people, with no other means of support except theft, similar to the bandits led by Bulla in Italy during the reign of Severus, or the so-called Bagaudae in Gaul in the late third century. A set of stone walls and some sturdy town gates would be a useful asset if this were the case. The possible attacks on the coasts, mentioned above, may have rendered even the inland towns vulnerable, or at least nervous. There may even have been some official encouragement to build town walls in Britain, since a town that was able to defend itself from low-level attacks would relieve the army of the necessity of coming to the aid of temporarily beleaguered towns. Only in cases of real sieges would the army have to send detachments to assist.

Defence works can deter attackers, but walls cannot stop determined invaders, unless they are properly manned. Unfortunately nothing is known about how the towns were actively defended. The Romans generally discouraged the establishment of semi-military formations, and even the desire to create a fire brigade was subject to careful Imperial scrutiny. The town councils may have appointed various inhabitants on a rota system to guard the gates, or at least to open and close them and keep the keys, but defending walls would surely require practice sessions and weapons training, and nothing has come to light to elucidate this problem. Detachments of troops may have been stationed in the towns. There is a lack of inscriptions to support this idea, and even if altars and gravestones turn up in towns, naming individuals from military units, it does not mean that whole units were garrisoned there.

The building work in the towns and at various villa sites is difficult to date accurately but archaeologists have repeatedly found that there was an upsurge in construction and refurbishment, starting *c.*250. A Roman-style house with painted plaster was built at Droitwich. At Brough-on-Humber, a *civitas* capital that seems to have been a late developer, stone buildings started to appear. The rate and the quality of construction increased between 270 and 275, not just of workmanlike structures but of well-appointed dwellings. A villa at Whitcombe, already showing signs of development as a large concern from *c.*250, was embellished and altered *c.*275, and another at Frocester Court had a formal garden laid out – not the sort of thing to contemplate if the country was under some dire threat. Several villas appeared around the town of Bath. Villas on the Gallic pattern, with a large central courtyard, or a central room within the villa, started to appear in the later third century. The most common suggestion is that these villas represent an influx of farmers and wealthier people from Gaul, possibly when the troubles began that gave rise to the formation of the Gallic Empire, or perhaps some people migrated when Aurelian approached, not knowing what his policy would be towards supporters of the Gallic regime. Without evidence as to who were the owners of these buildings in Britain, this is all that can be said, but the appearance of such houses dispels the idea that the third century was a period of decline in the whole of Britain.

One cause for complaint seems to have been Aurelian's monetary reforms, which were entirely necessary, but the reforms of the currency weighed heavily on the inhabitants of Britain, because the Emperor insisted that his new coins should be adopted and exchanged for the old ones at a very disadvantageous rate. This may be one of the reasons why there was some kind of rebellion, in one of the two British provinces, in 276, a year after Aurelian was assassinated as he was about to embark on a campaign against the Persians.

9

Brief Independence AD 275 to 305

After the Gallic Empire was re-absorbed into the Roman world, it is not known how the two British provinces were governed, or who the governors were. If the normal state of affairs was resumed, there should have been a consular governor in London and a praetorian commander in York, in charge of VI Victrix and the Lower province, but inscriptions are lacking and the literary sources do not elucidate what happened in Britain, nor were the ancient historians much concerned with the little island, when all over the rest of the Roman world frontiers were threatened and new Emperors came and went in rapid succession.

Aurelian fell victim to a plot hatched by some of his officers. One of the officials of the Imperial court allegedly found a list containing the names of men who were about to be executed, so the officers feared for their lives, and struck down the Emperor before he could strike them. The assassination of Aurelian seems to have been an ill-considered moment of panic, with no consideration for the immediate future. The conspirators were so interested in ridding themselves of the danger that Aurelian allegedly posed that they overlooked the fact that another Emperor would be required quite quickly. Consequently there was no one waiting in the wings for them to support as a candidate for the purple. Aurelian's death left a legacy of unfinished business. He had been on his way to make war on the Persians, the perennial thorn in the side of the Roman Empire, but this momentous task was bequeathed to his successors. He and his army were in Thrace when he was killed and his funeral was held there. He was the first Emperor whose remains were interred somewhere other than Rome.

The soldiers were angry that their Emperor had been killed and made it quite clear that they were disinclined to support any of the remaining army officers as the next Emperor. It was almost unprecedented in these turbulent times for the Senate to be involved in the choice of the next Emperor, though the senators were usually asked to ratify the choice and to bestow Imperial powers upon him. But this time the Senate's role was more decisive. The soldiers refused to declare for anyone at all, and they sent an embassy to Rome to ask the Senate to choose a candidate for them. The senator Marcus Claudius Tacitus was in Italy when he was made Emperor, and though quite elderly, he rose to the task. He had Aurelian deified, which was the normal procedure except for Emperors of ill repute, but it is permissible to wonder how posthumous deification could have bettered the position of Aurelian, who was a self-declared god during his lifetime. Next, Tacitus rounded up and executed most of the men who had assassinated his predecessor, though some of them escaped. Tacitus spent his short reign fighting the Goths, but he died, or was killed, after about six months. No one seems certain how he met his end. He had made his brother Florian Praetorian Prefect, and the army declared for him as the next Emperor, but at the same time the governor of the provinces of Syria, Phoenicia and Egypt, Marcus Aurelius Probus, was also elevated by his troops. There was a skirmish between the rival armies, but Florian lost, and Probus became Emperor in 276.

The main source for this period is the late author Zosimus, but his work covering most of the reign of Probus is lost. There are two brief references to Britain in what survives of his work:

[During his campaigns on the Rhine] Probus captured some Burgundians and Vandals and sent them to Britain. Living in the island they were useful to the Emperor when someone rebelled. (Zosimus 1.68.3)

> Through the Moor Victorinus, Probus suppressed a rebellion in Britain. It was
> at the suggestion of Victorinus that he had appointed the rebel to be governor
> of Britain. Probus sent for Victorinus, blaming him for the advice, and then
> despatched him to fight the rebel. He set out immediately and disposed of the
> usurper. (Zosimus 1.66.2)

This story is also relayed by the author Zonaras, but with a few more
details. He says that Victorinus asked to be sent to deal with the man
he had recommended, and then he set off, pretending to be a fugitive
from Probus so that he could be received as a friend at the governor's
headquarters. Then he killed him in the night and returned to Probus.
In this version of the story, less vague than that of Zosimus, there is no
question of battles and slaughter, or any involvement of the army, just a
quick assassination.

It is not clear whether there were two rebellions in Britain, or only
one, because Zosimus describes the capture of the Burgundians and
Vandals, and their subsequent assistance to the Emperor in suppressing
a rebellion, after he tells the story of the rebel governor despatched by
Victorinus. Also it is not clear whether the governor who rebelled was
the consular governor of Upper Britain, and if it was this rebellious
governor that the tribesmen helped to quell, it is not known how they
did so. Were they living in Britain as settlers on the land, perhaps with
obligations to provide recruits, or were they formed into military
units like the *numeri* of the northern frontier, and if so, where were
they stationed? Some of the tribesmen who were settled on vacant
territories in Gaul in the late Roman Empire were called *laeti*, and they
were granted farming lands on condition that they provided soldiers.
In Norfolk, it is known that there was a group of Germanic settlers,
assumed to be *laeti*, in the late Roman period, but it is impossible to
demonstrate any link with these tribesmen and the Burgundians and
Vandals sent to Britain in Probus's reign.

Aurelian had been preparing an expedition against the Persians when
he was assassinated, which left this important task for his successors
to carry out. For some time Probus had been too occupied with the

problems of the west and the security of the frontiers. He dealt with several would-be usurpers and invading tribesmen at the same time, and he even took the war into barbarian territory across the Rhine, establishing some forts beyond the frontiers. Unfortunately it is not known where these forts were located. When the fighting was over he was said to have restored sixty towns in Gaul, which indicates how widespread the damage of the invasion in the 260s had been. Probably in 278 or 279, he turned his attention to the Danube, and when peace was made with the tribes, he began to plan for another eastern campaign. It was an auspicious time to attack, because the Persian king was in no position to fight an external enemy while he was trying to re-establish his authority over his own dominions.

For reasons which remain unknown, the army was tiring of Probus, even though his reign was so far successful. The soldiers may have been upset because he allegedly boasted that soon there would be universal peace, and there would be no further need for armies, which is similar to modern times, when people are told that they are all redundant but would they just carry on working hard, please, until the management can decide when their dismissal will occur. Probably in 282 the Praetorian Prefect Marcus Aurelius Carus rebelled. Troops were sent against him but they went over to him instead. Probus was killed by his own soldiers, perhaps just before Carus was declared Emperor towards the end of 282. The new Emperor had two sons, Carinus and Numerianus, and like Valerian and Gallienus before them, Carus and Carinus each took responsibility for one half of the Empire, Carus and his younger son Numerianus taking the east and continuing with Probus's Persian campaign, and Carinus going to the west, but firstly to Rome, where he was to get married. It is assumed that he asked the Senate to ratify the army's choice of Emperor Carus, who elevated both his sons to the rank of Augustus.

The only reference to Britain during the short reign of these three Emperors is the title that Carinus adopted, Britannicus Maximus, in 284. It implies that there had been a successful campaign in Britain, but against whom, and why, is not explained in the sources. It is not even known if Carinus himself came to Britain, or whether he won a victory through one of his generals. The reason for the campaign may have concerned a rebellion by one of the governors, or the army, in protest against the death of Probus, or to make a rival claim as Emperor. Or it could have been a skirmish against the Frankish and Saxon pirates who appear to have gained control of the North Sea and the coasts of Gaul and Britain at about this time, and very soon a general called Carausius was charged with the task of rounding them up. Shortly afterwards he seized power in Britain.

Diocletian, Maximianus and Carausius

The Emperor Carus gained a victory against the Persians, marching into the capital at Ctesiphon, and earning the title Parthicus Maximus. He did not live to enjoy his success, though no one is certain about the cause of his unexpected death, whether it was from disease, which was quite likely since he was not a young man, or whether he had been murdered. His son Numerianus succeeded him, but on the way back to Rome, he too died, or was killed. Suspicion fell on the Praetorian Prefect Lucius Aper, who apparently tried to conceal the death of Numerianus, explaining to the troops that the young man suffered from an eye complaint and had to travel in a closed litter to avoid the sand and dust. This ruse could not go on indefinitely with a corpse in a closed litter in a hot climate. A member of the Emperor's bodyguard revealed the truth of the situation, and personally executed Aper. This soldier was called Diocles, but when the troops declared him Emperor in November 284 he took the name Gaius Aurelius Valerius Diocletianus.

In the west, Carinus's days were numbered. He was killed by one of his officers, or perhaps by his Praetorian Prefect, and his army declared for Diocletian. It was some time before Imperial attention turned to Britain. Diocletian decided that the Empire was too large for one man to govern and to protect, and chose a colleague to rule with him, Marcus Aurelius Maximianus, who was perhaps made Caesar *c.*285. His rank is disputed, and it is quite possible that he did not serve a brief apprenticeship as Caesar at all, but was made Augustus immediately.

Received opinion inclines to the theory that he was Caesar in 285 and elevated to full Imperial colleague as Augustus in the following year.

Maximianus's first task was to rid the Gallic provinces of a group of bandits called the Bagaudae, probably comprising deserters from the army, poverty-stricken people who had abandoned their homes, plus a selection of assorted adventurers. When Severus had faced a similar problem in Italy at the beginning of the third century, the bandits were led by a man called Bulla, about whom various stories were related in the ancient sources, but in the case of the Bagaudae, no such details are known, and even the meaning of the name Bagaudae is obscure. During the campaign, Maximianus was ably assisted by Marcus Aurelius Mausaeus (or Maesius) Carausius, who, according to the ancient sources, was given a command at Boulogne (ancient Bononia). He may have been appointed by Carinus, and Maximianus may have confirmed him in his post, or it may have been Maximianus who chose him, but whatever command Carausius held, and what his title was, is not clear.

Carausius was a successful commander under Maximianus in the campaign against the Bagaudae, and was then given another command, to rid the coasts of Gaul and Britain of the Frankish and Saxon pirates. According to the late historian Aurelius Victor he was put in charge of preparing a fleet, which has been taken to mean that there was no fleet to speak of at the time, and a new one had to be created. This theory is derived from the fact that the *Classis Britannica*, originally based at Dover and Boulogne, disappears from view about 244 in the reign of Philip the Arab, and the base at Dover appears to have gone out of use in the 270s. It is hard to believe that the fleet had been allowed to decline, let alone disappear altogether, so an alternative theory is that it had been distributed among different bases, perhaps at the coastal forts such as Reculver and Brancaster, and at the slightly later fort at Richborough, among other places. Some support for this is found in one of the panegyrics to the Emperors that became fashionable from the late third century, this particular one being addressed to Constantius, stating that when Carausius rebelled he took over 'the fleet that used to protect the Gauls', indicating that it was a fleet of some long standing.

If this fleet was not called *Classis Britannica* at the time and had been relabelled, it would seem that it contained at least some remnants of the old British fleet.

Whatever Carausius's title may have been can only be speculated. He was not limited to naval matters, having some land forces under him, at least in Gaul, consisting probably of vexillations of several legions, including the British ones, all attested at a slightly later time on his coinage. By the end of the third century the title *Dux*, literally meaning leader, had come into fashion, usually denoting a military commander, as opposed to the civilian governor, who was usually called *praeses*. The *Dux* could command all the troops in a single province, but was more usually in charge of all the armed forces of a group of provinces, to protect the frontiers. Carausius's command fits this pattern, but he may also have been *praepositus*, a term that did not denote any specific rank. It was usually applied to any officer, whatever his original function and status, who was temporarily in charge of anything from one unit to a collection of different troops. Since the command against the pirates was, hopefully, intended to be a temporary one, Carausius also qualifies for this title. Unfortunately nothing has been found to suggest what his title was.

Carausius employed some Frankish troops in his land forces, and after some successful operations against Frankish and Saxon pirates, suspicions grew that the perhaps the Franks in his army were in collusion with their fellow tribesmen as double agents, giving Carausius information about where the next raids would occur, so that he could allow the pirates to land and march inshore, seize all the portable wealth they could find, then he could pounce on them, kill or capture them, and recover the booty. The trouble was that he did not seem so keen to redistribute it once he had retaken it. The suspicions grew to such proportions that Maximianus, to whom Carausius was responsible, had to be seen to take some action against him, otherwise he might have been accused of co-operating with his subordinate and quietly taking his share of the goods. In 286, or possibly the following year, Carausius decamped and sailed for Britain, before Maximianus could apprehend him.

THE EMPIRE OF CARAUSIUS

When he set up headquarters in Britain, Carausius still controlled the fleet, and the coast of Gaul with the port of Boulogne, and territory as far inland as Rouen. He was accused of stealing the fleet:

> By a nefarious act of theft, this fugitive pirate stole the fleet that used to protect the Gauls, and besides this many ships were built after the Roman fashion, a legion was taken over, some units of foreign troops were excluded [from the Empire], merchants from Gaul were levied, numbers of barbarians were brought over attracted by the spoils to be found in the provinces, and all of these were trained in seamanship … (*Panegyric addressed to Constantine*, AD 297)

The same panegyric makes it clear that the forces of the legitimate Emperors were in no fit state to wage a naval war. It seems that Maximianus had few if any ships, having lost some in a storm. So for the time being Carausius was secure in Britain.

There seems to have been no protest from the inhabitants or the army of the British provinces when Carausius took over. Surely if there had been any disruption the authors of the panegyrics in honour of the Emperors would have made some mileage out of it, but the only word about the attitude of the Britons was that they rejoiced when they were brought back into the Empire by the Caesar Constantius in 296. Carausius may have had contacts with the governors and officials of the British provinces while he was engaged in campaigns against the pirates, and he was already acquainted with the legions or at least some detachments of them. Otherwise he cultivated the Britons by sensible arrangements that benefitted them. His coinage was of a better standard than the Imperial coinage of the western provinces, which fostered trust and support for him, and facilitated trade. Aurelian had tried to reform the monetary system during the 270s, but the measures had been resented, so Carausius restored confidence by improving the coinage minted in Britain. He used the coins to represent himself as saviour, proclaiming himself *Restitutor Britanniae*, the restorer of Britain, and celebrating the spirit of Britain, *Genius Britanniae*, concentrating on

Britain as a country rather than a divided province. Some of his coins bore quotations from Virgil, emphasising that Carausius was the saviour of the provinces. On one of them, the reverse shows the personification of Britannia welcoming Carausius, and the words *expectate veni*, which is from Virgil's *Aeneid*, loosely translated meaning 'come, the one we long for'. Many of the coins display the letters RSR, which used to be interpreted as signifying *rationalis summae rei*, referring to an official in charge of financial affairs, assuming that Carausius had appointed such an official. One of the RSR issues also shows an abbreviation that for some time defied explanation: I.N.P.D.C.A. It has now been interpreted by historian Guy de la Bédoyère, who noted that these two sets of initials are also from a Virgilian quotation, in this case from a passage in the Fourth Eclogue: *redeunt Saturnia regna, iam nova progenies caelo demittutur alto*, the reign of Saturn returns, and a new progeny is sent down from on high. This remarkable coinage demonstrates the way in which Carausius portrayed himself as the saviour of the British provinces, and also shows that at least some of the officials, army officers and inhabitants possessed a high degree of literacy and were familiar with the classic works of a previous golden age. The coinage of Carausius was distributed in Britain and Gaul, and would send an unequivocal message to Maximianus and to Diocletian that the British provinces were better protected now than they once were.

LITERACY IN ROMAN BRITAIN – Text Box

The language of administration, government and law in Roman Britain was Latin, but since the native British languages were not eradicated, it is assumed that many of the Britons would be bilingual, speaking Celtic at home and using Latin for the business of the town councils and dealing with the Roman authorities. Written language in pre-Roman Britain is hardly attested, but there is evidence that papyrus was imported before the Roman conquest, suggesting that some form of writing was known, but which language or languages were written down remains obscure. The Gauls used Greek characters in writing, not Roman ones. British coinage used Latin terms such as *Rex* (king) and the Britons of the south who imported Roman goods perhaps dealt with traders in a mixture of Celtic and Latin.

When the Romans arrived, the predominant literate people would be the soldiers, perhaps not all of them, but because the Roman army was nothing if not bureaucratic, and records were kept for all manner of purposes, a proportion of military men perhaps spent their lives pen-pushing in offices in the headquarters buildings of various forts. Along with the Roman officials, from the earliest times after the conquest a whole host of traders and businessmen would take up residence in the new province, or set up offices to be run by subordinates while they themselves lived in other provinces. Wooden writing tablets have been found in a first-century context in London, clearly business documents, for which purpose literacy and numeracy would be vital in accounting and for formulating contracts and concluding business deals.

How far literacy spread among the Britons other than the town councillors and aristocracy is not known. Most especially in the rural areas there were probably many people who were bilingual but who perhaps had no use for writing skills. The workers in potteries and tile manufacture clearly had some knowledge of literacy, judging from the many graffiti on potsherds, whole pots, and tiles, the most famous being the enigmatic phrase incised in a tile '*Austalis dibus tredecim vagatur sib cotidim*', Austalis has been going off on his own for thirteen days. No one knows who Austalis was, or why a co-worker felt the need to proclaim to the world in writing what he had been doing, but the graffito attests that at least one of the workers could read and write.

Potsherds were often used for writing notes in the Roman world, probably to keep rough records for copying up later on papyrus. Potsherds from a variety of places in Roman Britain, including Colchester, Chelmsford and Chedworth villa, have been found with alphabets incised on them, rarely the full panoply of all the letters, but clearly enough this was a way of teaching the form of capital letters, though to whom and by whom cannot be known. Capitals were used for inscriptions and in some instances the stone carvers made mistakes in spelling, though like typing errors which indicate a bad aim on the part of the typist rather than illiteracy, this may be due to a lack of concentration.

For documents, the Romans used cursive script, a form of handwriting that differs from the capitals used on inscriptions as much as handwriting diverges from printed texts nowadays. During the Republic, records were kept of debates in the Senate and a form of shorthand was invented to cope with the rapidity of speech. The military and civil officials probably used the same technique, and the records that have survived on papyrus from Syria and Egypt show that many abbreviations were used in official documents. The writing tablets from Vindolanda provide the best examples of the cursive form of handwriting, and it is even possible to distinguish the writing styles of different people who wrote the documents and letters; for instance the famous invitation to the birthday party from Claudia Severa to the wife of Cerialis, commanding at Vindolanda, was probably written by a secretary, most likely a slave, and signed by Claudia.

If literacy was confined to the elite few and the officers of the Roman army, it does not imply that Britain was wholly devoid of culture. At Brough on Humber, a theatre was built and paid for by one of the town councillors, although it is not known where in the town it was situated. Someone presumably organised performances in it. The theatre at Verulamium looks like a cross between a theatre and an amphitheatre, but like the example at Brough, it would not have been built unless there was some possibility of using it, whether that involved the production of plays, poetry readings or something similar. Nothing is known of the book trade in Roman Britain, but the coinage of Carausius with Virgilian quotations indicated only by initials suggests that there were people who knew what the quotations were all about and had access to books of their own, rather than relying upon recitals or teaching in schools, and that literature of a former age was still available.

Little is known about how the government of the two Britains was carried out under Carausius. There may have been a *praeses* at York commanding the VI legion and the province, but no names have been preserved. What happened to the governor of Britannia Superior is not known. He may have survived and remained in his post as a subordinate to Carausius. On the other hand since Carausius made himself consul, it is likely that he governed the whole province, presumably with subordinates carefully chosen by himself and placed in administrative posts and in army commands. He represented himself as the saviour of Britain, not the Britains. How far his authority extended is debatable, but a milestone from Carlisle bearing his name shows that his writ ran in the north-west, in what was technically the province of Lower Britain. The important factor is that he protected the provinces, and probably kept the coasts as clear as possible of pirates.

The way in which he did so must be primarily due to his command of a fleet, but he may also have begun the process that welded the disparate forts of the south and south-west coasts into what later became the Saxon Shore. This topic recurs under several headings because its development took place over a long period of time and under different officials, but the name Saxon Shore is so entrenched that it seems as though the whole system sprang up all at once, fully fledged and with exactly the same purpose, under one or other of the commanders from the third to the fourth century, and that it functioned in the same way through all that period of time. This is not the case. Forts were built on the coasts at different times, most likely in response to slightly different circumstances. Reculver and Brancaster have already been mentioned, probably the earliest of the forts to guard the approaches to Britain along the Thames estuary and via the Wash. They were previously dated to the early third century but more recent scholarship has reassigned them to the mid-third century, perhaps contemporary with the first appearance of Frankish and Saxon pirates. At some date between 270 and 290 forts were added at Burgh Castle, Bradwell, probably Walton Castle, Richborough, Dover and Lympne. It is suggested that Carausius added the large fort at Portchester, where the later Norman castle, neatly ensconced in one corner and almost dwarfed, demonstrates just how enormous the Roman fort was.

The suggestion has been made that Carausius created the chain of forts or moulded the existing ones into a system to protect himself against attack from Maximianus. This is not generally accepted now, since it was just as much in Carausius's interests to protect the island from attack by pirates, who threatened the livelihood, if not the actual lives, of the people living near the coasts, and by their disruption of trade, the pirates threatened more than just the coastal population. If Carausius failed to protect the inhabitants and their business interests, he would very quickly have lost all credibility. It has been suggested that Diocletian's victory title of Britannicus Maximus was assumed because of Carausius's victories over the pirates before he was suspected of foul play. Subsequently Diocletian dropped the title, so it suggested that this was because Carausius was no longer the hero, but the villain who had rebelled. Whether or not this is correct, it is probable that his success against the pirates was one of the reasons why the British provincials, officials and soldiers accepted Carausius as their new commander-in-chief.

Maximianus was powerless to oust Carausius for some three years, because the invasions into Gaul and the problems of the Bagaudae kept him busy. He had no fleet to speak of at first but by 289 he seems to have been ready to tackle the independent Empire across the Channel. There is no information about this planned expedition other than that it failed, which the panegyrists put down to the weather. That is not unlikely, given the vagaries of the British climate and the dangers of crossing the short stretch of sea between Gaul and Britain. It is not even certain if Maximianus ever put to sea. This failure ensured peace and quiet for Carausius for the time being. Aurelius Victor says that Carausius was allowed to retain Imperial power, meaning that Diocletian and Maximianus had other things to think about and were content to leave Carausius where he was. He had shown no signs of wanting to invade the rest of Gaul even though he had a base at Boulogne and his troops covered Gallic territory for some distance inland. The danger that he represented was perhaps less than originally thought, but all parties could be certain that he would not be allowed to remain where he was, in command of the British provinces and the sea, on a permanent basis.

Carausius, like Albinus at the end of the second century, could not realistically share in the Imperial government of the Roman Empire, but he required the relevant Imperial titles because they shored up his authority, enabling him to govern Britain and command the troops. This was the dilemma that all so-called usurpers faced, some of them only anxious to take charge of their own territory and protect it, but without some accepted form of authority they could not command their subordinates, and in assuming that authority, they incurred the suspicion and wrath of the legitimate Emperors. In the 290s, Carausius started to issue coins declaring his equality with the existing Emperors. One of his coin legends proclaimed Imperial peace, *Pax Auggg*, the abbreviation signifying *pax Augusti*, and the three letter Gs each stood for an Emperor, indicating that Diocletian, Maximianus and Carausius himself all ranked as Augustus. Another legend was *Victoria Auggg*, but the coin that unequivocally expressed the status that Carausius claimed for himself was the one that he issued in 292, perhaps because he had got wind of further plans to oust him. It bears three portraits, Diocletian in the centre, flanked by Maximianus and Carausius, with the legend *Carausius et fratres sui*, Carausius and his brothers. Carausius needed to persuade the population of Britain that his rule was legitimate and approved by the other Emperors.

No confirmation of this status or offers of power-sharing ever issued from the Imperial court. Instead, Diocletian established the Tetrarchy, the rule of four Emperors, on 1 March 293. He and Maximianus remained as Augusti, and each chose a subordinate with the title of Caesar. Galerius became Caesar to Diocletian in the eastern half of the Empire, while Constantius was subordinate to Maximianus in the west, adopting the names Flavius Valerius Constantius. He was colloquially known as Constantius Chlorus, from his pale complexion.

In the same year that he became Caesar, Constantius prepared an attack on Carausius's Gallic possessions, and captured Boulogne. This was a blow to the British regime, and Carausius lost favour. One of his officers called Allectus, probably his Praetorian Prefect, assassinated him, and took over his powers, retaining them for about three years.

THE TETRARCHY AND DIOCLETIAN'S REFORMS

The term Tetrarchy is not one that Diocletian would have used to describe his new Imperial system. It is a Greek term describing a territory divided into four regions, each ruled by a Tetrarch, who is strictly a subordinate officer to an overall ruler. Diocletian had no intention of being a subordinate, but the rule of four men is neatly described by the old Greek term, employed by modern historians. The Roman world was too large even in peacetime for effective rule by one man, but in war, with so many problems caused by internal unrest in many provinces and by external threat to most of the frontiers, the task was superhuman to say the least. The theory behind the Tetrarchy was that the Empire could be divided into four zones with a senior or junior Emperor in charge, taking care of administrative and military affairs through their various subordinates. All the four men who shared power in the Tetrarchy were native Illyrians, and they were bound together with marriage ties, in the hope that this would ensure peace and harmonious relations between them. Constantius was already married, or had formed an association with Helena, a tavern keeper's daughter from Naissus. She had given him a son called Constantine. At the formation of the Tetrarchy, Constantius divorced her to marry the stepdaughter of Maximianus. Galerius married Diocletian's daughter. Marriage alliances were always a part of Roman political life, but had never averted wars when individuals started to pursue different ambitions that departed from the original agreements.

In the end the system failed, because human characteristics do not generally allow continuous agreement between all parties about how things should be done, and greed for power affected all the participants eventually. But what the Tetrarchic system did achieve was to provide extra commanders who could protect the provinces and the frontiers, leaving Diocletian as senior Emperor to look more closely at the administrative and military functions and to discern what was wrong with them. No Emperor for the past several decades had been granted the time or opportunity of attending to these matters. Aurelian had paved the way, attempting to reform the currency and the government, and establishing the divinity of the Emperors that created considerable distance between the populace and their rulers. But it was Diocletian who initiated the most sweeping changes.

Diocletian's reforms are not as well documented as might be hoped. Most evidence derives from a period after his reign, and from the reign of Constantine, so that the finished picture that emerged under Constantine is all that remains, and it is difficult if not impossible to disentangle who was responsible for instigating which measures. Therefore it is convenient to outline the fully fledged reforms, regardless of whether they belong wholly to Diocletian or to Constantine, who was sometimes responsible for completing the measures and putting them into effect.

The British provinces could hardly have been affected while Carausius and then Allectus ruled the island, but an overview of how the Roman world changed at the end of the third century and the beginning of the fourth provides a background for the later Roman period in Britain.

The Roman world until the reign of Diocletian was described as the Principate, based on the ideology of Augustus, who promoted himself as *princeps*, loosely translated as first among equals. His title Imperator, indicating his command of armies, belied this concept, but he had no intention of acting the tyrant and being assassinated before he could put into effect all the measures that he wanted to achieve. He was granted a very long reign in which to change the way in which the Empire was governed, and never seems to have been the object of widespread conspiracies to remove him. Diocletian was not granted such a long reign and was probably painfully aware that time was short, while the need for reforms was urgent. From the end of the third century, the Principate was transformed into the Dominate, which needs no helpful interpretation. All inhabitants of the Empire were affected by his reforms. Imperial control became more intense and more detailed, reaching into all aspects of local government and personal life.

One of the most obvious targets for reform was the army and the frontiers. Diocletian was concerned to strengthen the frontiers and garrison them more fully. Forts began to diverge from their earlier styles, acquiring projecting drum towers at intervals along the walls, sometimes blocking in some of the gates, where a single projecting tower from one side of the gate to the other replaced the more usual towers flanking the gate. On the Danube, fan shaped towers appeared at the corners of the forts, giving a view along both the walls running from the corner. The whole method of protection and control of earlier times, where the army was housed in forts, but fought in the open, was changing to one of more static defence. In previous centuries the forts were not used like medieval castles, but now they began to appear as strongholds where soldiers and supplies could be protected. Landing places on rivers were fortified, and watchtowers guarded routes. There was no central guidance on the walling of cities, so these affairs were left to private and personal enterprise, and paid for out of local council funds. Diocletian probably could not afford to spend resources on civil defence of towns as well as provincial and frontier protection.

The number of legions was increased, almost doubled in fact. For some time modern historians argued that the new legions were much smaller than those of the Principate, at best containing only 1,000 men, but now it seems more likely that the normal strength of about 6,000 men was retained for all legions, but they were split up into smaller packets and stationed at different locations, perhaps 1,000 men in each fort, with headquarters somewhere that organised the legion's pay, record keeping, and administration. Much debate revolved around the possibility that it was Diocletian who created the central mobile cavalry armies, the *comitatenses*, which evolved from the *comitatus*, a collection of different personnel, friends, advisers, administrators and bodyguards, all of them qualifying for the description *comites*, who surrounded all Emperors, at home or on campaign. Diocletian certainly had his own *comitatus*, which perhaps contained some mounted troops, but it is not certain how it was organised or what the term signified in his day. The *comitatus* had become steadily more formalised from the reign of Marcus Aurelius onwards, and from Severus's reign it was always styled *sacra*, sacred, just as the Imperial court and family gradually morphed into the *domus divina*, or sacred household. There are two opposing opinions about Diocletian's *comitatus*, one that it was the same as it always was, a group of companions and bodyguards of the Emperor, and the other is that it changed into a military organisation, providing the nucleus of the mobile army of the *comitatenses*, which Constantine simply had to modify and augment in order to establish his own central mobile cavalry army, and then the provincial versions. This argument rests on personal preference, and cannot be properly resolved until more evidence can be found. If he did not establish the mobile field armies, Diocletian did create the *scholae*, the Imperial bodyguard, even though the Praetorian Guard was still in existence at the time, but not for much longer, as Constantine abolished it.

Another of Diocletian's reforms, probably wholly attributable to him and simply developed by Constantine, is the separation of civil and military commands. The trend for specialisation in one branch or the other had begun in the second century, but from now on the split was almost complete. In some small provinces the governor also commanded troops, but in general, the civil governor was called *praeses*, and the military commanders were equestrian *Duces*. Senators were not entirely divorced from provincial government, but regardless of rank, the governor was subordinate to the *Dux*. The term *Dux* means leader, but that does not convey the power and authority that was invested in these commanders. More often than not the *Dux* commanded frontier troops over more than one province, enabling him to move to the scene of the action in his zone or section of the frontiers without having to liaise with another commander. He and the *praeses* in each province would have to co-operate over supplies.

The provincial reorganisation was perhaps the more far-reaching of the reforms. Diocletian reduced the size of most provinces, splitting them into much smaller units. This doubled the number of provinces, which in turn doubled the number of administrative personnel required to govern them, and increased the costs. It is not known when this was begun, or when it was completed, perhaps only coming into full force under Constantine. The changes will have taken place over a period of time, since replacing the existing governors and finding new ones for the newly created smaller provinces cannot have happened in a day or two. All new boundaries would have to be surveyed and redrawn, administrative procedures adapted, extracting relevant information from the offices of what was once a larger province. In the end there would be some benefits, in that the governors of the smaller units would be able to devote more time to the supervision of towns and cities, and to the organisation of transport and communications, and there would be a reduced number of cases coming to court from a smaller population. Since tighter control was now the order of the day, tax collection could be more fully scrutinised.

The second part of provincial reorganisation was the grouping together of several provinces into a larger unit called a Diocese, with a *vicarius* in control, responsible ultimately to the Praetorian Prefects. The appointment of the *vicarii* provided an extra tier of government, but there does not seem to have been a strict hierarchy of command, since the Emperors or the Praetorian Prefects could communicate directly with the *vicarii* or with the provincial governors. Hopefully if they ever did this, the Emperors and Prefects sent copies of all communications to everyone concerned, otherwise the provincial governors and the *vicarii* could find themselves working at cross purposes.

In the financial sphere, Diocletian had less success with his reforms. Agriculture was the backbone of the Empire and produce was the single most important item that could be taxed. Diocletian tried to spread the burden more fairly, by establishing tax assessment via the *iugum*, a unit of agricultural land, but not one of a standard size. It was variable, adapted to the type of soil and the amount of labour that was required to produce different kinds of crops. Another assessment had to be made concerning manpower, based on a poll tax, the *caput*, but like the *iugum* this was not assessed to a single rigid standard; for instance a woman's labour was assessed at half a *caput*. A census was necessary to assess the *capitatio* of a region or province, and then the *capitatio* and the *iugatio* were used in association to establish the rate of taxation. The reports were sent to the Praetorian Prefects, who had by now lost their military functions and were in charge of supplies, among other duties. They apportioned the amount of tax to be paid by the province, and the various towns and cities were responsible for collecting it from their attributed territories. If there was a shortfall, the councillors were obliged to make up the difference from their own pockets. It was therefore in their interests to find farmers for all the lands attributed to their towns, otherwise areas lying vacant represented a loss. In the Empire there always seemed to be an abundance of vacant lands for the settlement of tribesmen, who came into the Empire in their thousands and were given lands to farm on the understanding that they provided recruits for the armies. Given the enormous increase in armed forces throughout the Empire, this was a very necessary undertaking, and without the vast numbers of the so-called barbarian soldiers who served in the Roman armies, the Empire would probably have fallen long before it eventually did.

The most famous of Diocletian's financial reforms is the Price Edict. The currency edict preceded it, and neither of them could be described as successful. He tried to regulate the value of coinage, just as Aurelian had done, but coins were only as good as their precious metal content, and as they became more and more debased, the good coins went underground and disappeared, and prices rose. The edict was supposed to cap all prices across the Empire, but for one thing there were too many regions with different produce and tastes, and for another it was largely ignored. Inflation reached unprecedented levels, and probably widespread barter replaced cash transactions. The edict was withdrawn, but versions of it survived in different parts of the Empire, and it is a fascinating document, providing historians with hours of study of produce and values in the later Empire.

Supplies for the armies and the teams of administrative staffs were not wholly covered by the taxation system, so for some time payments in kind were instituted. Money payments did not disappear altogether, but soldiers were often paid in rations. Requisitioning of produce and of services became more tightly controlled in order to keep the system functioning. Mines and quarries had been under Imperial control for some considerable time, but now centralised control extended to factories and businesses as well, especially those that produced goods with any relevance to the army. Production of arms and armour, textiles and clothing were managed and operated by military personnel. The expertise of skilled craftsmen was highly valued, so such people were obliged to join a guild or corporation, and were not allowed to leave their trades or jobs. They were also commanded to train their sons in their professions, so that vital skills should not be lost. All this did not come into force until the fourth century, but it was Diocletian who initiated the scheme. The consequent loss of personal freedom and social mobility stifled daily life, and reveals how the Emperors perceived the situation of the Empire as altogether desperate.

Agricultural workers were also compelled to remain on their lands, because when forced to stay and cultivate their farms, they produced crops and these could be taxed, as well as supplying food for the soldiers and people. The *colonus* or labourer was originally much more of a free agent, but a combination of bad harvests and endemic insecurity in some provinces had forced many farmers off their lands. Eventually the landowners and the *coloni* were thrown into each others' arms, the landowners requiring labourers to farm their estates, and the *coloni* requiring some influential person to sustain them through bad harvests and to protect them from the ravages of the tax gatherers. In this way, people fled from central and local government, where the burdens were too great, and set up almost independent little kingdoms in the rural areas. Fragmentation was only a short step away.

BRITAIN RECLAIMED

After he had captured Boulogne in 293, Constantius could not devote his attention to Britain for another three years, for the same reasons that Maximianus had been unable to leave Gaul or the frontiers and concentrate on a campaign across the Channel. The disruption in the provinces and the threats to the frontiers were of much more importance to Rome than the island on the north-western fringe of the Empire.

Allectus was therefore granted some time to govern the Empire he had wrested from Carausius. It was once considered that he was a financial official in Carausius's court, but that was derived from the coins bearing the legend RSR, which was related to a literary passage in the work of Aurelius Victor, originally thought to refer to financial matters. Victor's phrase *summae rei praeesset* refers to Allectus being left in charge of, literally translated, 'the highest things' by Carausius. This was related by modern historians to the post of *rationalis summae rei*, the title of a finance official. It seemed to be supported by the coin legends RSR, so Allectus was for a long time assigned by historians to a financial realm. The reinterpretation of the coin legends as quotations from Virgil now makes the financial connection redundant, so it is suggested that Allectus was Carausius's Praetorian Prefect. Assassination of Emperors by Praetorian Prefects was a long-standing tradition in the Roman Empire.

Allectus continued the policy of issuing good-quality coinage, much of it in gold. His coins have been found in Gaul with much the same distribution pattern as those of Carausius, so it is questionable whether the loss of Boulogne was so devastating to the British Emperors. Just as Carausius had done, Allectus attended to coastal defences. It used to be thought that the fort at Pevensey was built much later, perhaps in the fourth century, but it now seems that it may have been founded by Allectus, perhaps another continuation of the policies of Carausius. Allectus was also responsible for a large building project in London.

He may have known that his days were numbered if news reached him from Gaul, where Constantius was preparing two fleets, one at Boulogne which he commanded himself, and another at the mouth of the River Seine under his Praetorian Prefect, Asclepiodotus. In 296 they sailed. Asclepiodotus landed near Southampton Water, burned his boats and marched inland, while a feint by Constantius's fleet persuaded Allectus to draw up his troops in the wrong place, too far to the east of Asclepiodotus's troops. When he realised the mistake, Allectus rushed into London, and was temporarily saved because Constantius was forced back to Gaul in the fog that descended on the sea. Ultimately, Allectus fared badly when he faced Asclepiodotus, and there were considerable casualties, among them Allectus himself. The Frankish mercenaries in Allectus's army marched to London, but were rounded up and killed.

Allectus's followers would be purged, but in an excess of enthusiasm, the British population, according to the ancient historians and the panegyrics addressed to Constantius, were overjoyed to greet him, much as the population of England were overjoyed to see Charles II when he returned to claim the throne, all of them earnestly declaring that they had never supported the previous regime. Portraying himself as the saviour of Britain, Constantius issued a medallion from the mint at Trier, a fine piece showing the inhabitants of London greeting him, with the legend *Redditor Lucis Aeternae*, Restorer of the Eternal Light. The theme of restoring the light is repeated in the literary sources. It is permissible to wonder if it had really been so dark in Britain under Carausius and Allectus. The panegyrics give the real reason for the recovery of Britain:

> [Britain] was no slight loss to the Empire, a land so fertile for all kinds of cereals, rejoicing in a great number of pastures, so abundant in metals, so productive of tax revenues [*vectigalia*], so well provided with harbours … (*Panegyric addressed to Constantius*, AD 297)

In other words the British provinces were well worth hanging onto. Another reference from the reign of Julian in the mid-fourth century makes it clear that for a long time Britain had exported wheat to the Continent, to supply the troops. Such a province should not be discarded lightly.

THE SECOND DIVISION OF BRITAIN

It was probably after his victory against Carausius that Constantius oversaw the division of Britain into three or possibly four provinces. This was in keeping with Diocletian's policy of dividing all the provinces into smaller units, which had begun before Britain was recovered for the Empire. When the Verona List (*Laterculus Veronensis*), which was started in 303, was finally drawn up in 314 listing all the provinces, Britain was divided into four, but it is suggested that originally Constantius's arrangements were for three provinces, Britannia Prima, Britannia Secunda, and perhaps a larger one called Caesariensis. The last named province was probably soon afterwards divided into Maxima Caesariensis and Flavia Caesariensis. These are the four provinces named in the Verona list, and they are also reflected in a later document called the *Notitia Dignitatum*, which lists all the garrisons and offices of the high officials all over the eastern and western Roman Empires.

The province of Maxima Caesariensis was the only one with a consular governor, with headquarters presumably in London, though there is no actual proof for this. The other provinces were governed by *praesides*. Secunda was probably based on York, and Flavia Caesariensis at Lincoln. Britannia Prima is thought to have been governed from Cirencester, since an inscription was found there recording the *primae provinciae rector*, dating to the mid-fourth century, though this does not actually state that Cirencester was the capital of the province. Since the other provinces of Britannia Secunda and Flavia Caesariensis were governed from the *coloniae* of York and Lincoln, for Britannia Prima the *colonia* of Gloucester is at least as likely as Cirencester to have been chosen as the administrative centre. It may be that successive *rectors* dealt with some official business at Cirencester, possibly on a regular basis.

The new, smaller provinces were grouped together in the Diocese of the Britains, with a *vicarius* in charge, though none is attested until 319. The *vicarii* of the British Diocese were responsible to the Praetorian Prefects of Gaul, and they most probably combined both military command and civilian administrative functions at first, until the appointment of the first *Dux*, after which the *vicarii* would attend to all civilian affairs, and all military matters would be in the hands of the *Duces*. It is not known when the first military commander was appointed. As for other officials, only one is known before 305, a *praeses* named Aurelius Arpagius, recorded on an inscription from Birdoswald. His province was most probably Britannia Secunda. The Birdoswald inscription is not securely dated, but clearly belongs somewhere between 296 and 305, and it supports the suggestion that the early *vicarii* combined military and civil duties, since Arpagius was the civil governor, but he still commanded troops. The division of civil and military commands that Diocletian had put into effect was clearly not rolled out to Britain immediately after the defeat of Allectus.

The Birdoswald inscription records the fact that the resident cohort, for which no name survives on the stone, had rebuilt the commander's house inside the fort, which had collapsed and been covered with earth, and they had also rebuilt the headquarters building, and the bath house. Such a description of a building fallen down through age and so on is often taken to be euphemism for destruction by enemy action, but in this case it is possible that no commander had been living in the house for a long time, even though the unit remained there. Flavius Martinus, a centurion with the title *praepositus* is attested as the supervisor of the building work. The title *praepositus* implies that Flavius Martinus was an acting commander, not the regular one. There may have been a succession of temporary commanders, and the reconstruction of the house suggests that there was soon to be a new more regular officer to live in it.

It is assumed that Constantius instigated a whole series of restoration works on Hadrian's Wall and the northern forts in 296, though the evidence for such an organised rebuilding programme is slight. Archaeological evidence attests building work in several of the northern forts, loosely dated to the beginning of the fourth century.

It used to be thought that there was serious trouble on the northern frontier in 296 because Allectus had probably withdrawn some of the troops when Constantius attacked, and that consequently there was considerable damage that required repair, hence the building work detected at several sites. However, it has been pointed out that there is no mention in the panegyrics addressed to Constantius of any invasion or a punitive campaign in 296, and it is rare that a dedicated panegyrist would neglect to mention such an event, so it looks as if the theory of a disaster in that year is as ephemeral as the supposed invasion of 197 after Clodius Albinus withdrew troops and was defeated in Gaul.

There was perhaps a new assessment of defensive needs in northern Britain. New forts were built at Piercebridge, perhaps at this period, and also at Newton Kyme. Piercebridge is on the southern section of Dere Street, running north towards Chester-le-Street, and it is an exceptionally large fort, near the bridge across the River Tees. Its function was most likely to protect communications. The Roman road survives as the B6275, running in a straight line to the west of the A1(M) from Scotch Corner. The village preserves part of the road system of the fort, and parts of the fort wall, and of the bridge across the Tees, are still visible.

The repairs to the walls of the legionary fortress of Chester are not closely dated, and can only be said to belong to a period after 270, so it cannot be categorically stated that it was Constantius who authorised the rebuilding, but his presence in the island for a short time may have been the occasion for an overhaul of the forts and fortresses. The repair work on the walls of the Chester fortress did not extend to the entire circuit. In sections of the repair work, gravestones were used, the latest from the reign of Elagabalus. This could be interpreted as a need for haste, and could possibly be linked to attacks by pirates from Ireland, threatening the River Dee, but there is nothing substantial to support this suggestion. The York fortress was even more spectacularly embellished, perhaps under the orders of Constantius, but this too is only speculation. There is no firm dating evidence, and the vagueness of a post-270 date leaves the question open as to whether it was Aurelian who started off the York defences, soon after the Gallic Empire was re-absorbed into the Empire in 274, close to the date when he ordered the walls of Rome itself to be built. However, since Constantius campaigned in northern Britain, the association with him is perhaps more likely. On the side of the fortress facing the River Ouse and the *colonia* eight externally projecting multi-angled towers were added, one of which can still be seen in the gardens around the museum. These towers present a far more elaborate facade than a mere defensive wall with a few ordinary stone towers would have done, and it is tempting to associate them with Imperial planning.

Before he returned to Gaul in 297, Constantius commandeered a group of craftsmen (*artifices*) from the British provinces, to send them to Autun, where there had been a siege in 269 by the army of the Gallic Empire. It is eloquent of the turmoil in Gaul that twenty-eight years had passed and the city was not yet fully repaired, but with the arrival of the British workers perhaps the rebuilding was hastened. If such craftsmen could be spared from Britain, it suggests that there was no pressing need for rebuilding in the island, and that it was comparatively peaceful. Nearly another decade would pass before the presence of Constantius was required again in Britain. In the interim, it is not known how the provinces were governed, or when Diocletian's reforms were put into effect, how the soldiers were paid in cash or in kind, or when the civil governors ceased to command troops. All the inhabitants would be assessed for the tax on agricultural produce, surveys would be made of all agricultural lands to apply the *iugatio*, and a census would be taken to assess the *capitatio*, though nothing is known of when or how it was done, nor how the taxes were allocated and levied, until 319 when the *vicarius* Pacatianus raised a problem requiring an Imperial reply, the gist of which was that decurions of town councils could only be sued in respect to their own lands, and should not be held responsible for anyone else's territory. Perhaps a decurion had defaulted and the tax gatherers had tried to make another man pay up.

A major change occurred at the beginning of May 305, when Diocletian abdicated. He had been ill for some time, but he had created what ought to have been a self-perpetuating system of government, with two senior and two subordinate rulers who could share the burden of Empire, and so in theory the edifice ought to have been able to sustain itself. He forced Maximianus to abdicate at the same time, and so Constantius and Galerius were raised to Augusti, and they appointed subordinates as their Caesars, Flavius Valerius Severus under Constantius in the west, and in the east Galerius appointed his nephew, Maximian Daia. Almost as soon as he was declared Augustus, Constantius prepared another expedition to Britain, summoning his son Constantine to join him.

IO

Britain in the New World of Constantine & his Successors AD 306 to 367

Before he embarked on his British expedition, Constantius sent for his son Constantine, who was in the eastern half of the Empire, possibly as a hostage of Galerius, no friend of Constantius. Aurelius Victor carries this story, but Zosimus does not mention it, simply stating that Constantine was residing in the east when he was summoned by his father. Constantine himself either knew, or imagined, that he was in danger, so he set off in full flight, anxious to avoid Severus, who was Caesar in the west under Constantius but in reality an ally of Galerius. In order to prevent anyone from following too closely, when he reached a post house to change horses he took fresh mounts and killed or maimed the ones that had carried him there. Depending on one's sympathies, this is a shrewd piece of self-preservation, or an act of wanton cruelty. Either interpretation is indicative of the man. He reached Boulogne safely to met Constantius, and embarked for Britain.

Virtually nothing is known of the campaigns of 305–306 in Britain. York was probably made the headquarters of the army, just as Septimius Severus had made it his military and administrative centre almost a century earlier. It is assumed that the fighting was in the north, because in a panegyric addressed to Constantine at Trier in 310, it is stated that

Constantius knew that he was soon to die, and before he entered the eternal light himself he wanted to go and see the ocean in the far north where the daylight was almost continuous. In a different passage, the author says that when the gods were already calling him, he wanted to go to the furthest edge of the world. This implies that the army did reach the far north, but merely wishing to see the midsummer sun skirting the horizon would seem to be an imponderable reason for marching an army through Scotland to the northern coast.

There are few if any clues as to why this campaign was mounted. On several further occasions after Constantius's expedition, most of the troubles that beset Britain arose in the north, so it can only be concluded that the tribesmen were particularly warlike, with each new generation seeking battle honours and plunder in or near the Roman province. The panegyrist of 310 says that Constantius did not annexe the territory he had overrun, and describes it as mostly forests and marshes, with the unspoken subtext that it was not of great value. Pottery of roughly the appropriate date has been found at Cramond and Carpow, suggesting that like Severus and Caracalla, Constantius marched up the eastern side of the island, and used the fleet to support the army and bring supplies. None of the well-known series of marching camps in Scotland has been assigned to Constantius's campaigns, and it is not even known if the army still built camps in the old way when on the march.

The parallel with the campaigns of Severus was not limited to the march to the north. In 306, Constantius died at York. Technically, his Caesar, Severus, ought to have been chosen as the next Augustus, but heredity won out over the Tetrarchic arrangements, and the army in Britain declared for Constantine. Aurelius Victor says that a king of the Alamanni called Crocus helped to bring this about, but offers no details of how he did so. Though the text merely says that Crocus had accompanied Constantius to give military assistance, it is probable that the Alamanni contributed soldiers to the campaign army, commanded by their king, which harks back to the much earlier practices of the Republican army, where tribesmen were recruited and fought as separate units under their native leaders, returning home when the campaign ended rather than signing up for a specific term.

The situation could have got out of hand if Galerius in the east had chosen to regard Constantine as a usurper. Remembering Carausius and how difficult it had been to winkle him out of the island, it would have been wasteful to start a civil war when there were other problems to deal with, somewhat closer to Rome. Constantine was officially made Caesar, and Severus was raised from his rank as Caesar to Augustus. This would probably take several months to arrange, for messages to travel to and from Galerius's headquarters, and Constantine waited patiently in Britain. He too probably considered that it was not worth starting a civil war over a proclamation by the troops, especially since at the moment he only had the support of the army of Constantius and the solders of the British provinces. He put the waiting time to good use, improving roads and perhaps initiating building and rebuilding projects. He accepted Galerius's pronouncements, and carried on with the roadworks, as attested by no less than six milestones, all displaying his title of Caesar.

It is not known when he left Britain, and he may have revisited the island in *c.*307, though this is only a tenuous suggestion. There was a long way to go before he would become Augustus in his own right, which was probably his long-term goal from the start of his career. There were several rivals to overcome. In 306 the Praetorians in Rome declared for Maxentius, the son of Maximianus, who had been forced to retire when Diocletian abdicated in 305. Severus, Augustus in the west, was sent against him, but lost the fight, and was executed, possibly on the orders of Maxentius. Allying himself with Maximianus, Constantine married the former's daughter Fausta in 307, and Maximianus promoted him to the rank of Augustus, possibly even before Severus was eliminated. Shortly afterwards, Maximianus and his son Maxentius quarrelled, and Maximianus turned up at Constantine's headquarters at Trier, while Constantine campaigned on the Rhine. Since things were getting seriously out of hand, Galerius called for a conference at Carnuntum on the Danube towards the end of 308, bringing Diocletian out of retirement, to become Emperor for a second time, or at least to arbitrate. Diocletian would not be persuaded to take up the reins of state, and as a result, Maximianus was forced to retire once again. A new Augustus was elevated, Licinius, a colleague of Galerius, which offended Galerius's existing Caesar, Maximinus. No one mentioned the name of Maxentius in all the new arrangements, so it was clear that he was not considered part of the legitimate government.

By 310, war broke out because Maximianus would not accept his enforced retirement, but he committed suicide at Marseilles when Constantine besieged the town. Probably in May 311 Galerius died, leaving Licinius, Maximinus and Maxentius as obstacles on Constantine's path to power. Around this time Constantine may have returned to Britain. A series of coins datable to 310–312 and 313–314 were issued from the mint at London, announcing *Adventus Aug[usti]* or the arrival of the Emperor, possibly for another campaign, on at least one occasion, or perhaps twice. His biographer Eusebius says that he campaigned against the Britons who live at the edge of the Ocean where the sun sets, and in another passage he says that Constantine crossed the sea to the island and brought the Britons to terms, but it is not clear what this was all about, or what terms were imposed on whom. It is likely that Constantine also recruited soldiers or took troops from Britain *c*.311 for the coming battle against Maxentius. According to Zosimus he led to Rome an army of 90,000 infantry and 8,000 cavalry, containing conquered German tribesmen, other Celtic people and those collected from Britain. With this army, Constantine defeated Maxentius at the Battle of the Milvian Bridge in Rome in 312. Maxentius was killed. The night before the battle, so the story goes, Constantine had a vision of the Christian symbol of the cross, and heard the words, 'In this sign you shall conquer.' He ordered the soldiers to paint the cross on their shields, and he conquered.

Constantine did not personally embrace Christianity, preferring to hedge his bets by also honouring pagan gods, especially Sol Invictus, the Unconquered Sun, but he gradually promoted the religion. His father Constantius had been ordered to stamp out Christianity in Gaul and the west, but had not actively persecuted anyone, limiting his activity to destroying some churches. Persecution and toleration of Christians alternated throughout the later Empire until Constantine's reign. Galerius had been a strong advocate for eradication of the religion, and in the east Maximinus was still assiduously persecuting Christians. In 313, the year after the victory over Maxentius, Constantine met Licinius in Milan, and from this meeting an edict was issued, tolerating all religions. Conveniently, Licinius eradicated Maximinus that same year. For just over another decade the two Augusti ruled the eastern and western parts of the Empire, until Constantine defeated Licinius and emerged as sole Emperor in 324. He did not take a colleague.

Constantine's Reforms

Many of the reforms instituted by Diocletian were brought to fruition by Constantine, who contributed ideas of his own, but the whole process is so intertwined that it is difficult to unravel precisely which of the two Emperors was responsible for the commencement and the completion of individual reforms. Constantine for the most part left provincial boundaries as they were intended to be under Diocletian, and he made no changes to the laws tying people to their professions. He shored up the senatorial class by bestowing the rank of senator on individuals from a broad base of personnel across the Empire, relieving them of the obligation to live in Rome or to attend meetings of the Senate. These new senators governed some of the consular provinces and were made prefects of the city of Rome, but although the senatorial class was revived there was no policy of removal of equestrians from government posts.

Changes to the army saw the full development of the *comitatenses* or mobile field armies, and the billeting of troops in the towns began, while the frontier *alae* and *cohortes* were downgraded and became the *limitanei*, from the Latin for frontier, *limes* (plural *limites*). Originally this word simply meant the road into enemy territory, but when physical barriers were set up to mark the frontiers the term was applied to the frontiers themselves. At this stage in the reign of Constantine, these troops were part of the regular army, but confusion arose because in the much later army the same name applied to the frontier militia, farmer-soldiers defending their homes, so in some late Roman historical sources for the fourth century the two kinds of troops became confused.

The Christian authors who could find no wrong in Constantine praised him for these developments, but Zosimus condemned him, complaining that he ruined Diocletian's system for the protection of the frontiers, by taking the soldiers away and putting them in cities which did not need them.

After the Battle of the Milvian Bridge, Constantine disbanded the Praetorian Guard. The Guardsmen had proclaimed Maxentius as Augustus, so they were deprived of the power to repeat their actions by proclaiming someone else. As a new guard, Constantine adopted the *scholae*, which had been created by Diocletian. The Praetorian Prefects were retained, but now lost their military functions completely, and two new supreme commanders were created, the *magister militum*, literally the master of the soldiers, commanding the infantry, and the *magister equitum*, commanding the cavalry. Constantine may also have instituted the title *Comes*, signifying a proper rank, as opposed to the non-specific *comes*, meaning companion of the Emperor.

DIOCLETIAN'S PRICE EDICT AND BRITISH WOOLLENS – Text Box
One of Diocletian's attempted reforms was not adopted and developed by Constantine. The edict on prices (*de pretiis*) was issued in 301 in a period of rampant inflation, to try to prevent the dramatic rise in prices from spiralling out of control. The Romans had no budget to work to, and no economic theory, though it is doubtful if such theories are effective even today. Diocletian was trying to govern an Empire that was almost totally geared up for war on several fronts at once, as pressures on the frontiers mounted, and as part of his measures to protect the Empire and provide essentials, he put virtually everything under strict state control, such as bakeries, arms factories, and textile

and clothing establishments. He was convinced that the problem of rising prices stemmed from greedy merchants and officials who charged exorbitant amounts for goods and services, so he had an extensive list produced giving maximum prices for all manner of commodities, all listed in categories, such as food, clothing, raw materials, transport, wages and services. It did not work and was not renewed or kept up to date, but it is a fascinating document offering historians a wealth of information about products of the different provinces and their relative values. For textiles, silk was the most expensive of all, then woollens, then linen, followed by coarse linen for commoners and slaves.

The fact that British woollens find their way into this document shows that by the fourth century the industry had made its mark on the whole Empire. Cloaks and tunics were rated in the price edict by their weight, and by their origin. The *birrus Britannicus*, or semi-circular cloak, was rated less highly than the hugely expensive cloaks of the Nervii from Gaul, but it was still a valuable item. No wonder that several leaden curse tablets from Britain are concerned with the retrieval of stolen cloaks. It has been pointed out that the descriptive term *birrus Britannicus* may refer to a style of cloak rather than clothing specifically made in Britain, but even if this is so, the label 'British' ought to mean that the garment originated there and was probably still produced there, even if other manufacturers in other places also made it. Another British product was the woollen rug, called *tapete*, which was listed as a high-quality item. The same type of rug may have been called *tossia Britannica*, which is mentioned on an inscription from Gaul as the gift of the governor of Britannia Inferior, which pre-dates the division into four provinces under Diocletian, but it is to be presumed that the governor would hardly send anything other than the highest-quality British rug to his associate in Gaul.

The spinning and weaving of wool had a long history in Britain and was well established before the Roman conquest. Sheep's wool remained the most important fibre in Roman Britain, but it is not known if all the wool used in textile manufacture was home-grown on the farm estates. It is suggested that wool was brought in from other areas, possibly from Scotland. If there was any attempt to improve sheep breeds to produce better-quality wool, this would be very hard to detect by archaeological means, but in the long period of the Roman occupation it would seem likely that at least some breeders attempted to do so.

There was an extensive industry producing woollen goods in East Anglia. Carding combs and other pieces of equipment have been found at Caistor-by-Norwich, and cropping shears for clipping the finished items to give them a smooth surface were found at Great Chesterford. The factories were probably based in towns, unlike most industries, which were located in rural areas. At least this was the norm on the Continent, where factories were based in Rheims, Tournai and Trier. The wool was not made into bolts of cloth as in modern-day factories, to be sent to other manufacturers to be made up into clothes, but complete woollen garments were produced. This would make sense especially if the factories were producing goods for the army, where finished items would be somewhat more useful than lengths of cloth to be made up. How the woollen garments reached other customers is a matter for debate. There may have been middle men who sold the finished items.

From the late third century the government controlled weaving works and textile manufacture. A factory was called a *gynaecium*, and weaving establishments are noted under this title in the *Notitia Dignitatum*. In Britain, the *procurator gynaecii in Britannis Ventensis* was responsible for the production of goods, but it is not certain where the factory was. The officials who compiled the document perhaps did not know either, since they were working in the fifth century, using out-of-date information reflecting the period before Britain and the Empire parted company. The factory was in Venta, but does this mean Venta Belgarum (Winchester), Venta Silurum (Caerwent), or Venta Icenorum (Caistor-by-Norwich)? Some scholars argue for Winchester, but since the evidence for a developed weaving industry derives from East Anglia, perhaps Caistor-by-Norwich was where the *procurator gynaecii* operated.

Before and during the Tetrarchy, several large cities of the Empire had become Imperial residences where the Emperors could administer their territories and from which they could mount campaigns. These cities included Milan in northern Italy, which was within reach of the Rhine and Danube, Trier in Gaul where Constantine resided as Augustus, and in the east Nicomedia and Sirmium where Diocletian set up headquarters. Rome was now too far away from the scene of most of the action. The frontiers were most threatened from the north, where tribes pressed upon the Rhine and Danube, and in the east where the Persians represented a sometimes exaggerated perceived threat, because the Persian kings could call upon better organised armies than the tribal warriors could command. For some time now Rome itself had been declining in importance, and the city of Byzantium, close to the east and the River Danube, had earned the name *Roma altera*, another Rome. In 330, Constantine officially moved the capital of the Empire to this city, and renamed it Constantinople, or the *polis* (the Greek term for city) of Constantine. Modesty was of little use to Roman Emperors, so Constantine never cultivated it.

THE EXPEDITION OF THE EMPEROR CONSTANS TO BRITAIN
The provinces of Britain enter the historical record at sporadic intervals, usually because there was some trouble in the island and the Emperors had to send a general to sort out the problems, or mount an expedition in person. Between these episodes there is complete silence in the historical sources, except for archaeological evidence, which can be interpreted only with difficulty, since dating materials are usually lacking. The habit of setting up inscriptions declined from the third century onwards, and for the fourth century coins and pottery are much scarcer than for the earlier periods. Without some attested context as background

information, signs of destruction and demolition at individual sites do not yield very much.

After the death of Constantine in 337, the Empire was split between his three sons, Constantine II, Constantius II, and Constans. Constantine II took over the west from 337 to 340, when the troops of his brother Constans murdered him, and for the next decade Constans ruled the west. The Franks were defeated by Constans in 342, and almost immediately after this campaign, he sailed at the beginning of 343 to Britain, for reasons which are not clear. The ancient authors are more concerned with his bravery in crossing the Channel, probably in January or February when it was particularly dangerous, than in recounting why he did so or what he accomplished in Britain. The relevant books of Ammianus Marcellinus's history, which would have been invaluable, are lost. Fortunately, in his accounts of later episodes in Britain, he refers briefly to what he wrote about Constans in his earlier books. In his account of trouble in Britain nearly two decades later, just before the Caesar Julian was declared Augustus by his soldiers in Gaul, Ammianus says that Britain had been overrun by tribesmen from the Scotti, or Attacotti, and Picts, but Julian was preoccupied in Gaul, where the Alamanni were poised to invade, and so he could not go to Britain himself, as Constans had done.

The outbreak of hostilities was most likely in the north of Britain, possibly from beyond Hadrian's Wall, and may have concerned a group of military scouts called the *areani*, who were probably not the main cause of the trouble in this particular instance. Writing of the exploits of Theodosius in Britain in 367 and 368, Ammianus says:

> The *areani* were a group of men established long ago, about whom we reported a certain amount in our account of Constans ... Their task had been to move back and forth across a wide area and report to our generals [*duces*] any threatening behaviour among the neighbouring peoples. (Ammianus Marcellinus 28.3.8)

These are probably the tasks that the *exploratores* had fulfilled, going out on scouting expeditions from their bases in some of the forts on

Hadrian's Wall and in the outpost forts. Direct connections between these and the *areani* cannot be demonstrated, but the need for the gathering of intelligence clearly remained the same. Perhaps on this occasion, the *areani* had provided useful information that led to the campaign under Constans. If they had been the prime cause of the trouble in Britain, it is probably safe to hazard a guess that Constans would have disbanded them, as Theodosius did in 367 or 368.

Whenever disturbances erupted in Britain, the accounts of the ancient authors very rarely mention any of the existing troops in the various British provinces, nor do the units themselves leave much trace of their whereabouts and exploits on inscriptions. Though the full complement of troops may have been severely depleted, and recruitment was known to be increasingly difficult in the later Empire, it seems that the armies of the Diocese of Britain were too weak or incapable of dealing with the various crises that broke out from time to time. Perhaps there were other episodes of fighting and policing which received no mention in the works of the ancient historians, who took notice of only the most severe problems, which involved intervention by the Emperors, or generals appointed by them. The participation of soldiers from British units in the various campaigns is to be assumed, if not attested. According to the ancient author Libanius, Constans embarked for Britain with one hundred men. This may mean that he gathered a few soldiers in a hurry, relying on the army of British provinces to maintain the situation until he got there himself. He could have given orders for more troops to follow him. It has been suggested that some units of the mobile field army may have come to Britain at this time, commanded by Gratian, the father of the future Emperors Valentinian and Valens. Ammianus describes him as *Comes*, usually rendered in English as Count. Gratian held this post first in command of the army in Africa and then in Britain with the same rank. There is no firm evidence for this command, and no trace of any campaign, but there is no other recorded context for his presence in Britain with the rank of *Comes*.

At some time after the reconstruction under Constantius at the beginning of the fourth century, and before the disaster of 367, the outpost forts north of Hadrian's Wall at High Rochester, Risingham and Bewcastle were destroyed. The last two were rebuilt but not High Rochester. It is not certain what happened at Netherby. The destruction has been linked to tribal warfare that preceded the campaign of Constans, without solid evidence. All that can be said is that Constans sailed to Britain early in 343, and coins were issued proclaiming a victory. Nothing is known about what terms he may have imposed on the tribes, except that the tribes broke their promises later on, and it is most likely that these promises were made to Constans.

DID CONSTANS CREATE A NEW PROVINCE?

One of the most intriguing problems of fourth- and fifth-century Britain concerns the province called Valentia. From the end of the third century, there were four provinces, probably created by Constantius in 296 after his northern campaigns, but in the *Notitia Dignitatum*, a document drawn up much later and listing all the provincial governors and military commanders, there are five provinces in Britain. The list names the four original provinces of Britannia Prima, Britannia Secunda, Flavia Caesariensis, Maxima Caesariensis, and adds a fifth one, Valentia, which was governed by a consular governor. The trouble is, no one knows where it was.

Ammianus Marcellinus says that in 367 the general Theodosius recovered the province that had been overrun by the tribes, and after the news reached the Emperor Valentinian, the province was given a legitimate governor (*rector*) and by the Emperor's decision it was called Valentia, relating it to the victory won under Valentinian. It may be that Theodosius created this province, but it is described as being recovered, not newly established. It has been suggested that it was Constans who carved a new province out of what was Britannia Secunda, and it possibly comprised the frontier area of Hadrian's Wall, under a different name, which was then changed by Valentinian. Without further evidence it is not possible to confirm or refute this theory. No information as to who governed this province has survived.

DID CONSTANS ESTABLISH THE SAXON SHORE?

As previously mentioned, the Saxon Shore turns up in the accounts of several episodes in the history of Roman Britain, because the various coastal forts have such a long history before they were co-ordinated and welded into a single system, and the date when this happened is far from certain. Though the forts already existed all along the south and south-east coast, the command of the *Comes Litoris Saxonici* is not attested until the end of the fourth century. This title may not have been properly established until other variants had been tried; for instance, in the disaster of 367, the approximate date of the so-called *conspiratio barbarica* when Britain was attacked from all sides including the sea, a commander called Nectaridus, otherwise unknown, was killed. He is described by Ammianus Marcellinus as *comes maritimi tractus*, which could have been simply a literary version of the title of the command of the Saxon Shore, or since Ammianus was not usually so vague about such matters, it may have been an official post that preceded the *Comes Litoris Saxonici*. The first mention of the Saxons does not occur until *c.*370, in the work of the late author Eutropius. Given that there may once have been other works by known or unknown authors that have been lost, this does not mean that the Saxons appeared for the first time in the flesh around 370 or a few years before, but the thirty-year gap between Constans and the statement of Eutropius give reason for caution in assigning the Saxon menace to the middle of the fourth century.

There may have been threats from sea-borne tribes other than the Saxons, which made it necessary to defend the coasts. The wide range of foundation dates for the forts of the Saxon Shore suggests that there was an ongoing problem, which the Romans dealt with by increasing the fortifications, and it is possible, even likely, that while Constans was in Britain he attended to whatever problem of coastal defence he encountered in the 340s, possibly creating a prototype system for the later Saxon Shore.

THE REBELLION OF MAGNENTIUS AND ITS AFTERMATH

Constans ruled the western half of the Empire for a decade, until the troops proclaimed Flavius Magnus Magnentius as Augustus at Autun (ancient Augustodunum) in 350. Constans was killed shortly afterwards.

Constantius II defeated the army of Magnentius at the Battle of Mursa in 352, but did not capture or kill the usurper, who clung onto his rule until the following year, until he was finally eliminated in Gaul, and the retribution began. Constantius II hunted down collaborators of Magnentius in Gaul, and despatched to Britain one of the palace officials called Paulus, to round up and bring back any supporters of the usurper. This thoroughly unpleasant individual was known as Catena, 'the Chain', from his ability to weave chains of intrigue around his victims. He realised that there was no one with sufficient energy to oppose him in Britain, so he began an inquisition of his own, exceeding his original brief. Innocent people were arrested and fabricated charges were laid against them, until the *vicarius* Martinus protested at the ill treatment of the provincials. Paulus responded by arresting several more military men and officials, including Martinus himself, preparing to have them taken to the court of Constantius. Since his fate was no doubt to be execution, Martinus attacked Paulus with a sword, but missed his target, and killed himself instead.

After leaving Britain, Paulus became an expert at tracking down usurpers and so-called traitors and their supporters, but he met his end at the hands of the Emperor Julian, who brought him to trial in Chalcedon, probably in 361 or the following year. It is somewhat satisfying to report that Paulus was burnt to death.

THE BRITISH PROVINCES IN THE REIGN OF JULIAN

Julian was the nephew of Constantine I and therefore cousin to Constantine II, Constantius II and Constans. He was created Caesar in 355, and was based in Gaul. In 360, he was declared Augustus by his troops. His connections with Britain are better documented than any other later Roman Emperor.

After the episode of Paulus and Martinus, the *vicarius* or possibly the *vicarii* of the Diocese of Britain are unknown, until Julian's friend Alypius was appointed probably in 357. Two personal letters written to him by Julian have survived, referring to their long friendship, and to the receipt of a map that Alypius had sent to the Emperor.

While Alypius was *vicarius*, Julian set up an enquiry into what sounds like a case of embezzlement by army officers, in 359. The report derives from the author Libanius, who describes how money that was destined for military purposes was being diverted into the pockets of some generals. Perhaps they were falsifying their expense accounts. Such practices have a long history, and corruption in the Roman army was not new. A case is documented of an army commander, not from Britain, who sold all the horses of a cavalry unit, and the Roman soldiers had already thought of the ruse of claiming dead men's pay. Libanius does not elaborate on what happened to the men who were found guilty of these charges, nor does he mention Alypius, but it is assumed that the *vicarius* would be involved in the investigations and the punishments.

Another of Julian's achievements throws light on the wealth of the British provinces that was outlined by the panegyrist of Constantius, concerning the fertility of the island and its production of crops. There is ample documentation about Julian's efforts in 359 to reinstate the regular shipments of grain from Britain to the Rhine that had been organised at some time in the past. Without this documentation, there would probably have been no hint of how much surplus Britain was capable of producing in the Roman period, even though the panegyrists, describing how the loss of Britain would be detrimental to the Empire, wax lyrical about the fertility of the British provinces and the crops that they produced.

The shipments had ceased because the Germanic tribes of the Salii and Chamavi had taken control of the estuary of the Rhine and the land on both banks, and prevented the Roman ships from approaching. Some cargoes of grain were delivered to other areas on the coast and then loaded onto wagons to be transported by road, which was labour-intensive and slow. As part of his reconstitution of the devastated cities of Gaul, Julian determined to eradicate this problem and resume the grain transports. When he had recovered many of the Gallic cities, he collected 200 ships from Britain and elsewhere, and he had some 400 new ones built. In one of his letters to a friend Julian gives these numbers, which by the time that Zosimus wrote his account had been inflated to

800 ships. With this fleet Julian cleared the Rhine of the tribesmen, who were supposedly terrified at his approach and made terms. Ammianus says that when rebuilding the cities in Gaul, Julian also repaired the granaries that had been burnt down, so he would be able to store the British grain. It is unfortunate that not much is known about where the grain originated, how it was collected, or who shipped it.

In the winter of 360, after Julian restored the grain transports from Britain, more raids started from the north of the island, and perhaps from Ireland, by sea. Ammianus dates the events securely:

> In the tenth consulship of Constantius and the third consulship of Julian, the Scotti [or Attacotti] and the Picts, wild tribesmen, invaded and broke the peace that had been agreed. They were devastating the places close to the frontier and fear was spreading throughout the provinces, worn out by the previous disasters. (Ammianus Marcellinus 20.1.1)

The peace that had been agreed was most likely arranged by Constans, seventeen years before, though neither Ammianus nor any other source verifies this assumption. Since Julian himself was fully occupied in Gaul because the Alamanni were restless and could invade at any time, he sent to Britain his recently appointed *magister equitum*, Flavius Lupicinus. Ammianus makes Lupicinus sound like a bit of a ham actor, full of bluff and bombast. He also says that it was debatable whether Lupicinus was more greedy than cruel.

No information survives of what Lupicinus achieved. He took with him some light-armed troops, the Heruli and Batavi, and some Moesiaci, landing at Richborough, and making straight for London to find out what had happened. No *vicarius* is named, but it is at least possible that such an official was in post, and Lupicinus met with him to discuss the problems and how to deal with them.

Soon after the departure of Lupicinus, a letter arrived at Julian's headquarters from Constantius II, asking for troops to be sent to the east, with Lupicinus as their commander. Constantius had not yet heard what was happening in Britain, but the unavailability of the *magister equitum* very quickly became of less concern to him than the fact that in February 360 Julian was declared Augustus by his army. Inevitably, Constantius would take a very dim view of this, and Julian was uncertain of where Lupicinus's loyalties would lie, so he prevented ships from sailing to Britain so that the news of his own elevation to Augustus would not reach his general. He allowed the British campaign to take its course and then arrested Lupicinus when he returned to Gaul.

For the next seven years, nothing is known of Britain. Constantius II died in 361, leaving Julian as sole Emperor. He went to war against the Persians, and was killed in battle in the summer of 363, succeeded briefly by Jovian, who died in February 364, suffocated by fumes from a brazier that was left in his bedroom, allegedly by accident. Valentinian, the elder son of the *Comes* Gratian, was declared Emperor immediately and a month later his younger brother Valens was made his colleague. The two Emperors shared the government of the Empire, Valens in the east and Valentinian in the west.

It is sometimes stated that there were further troubles in Britain in the first year of Valentinian's reign, but it has been pointed out that this derives from Ammianus, who gives a short summary of the main events that occurred all over the Empire under Valentinian and Valens, placing the passage at the beginning of their reigns in 364, as though it all happened at once. The description of the tribes of Scotti, Attacotti, Picts and Saxons all attacking the British provinces in 364 more likely refers to the so-called barbarian conspiracy of 367.

THE CONSPIRATIO BARBARICA

The concerted attacks of the tribesmen in 367 seemed to the Romans to have sprung from an agreement between all the savage peoples surrounding the Roman provinces of Britain, and the movement was labelled as a barbarian conspiracy by Ammianus. Some modern authors accept it as such, suggesting that there must have been a leader who co-ordinated the attacks. This may be true, but it is not likely that the tribesmen could have formed an alliance and maintained it for very long. What their main aim was is the subject of conjecture, but it was probably to gather plunder and portable wealth, and to gain status as warriors within their own tribes. Co-ordination between the Saxons and the tribes from Scotland and Ireland is harder to contemplate, since the seaborne pirates were perhaps not likely to sail towards a meeting place with the tribes on land in order to share their booty. It has to be admitted that the Saxons were said to have harassed the shores of Gaul, and are not stated to have attacked the British coasts, though if there was plunder to be had there, then it is likely that they did not pass up the opportunity.

The concept of a 'conspiracy' gives the impression that the tribes had created some kind of united army, intent on destroying the British provinces by their combined efforts. There was perhaps never any such intention, and no army to speak of, only disjointed bands of warriors looking for adventure and profit. This is not to diminish the effects that the attacks would have on the provincials in Britain, or on the military commanders who had to deal with them, but rather than a conspiracy there was probably an outbreak of simultaneous opportunism at a time when the army was too weak to prevent attacks on several fronts.

Ammianus reports that the news of the serious nature of the attacks reached Valentinian when he was travelling from Amiens to Trier in summer 367. In the fighting in Britain, Nectaridus, described as *comes maritimi tractus*, had been killed, and the *Dux* Fullofaudes had been defeated. Ammianus does not say that Fullofaudes had also been killed, but implies that he had been surrounded in an ambush, perhaps a sufficiently dire scenario to obviate the need to finish the sentence. Valentinian despatched one of his officials, Severus, *comes domesticorum* since 365, to deal with the situation in Britain. It is not known whether he took troops with him or what he achieved before his replacement by Jovinus, Valentinian's *magister equitum*. The text of Ammianus breaks down at this point, but enough of it remains to be certain that Jovinus could not prevail over the tribesmen, and that he urged Valentinian to be allowed 'to seek the support of a strong army'. It was time to send for Count Theodosius.

11

Destruction & Reconstitution
AD 367 to 395

Count Theodosius, as he is referred to in modern literature, is not generally titled *Comes* in the ancient histories. More usually he is *dux*, perhaps in its general sense meaning leader or general, rather than *Dux* in its specific sense, as Fullofaudes was called, meaning an officially appointed military commander with a brief to protect the frontiers and the provinces. It is suggested that he was *comes rei militaris*, as Gratian probably was under Constans.

Theodosius was of Spanish origin, though efforts to trace his ancestry back to the family of Trajan may have been deliberately fabricated. His second son was the future Emperor Theodosius I, called the Great, whose reign spanned the last decades of the fourth century. This Imperial connection ensured that more attention would be paid by the historians to Count Theodosius's military exploits than was paid to other generals, so for the British provinces his campaign is described in a little more detail than usual, starting with Ammianus Marcellinus, who wrote while Theodosius the Great was Emperor. This work is the best source, but still does not give sufficient information to reconstruct exactly where the campaigns took place, which troops took part, and what happened. These facts would perhaps not be as interesting to contemporary audiences as the life story of the Emperor's father. Britain was a long way from Rome and even further from Constantinople, so the addition of a few place names in Ammianus's text, which would have been invaluable to archaeologists and modern historians, would have meant very little to the Romans of the later fourth century.

The overall impression of the work of Theodosius in the British provinces, reiterated in later sources after Ammianus wrote his history, is that it was all a tremendous success. With the proviso that probably no writer would criticise the father of Theodosius the Great, this is perhaps correct. He cleared the provinces of the marauders and seems to have strengthened it against further attacks, which is all that could have been asked of him.

Ammianus says that before he set off for Britain, Theodosius enrolled legions and cohorts of spirited young men. If he created new units it is not known what they were called, or what became of them after the campaigns. Units of the field army were also summoned, the Heruli, Iovi and Victores. It is estimated that Theodosius took an extra 2,000 men with him, which suggests that the existing units in Britain formed the larger part of his army, but there is no mention of them in the sources. There is no named general, no *Dux*, no hero who had tried to save the provinces, in any of the literature. The Britons and the Roman government officials alike seemed to be floundering helplessly, unable to control the invaders, or to protect themselves. If Severus and Jovinus had achieved anything in their brief commands, it is not described, perhaps because they had been ineffective, or possibly their activities were deliberately passed over so that Theodosius could garner all the credit.

The state of Britain bordered on the desperate. The Picts, who according to Ammianus were now divided into two groups called Dycaledones and Verturiones, and the Scotti, from Ireland, and the Attacotti (who may be the Scotti under a different name) were roaming free all over the country. All the tribesmen were wild and savage, and the last named were said to be cannibals. Perception of what they were like and what they could do was probably inflated, and fear of them would escalate with each reported incident. The tribes were perhaps attacking from the sea, on the west coast opposite Ireland, and the rest attacking as they moved on land. As for the Saxons, the ancient historians report that they attacked the coasts of Gaul, but it is equally possible that they may have attacked Britain as well. On the south and east coasts the Saxons may have been going after shipping, threatening river estuaries, and landing occasionally to plunder. Since no part of Britain is more than 70 miles from the sea, the perceived threat from pirates was probably very great.

The military response to the attacks seems to have been to bury communal heads in the sand, though reports may have been exaggerated to inflate Theodosius's difficulties and his success in overcoming them. Soldiers are said to have deserted in droves, while others claimed that they were on long-term leave. It is a natural response to difficult and dangerous situations, but suggests a complete lack of discipline and ineffective officers.

Some modern historians have suggested that the problems in Britain were internal upheavals, caused in part by this lack of discipline and lawlessness, but it could be that the external threats had created the situation, just as it did in other provinces, where a so-called usurper was sometimes declared Emperor, or set himself up as Emperor, in order to protect their homelands. Not all of these were military men; in the east in particular it was sometimes the leading men of the civil community who tried to remedy situations that the legitimate Emperors could not deal with. In Britain in the fourth century no one had been chosen as leader or had decided to take the matter in hand. Theodosius therefore had an uphill task.

He sailed from Boulogne to Richborough, and started off for London, which Ammianus says was now called Augusta. This probably means that the city had been made a *colonia* but this is not proven. On the way to the city, Theodosius encountered some brigands laden with booty, probably on their way back to the coasts. He divided his forces into detachments, and trapped and defeated them, reclaiming the booty. Most of the stolen goods were returned to their owners, except for a small proportion that he gave to his soldiers, who were exhausted. Part of this may have been food supplies that had been gathered by the tribesmen, but most Roman generals were wise enough to allow the troops to have their tangible rewards after a successful action.

The inhabitants of London greeted Theodosius with adulation, not to say relief. He required information about what was going on in the province, and may have put out an appeal for informers. He also questioned captives, who explained that the only way to defeat the tribesmen was to use stratagems and ruses, and lay ambushes. There was probably no large horde, led by one chieftain, for Theodosius to fight, but perhaps a whole series of tribal groupings and their leaders, sometime combining and sometimes operating independently. This was to be guerrilla warfare rather than a campaign of set battles. Before he marched from London, Theodosius recalled the men who claimed to be on leave, with no questions asked, and also issued a proclamation offering amnesty for deserters. Ammianus says that most of the missing soldiers came back to join their units.

It seems that Nectaridus and Fullofaudes, the officials who had been killed when the attacks began, had not yet been replaced, or at least it is likely that there was no Diocesan *vicarius* in post, and no *Dux* in Britain. Civil government and military command having lapsed for a short time, Theodosius was anxious to find personnel to take charge of these affairs before he set off on campaign, and asked for Civilis to be sent as *vicarius*, or as he is described by Ammianus, *rector pro praefectis*, deputy for the Prefect of Gaul, which amounts to the same thing as *vicarius*. He also asked for Dulcitius as *Dux*. Apart from this mention in Ammianus's work, nothing is known of these individuals.

The actual campaigns of Theodosius are described in very general terms, so it is impossible to discern where the army was operating. Theodosius frustrated the tribesmen by choosing places for laying ambushes, and he never asked the soldiers to undertake tasks that he would not willingly do himself. This is the sum total of information about how he cleared the island of invaders and 'put all his enemies to flight'. When he caught the first band of tribesmen while he was marching to London, Theodosius divided his forces into several detachments, so in clearing the rest of the country he probably used the same tactics, rather than marching in one great column hoping to find an enemy to fight. Good intelligence services would be in demand to track down the groups of attackers. An army moving in separate detachments would also require good communications. None of these details are known, and if Theodosius's troops built marching camps, nothing from the archaeological record has been assigned to them.

RECONSTRUCTION

The whole operation to clear the bands of marauders from the whole country may have taken a full year, spilling over into 368, and the reconstruction work that Theodosius put into effect was perhaps not started until 369. According to Ammianus:

> [Theodosius] completely restored cities and forts that had been affected by multiple damages, and fortified them so as to ensure peace for a long time. (Ammianus Marcellinus 28.3.2)

There are different interpretations of this phrase, one of them suggesting that the cities had been fortified to ensure peace, but had nonetheless suffered damage, which emphasises the degree of destruction that had occurred, and also belittles the efforts of the town councils and the military authorities to fortify their towns and forts effectively enough. This is a negative comment on Britain and casts doubt on its future chances of survival, since it implies that it could all happen again. This is not at all what one would expect of Theodosius's achievements. It is more fitting to end on a positive note, with all due credit to Theodosius, and the assertion that he had made the British provinces safe for the future.

Tracking down where the late fourth-century reconstruction was done is not as easy as it might sound. From the archaeological standpoint, the towns do not seem to have been so badly damaged, and even many of the villas seem to have emerged for the most part unscathed. Insufficient numbers of villas have been fully excavated to be able to say what proportion of them escaped damage, and in any case it is not always easy to put a precise date on destruction even if it is found in the archaeological record. There is one grisly case at Brislington in Somerset, where human heads and burnt tiles had been thrown down the well, and no one came back to tidy it all up, which may represent an attack by roving bands looking for loot.

Any damage such as burnt crops or stolen harvests would be impossible to trace by archaeological means, but it is more likely that the countryside was where much of the damage occurred. Since most of the small industries were located in rural areas, it was probably manufacturing that was worse affected, especially as communications would be disrupted while the pirates and tribesmen were at large, so even if the factories were not damaged, the distribution of goods would probably cease for a while. Pottery studies have revealed that Crambeck ware supplied to the troops suddenly blossomed at about this time, perhaps because rival firms had gone out of business, so the factory owners seized the gap in the market – it is an ill wind that blows nobody any good.

Although the towns do not appear to have suffered severe structural damage, the inhabitants would have been shaken by the invasions, which would have been, in modern parlance, a wake-up call. Now the town councils put their efforts into enhancing their fortifications. It may have been Theodosius who encouraged them, or the new building may have arisen spontaneously in separate towns. Externally projecting towers began to be added to existing walls, with artillery platforms on top, suggesting that probably the tribesmen had succeeded in getting uncomfortably close to the town walls, and the councils were determined not to let them repeat the process with impunity. The possibility of help from the military in building the towers is dismissed, because the quality of the work varies, as though different gangs with divergent skills were used at the same time, possibly indicating that town councillors paid for the work themselves and employed their own builders. Multiple gangs would enable the work to be done much faster, and it is not unlikely that the able-bodied inhabitants of the towns were coerced into doing at least some of the work, which may account for the varied quality of the construction.

Though the army may not have assisted with the building work, there may have been a military presence in the towns. Defensive walls, even if well stocked with weapons and ammunition, including artillery engines, would be of no use if there were no trained personnel to operate them, so it is possible that at least at first some soldiers were billeted in the towns, either to operate the machinery or to train townspeople in their use. In the other provinces of the west it was quite normal for troops to be billeted in the towns, so it would not be out of the question to do the same in the British provinces, except that there is no absolute proof for this. There is one factor that may be an indication that British towns did possess a garrison of some kind. In the *Notitia Dignitatum*, the list of officials and military units and commanders, probably drawn up in the fifth century, an illustrated page with the relevant insignia is included for each high-ranking official. The *vicarii* are normally indicated by various figures of maidens, but the *vicarius* of the Diocese of Britain is given a page showing diagrammatic towns with castellated walls, which may indicate that the *vicarius* was not limited to civilian administration but also commanded some troops.

Rebuilding and repairs at military installations have been found in archaeological excavations at forts in the north, such as Ilkley, Bainbridge and Chester-le-Street. On Hadrian's Wall, a coin of Valentinian was found under a rebuilt section. On the Wall itself, this may be the occasion when people from the *civitates* were brought northwards to repair parts of the stone curtain wall. They left some undated inscriptions recording their work, which is of inferior quality and not in the usual military style, but at least their work restored the defences. Some of the Wall forts were remodelled internally. The headquarters buildings at Housesteads, Chesters and South Shields seem to have been converted into stores and dwelling spaces, and at Housesteads pottery found in the granary suggests that people were living there too. The late Roman barrack block in the north-eastern sector of Housesteads fort, conserved for visitors to see, was built more or less on the line of the previous barracks, but each house was built separately, with a very narrow gap between each one, which may indicate a change of garrison. Archaeologists labelled these buildings chalets, because they are reminiscent of holiday camp accommodation. Certain finds such as hairpins and sewing equipment from inside some of the forts was taken as an indication that they were used by civilians rather than soldiers (though soldiers of all periods were usually quite skilled with needle and thread). This evidence was connected to the apparent abandonment of some of the *vici* outside the forts, to produce a scenario of soldiers and their families all living together within the walls for protection. It would be a perfectly normal reaction after a period of great distress, but it has to be admitted that until all the *vici* and all the forts have been excavated it cannot be said that it was a universal trend in the Wall area to bring families and other civilians into the forts.

Since there is an understandable tendency to relate archaeological findings with known personalities and events, the blocked gates at some of the forts have been linked to Theodosius's reconstruction of the frontier. Usually one portal was blocked up, and perhaps the guard chambers re-orientated to accommodate the change. As a result, at some of the forts where the remains of a double portal gateway are visible, one threshold is worn and the other almost new. Blocking the gateways was not an unusual feature of late Roman forts, especially on the Danube frontier where projecting towers were built right across some of them, blocking them entirely.

The troops which manned the Wall forts are not known, since hardly any inscriptions have been found dating to the late fourth century. In the *Notitia Dignitatum* the information about British garrisons does not seem to be contemporary with the rest of the listings, and shows that old-style *alae* and *cohorts* existed along the Wall. No other province contains such units, so there are several questions to be asked about the information. Is it correct, and were the old style units really still in place at the end of the fourth century? Or did the compilers of the document have no access to up-to-date information, and therefore used whatever they had to hand? There is such controversy over the date of composition of the whole document in general and the British sections in particular that it would occupy half a chapter simply to enumerate all the theories.

North of Hadrian's Wall, the outpost forts appear to have been given up, making the Wall itself the most northerly point that was manned by Roman troops. Patrols to reconnoitre the tribal territories probably also ceased. Theodosius disbanded the *areani* because they had colluded with the barbarians:

> He removed from their posts the *areani*, a group of men set up long ago, about whom we related certain things in the account of Constans. They had lapsed into evil ways, and were openly convicted of passing onto the barbarians information about what was happening on our side, seduced by the receipt of, or promises of quantities of booty. (Ammianus Marcellinus 28.3.8)

During the onslaught of the tribes, much of the damage was done by seaborne tribes and pirates, so it is possible that Theodosius established the watchtowers of the east coast, running from Flamborough Head, probably up to the entrance to the Tyne. Ammianus says that Theodosius protected the frontiers with watchtowers and defences, which could just as easily refer to Hadrian's Wall as to the coasts, but the late Roman towers of the Yorkshire coast were definitely built by someone, and an Imperial expedition, either Constans in the 340s, or Theodosius in the 360s, is as good an occasion as any for their establishment. It is clear now that the west coast was not neglected, and towers have been found there that probably date to the fourth century. Further south a fort was built at Caernarvon, and at Caer Gybi near Holyhead the late Roman structure is reminiscent of the late Roman fleet bases on the Rhine. It is conjectured that all these towers and forts may have been commanded by the Count of the Saxon Shore (*Comes Litoris Saxonici*). It would certainly make sense to amalgamate the coastal areas under one command, but this remains conjecture, since the *Notitia Dignitatum* only lists the south coast forts under the count of the Saxon Shore.

Forts by themselves cannot protect the coasts, but only give advance warning to inland troops of an impending attack. With the addition of a fleet patrolling the seas the task of the coastal forts and towers would be much enhanced, giving the opportunity to attack pirate vessels before they came to shore, or to intercept them on their way home. There is no proof for this, especially as the main fleet base in the later Roman period was at Boulogne, and the attacks on the coasts that are reported in the ancient sources were directed at Gaul. The late Roman author Vegetius describes the fleet operating in northern seas in the late fourth century:

> Scouting vessels are associated with the larger galleys, with twenty oars on each side. The Britons call them *Picati* [meaning daubed with tar]. These are intended to locate and sometimes intercept enemy ships and to discover their arrival or what their plans are. In order to prevent the scouting ships being easily seen through the brightness of their appearance, the sails and rigging are dyed sea-green, and even the pitch with which they are daubed is the same colour. The sailors and marines wear sea-green clothes so that as they are scouting they may escape detection by day as well as by night. (Vegetius *Epitoma Rei Militaris* 4.37)

One wonders whether, for British waters, slate grey might not have been a better option for sails and clothing. The operations of the fleet may have been carried out in association with the coastal towers and the forts all around Britain, not just the forts of the Saxon Shore in the south.

WHERE WAS THE PROVINCE OF VALENTIA?

This problem has already been mentioned in connection with the campaigns of Constans, but since the evidence for it derives from Ammianus's account of Theodosius's campaigns, it requires further consideration. It has been suggested that the province already existed when Theodosius restored the provinces of Britain, perhaps created by Constans, and then renamed for Valentinian and Valens when Theodosius recovered it. The main trouble, apart from lack of information about *when* it was created, is that no one knows exactly *where* it was.

In Ammianus's account, the story of the recovery of the province and its renaming is told after the dismissal of the *areani* who operated in the north, most likely beyond the Wall. Therefore it can be argued that when he moved on from that story, Ammianus was still dealing with the north when he wrote about Valentia. One suggestion is that Valentia was carved out of the northern half of Secunda, which was based on York, and another is that Valentia covered the whole frontier area of Hadrian's Wall and some of its hinterland, with a capital at Carlisle. A *civitas* capital had been established there, and was still flourishing in the later Roman period and even in post-Roman times. It has also been suggested that the province was in the west, in modern Cumbria, where the threats to the coast and the western end of Hadrian's Wall had increased when Irish pirates took to the seas.

It was clearly an important province, since in the *Notitia Dignitatum* it is listed with a consular governor, putting it on a level with Maxima Caesariensis with its capital at London. A case has been made for the two consular provinces being one and the same, so that Maxima Caesariensis became Valentia. This was the suggestion of a modern scholar who inserted an ingenious amendment to the two entries in the *Notitia Dignitatum* where both provinces are listed, but if the word *nunc* meaning 'now' is inserted between the two names, rendering them as Maxima Caesariensis, now Valentia, it can be argued that Valentinian renamed the most important of the British provinces after himself and his brother Valens.

There are no other references to Valentia in the existing literature. What is required is an inscription from some late Roman site tying it unequivocally to this peripatetic province, but unfortunately the people of fourth-century Britain had for the most part lost the habit of setting up inscriptions.

THE REVOLT OF VALENTINUS

One of the problems that Theodosius had to deal with was an attempted usurpation by a certain Valentinus, which Theodosius managed to nip in the bud before it could spread. Valentinus was originally from Pannonia, but after he committed some serious offence he had been exiled to Britain. He sounded out some of the soldiers and other exiles, and promised them money, but Theodosius had a thorough intelligence network, and was informed of the plot. The plan was perhaps to break out while Theodosius and the army were in the far north, but it was foiled and Theodosius gave orders to the *Dux* Dulcitius to round up Valentinus and some of his followers and execute them. One of the interesting features of this episode is that there seems to have been enough exiles in Britain for Valentinus to imagine that he could find considerable support among them. While one modern author denies that Britain was the Roman version of Botany Bay, the island would be an ideal place to send dissidents since they would have to make extra efforts to leave the province across the Channel or the North Sea, and there would always be a bevy of helpful informers to watch their movements.

AFTER THEODOSIUS

It is impossible to produce a continuous narrative of events in Britain for the last quarter of the fourth century, because there are only sporadic fragments of information concerning the British provinces from time to time, leaving great gaps where nothing is known, except from archaeological excavations. One general observation can be made, that there are signs of widespread prosperity in the last years of the fourth century, which must at least in part be attributable to Theodosius' success in restoring order, and along with it, renewing confidence among the Britons.

For a few more years, Theodosius went from strength to strength. He was appointed *magister equitum* when he returned to the Imperial court, and then campaigned against the Alamanni in Raetia. He moved on to Africa to suppress a rebellion in 373, and remained there till

375, but was suddenly arrested and executed for reasons unknown. His execution was probably ordered by Valens, because his brother Valentinian died in that year, and Valens had been told by an oracle that he would be succeeded as Emperor by a man whose name began with Theod-, so he removed the candidate that he thought the most likely successor. Perhaps it was a good thing that he ignored the fact that Theodosius's second son was named after him, and became the Emperor Theodosius the Great, a year after Valens was killed at the Battle of Adrianople.

In Britain the peace established by Theodosius was broken in 370 when the Saxons struck again. Ammianus recounts how Nectaridus stopped the invasion but was wounded and lost a lot of men, so he appealed to the Emperor Valentinian, who sent the *magister militum* Severus to deal with the situation. It is conjectured that Nectaridus may have been *Comes Litoris Saxonici* though he is not named as such by Ammianus.

Two years later Ammianus records that Fraomarius, a chieftain of the Bucinobantes, a branch of the Alamanni settled near Mainz (ancient Mogontiacum), was sent to Britain to take command of a *numerus Alamannorum*. This unit is not attested in any other source in Britain, and it is not known where it was stationed. It is one illustration of the increasing use of Germanic troops in Britain. The archaeological evidence that was once thought to relate to such Germanic troops has been re-evaluated. The first finds of military equipment that were classified as Germanic in origin were used to build up a theory that many Germanic mercenaries had been settled in the south of Britain in the late Roman period, which gave rise to a further suggestion, that the Saxon Shore was not named for defence against the Saxons, but for the area which was settled by them. However, further discoveries have revealed that the military items were not necessarily related to German tribesmen, either as mercenaries or soldiers of the regular Roman army, because Roman factories were producing them en masse and distributing them to all units.

There is a dearth of information about Britain for the next decade, but there were momentous events in the Empire. Valentinian died in

375, allegedly because he had an apoplectic fit after dealing with a particularly difficult embassy. He was succeeded in the west by his two sons, Gratian and Valentinian II, while his brother Valens governed the east. Three years later war broke out with the Goths on the Danube, where the tribesmen had been treated very insensitively by the Romans. They wanted to settle on lands within the Roman Empire, but promises made to them were broken, and they were herded together and denied food. They sold their children into slavery to avoid starvation. The end result was the eruption of the Goths and the Battle of Adrianople in 378. The Emperor Valens engaged the tribesmen without waiting for Gratian to arrive with more troops. Valens was killed, and most of the eastern army was destroyed. Ironically, in the longer term, it was the west which declined and not the east, because the eastern Emperors were forced to reorganise, and they possessed the wealth to do so. The successor of Valens was the man of the prophecy, with the name beginning with Theod-, the son of the executed Count Theodosius, called Theodosius I, or the Great.

VILLAS – Text Box

In the fourth century villas in Britain flourished, reaching a peak of development around 350. The builders and inhabitants of villas at that time probably had no inkling that this would be the last phase of development and expansion. Villas had a long history in Britain, and the study of them continues without producing a definition of the term villa, or a classification of villa types. About fifty to sixty years ago, there were fewer examples of excavated villas, and it seemed as though they could be understood principally as farms, and that it was possible to categorise them into specific groups. All this has changed in recent years as more and more information has been gathered, and the confidence of historians and archaeologists in the early years of villa studies has been eroded. To categorise the many examples of villas would be like trying to categorise houses in the British countryside today, ranging from enormous country houses of the diminished aristocracy, through lesser houses, to large farms. If these were to be studied by archaeological methods, using only the ground plans and artefacts that turned up, it would be impossible to say how much land was attached to them, whether their main occupation was agriculture, whether nearby buildings that looked like storage facilities housed their produce, and if the cottages for a few miles around belonged to the estate or were independent dwellings. Archaeology cannot fully elucidate ownership, tenants or occupations.

In the third century it seems that there was an increased interest in villas in Britain, but it is not known whether wealthy people were investing in land and buildings to cream off the profits, or whether they actually lived in the villas themselves. People in other provinces may have bought villas in Britain and installed managers or bailiffs to run them, or they may have migrated from Gaul or Germany where conditions were less secure, and bought or built villas in Britain. There were several Imperial estates in other provinces run on behalf of the Emperor by his appointed staff, and though there were probably at least a few in Britain, it is not known where they might have been; we can only guess. Even in rare cases where there is some evidence of an owner, such as Tiberius Claudius Severus at Piddington in Northamptonshire, whose name appears on tile stamps, there is no information as to his status, or his wealth and where it came from, or if he lived in the villa himself.

It has been suggested that in some cases there may have been multiple occupancy of a villa, perhaps in those where two sets of bath houses are known, as at Chedworth, where there are also two sets of living accommodation. This can be explained by the theory that Chedworth may have been a religious establishment, but the theory of multiple occupancy remains valid.

Multiple occupancy of a different kind is in evidence at the great villa estates. At Rockbourne in Hampshire, there were two sets of baths, but this seems to have been a large estate where the owners lived in the main house and the estate workers dwelt in humbler accommodation with their own communal baths. The enormous villa at Woodchester comprised a very large house set around a courtyard, and several quite substantial buildings around it, the whole complex surrounded by a wall with gates and towers at the main entrance. It is best interpreted as an estate like Rockbourne with its workers housed near to the main house.

The inhabitants of villas close to towns are assumed to be Romanised British people, possibly town councillors who may have had town houses as well for the days when official business obliged them to be there. Some villas have been shown to have started life as Iron Age roundhouses, replaced by Roman-style houses, sometimes by a succession of ever more elaborate houses, or improvements were made to the original house by enlarging it, adding new wings on either side or sometimes completely enclosing a courtyard. The villa at Lockleys in Hertfordshire was built over an Iron Age house, first as a timber house dating from 50 to about 120, then after a gap a stone house appeared around 300. It cannot be known whether this villa remained in the same family, descended from those who were originally living in the roundhouse that preceded the first villa.

Agriculture was the basis of wealth in the Roman world, so it is likely that many of the villas in Britain were principally occupied with producing grain, wheat being the staple commodity, followed by barley and oats. The wheat that was exported to the Rhine from Britain, as attested by Ammianus, must have been grown on farms, some of which might be classifiable as villas. Even modest farms would probably cover a large area. Animals would be needed for transport and farm work; stables and sheds would be required to house them. Cart sheds and workshops may have been built, for the repair or even manufacture of tools and implements. Houses for labourers and slaves and their overseers would be located nearby. An archaeological investigation of such a vast area would be expensive and of a longer duration than most digs usually are nowadays, but an investigation of one or two buildings cannot reveal the complexity of villas or give any clues as to what their function was. There may have been some villas where the main function was small-scale industrial production, for instance of tiles or pottery, where the owner made enough profit to build a well-appointed house which was not primarily a farm, though some crops and vegetables may have been grown to provide for the family and workers.

There was a detectable increase in the number of villas in the fourth century, which has been explained by people fleeing from Gaul and setting up home in Britain, and also by the possibility that British farmers could now afford to build a modest villa. Though the number of villas increased, the days of the large villa were over, and no such new building has been discovered dating to the fourth century. The existing large villas did not yet go out of use. Lullingstone in Kent reached a peak of development around 350. At that period many villas displayed painted walls and mosaic floors, the typical attributes of villas, but it was soon to change. The upheavals of 367 may not have destroyed many villas but probably any further development was halted. What happened between the middle of the fourth century and the end of the fifth is imperfectly understood. Some villas continued to be occupied but it is not known by whom. Where definite changes are detectable, such as evidence that fires were lit on top of mosaics, or in one case at Sparsholt in Hampshire where a corn dryer was dug through a mosaic floor, it is usually suggested that the original owners or occupiers must have abandoned the villa and others with fewer scruples took possession, but more recently it has been pointed out that there may have been a change of use and an adaptation to reduced circumstances by the original inhabitants. A mosaic floor does not feed the family, whereas a corn dryer brought into the house would be of more help. It seems that around villas where there was a decline in standards in the living accommodation the land was still farmed. At Sparsholt the villa eventually crumbled and a timber hall was built near the ruins, but farming continued. There is a modern parallel, not quite so dire, but many farms are now diversifying, not just as bed and breakfast establishments, but they are also setting up shops for the sale of produce not necessarily grown on the farm, together with cafés, craft shops, family attractions and so on. The fields around the farm are still planted and harvested, cattle and sheep graze the pastures, but none of this is any longer the concern of the owner or tenant farmer, whose fields are now farmed by large contractors with all the up-to-date machinery. Archaeological investigations would merely be able to illustrate the facts that the farm was occupied and the land was farmed.

There is a darker side to villas, found in several excavations. It is clear that it was customary to bury newborn or very young babies in the grounds of the villas or under the doorsteps. The infant mortality rate was probably very high, so these babies may not necessarily have been killed, and in Romano-British society burials under the door or within the house may have been carried out to propitiate deities and ensure protection of the household. But the case of the villa at Hambleden, where nearly one hundred dead babies were buried over a period of time, may indicate deliberate elimination of unwanted children, perhaps born to slaves. Exposure of unwanted infants was still carried out in the Roman world, despite the enactment of laws to prohibit the practice. These factors erode a little of the glamorous picture of life in the villas with mosaic floors, painted walls and central heating.

THE REVOLT OF MAGNUS MAXIMUS

Maximus was said to be a relative of Count Theodosius, and had accompanied him to Britain for the war of 367, but it is not known where he went after the campaigns ended. He reappeared in Britain in 383, obviously with some high rank, but there is no information as to his title. Since he is credited with campaigns against the Scotti and the Picts, it is possible that he was *Dux* in the north, but it is also suggested that he may have been *Comes Litoris Saxonici*. Suggestions that his title was *Comes Britanniarum*, in command of all the British provinces, have been dismissed since this post is not attested until a later period.

As a usurper who ultimately failed, the sources are mostly hostile to Maximus, except that the late author Orosius says that he would have been worthy of being Emperor if only he had not acted illegally. The reasons why Maximus rebelled are obscure. The Greek historians, reflecting the views of the eastern half of the Empire, were certain that he was jealous of Theodosius I, to whom he was probably related, and with whom he had served while participating in the elder Theodosius's British campaigns. This makes it seem as though he had always harboured a desire to be Emperor or at least to gain some higher office than he held at the time of the revolt. More sober authors claimed that the soldiers had declared for him, and this is the excuse that Maximus used himself, although he elevated the matter from the human to the divine plane, insisting that it was the will of God.

Maximus could not have led a revolt without the complicity of his troops, who seemed perfectly content to declare for him, so this suggests that there were genuine grievances against Gratian and Valentinian II. Maximus soon left Britain for Gaul. He was already a Christian, but he was baptised and embraced the Catholic doctrine at Trier. It is debatable whether he stripped the garrisons from Britain, or whether he took only a select few soldiers and made arrangements for defence of the British frontiers. He may have taken auxiliaries from the forts of Wales and the Pennines, and he probably removed XX Valeria Victrix to Gaul. The Chester fortress seems to have been disused from about this time onwards, but the legion could have been split up and put into smaller forts in Wales and along the west coast. If this was the case there is no trace of it.

The possibility that Gratian had fallen into disfavour at least with the armies is supported by the ease with which his troops deserted him and went over to Maximus once the British Emperor arrived. Gratian was killed, leaving Gaul and Spain open to Maximus. Theodosius I officially recognised Maximus in 384, rather than go to war against him immediately, so for a few years there was peace and good government. Maximus converted the recognition of his Imperial title from mere acceptance to acknowledged support from Theodosius for his regime, which would have encouraged his troops and the provincials under his rule. Nothing is known of how he administered the dioceses of Gaul, Spain and Britain, except that he may have appointed a *vicarius* to one of them, named Desiderius. The evidence comes from an Imperial reply, or rescript, to a question about a legal matter. It is dated by the names of the two consuls to 385, when Maximus was established as Emperor, but the names at the top of the letter, which was reproduced in the law code drawn up in the reign of Theodosius, are those of Valentinian, Theodosius and his son Arcadius, with no mention of Maximus. Perhaps when the usurper had been overthrown the record was altered to fit the revised circumstances before it was included in the law code.

Valentinian II was in Italy while Maximus ruled the western provinces, but in 387, having had plenty of time to recruit soldiers and enlarge his army, Maximus descended on Italy and forced Valentinian to flee to the court of Theodosius, who was probably already preparing to deal with Maximus. In 388 war broke out. Theodosius destroyed Maximus's fleet, then his army defeated him in a few skirmishes on land. Finally Maximus was captured, and tortured to make him renounce the idea that he had ever been supported by Theodosius. It was important for the Emperor to justify his action against Maximus, since if he had actively supported him and then turned against him it would seem like a perfidious betrayal. Maximus was executed and Valentinian II was restored as Emperor of the western half of the Empire.

For the next few years, events in the western and eastern halves of the Empire did not affect Britain directly. Even when Theodosius was persuaded by Bishop Ambrose in 391 to issue a decree outlawing all pagan practices, and a second more radical one to stamp out the worship of the Roman domestic gods, the *lares* and *penates*, paganism in Britain was not rooted out. The other western provinces took exception to this last law, and a revolt broke out under the pagan general Arbogast, but he had further reasons to rebel, apart from religious ones. Theodosius returned from the west to Constantinople, leaving Arbogast to watch over Valentinian II, who was only twenty years old. In May 392 the young Emperor was found dangling at the end of a rope. If he had committed suicide, no one believed it, so Arbogast fell under suspicion. Three months went by without an official ruler, until Arbogast declared another devotee of paganism, Eugenius, as Emperor. Once again Britain was included in a rebel Empire, until Theodosius eradicated both Arbogast and Eugenius in September 394. Within five months Theodosius himself was dead.

BRITAIN IN THE LATE FOURTH CENTURY

Perhaps some of the units that Maximus took with him to Gaul were returned to Britain, but since it is not known which ones he removed it is difficult to isolate any troop movements within the five-year period of his reign. Valentinian II would have sufficient time to remedy the military situation in Britain if there were deficiencies after Maximus was killed, but there is no record of replacements being sent to fill gaps. It is pointed out that in the army of Illyricum as listed in the *Notitia Dignitatum* there is a unit called Seguntienses, which may have started out at Segontium, near Caernarvon in north Wales. If so Maximus may have taken it with him, and when he was defeated it was sent to a different posting.

The Welsh connection is of course very strong, since Magnus Maximus is Macsen Wledig, one of the heroes of the old Welsh tales related in the *Red Book of Hergest*, and the *White Book of Rhydderch*. Both of these are collections of narrative prose stories and poetry from a long-standing oral tradition, compiled in written form in the fourteenth century. Macsen was a Roman Emperor who married a Welsh woman, and his brothers helped him to regain his throne. Somewhere there is a tiny kernel of truth in this tale, and the rest is fantasy.

Some of the native chiefs of the tribes of the north and Wales may have been empowered by Maximus when he left, in order to protect the frontiers by employing the tribal warriors. It was normal practice on other frontiers to use tribesmen almost as a buffer on the frontiers, perhaps because they were considered expendable, and possibly cheaper to employ, but they were not usually employed in the provinces where they were raised. Nothing can be proved for this theory, but Maximus features in the genealogies of the tribes of Galloway as well as those of Wales.

Towards the end of the fourth century, the Irish had begun to settle in Wales, in the Lleyn and Gower peninsulas, but they do not receive as much attention as the Saxons, perhaps because they did not evict or kill the existing inhabitants, or possibly there were vacant lands for them to cultivate. On the other hand some authors suspect that they may have attacked places within reach of the coasts, for instance Wroxeter, where a skeleton of an old man together with some coins was found in the hypocaust of the baths, as though he had hidden there and died, never having been rescued.

Exactly what state the army was in is hard to judge. All over the Empire recruitment of provincials had become more and more difficult in the second half of the fourth century, and there is no reason to imagine that Britain was an exception to the rule. From Diocletian's reign onwards sons of soldiers were compelled to become soldiers themselves, and a series of laws outline how all the usual qualifications for joining the army had been relaxed. The upper and lower age limits for recruits were widened to bring younger and older men into service, and then the height qualification was reduced. It seemed that anyone with all four limbs would be accepted as a soldier, but laws were issued to force landowners to contribute healthy men to the levy instead of homeless vagrants, a ploy that many of them had begun to use so that so that they could retain their own agricultural labourers on their estates. Men began to cut off their fingers or thumbs to avoid the service, as more laws attest. In 368 Valentinian dealt harshly with all men who had deliberately mutilated themselves, condemning them to be burnt alive, thus removing them altogether from the available pool of recruits. Theodosius took a more sensible line, allowing any men with only one or even no thumbs to join, but if a local landowner presented such a defective candidate for the army, he was obliged to provide an extra man so the two of them combined would make up one good soldier.

The difficulty of recruiting provincials only increased the reliance upon tribal warriors, either brought into existing units or enlisted in groups, perhaps as the *numerus Alamannorum* had been, commanded by Fraomar, who was probably an Alamannic tribesman himself. Across the Empire there was a gradual reversion to the Republican practice of enlisting whole groups of tribesmen, commanded by their own officers, who were with, rather than in, the Roman army, and were allowed to return home when the campaign for which they had been engaged was over. The Alamanni were probably part of the regular army in Britain, but they are not attested after this reference in the history of Ammianus. It is perhaps more likely that with an Alamannic officer they may not have been a permanent part of the military establishment. Other such units, not part of the permanent military establishment, may have existed in Britain, making it difficult to enumerate the full complement of troops in the five provinces of the Diocese.

The governors of the British provinces and the local councillors may have been guilty of a reluctance to serve, and when in office they may have displayed a lack of interest in their duties in the late fourth century. One of the greatest contributions to ancient history was made by the eastern Emperor Theodosius II when he ordered the lawyers to collect and record all the laws that were still relevant, including the rescripts of the Emperors clarifying various points of law. From this compilation of laws it is known that in 369 Valentinian I issued a law instructing the Prefects to ensure that all provincial governors should keep their appointed residences in good repair, and he urged that they should live in them, rather than going off to live on the estates of wealthy hosts in comfort and luxury. The fact that the law had to be issued at all indicates that the lax behaviour was widespread, and also that someone was reporting on it.

Local government was perhaps not so badly afflicted and was certainly not in abeyance, but the decurions in Britain were probably also living more and more in their villas outside towns rather than in their town houses. This may mean that the provinces of Britain were peaceful and so they did not feel under threat of attack. Therefore they could forgo the protection that living within the walls of the towns would offer. It is known that there was considerable reluctance to take up office in the town councils, and it had become customary to commiserate with men who had received an appointment rather than congratulating them. Although it was still an honour to serve, it was onerous financially, at a time when inflation and taxes bit deep. The trick was to hold office for as short a time as possible. Decurions were expected to finance entertainments and civic services and amenities out of their own pockets, which probably bankrupted some of them. The individual decurions may have been responsible for building the projecting towers that were added to some of the towns, and the varied style and quality of the work in some of them may reflect variations in the financial status of those who paid for them.

Nonetheless there were some wealthy people who were able to afford reconstruction and refurbishment of villas in the late fourth century, notably at Great Casterton and Huddlecote, where new mosaic floors were laid, and someone built a lavish town house at Verulamium at about the same time. Trade and industries seemed to have continued to flourish in the last quarter of the fourth century, one particular instance being pottery manufacture in the factories in Hampshire, where new designs were introduced at the end of the century, which does not suggest impoverishment or insecurity.

With the benefit of hindsight, because the Empire was about to encounter difficult times within a few years of the end of the fourth century, and Britain was shortly to be divorced from the Empire, it seems that the decade after the rebellion of Magnus Maximus ought to have been full of doom and gloom, but there were no discernible hints in the lives of the majority of Romano-Britons that change was on the way.

12

Transition & New Beginning
AD 395 to c.450

The death of Theodosius I could be said to mark the transition from the old unified Empire, governed by two or more Emperors in the eastern and western sectors, to the division into two distinct Empires, but although succeeded by his two sons, Arcadius in the east and Honorius in the west, this was far from the complete division into two separate Empires. For many years the same laws were promulgated in east and west, and troops were sent from one half to assist the other. One of the differences between the earlier Empire and the late Empire was that the Emperors no longer accompanied the troops on campaigns, as they had been accustomed to do from Marcus Aurelius to Constantine and his heirs. From the fourth century, the most important military commanders were the *magistri* in charge of the field armies, many of whom were of German extraction, or originally from other tribes. These powerful military commanders were thoroughly Roman, and were loyal to Rome and Constantinople if not always to the Emperors.

The officer with the most prestige and power when Theodosius died was Stilicho, by birth a Vandal. He was closely associated with the Imperial family, having married Theodosius's niece, who had been adopted as the Emperor's daughter. Stilicho's own daughter married Honorius, so he was the son-in-law of an Emperor and after 395 the father-in-law of another. Stilicho always maintained that according to Theodosius's last wish, he was to supervise both Arcadius and Honorius, which would give him ascendancy in both halves of the Empire. Unfortunately this last wish had never reached the stage of a public pronouncement, so there was considerable doubt about Stilicho's honesty and motives.

One of the most visible changes in the Empire was in the composition of the army. There was no sudden sweeping alteration, but a gradual conversion from a mostly Roman or provincial army to one containing a large proportion of tribesmen, who were unhesitatingly called barbarians by the Romans. The difficulties of attracting suitable provincials had started in Severus's reign, when this Emperor realised that service in the armies had to be made more appealing if new recruits were to be found in the vast numbers that were perpetually required. Consequently he raised pay and allowed the soldiers some privileges such as the permission to marry. In the fourth century these problems of recruitment had intensified, and as the enrolment of tribesmen had been practised for some time and was for the most part successful, the Romans continued to employ tribesmen, on an ever widening basis. For a long time tribes such as the Franks and Alamanni had been at one and the same time enemies fighting against the Romans and soldiers fighting for them. The tribesmen seemingly had no problems in going to war against their own kind, though units raised in one area did not normally fight near their homes. Tribesmen serving in the Roman army were nothing new. When large groups were officially settled within the Empire on vacant lands, they were often given the status of *laeti*, the meaning of which is not entirely clear, but may mean that they were only half free. This fits well with the terms of the treaties that were made with them, stipulating that they should farm the land and also provide recruits. By the middle of the fourth century, there was a change in the way the tribesmen were employed, in that some of the units raised from tribesmen often remained near their homes. One of the reasons why Julian was made Emperor by his troops in Gaul was that the soldiers protested against being called upon to fight in another part of the Empire. This was contrary to the terms upon which they had been engaged, which promised them that they would remain close to their own lands.

The Romans were well served by the tribesmen in the army, and the Emperors did not prevent any tribesman with abilities from rising to high rank. Gradually the so-called barbarians reached the position of supreme commanders, and as the Emperors became increasingly like mere figureheads, the generals acquired real power. Stilicho was just one in a long line of barbarian generals, who wielded great power, but rarely if ever made themselves into Emperors, preferring to raise an Emperor as figurehead, and then manipulate policy and practice from behind the scenes.

BRITAIN IN THE EARLY FIFTH CENTURY

At the end of the fourth century the provinces of Britain were still prosperous, with a hierarchical government descending from the Emperor via the Prefects and the *vicarii* down to the governors and the provincials themselves. As the fifth century opened it probably seemed that this system would be eternal, albeit with a few crises to overcome here and there. Within a decade all had changed and Britain was once again outside the Roman Empire, never to be taken back into the fold.

It is difficult to discern the state of the Roman army in Britain, and what its overall strength was. It is usually assumed that Magnus Maximus had taken most of the troops to the continent in 383, and perhaps few if any had returned. But the wholesale recruitment of groups of tribesmen, who were perhaps not listed with the regular army, may have swelled the establishment in Britain without leaving any traces. These soldiers would perhaps have been more mobile and the military situation more fluid than it was when whole units occupied single forts where their headquarters were located. It certainly seems that the army in the British provinces could not cope with the various attacks that were made in the latter years of the fourth century, and always had to ask for help from the Emperor, who sometimes sent a general like Count Theodosius and some extra troops from the field army. The numbers of extra troops, if correctly reported, never seemed to be enormous, so it is likely that the British troops played a large part in suppressing attacks, but these soldiers are not mentioned in the sources. Possibly the British units managed very well against less serious attacks, but perhaps these have not been recorded either, and only the most serious ones made it into the pages of the ancient historians.

In 398 there was a successful action against pirates, in which Stilicho was involved. The source is the adulatory poetry of Claudian, whose flowery language makes it difficult to discern what was going on. It is likely that Stilicho sent some troops and a reliable commander but did not come to Britain in person, otherwise Claudian would have composed some suitable lines to commemorate Stilicho's arrival, exploits and departure. As it is, he gives a voice to the personification of Britannia, explaining how Stilicho had fortified her against Irish pirates, and how she no longer feared every tide that might bring the Saxons. There is some support for a mission sent to Britain by Stilicho in the works of the historian Gildas, who composed his account of the destruction of Britain (*De Excidio Britanniae*) probably in the middle of the fifth century or later, though there is no agreement on the date of composition. He says that the Romans once sent a *legio* to the aid of the Britons, but there is no firm date for this and his account could apply to other occasions. However, it might belong to the period when Stilicho was in power.

Stilicho may have been responsible for the creation of the post of *Comes Britanniarum*, or count of the provinces of Britain, which is known to be a late innovation, but could possibly have been established earlier than *c.*398. This post is listed in the *Notitia Dignitatum* where the *Comes Britanniarum* commands units of the field army, more than half of them cavalry. He is listed along with the other officials, the *vicarius* in charge of the five provinces, the *Dux Britanniarum* who commands the northern army units, including VI Victrix at York and the *alae* and *cohortes* along the line of Hadrian's Wall (*per lineam valli*), and the *Comes Litoris Saxonici* whose responsibilities cover the south and south-east coasts. This list of officials and units seems at first sight to provide a clear picture of where the army officers and their troops were located in the British provinces, but it is notoriously problematic to pinpoint the date of the military situation that is outlined in the document. Since no one can agree when the *Notitia* was compiled, it cannot be stated categorically that the information concerning Britain was written down when the province was still part of the Empire. It probably pertains to the late fourth-century dispositions, but no one can be certain, especially as the garrisons listed for Hadrian's Wall seem to represent a much earlier establishment than the units listed for the other sections on Britain. If the *Notitia* belongs to the second decade of the fifth century, it could not have included contemporary information about Britain, because the island was no longer under Imperial rule, and so the *Notitia* entries represent a situation that was already historic, perhaps retained as wishful thinking that one day the British provinces might be regained.

Constantine III

The ambivalent attitude of the Romans to the so-called barbarians is illustrated by the way in which they dealt with Alaric and his bands of Goths. Alaric wanted an officially sanctioned post in the Roman army, so that he could employ his tribesmen in the service of Rome and also feed and equip them at Imperial expense. He had alternately attacked the Romans and worked with them, and the eastern Emperor used the Goths and discarded them as it suited his needs. The Goths engendered fear and loathing among the Romans, but the same Romans did not mind if Alaric expended his energies and his men in their service, so eventually he obtained a post as *magister militum per Illyricum*. This brought him close to Italy, which he descended upon in 401. Stilicho met him and fought him to a standstill, but did not kill him. For this battle he may have taken some troops from Britain, which, if true, could have caused some disquiet.

In 406, there was a serious incursion across the Rhine, and the Frankish allied soldiers, the *foederati*, were overwhelmed and scattered. In the same year a rebellion broke out in Britain. It is not known which of these events came first. If the invasion of Gaul occurred before the British army units rebelled, then it could be said that the troops and perhaps the population feared that the Roman field armies were unable to protect them, and so they raised their own Emperor in case the tribes rampaging through Gaul should threaten them too. On the other hand if the rebellion occurred before the invasions across the Rhine then alternative reasons may have been dissatisfaction with the rule of Honorius, and perhaps lack of assistance against attacks from pirates. No reasons have been recorded for the action of the troops.

The soldiers chose two Emperors in rapid succession, one called Marcus, and the second called Gratian, but they were killed because neither of them proved suitable, which probably means that they did not give the soldiers what they wanted, though it is not recorded what that was. Then they chose Constantine, allegedly because of his name and for no other attributes. It was a fortuitous name for the British troops, redolent of past successes. It is said that Constantine III, as he was soon labelled, was of lowly origin, but that does not preclude his rank at that time, which may have been reasonably high.

History repeated itself as Constantine III crossed the Channel to Gaul with his troops. The old problem recurs: how many did he take and what arrangements did he make for the protection of the provinces? Once he had taken over Gaul he could recruit more soldiers, and he quickly took Spain, via Gerontius, a Briton who had become his general, and his own son, Constans. The ease with which these provinces agreed to his rule suggests that discontent was widespread and that there were great hopes for the new Emperor. Just as Theodosius had recognised Magnus Maximus *c.*384, Honorius recognised Constantine III as Augustus, largely because he could do little else for the time being. The Empire was in retreat, the capital at Milan was eventually given up in favour of Ravenna, more easily defended, and the northern capital of Gaul at Trier was abandoned in favour of Arles in the south. Despite the problems, there was stable government in the west, the Prefecture of Gaul was intact, and there was a sort of peace.

The situation changed in 409 when Arcadius, Emperor at Constantinople, died. Stilicho had not renounced his claim to be supervisor of both east and west, and came under suspicion at the court of Honorius, where it was also rumoured that he was too friendly with Alaric. He was executed, thus removing perhaps the only man in the Roman world who could have dealt with Alaric and the Goths. In 410, Alaric sacked Rome. The event has been played down by modern historians, because the Goths were only there for three or four days and they spared the Christians. The actual physical damage, however, was not what counted. It was the psychological impact that shook the Romans. The city of Rome, walled since the days of Aurelian, and never taken by force since the fourth century BC, had been sacked by a band of barbarians, who were not supposed to be able to do such things, and where was the Roman army in all this? Life went on in the Roman world, but that world was never quite the same.

BRITAIN BREAKS AWAY FROM THE EMPIRE

The people of the British provinces might have shrugged and said 'So what?' when they heard about Alaric's descent on Rome, since they had probably already broken away from the Roman Empire. It was becoming clear that Constantine III was not going to be able to protect Britain from attacks on the coasts and from the tribes of the north, and if, as seems likely, he had taken away some troops to help him stake his claim as Emperor, then the Britons would have to look to their own defence. Attacks in 408 may have triggered this decision, which seems to have been taken in 409. Zosimus reports that it was during the reign of Constantine III that:

> [The] situation in Britain made it necessary for the inhabitants of Britain and some of the Celtic nations to revolt from Roman rule and live on their own, and to obey Roman laws no longer. The Britons took up arms, and braving danger because they were now independent, they freed themselves from the barbarians who were threatening them. (Zosimus 6.5.3)

The reasons behind this drastic decision probably derived from the realisation that paying taxes for the upkeep of an absentee army was a waste of time and effort, and the same taxes could be diverted to pay an army that did what the inhabitants wanted. Freed from Roman control, the Britons could distribute the money from the taxes as they wished, and act as they wished, all of which was impossible with a government administered by Roman officials. The provincials were forbidden by law from carrying arms, though it was becoming more common for groups of people to protect themselves. Honorius had ordered the cities of northern Italy to take measures for their own defence when the Goths were on the march. It is usually suggested that he also wrote to the Britons in 410 to instruct them to organise their own defence, though some doubt has been cast on the intended destination of this letter. The ancient name for Bruttium in southern Italy was Brettia, and there may have been some confusion in the ancient sources, in this case the work of Zosimus, over the place name. Since the cities of northern Italy had been left to their own defence it is just as likely that Honorius instructed the southern Italian cites to do the same, and it is not without significance that this was where Alaric headed after the sack of Rome. Whether or not Honorius wrote to the Britons or the Bruttians, it was indicative of the era, as some provinces or parts of them in Gaul turned away from Rome, and Rome declared an inability to protect them. The western Empire was beginning to fragment under an onslaught of external attacks and internal unrest. The surprising thing is that the western provinces staggered on for as long as they did, for another six or seven decades at least, and re-emerged with some Roman underpinning and a Gothic or Germanic facade.

Nothing is known of how the Britons expelled the Roman officials. It is possible that some of these officials joined the independence movement and stayed in the island. On the other hand it is also possible that there was bloodshed. When they were alone, the Britons perhaps retained some of the Roman administrative systems, but it has been pointed out that while the Gauls shared in government and filled several official posts, the native Britons did not seem to have gained widespread experience of government, and so there was perhaps no solid core of personnel around whom to form a new government. From the start, it is probable that the whole country quite quickly divided up into regional enclaves, not necessarily based on the five provincial areas that had been drawn up approximately a century earlier.

Without centralised control within each province, the system of government would break down. Protection, supply and communications probably depended on the strongest group or even one individual, but now encompassing a smaller and more manageable area. It is not known if all the troops were withdrawn from Britain as the Imperial court at Ravenna demanded more men to defend its own headquarters and as much of Italy as it could. It is likely that many soldiers remained in the northern forts with their families. It would not take too long to realise that they were now on their own – parallels are known from other parts of the Empire, where the soldiers sent a few men to provincial headquarters to enquire what was happening and when their pay was to arrive, and these unfortunates either brought back the news that pay and supplies had ceased, or more likely they failed to return at all. In one instance at a fort on the River Inn in present-day Austria, the bodies of the men chosen to go on this mission floated past the fort some days later.

The alternative would be to live in the forts and farm the land, which is how some of the frontier units were employed in other parts of the late Empire even while it was still intact. In Britain, there is some evidence of continued occupation inside forts, but nothing about who the occupants might have been. In the villas, military equipment has been found, but its significance is down to guesswork. Perhaps landowners, self-appointed rulers of their regions, hired soldiers for protection, or soldiers took over the houses and possibly the estates. On the other hand, if there was some semblance of government and administration still functioning, there may have been a policy of billeting troops as a means of feeding and housing them. It is impossible to say what sort of army remained in Britain after the inhabitants expelled the Roman officials.

The hire of tribesmen as soldiers is not out of the question. These would perhaps be Saxons, though some clarification is required as to what this label meant. The Romans often applied an all-embracing term to different groups of tribesmen, no matter what their ethnic origins, and would not usually distinguish between the groups from different regions quite as precisely as modern scholars would like. For some time, the enemies of the eastern parts of the Empire were called Scythians by the Romans, but the term obscures the fact that several different tribes were grouped under this heading. Similarly in Britain, archaeologists separate the later arrivals of tribesmen into Angles, Saxons and Jutes, but for the most part in late Roman Britain any evidence that suggests the settlement of Germanic people tends to be categorised as Saxon.

While the finds of Germanic types of military dress have been dismissed as a means of identifying the kind of troops involved because such items were standard issue, it is known that Saxons had been brought into Britain on an official basis long before the fourth century, and that they settled near Roman centres of administration or near to fortified towns and coastal forts, and even near to Romano-British villages. Not much is known about where they were housed, but the numbers of settlers can be very roughly estimated from the cemeteries that they set up near these places, especially at York, Colchester and Caistor-by-Norwich. It was only much later that the Saxons avoided Roman sites. There is some evidence that Romano-Britons and Saxons lived side by side, in the Wolds of Lincolnshire and in East Anglia, where Romano-British pottery and early Anglo-Saxon types are found together. The presence of Saxons is strongly represented on the east side of England, and particularly near the forts of the Saxon Shore, lending some credence to the theory that the area and the late Roman military command were so named because of the new settlers, and not for the fact that the forts were built to defend the country from the Saxon pirates.

The most important point is that the inhabitants of Roman Britain would have become quite well accustomed to interacting with the Saxons and other Germanic tribesmen before the island separated itself from the Roman Empire. There had been other Germanic soldiers on Hadrian's Wall in the later third century, probably Friesians, using pottery that was very similar to the types used in the Netherlands.

Burgundians and Vandals had been settled in Britain by the Emperor Probus, Franks had been engaged by Carausius, and in the late fourth century at least one unit of Alamanni had been located somewhere in Britain. After the island became independent, the hire of fresh groups of immigrant Saxons to provide military protection would not be regarded with suspicion.

THE ADVENTUS SAXONUM

In his account of the destruction of Britain (*De Excidio Britanniae*) the late fifth-century or sixth-century author Gildas employs only a few paragraphs to describe the arrival of the Saxons and their subsequent history in Britain, ending with a brief mention of the Battle of Mount Badon, when the Britons under Ambrosius defeated them. Gildas's chronology is less than precise, and perhaps some of his facts are suspect, but his work is the closest to a contemporary account for the post Roman period, though no one can agree on the dates when he wrote his history. He may have started in *c.*490, or he may have worked as late as the 540s.

The title of his work indicates Gildas's attitude to the Saxons. Between the later third century and the early to mid-fifth century, something had gone wrong with the relationship between the Britons and the Saxons. According to Gildas, before they left the island, the Romans had taught the Britons to build a wall of turf and another of stone, which sounds like an explanation of the Antonine Wall and Hadrian's Wall. But then, according to Gildas, the Scots and Picts took over the country as far as the wall (which one?), and the useless garrison there could not stop them from overrunning it. There is a description of deserted towns and horrible massacres, and then the miserable Britons, hard pressed by attacks of the barbarians, sent a letter asking for assistance to a Roman general in Gaul called Agitius, consul for the third time. Although there was a general called Agidius, it is generally agreed that this man called 'Agitius' must have been the *magister militum* Aetius, who had been the most powerful individual in the western Empire since 433. He was consul for the third time in 446, as stated in the text of the letter, which is known as the Groans of the Britons. This provides a probable date for the letter, stating that:

> The barbarians drive us to the sea, the sea drives us back to the barbarians, [so] between these two forms of death we are either slaughtered or drowned. (Gildas *De Excidio Britanniae* 20)

The account continues with the lament that no help was forthcoming from the Romans, so some of the Britons continued to resist the attacks, hiding in their mountain fastnesses and caves, until finally they got together and defeated the barbarians. There was peace and prosperity for a while, but then corruption and vice took over (the Christian ethic had taken firm hold by the time that Gildas wrote his book). Several rulers were created and deposed. Then after a plague, the council met to decide on the best ways of overcoming their enemies. This indicates that at least some form of government still existed, running in Roman fashion. According to Gildas, the 'blind tyrant', blind not in the physical sense but blind to his actions, called in the fierce Saxons to help to fight the various enemies threatening Britain. This is assumed to be Vortigern, though he is not actually named in the narrative. The Saxons soon complained that they were not getting enough supplies, and turned against the Britons and went on the rampage. Then Ambrosius emerged as military leader and after some reverses he defeated the Saxons at Mount Badon.

The order in which these events really occurred has been debated, since it has a bearing on when the Saxons were called in by Vortigern. There are two possibilities, the first just as Gildas suggests, the appeal to Aetius was sent some time before the Saxons arrived, or secondly, it may be that Vortigern called them in, they rebelled, and then only after that was the appeal sent to Aetius to help curb them. This second alternative satisfies the theory that the council meeting and the decision to send for the Saxons belongs to the 430s. Aetius was consul for the third time in 446, so it might seem that for a few years all went well and then the trouble started with the Saxons, who proved to be discontented soldiers, and the Britons were powerless when their Saxon troops turned on them. On the other hand, if all the events enumerated by Gildas occurred *after* 446, the date of Aetius's third consulship, then the arrival of the Saxons did not come about until the mid-fifth century. This finds some support in the relatively low numbers of Anglo-Saxon finds in archaeological excavations until about 450, when there is a noticeable increase in artefacts and pottery. But according to tradition, the first Saxons arrived in three ships, so their numbers could not have been great, just enough to form a small army.

It has been suggested that it may have been Aetius who advocated the call to the Saxons. He had employed Huns to fight for Rome, and barbarian troops were commonly used for frontier defence, so the summons to the Saxons would be perfectly normal procedure for the time. The meeting of the council where Vortigern made the decision suggests that there was still a vestige of normal Romano-British administrative procedure in the independent island. At some point in the proceedings, Vortigern was said to have given lands in Kent to the Saxons, and this too was normal. Tribesmen had continually been brought into the Empire and given lands since the days of Augustus. It is suggested that some of the Saxons were employed in the protection of London, and there are signs that there was a Saxon presence there in the fifth century. In Roman terms, all this was acceptable policy.

Unfortunately, on occasion, it was also acceptable Roman policy to underestimate and mistreat the so-called barbarians. Only about seventy years before the trouble with the Saxons broke out, the Romans in the east had dealt so miserably with the Goths that the tribesmen had nothing to lose when they decided to fight the Romans instead of trying to negotiate with them. They destroyed the eastern Roman army at Adrianople. Perhaps the recorded complaints of the Saxons that they had not been given enough rations were based on fact.

AMBROSIUS AND ARTHUR

The Saxons were probably well established in Britain by the middle of the fifth century, but they were perhaps not in the ascendancy until the sixth. Gradual penetration into the country is indicated by pottery finds. The older theory that the Saxons drove the Britons into the west, to settle in Wales and Cumbria, is not tenable. In many places the Anglo-Saxons probably integrated with the Britons rather than slaughtering them.

It is accepted that there would have been some resistance to the Saxons, and two names have been handed down in the sources, with legendary overtones. Gildas says that the parents of Ambrosius Aurelianus had worn the purple. Since they were not Roman Emperors themselves, this may mean that they were related to someone who had been, or had tried to be, an Emperor. The possession of illustrious ancestors was equally important to Romans and Britons. It is not known if this Ambrosius in the pages of Gildas is the same as the opponent of Vortigern described by Nennius in the *Historia Brittonum*. Much depends on the dating of the activities of Vortigern and the Saxon revolt, a problem that will probably never be solved. The Battle of Mount Badon is also difficult to date. Modern theories suggest that it was fought somewhere around the very end of the fifth century or the beginning of the sixth. Though it was a victory for the last of the Romans, it did not bring back the Empire or stop the growth of the Anglo-Saxon kingdoms.

Arthur, who is said to be the victor of the Battle of Mount Badon, is so deeply embedded in British mythology that it would be very difficult to extricate him, but although belief in him is strong there is no solid evidence for his existence. Several places in Britain have been associated with Arthur without any real proof, save for the late Roman background against which he may have lived. His legend begins in Celtic sources, which have been dismissed as unreliable, and it is continued in the medieval period when Arthur became a cult figure with so many knightly attributes that he lost his supposed Romano-British roots. Instead of trying to prove that he was a real person by writing of his life and times, it is only possible to write of his times, and perhaps to subscribe to wishful thinking that if he didn't exist then it would be necessary to invent him. With the voluntary suspension of disbelief, it is still a good story.

What Survived into the Fifth Century?

For a while, the newly independent Britons probably kept up as much as they could of the Roman administration, but corporate government would perhaps not be possible except for small areas, especially if communications and safety were threatened. Vortigern is presented as ruler of the country but perhaps only ruled the south-east and the environs of London. For the rest of the country, local landlords and tribal chiefs perhaps took over responsibility for their territories.

The upkeep of roads was probably the first thing to suffer neglect, and it seems that trade and industry declined quite soon after the beginning of the fifth century. Money economy disappeared after about 420 when coins die out from the archaeological record. The more prosperous towns had a better chance of survival, still linked to the surrounding countryside and able to provide food and home-made commodities. Though the decurions of the later fourth century had displayed reluctance to serve on the councils, there would at least be a number of men with experience of government and the authority to organise defence, building work, sanitation, and perhaps markets. Although long-distance roads were not repaired, at Lincoln a coin of the late fourth century buried below three layers of repairs shows that someone was in charge of the local roads, and at Cirencester someone kept the Forum in good order into the fifth century. In a town house at Verulamium, a corn dryer was installed in one of the rooms with a late fourth-century mosaic floor, so pragmatism won over aesthetics. Later in the fifth century the house was demolished and a stone barn was built over it, possibly for storage of grain inside the town, or perhaps the building was intended to be a meeting hall. The building was not erected until a water main had been laid across the site, indicating that some form of corporate government still operated there. At Wroxeter the basilica attached to the baths was used until the late fifth century, as was a bread oven, and in the sixth century the basilica was pulled down and a timber building put up in its place.

Occupation of some villas continued into the sixth century, but it is not known who lived in them. It is suggested that squatters took over, but in at least some of them it is possible that there was some continuity and the land was perhaps still farmed, though it is impossible to say who was farming it. The Saxons tended to avoid Roman sites, possibly because they used different farming methods, but the notion that all Roman agricultural lands were abandoned cannot be demonstrated.

In some areas, insecurity drove people to seek fortified sites and turn them into dwellings. Timber buildings on the site of the granary at the fort of Birdoswald were occupied into the sixth century, perhaps by a local chieftain. Other people took to the old hill forts, as at Dinas Powys, Cadbury and Congresbury. At Tintagel, life was perhaps more comfortable than might be expected, with pottery from the Mediterranean still reaching the inhabitants, and perhaps other more perishable goods were brought in as well.

One of the towns of Roman Britain seems to have survived well beyond the fifth century. When St Cuthbert visited Carlisle, the inhabitants proudly showed him their defensive walls, and a fountain, made by the Romans, they said, and still working.

St Germanus and St Patrick

Contact with the Roman Empire of the fifth century continued through the officials of the Christian Church, a powerful organisation which had survived the severe persecution of the Tetrarchs, and finally emerged almost as another state within the Empire. After Christianity was legalised by Constantine the influence of the Church was felt all over the late Empire, especially as it rapidly accumulated wealth and ever more political power. However, there was no single monolithic structure that bound everyone together in identical beliefs and doctrines. From the start the new religion was rent by differences of opinion that sometimes escalated into bloodshed. It has been suggested that Constantine hoped that the spread of Christianity would provide some means of uniting the Empire, but if so he was probably disappointed that the Church was often divided against itself, and he and successive Emperors sometimes had to intervene.

Pagan religions survived in Britain perhaps until the end of Roman rule, though some temples went out of use towards the end of the fourth century, while others were probably pillaged. Some wealthy inhabitants of Britain displayed their adherence to Christianity by including relevant symbols in the mosaics and perhaps other art forms in their villas. By the middle of the fourth century Christianity had taken firm hold, and Constantius II made it the sole religion of the Empire.

Two men from late Roman Britain are associated with the Christian religion. One is Pelagius, who is generally agreed to have been born in Britain. He went to Rome in 380 to study, but emerged as more of a free thinker than was comfortable for the Church. He took exception to the idea of original sin, and argued strongly for freedom of choice. Even though he did not live in Britain, the Pelagian heresy as it was called attracted many adherents, becoming serious enough to occasion a visit from bishops of the Roman Church in 429, two decades after Britain and the Empire had parted company. The meeting of Catholics and Pelagians probably concerned only the wealthiest and most influential Britons, leaving the majority of poorer people completely unconcerned about the finer points of Christian beliefs. The Roman delegation was chosen by a council of bishops of Gaul, at the instigation of the Pope, with whom British opponents of the Pelagian heresy had been in contact. The leader of the Catholic group was Germanus, bishop of Auxerre. He was said to have been a soldier, perhaps even an officer. He brought with him Lupus, bishop of Troyes. The information about the meeting, which may have been held at Verulamium/St Albans, comes from the *Life of Germanus* in which the Pelagians appear sumptuously dressed, ostentatious in their display of wealth, and surrounded by a multitude of people fawning upon them. It has been pointed out that this sounds very much like a group of Roman senators with their clients, and the description also suggests that, two decades after becoming independent, the inhabitants of the former Roman province were not quite as oppressed as they claimed to have been when the letter outlining 'the Groans of the Britons' was addressed to Aetius.

When it was clear that the Catholic party was the outright winner, having persuaded the mass of people by their effective preaching, Germanus then led the Britons in an attack on the Scots and Picts. The battle may have taken place in north Wales. This is not actually stated, but the terrain is described as mountainous, with a great river running through it. The coast of Wales would be an easy target for sea raiders. Germanus baptised the British troops en masse, which presumably means that they were all pagans, and demonstrates the survival of the old religions among the common folk into the fifth century. Germanus taught the soldiers to shout 'Alleluia' as they went into battle. This so frightened the tribesmen that they turned and fled, and thus the victory could be safely ascribed to God, by dint of His good grace to those who worshipped Him in the correct manner.

Germanus returned to Britain for a second visit which is not precisely dated. It has been suggested that this may have been in 446, after the letter from the Britons reached Aetius, and the visit may have been instigated by Aetius himself, as a substitute for sending some of his troops. Germanus had won a victory before and the Britons would have faith in him. He may also have had an opportunity to ensure that the Pelagians did not resurface in Britain. Nothing is known of what he achieved during his second visit.

One of Germanus's pupils may have been Patrick, who sought the religious life after his experience as a slave in Ireland from the age of sixteen to twenty-two. The course of Patrick's youth, his capture by Irish tribesmen, and his subsequent history are documented, but none of the details can be firmly dated, so the context is not known. It is not even known where he was born, though a case has been made for Carlisle. His unruly boyhood may have been spent during the final years of Britain as a Roman province. Raids on Britain occurred just as the Britons decided to expel the Roman officials in 409, so he may have been captured at that time, and when he escaped he would return to an independent Britain. His grandfather Potitus, and his father Calpurnius were probably decurions on the town council of his *civitas*, wherever that may have been, and the story goes that when he returned from Ireland, his father tried to persuade him to undertake *munera*, which term normally means the duties of public office. This has been used by some authors to suggest that local government continued on Roman lines well into the fifth century, but has been disputed by others.

To provide a cut-off date for Roman Britain and a start date for Anglo-Saxon England and the Celtic kingdoms is an artificial device, helpful to historians, but not representative of real life. The change did not happen all at once, and though archaeology can demonstrate considerable differences in lifestyle between Romano-Britons of the late Empire and the Anglo-Saxons, there was no single instance when it could be said that one culture died out and another took its place. Changes occurred all the time during the history of Roman Britain and the Roman Empire, and the people who lived through these changes would observe them slowly and gradually over their entire lifetimes, and perhaps in some circumstances they would not even notice that there had been a change. Not all of the changes would be sudden, violent or harmful. Rome influenced Britain long before the conquest and ruled the island for nearly four centuries, and to appreciate the changes, or evolution and development through all that long time span, it is only necessary to review the four centuries before the present time, looking back through the eras of the Edwardians, the Victorians, the Hanoverians, the Stuarts, the Civil War and the very end of Queen Elizabeth's reign. Life is not uniform or static, beliefs and fashions come and go, prosperity and austerity alternate, nadir follows zenith, but people have a remarkable capacity to survive and adapt. Though they disappear from view, the Romano-Britons of the late Empire would possess that same capacity.

Chronology

This list includes some of the more important events in the Roman Empire which may have affected Britain indirectly, but provide a background against which the Roman province developed.

59 BC	Julius Caesar elected consul
58–56	Caesar campaigns in Gaul, and gains broader knowledge of Britain
55–54	Caesar invades Britain on two separate occasions
52–51	Revolt of Vercingetorix in Gaul
49–45	Civil war begins between Caesar and Pompey; Pompey defeated at Pharsalus and killed in Egypt; in the Alexandrian war, Caesar makes Cleopatra VII Queen of Egypt
Before 44	Caesar doubles army pay
44	Caesar assassinated
43–30	Octavian allies with Antony and Lepidus, the second Triumvirate; civil war between Antony and Octavian, ending with the fall of Alexandria in 30
27 BC to AD 14	Principate of Augustus
AD 6	Augustus forms *aerarium militare* to fund pensions for veterans
Before AD 14	British kings Tincomarus and Dubnovellaunus come to Augustus for assistance to regain their kingdoms; on three occasions an invasion of Britain is planned, but in the end no Roman military expedition is mounted
14–37	Tiberius Emperor
37–41	Caligula Emperor
39–40	Adminius, son of Cunobelinus of the Catuvellauni, comes to the court of Caligula; an invasion of Britain is planned, troops march to the coast but the expedition is cancelled
41–54	Claudius Emperor
41–42	Verica is expelled and arrives at Claudius's court

43	Invasion of Britain
43–47	Aulus Plautius governor
43–47	Legions II Augusta, IX Hispana, XIV and XX fan out towards the north, the north-west and the south-west; future Emperor Vespasian commands in south-west campaigns with II Augusta; Caratacus defeated but flees to Silures of south Wales
47	Claudius grants Aulus Plautius an ovation in Rome, normally reserved for members of the Imperial family
47–52	Publius Ostorius Scapula governor
47	Scapula disarms the Britons, the Iceni revolt, but are suppressed; Scapula begins campaign in Wales
48	Trouble in Brigantia, Roman troops sent to assist Cartimandua
49	Colchester is made a *colonia*
51	Caratacus flees from Wales to Brigantia, and Cartimandua surrenders him to Romans
52	Welsh campaigns continue; Scapula dies in office
52–57	Aulus Didius Gallus governor
52–57	Campaigns in Wales; Roman troops sent to assist Cartimandua against her husband Venutius
54–68	Nero Emperor
57–58	Quintus Veranius governor
58	Quintus Veranius dies in office
58–61	Gaius Suetonius Paullinus governor
c.59–60	Campaign in Wales, attack on Anglesey; Gnaeus Julius Agricola military tribune
60–61	Rebellion of Boudicca; Colchester and Verulamium destroyed; Suetonius arrives at London and abandons it to Britons; fights battle probably in Midlands; Boudicca defeated
c.61–63	Publius Petronius Turpilianus governor
63–69	Marcus Trebellius Maximus governor
66 or 67	Nero withdraws XIV legion for campaigns in Caucasus
68	Death of Nero
68–69	Galba, Otho and Vitellius Emperors
69	Trebellius Maximus flees Britain; legionary legates govern province
69–71	Marcus Vettius Bolanus governor
c.69	XIV legion is sent back to Britain
69	Cartimandua is expelled from Brigantia, and is rescued by Roman troops
69–79	Vespasian Emperor
69	Revolt of Civilis and the Batavians on the Rhine, Quintus Petillius Cerialis is appointed general
70	XIV legion is sent from Britain to Germany
71–74	Quintus Petillius Cerialis governor
71	Legion II Adiutrix arrives in Britain

71–74	Cerialis campaigns against Venutius and overruns Brigantia; possibly founds the first fort at Carlisle; possibly moves IX Hispana from Lincoln to York fortress
74–77/78	Sextus Julius Frontinus governor
74–77/78	Silures defeated in south Wales; possibly fortress at Chester founded
77/78–83/84	Gnaeus Julius Agricola governor
c.77	Conquest of north Wales completed, attack on Anglesey
c.77–78	Campaigns in northern Britain; water supply of Chester fortress laid
c.78/9–83/84	Campaigns in Scotland; in seventh season, Agricola defeats Britons at Battle of Mons Graupius
79–81	Titus Emperor
81–96	Domitian Emperor
83/84–96	Sallustius Lucullus governor, executed by Domitian; unknown governor(s) succeed him
82–3 (?)	Domitian increases army pay from 225 *denarii* per annum to 300 *denarii*
85–87	Dacian wars; governor of Moesia killed; army under Praetorian Prefect Fuscus defeated
c.87	Domitian abandons Scotland; Legion II Adiutrix withdrawn for Danube wars at some time before 92
89	Revolt of Saturninus at Mainz; Domitian puts an end to two-legion fortresses
c.90–100	Lincoln and Gloucester made *coloniae*; London has stone fort built inside town
96–98	Nerva Emperor
c.98	Publius Metilius Nepos governor
c.98–c.101	Titus Avidius Quietus governor
98–117	Trajan Emperor
101–102	First Dacian war of Trajan
c.100	Northern boundary of Britain established between River Tyne and River Solway; Stanegate is most northerly road with forts and watchtowers, but not traced west of Carlisle or east of Corbridge; Britons recruited at this time and sent to Germany as *numeri Brittonum*?
c.103	Lucius Neratius Marcellus governor
105–106	Second Dacian war of Trajan; annexation of Dacia
108	Legion IX Hispana last attested at York; possibly moves to Nijmegen?
c.115–118	Marcus Atilius Bradua governor
117–138	Hadrian Emperor
118–122	Quintus Pompeius Falco governor
122–c.124	Aulus Platorius Nepos governor
122	Hadrian visits Britain; VI Victrix arrives at York fortress; building of Hadrian's Wall begins
124–126	Unknown governor
126–127	Lucius Trebius Germanus governor

*c.*131–*c.*133	Sextus Julius Severus governor
*c.*133–*c.*135	Publius Mummius Sisenna governor
*c.*135–138	Unknown governor
Before 138	Fire destroys much of London
Before 138	German frontier palisade and watchtowers begun; stretches of stone wall built in Africa
138–161	Antoninus Pius Emperor
*c.*138–142	Quintus Lollius Urbicus governor
138–142	Campaigns in Scotland
142–144	Unknown governor
*c.*143	Construction of Antonine Wall begins in Scotland; German frontier advanced a few kilometres to the east
*c.*145–146	Gnaeus Papirius Aelianus governor
*c.*146–*c.*157	Unknown governor(s)
*c.*155	Verulamium destroyed by fire
*c.*157–158	Gnaeus Julius Verus governor
Before 158	Serious trouble in northern Britain; Antonine Wall evacuated, Hadrian's Wall becomes frontier again
158–161	Marcus Pisibanius Lepidus governor (possibly)
161–180	Marcus Aurelius Emperor, with Lucius Verus as colleague 161–169
161–162	Marcus Statius Priscus governor
162–166	Sextus Calpurnius Agricola governor
167–180	Marcus Aurelius at war on the Danube against Quadi, Marcommani and Sarmatians
166–172	Unknown governor(s)
172–174/175	Quintus Antistius Adventus governor
175	Marcus Aurelius sends 5,500 Sarmatian cavalry to Britain
174/175–177	Caerellius governor
178–184/185	Ulpius Marcellus governor
180–192	Commodus Emperor
*c.*182–*c.*185	Warfare in northern Britain, Ulpius Marcellus wins victory; mutiny of legions in Britain
185	Soldiers from the army of Britain send delegation to Rome to demand from Commodus the dismissal of Praetorian Prefect Perennis
185	Marcus Antius Crescens Calpurnianus acting governor
185–187	Publius Helvius Pertinax governor
185	Mutinous legions try to make Pertinax Emperor; he refuses, and quells mutiny
187–191	Unknown governor(s)
193	Pertinax Emperor; Didius Julianus Emperor
193–211	Severus Emperor
193	Civil war between Septimius Severus and Pescennius Niger
192/193	Decimus Clodius Albinus governor; declared Emperor in 193 by troops
193–197	Britain ruled by Clodius Albinus as Caesar; declares himself Augustus and takes troops to Gaul; defeated by

	Severus at Lyon
197–211	Severus recognises soldiers' marriages and awards first pay rise since reign of Domitian
197–200	Virius Lupus governor
197	Repair and rebuilding of forts in northern Britain begins
200–c.202	Unknown governor
c.202–c.205	Gaius Valerius Pudens governor
205–207/208	Lucius Alfenus Senecio governor
205–208	Repair and rebuilding of northern forts continues; more inscriptions record Alfenus Senecio than any other governor
c.208–c.213	Gaius Junius Faustinus Postumianus governor
208–211	Severus campaigns in Scotland; his sons Caracalla and Geta accompany him; Severus dies at York, February 211
Between 208–211?	Albanus condemned by Geta and martyred at Verulamium, where the town was named after him, St Albans (the date is disputed)
211–217	Caracalla Emperor
211/212	Caracalla makes peace with northern British tribes; Hadrian's Wall is northern frontier, with outpost forts beyond it
c.211–213	Britain divided into two provinces, Britannia Superior with its capital at London, governed by a consular governor; Britannia Inferior with capital at York and equestrian *praeses* commanding VI Victrix and also governing the province
212	Geta murdered by Caracalla in Rome; Geta's name removed from all inscriptions
c.212/213	*Constitutio Antoniniana* gives citizenship to all freeborn inhabitants of the Empire
213	Gaius Julius Marcus governor
216	Marcus Antonius Gordianus governor of Britannia Inferior
217–218	Macrinus Emperor
218–222	Elagabalus Emperor
219	Modius Julius governor of Britannia Inferior
220	Tiberius Claudius Paulinus governor of Britannia Inferior
221–222	Marcus Valerianus governor of Britannia Inferior
222–235	Severus Alexander Emperor
Between 222 and 235?	Tiberius Julius Pollienus Auspex governor of Britannia Superior
223	Claudius Xenophon governor of Britannia Inferior
225	Maximus governor of Britannia Inferior
Between 226 and 234	Calvisius Rufus governor of Britannia Inferior
Between 226 and 234	Valerius Crescens governor of Britannia Inferior
Between 226 and 235	Claudius Apellinus governor of Britannia Inferior
235 to c.270	The age of the soldier-Emperors begins, civil war,

	invasions across frontiers all over the Empire
235–238	Maximinus Emperor
Before 237	York civil settlement given status of *colonia*
237	Tuccianus governor of Britannia Inferior
Between 238 and 244	Maecilius Fuscus governor of Britannia Inferior
Between 238 and 244	Egnatius Lucilianus governor of Britannia Inferior
242	Nonius Philippus governor of Britannia Inferior
Between 238 and 260?	Marcus Martiannius Pulcher governor of Britannia Superior
Later than 244	Aemilianus governor of Britannia Inferior
238	Gordian I and Gordian II Emperors
238–244	Gordian III Emperor
244–249	Philip the Arab Emperor
*c.*244	Last recorded evidence of the fleet *Classis Britannica*
249–251	Decius Emperor
251–253	Wars with Goths and civil wars
Between 253 and 258	Desticius Juba governor of Britannia Superior
253–260	Valerian Emperor with his son Gallienus as colleague
*c.*255	Wall at riverside built in London
*c.*258–259	Gallic Empire splits from Rome under Postumus
*c.*258 to 274	Britain administered as part of Gallic Empire
260	Valerian's campaign against the Persians ends with his defeat and capture
260–268	Gallienus sole Emperor
260–272	Odenathus of Palmyra and then Queen Zenobia rule in the east after Valerian's defeat
263–268	Octavius Sabinus governor of Britannia Inferior
267	Goths sack Athens
268–270	Claudius Gothicus Emperor
270–275	Aurelian Emperor
272	Aurelian reconquers the east and Palmyra
274	Aurelian defeats Tetricus and Gallic Empire ends
274	Britain back under control of Roman Emperors; unpopularity of Aurelian's monetary reforms
275–276	Tacitus Emperor
275–276	German tribes invade Gaul
276–282	Probus Emperor
*c.*277	Probus settles Burgundians and Vandals in Britain
282–284	Carus and Carinus Emperors
282–284	Persian campaign, Carus dies; Civil war, Diocletian disposes of Carinus in the west
284–305	Diocletian Emperor, with Maximianus as colleague from 286
286	Maximianus campaigns against Bagaudae in Gaul, Carausius rises to prominence
287	Carausius flees to Britain and takes control of the government and fleet
287–293	Carausius controls legions and fleet in Gaul, and base at

	Boulogne; he issues coinage in Britain. Last coin evidence for XX Valeria Victrix
293	Constantius I as Caesar to Maximianus captures Boulogne. Carausius assassinated by Allectus
293–296	Allectus rules in Britain; he starts building work on palace in London, and possibly founds fort at Pevensey
296	Constantius I regains control of Britain; campaigns probably in the north; perhaps divides Britain into four provinces within the Diocese of Britain
Between 296 and 305	Aurelius Arpagius *praeses* of Britannia Secunda
297	Constantius I sends craftsmen from Britain to carry out restoration work at Autun in Gaul
305	Diocletian and Maximianus abdicate, Tetrarchy of four Emperors set up, Constantius I Augustus in the west with Severus as his Caesar, Galerius as Augustus in the east with Maximinus Daia as his Caesar
305–306	Constantius I Augustus campaigns on the northern frontier of Britain with his son Constantine
306	Constantius I dies at York, Constantine declared Emperor by the army in Britain. Galerius recognises him but as Caesar, not Augustus
306	The Praetorians in Rome declare for Maxentius as Augustus; his father Maximianus comes out of retirement to join him
307	Maximianus makes Constantine Augustus
308	Galerius calls a council at Carnuntum on the Danube; Licinius made colleague of Galerius
310	Maximianus rebels against Constantine, and is killed or commits suicide
312	Constantine raises troops, some of them from Britain, and defeats Maxentius at the Battle of the Milvian Bridge in Rome
313	Edict of Milan, establishing the Peace of the Church
314	Council of Bishops at Arles, three British bishops attend
Before 319	Lucius Papius Pacatianus, *vicarius* of the Diocese of Britain
324	Constantine defeats remaining rival Licinius
324–337	Constantine sole Emperor
c.324 onwards	Constantine reforms the army; abolishes the Praetorian Guard, divides army into mobile field armies and frontier armies
330	Constantinople becomes the Imperial capital and residence of the Emperors
337	Constantine II, Constans, Constantius II Emperors
340	Constans defeats and kills his brother Constantine II and takes over the west; Gratian possibly *comes rei militaris* in campaigns
340–360	Attacks on Britain by the northern tribes, and from the sea
343	Constans visits Britain, campaigns in the north

350	Magnentius declared Emperor in Gaul, Constans defeated
350–353	Britain ruled by Magnentius; Constantine II defeats him in 351 and again in 353, when Magnentius commits suicide
353–354	Paul Catena in Britain to find supporters of Magnentius
353–354	Martinus *vicarius* of the Diocese of Britain attempts to kill Paul, but fails and commits suicide
355	Julian declared Emperor by troops, Constantius II makes him Caesar; Julian rules Britain and Gaul
c.358–360	Alypius *vicarius* of Diocese of Britain
359	Julian reinstates transports of grain from Britain to the Rhine
359	Council of Rimini, Bishops from Britain attend
360–363	Julian sole Emperor
360	Attacks on Britain from Scotti and Picts, campaigns of Lupicinus
363–364	Jovian Emperor
364–375	Valentinian I Emperor in the west
364–378	Valens Emperor in the east
367–383	Gratian Emperor with his father Valentinian I
367	Civilis *vicarius* of Diocese of Britain
367	*Conspiratio Barbarica*: combined attacks of Scotti and Picts in the north, Saxons and Franks raid coasts of Gaul and probably of Britain, two generals sent to combat them, appointment of Count Theodosius
367–369	Theodosius restores order, rebuilding begins; suppression of revolt by Victorinus
378	Valens defeated and killed by Goths at Adrianople
375–392	Valentinian II Emperor in the west
379–395	Theodosius I the Great Emperor in the east
383	Revolt of Magnus Maximus; defeat of Picts; Maximus goes to Gaul
383–388	Britain ruled by Maximus
388	Defeat and execution of Maximus
391	All forms of pagan worship forbidden by Theodosius I
392–394	Arbogast and Eugenius rebel, pagan worship revives, Britain ruled by Arbogast
394	Theodosius I recruits large numbers of tribesmen and defeats Arbogast and Eugenius at the Battle of the Frigidus
394	Rise of Stilicho as commander of all armies of the western half of the Empire
395–408	Arcadius, Augustus from 383, Emperor of the east
395–423	Honorius, Augustus from 393, Emperor of the west
395–406	Chrysanthus *vicarius* of Diocese of Britain; Victorinus *vicarius* of Diocese of Britain
c.395	Last record of VI Victrix and II Augusta
c.400	Possible withdrawal of troops by Stilicho
402	Imports of bronze coins to Britain ends
405	Irish raids on British coasts, possibly when St Patrick is

	captured
406–407	Troops in Britain declare for Marcus, then Gratian, then
	Constantine III
407–411	Britain under Constantine III, ruling from Arles
409	Britain rebels against Constantine III and expels Roman
	officials
410	Alaric the Goth sacks Rome. Traditional date of
	Honorius's letter to Britons saying they must look
	after themselves (disputed whether this is correct)
411	Constantine III captured and executed
416	Pelagian heresy, founded by a Briton, officially condemned
425	Aetius commands armies of Gaul as *magister militum*
429	St Germanus visits Britain as part of a delegation of
	Roman bishops to debate with Pelagians. St Germanus
	helps Britons to defeat Picts and Scots
Between 446 and 454	Alleged date of the Groans of the Britons addressed to
	Aetius, 'consul for the third time'
450s	Traditional date when Saxons assume supremacy over
	Britain
454	Aetius killed, armies of the west decline
476	Traditional date of the fall of Rome, last Emperor
	Romulus Augustulus deposed, Gothic leader Odoacer
	rules Italy

Glossary

Aedile: city magistrate originally responsible for supervision of the *aedes*, or the temples of the plebs. During the Republic there were two aediles subordinate to the tribunes of the plebs, and later two more were elected from the patricians (*aediles curules*). In the Empire the main duties of the aediles were care of the city, including keeping the streets clean, keeping public order, attending to the water supply and markets. They were also in charge of the public games (*ludi*) until Augustus transferred this duty to the praetors. All the municipalities of the Empire employed elected aediles fulfilling the same purposes as they did in Rome.

Aerarium militare: military treasury set up by Augustus in AD 6 to provide pensions for honourably discharged veterans.

Ala (plural *alae*): Latin term for 'wing', used to describe the traditional location of the cavalry on the wings in battle formations. The term was eventually applied to cavalry units of the Roman army. The soldiers would be recruited from non-Romans, who served for twenty-five years, and on honourable discharge (*honesta missio* q.v.) they were granted Roman citizenship and could draw their pensions. The cavalry *alae* were divided into smaller units called *turmae* (q.v.) each containing about thirty-two men, with two officers in command, the senior one being the decurion (q.v.).

Ala milliaria: auxiliary cavalry unit of *c.*1,000 men, in reality about 768 men, organised in thirty-two *turmae* (q.v.) each containing thirty-two men. The milliary *alae* probably did not appear until the reign of Vespasian, in the early AD 70s. There was usually only one of these 1,000-strong cavalry units in any province; in Britain the *ala Petriana milliaria* was based at Stanwix, Carlisle. It was the senior unit on Hadrian's Wall, and the most senior auxiliary unit in Britain. Its full title was *ala Augusta Gallorum Petriana bis torquata milliaria civium Romanorum*, indicating that the unit had been awarded torques, a reward for especial valour, on two occasions (*bis torquata*), and all the soldiers had been made Roman citizens (*civium Romanorum*), a distinction earned for extraordinary performance in battle, when the whole unit was enfranchised. The commander of an *ala milliaria* was a tribune, not a senator, but a man who originated from the *equites* (q.v.), or the equestrian class. At first sight this seems an extremely appropriate origin for a cavalry officer, but long before the Roman conquest of Britain, the term *equites* had become a mark of social rank, and had lost its association with the cavalry of the early Roman Republic. The tribunes were high-ranking officers with military experience in command of the auxiliary units and as an officer in the legions. See also *auxilia*; citizenship; decurion; *turma*

Ala quingenaria: auxiliary cavalry unit of *c.*500 men, made up of sixteen *turmae* (q.v.) containing thirty-two men, giving a total of 512 men, rounded down for administrative purposes to 500. These units were commanded by prefects (*praefecti*), men who were not senators but who came from the *equites* (q.v. and see the previous entry about *alae*).

Angusticlavius: 'the narrow stripe' signifying a man of equestrian rank; in Britain this term mostly concerns the *tribuni angusticlavii*, of which there were five in a legion, the senior tribune being a senatorial *tribunus laticlavius*.

Annona militaris: provisions for the army; in the later Empire the Praetorian Prefects were placed in charge of the supplies for the troops.

As: lowest denomination Roman coin, made of bronze or copper. Four *asses* (nothing to do with donkeys) made one *sestertius* (q.v.).

Auctoritas: a measure of the reputation and social and political standing of Roman senators and politicians. The literal translation 'authority' does not convey its true meaning. *Auctoritas* could be earned and increased by political or military achievements, or it could be lost after disgraceful conduct.

Aureus: Roman gold coin, worth twenty-five *denarii* (q.v.).

Auxilia: literally 'help troops', the term used by the Romans to describe the units recruited from non-Romans. During the Republic these troops were recruited from among the friendly local tribes wherever the Romans were fighting battles. They were hired for the duration of the campaign, fought under their own native officers, and were disbanded at the end of the war. When Augustus created the first standing army from the troops he inherited after the civil wars with Antony and Cleopatra, the auxiliary troops were converted into regular units, gradually organised as *alae* and *cohortes* during the Empire, though at the time of the Claudian invasion of Britain their organisation was probably still evolving.

Ballista: an artillery engine, which could shoot large arrows or stone projectiles.

Beneficiarius: a soldier with a special mission or on special duties; *beneficiarii consularis* were sometimes stationed on frontiers, perhaps to gather intelligence

Camp prefect: see *praefectus castrorum*

Canabae: the civilian settlement outside a legionary fortress. See also *vicus*.

Capitatio: a poll-tax, paid in cash.

Capitum: fodder; in the later Empire payments to the soldiers were made partly in kind instead of cash; the terms *capitum* and *annona* were used for supplies, respectively for the horses and for the men.

Censitor: census official

Census: before taxes could be levied the number of people in a province were counted, and their property assessed, which required a census to be carried out, usually every five years though procedure could vary. An Imperial procurator would supervise the census of the province, and two procurators of the census are known in Britain. Other census officers were assigned to specific areas or tribes to collect the information. The town councils in Britain would be responsible for carrying out the census of their districts.

Centuria: (i) century, or a division of a cohort in a legion, or in an auxiliary infantry unit, nominally of 100 men, but in practice of 80 men, from the late Republic and throughout the Empire; (ii) a voting unit of the people of Rome.

Centurion: commander of a century (*centuria*), in the legions and in the auxiliary infantry units.

Citizenship, Roman: during the Republic, as Rome expanded her territory, citizenship could be conferred on individuals or on whole communities, and did not entail an obligation to live in Rome itself. In the Empire citizenship spread in a variety of ways: individual grants could be made, and the beneficiary usually took the family name of the person who had conferred citizenship on them; auxiliary soldiers were recruited from non-citizens, but each soldier was granted citizenship on completion of service; non-citizen magistrates of higher grade towns were usually granted citizenship after they had served the full term of office. Until the third century, Roman citizens enjoyed privileges at law and a favourable tax status, but these privileges had been largely eroded by the time that Caracalla granted citizenship to all free born inhabitants of the Empire.

Civitas (plural *civitates*): a collective term used for the citizens of a community; in Britain it was applied to a tribal area, where the citizens of the community had a council and magistrates, and were responsible for local government, and collecting taxes and carrying out the census. In the western provinces where there was a lack of urbanisation, the system could operate without the focal point of a town, but most *civitates* eventually developed an urbanised administrative centre, referred to by modern historians as *civitas* capitals. These were usually distinguished by their tribal names, such as Venta Silurum, market of the Silures (Caerwent), or Venta Belgarum, market of the Belgae (Winchester). Some were more successful than others: Cirencester flourished, Brough on Humber did not.

Cohors (plural *cohortes*): a cohort. The term denotes two types of unit: (i) a division of a legion containing six centuries of eighty men each, giving a total of 480 men; (ii) an auxiliary infantry unit, either 500 or 1,000 strong.

Cohors equitata: part-mounted auxiliary unit, nominally 500 or 1,000 strong, containing both infantry and cavalry. The organisation of these mixed units is not fully clarified. It is suggested that there were 480 infantry, as in a purely infantry *cohors quingenaria* (q.v.), with perhaps *c.*120 cavalry added to the unit, but if there were four *turmae* each containing 32 men, the total would be 128 horsemen. For the milliary *cohortes equitatae*, the numbers were probably 800 infantry, or ten centuries of 80 men, and perhaps eight *turmae* of 32 men, giving a total of 256 horsemen. These numbers are not confirmed by any contemporary source and remain speculative. The cavalry in a *cohors equitata* were not just mounted infantry or messengers, but were split off from their units in battle to fight with the other cavalry.

Cohors quingenaria: auxiliary infantry unit containing 500 men, in reality about 480 men, divided into six centuries with eighty men in each. The commander of a quingenary cohort was a prefect, usually drawn from the equestrian class. For about two or three years he would remain in his post as *praefectus cohortis*, the most junior of the equestrian career opportunities, and then go on to an appointment in a legion as *tribunus angusticlavius* (q.v.).

Cohors milliaria: auxiliary infantry unit nominally 1,000 strong, divided into ten centuries each containing eighty men, giving a total of 800 men. The commander was a tribune, who had most likely served as prefect of a *cohors quingenaria*, then as *tribunus angusticlavius* (q.v.) in a legion, followed by an appointment as prefect of an *ala quingenaria*. The command of a milliary cohort was usually referred to as the fourth military command (*quarta militia*) going up the scale of military appointments.

Colonia: the highest status for a civilian settlement. In the early Republic colonies of Roman citizens were established on the borders of Roman territory, for the protection of strategic areas or routes, and also to drain off surplus manpower from Rome. The colonists received lands to farm when the colony was established. In Britain, *coloniae* were set up for veterans from the legions, providing a livelihood for the retired soldiers and also a reserve of manpower for the army in case of trouble. Colchester was the first *colonia* to be established, *c*.AD 49, followed by Lincoln, which became a colony after the legionary fortress was given up in favour of the new legionary base at York, and Gloucester was made a colony when its legion moved out. At the beginning of the third century, the Emperor Severus elevated the civil settlement outside the fortress at York to the status of a *colonia*. It is suggested that London was likewise elevated in status at some unknown time, but there is as yet no proof of this. A *colonia* was a chartered, self-governing settlement, with a town council (*ordo* q.v.) consisting of officials called decurions, elected from the citizens of the colony. The senior magistrates were the two annually elected magistrates, *duoviri iuridicundo*, who dealt with legal matters and the law courts, as well as chairing the meetings of the *ordo*. Two other annually elected magistrates, *duoviri aediles,* were the next most senior officials, responsible for the upkeep of public buildings and the streets. Decurions of the *coloniae* and other towns were expected to finance public buildings and entertainments, a financial burden which became so oppressive in the later Empire that many of them left their towns, and recruitment to the *ordo* became very difficult.

Colonus (plural *coloni*): (i) the inhabitants of a *colonia*; (ii) in the later Empire the term described the tenant farmers of a landowner. They were increasingly tied to their place of origin, or the place where they were registered, under the control of the landlords.

Comes (plural *comites*): the entourage of an Emperor consisted of his friends (*comites*) who were organised on an unofficial basis at first, but Constantine gave the title *Comes*, usually translated as Count, to his military commanders and provincial governors. There was originally no connotation of rank in the title, but with the passage of time three grades were established, called *ordinis primi, secundi,* and *tertii*. After the disasters in Britain in AD 367, the Emperor Valentinian despatched three generals in quick succession to restore order, the third one being Count Theodosius, the father of the Emperor Theodosius. The historian Ammianus Marcellinus describes in some detail the achievements of Count Theodosius in Britain.

Comes rei militaris: when *comes* became an official title instead of a general term for one of the Emperor's associates, the *comes rei militaris,* 'count of military affairs' was used for a senior military commander.

Comitatenses: collective name for the units of the late Roman mobile field army, comprising cavalry and infantry.

Comitatus: derived from *comes*, initially describing the entourage of the Emperor; by the fourth century *comitatus* denoted the field army.

Consul: except for the Dictator and the censors, the consuls were the most senior magistrates of the Roman Republic, elected annually in pairs, responsible for civil duties and command of the armies. They were responsible to the Republican Senate. During the Empire the consuls were still elected annually, but with reduced military responsibilities and subordinate to the Emperor.

Consul ordinarius: during the Empire there were often more than two consuls in the year. The *ordinarii* were the officially elected consuls, who might hold office for a month or two, giving way to the *consules suffecti*. The *ordinarii* were the eponymous consuls, giving their name to the year, and are sometimes cited in literature and on inscriptions, thus providing historians and archaeologists with firm dates (but not frequently enough).

Consul suffectus: the suffect consuls were those who held office after the *ordinarii*. They may have served for only a few months, but this period of office gave them experience of government, and conferred consular rank on them, enabling them to progress to other appointments.

Consularis (plural *consulares*): a man who had been consul. The governors of Britain were all *consulares* until the division into two provinces in the third century, when Britannia Superior was governed by a *consularis*, and Britannia Inferior was governed by a the legionary legate of VI Victrix, of praetorian status.

Constitutio Antoniniana: an act passed by the Emperor Caracalla in AD 212, making all freeborn inhabitants of the Empire Roman citizens.

Contubernium: tent party, or the soldiers sharing one barrack block, normally eight men.

Corrector (plural *correctores*): Roman officials with the title *corrector* were appointed from the reign of Trajan, originally for the purpose of attending to the financial affairs of free cities which did not come under the jurisdiction of the provincial governors. *Correctores* held military and civil powers. Their responsibilities eventually extended to any of the cities in a province, free or otherwise, if the Emperor wished to investigate provincial affairs.

Curator civitatis: the Emperors sometimes appointed a *curator* to investigate and regulate the administration of a town if things were getting out of hand.

Curia: originally applied to the Senate House in Rome, this term was used for a subdivision of a town, or in less urbanised areas it referred to an assembly.

Curiales: members of the city councils. See also decurion; *ordo*.

Cursus honorum: the senatorial career path; senators of the later Republic and the early Empire followed a roughly similar succession of civil and military appointments before reaching the consulship, and thereafter the higher military commands and prestigious provincial governorships were open to them. In the early Empire, Britain ranked as one of the most important provincial commands. After the later second century, separate civil and military careers began to emerge and specialisation in one or the other became the norm.

Decurion: (i) senior officer of a cavalry *turma* (q.v.); (ii) a member of a town or city council (*ordo*, q.v.).

Denarius: Roman silver coin worth four *sestertii*.

Diocese: administrative grouping of several provinces, instituted by the Emperor Diocletian. Britain was divided into two smaller provinces in the early third century, and then into four much smaller provinces under Diocletian, who grouped them all together in the Diocese of Britain, governed by the *vicarius Britanniarum*. The British Diocese belonged to the larger territorial unit of the Prefecture of the Gallic provinces, the *vicarius Britanniarum* being the Prefect's deputy in Britain.

Diploma: a modern term for the two-leaved folding bronze certificate awarded to auxiliary soldiers who were honourably discharged from military service. Roman citizenship and other privileges were granted to such men, but withheld from any soldiers who had disgraced themselves.

Divus: divine, usually applied to Emperors who had been deified after their deaths. This was not an automatic honour, and could be withheld by the Senate for Emperors such as Nero and Domitian.

Duovir (plural *duoviri*, sometimes rendered as *duumviri*): one of pair of magistrates elected from among the members of a town council (*ordo* q.v.). In the larger towns there were *duoviri iuridicundo* responsible for legal affairs, and *duoviri aediles* responsible for the upkeep of buildings and streets. See also aedile.

Dux (plural *duces*): literally, leader. In the later Empire the term was used for equestrian military officers in command of troops in the frontier regions, usually with the title *dux limitis,* sometimes accompanied by an explanation of where they operated, such as *dux limitis per Africam.* Their commands sometimes covered more than one province so that the *duces* could control long stretches of the frontiers. In late Roman Britain the *dux Britanniarum,* leader of the Britains, or British provinces, in the plural, indicates that his command extended over more than one province. His headquarters may have been at York. *Duces* were raised to senatorial status by the Emperor Valentinian I.

Equestrians: the Roman middle classes, composed of *equites* (q.v.)

Equites: (i) horsemen of a cavalry unit; (ii) the equestrian, or middle class of the Roman Republic and Empire, next in rank after the senators. They derived their title from the very early Republican cavalry, whose horses were supplied by the state; they were described as *equites* entitled to a public horse (*equites equo publico*). During the Empire there was a property qualification for membership of the equestrian order of 400,000 *sestertii.* Equestrians were the businessmen of the Roman world, or the backbone of local communities as magistrates and councillors. They also provided lower-ranking officers for the Roman army. As social mobility became more widespread in the second century, many equestrians were elevated to the Senate, and under later Emperors such as Severus, Gallienus and Diocletian, equestrians began to replace senators as army commanders and provincial governors. See also *praeses.*

Equites legionis: cavalry contingent of a legion, initially thought to number 120 men, but increased by the Emperor Gallienus to over 700 men.

Equites singulares: bodyguards of the provincial governor, usually organised in units *c.*500 strong, formed from picked cavalrymen seconded from the *alae.* An inscription from Carlisle shows that a trooper from the *ala Sebosiana* had been seconded to the *equites singulares* of the governor Agricola. The *equites singulares Augusti* were the Emperor's bodyguard.

Foederati: literally those who are allied in war, derived from *foedus,* a treaty, and denoting troops raised according to the terms of a treaty. The *foederati* of the later Empire were similar to the early auxiliary troops, raised from tribesmen to serve mostly on the frontiers. They should be distinguished from the sixth-century *foederati,* which were regular troops.

Frumentum: grain, but often used of the food supply in general.

Frumentarii: originally officials concerned with the supply of food. The legions each had a number of *milites frumentarii* attached to them, commanded by a centurion. In the second century the *frumentarii* were employed on different tasks, such as intelligence gathering for the army, and as Imperial secret police.

Gentiles: non-Romans, and also in most cases non-provincials. The term was used of free tribesmen beyond the frontiers, and also of tribesmen settled in groups within the Empire. It is also used of a unit of Britons (*Brittones Gentiles*) serving in a *numerus* (q.v.) or small unit of the Roman army at Walldürn in the province of Upper Germany.

Honesta missio: honourable discharge from a military unit after serving for the specified time, twenty-five years in the case of the auxiliary soldiers.

Iuridicus: high officials appointed by the Emperors to take charge of judicial affairs. In Britain, five of these officials are known, all of them appointed when there were serious or prolonged wars where the governor was unable to leave his military duties to attend to judicial matters.

Iugum: a unit of land used for tax purposes in the late Empire, not always a standard measure since the type of land and the crops grown were taken into consideration by the assessors.

Iumenta: baggage animals of the army, specifically mules.

Laticlavius: 'broad stripe' signifying a man of senatorial status; the senior tribune of a legion was the *tribunus laticlavius*.

Legatus: legate, a term used for various appointments, with different ranks. Governors of Imperial provinces were *legati Augusti pro praetore* or legates of the Emperor; the commanders of legions were also called *legati*.

Legion: the term *legio* originally meant the choosing, or the levy, and was eventually applied to the main unit of the Roman army. Somewhat surprisingly, there is no information from Roman times about the exact size of a legion. Modern scholars estimate that there were about 5,000 or 6,000 men in a legion, but it is possible that some of them were understrength or overstrength, and numbers may have differed in peacetime and wartime. The legion was primarily a heavy-armed infantry unit, but also contained some cavalry. Legions of the late Empire were smaller, newly raised Diocletianic units perhaps being only about 1,000 strong, but this is a subject fraught with debate.

Limes (plural *limites*): when the fashion for enclosing the Empire within fixed boundaries began in the second century AD, the frontiers of the Empire were called *limites*, from which is derived the English word limit. In the Republic and early Empire, when there was no concept of calling a halt to expansion, the term *limes* referred to a road into enemy territory.

Limitanei: frontier troops of the later Empire.

Magister equitum: literally master of horse; in the Republic this title was given to the second in command of a Dictator; in the late Roman army it was an important military post in command of the cavalry units.

Magister militum: master of the soldiers. Like the *Duces* the various *magistri militum* could be in command of the troops of a single province or a larger region, but the title sometimes denotes a supreme commander of the whole army, otherwise expressed as *magister utruisque militiae*.

Magister officiorum: late Roman head of the secretarial offices of the Imperial administration.

Magister peditum: master of the infantry of the late Roman army.

Maniple: literally 'a handful', a term denoting a unit of the Republican army consisting of two centuries.

Municipium (plural *municipia*): an urbanised settlement second in rank to a *colonia* (q.v.). In the western provinces these towns were established within an existing settlement, but the British tribes had not developed self-governing towns with a Roman-style administrative system, despite the description of their settlements in Latin literature as *oppida*, sometimes translated as 'towns'. The Romans established the first, and probably the only *municipium* in Britain at Verulamium, on the site of the older British settlement of Verlamion. The *municipium* of Verulamium was a chartered town with its own constitution, and its laws may have amalgamated local custom and Roman law. The council members would be drawn from the elite members of the community, whose wealth enabled them to undertake the functions and obligations of the council. See also decurion; *duoviri*; *ordo*.

Numerus: meaning a military unit in the general sense, this term was also applied to small so-called ethnic units of the Roman army, drawn from tribesmen and serving mostly on the German and Danube frontiers and in Africa. Several *numeri* of Britons are attested in Germany from the late first century onwards, and in the later Empire several units called *numeri* are listed as part of the British garrison.

Optio: second in command to a centurion.

Ordo: originally applied to the senate and the senatorial order in Rome, this term also embraces the equestrian order, and more pertinently for Britain it was the name used for the councils of the various towns of the Empire.

Ornamenta triumphalia: literally triumphal ornaments or decorations, awarded to victorious generals. After the accession of Augustus, a triumphal procession was the exclusive preserve of members of the Imperial family; other generals were awarded the distinction of a triumph but not the traditional parade through the streets of Rome to dedicate the spoils of war in the temple of Jupiter on the Capitol Hill. See also triumph.

Pater patriae: father of the country, or fatherland, a title and distinction that all Emperors could be awarded, but they did not necessarily adopt it as soon as they took power.

Peregrini: literally 'foreigners', or non-Roman citizens. Most of the Britons under Roman rule would be of this status, unless they had been awarded citizenship, or had served as magistrates of their town councils, when Roman citizenship was granted after their term of office.

Phalera (plural *phalerae*): military decoration worn on the breastplate.

Pilum: missile weapon used by legionaries, consisting of a long, thin metal shank with a pyramidal tip, attached to a wooden shaft, like a javelin. There were various different sizes and types of *pila*, and their origins are much disputed.

Praefectus: prefect, a title given to several different civilian officials and military officers. The 500-strong auxiliary infantry cohorts and *alae* were commanded by prefects, usually equestrians who were beginning their military careers. The prefects could be of any rank from lowly cohort commander to powerful Imperial official. In the later Empire equestrians were put in command of legions with the title prefect. The summit of an equestrian career was to be appointed to one of the four great prefectures of the Empire, the Prefect of the *annona*, in charge of military supplies (*Praefectus Annonae*); the Prefect of the *Vigiles*, the fire brigade in Rome (*Praefectus Vigilum*); the Praetorian Prefect (*Praefectus Praetorio*), and the Prefect of Egypt (*Praefectus Aegypti*). A few of the commanders of military units in Britain could aspire to these appointments, working their way up the career path, and hopefully being noticed by the Emperor.

Praefectus castrorum: camp prefect, third in command of a legion during the Empire. In Britain, the most famous or infamous camp prefect is Poenius Postumus, *praefectus castrorum* of II Augusta, who failed to order his troops to march to the aid of Suetonius Paullinus during the rebellion of Boudicca.

Praepositus: title given to an officer in temporary command of troops, sometimes units such as the *numeri* (q.v.) or of temporary vexillations or detachments made up of men from different units. The term does not denote any specific rank, and could be awarded to soldiers of different grades while they carried out special tasks. In Britain, the title *praepositus* is attested for two individuals, both of them legionary centurions commanding at Ribchester in Lancashire in the early third century, and both called *praepositus regionis*, implying that they commanded not only the fort and the unit there but also were responsible for the surrounding territory.

Praeses (plural *praesides*): provincial governor of equestrian rank, common from Severan times onward. Only four *praesides* are known in Britain, and only two of these are directly attested by evidence from Britain itself. The first *praesides* were responsible for military and civil affairs as previous governors were, but gradually civil governmental posts and military commands were separated, and in the late Empire the *praesides* were usually administrative officials with no command of troops.

Praetor: the praetorship had a long history. Originally the praetor was the chief magistrate in early Republican Rome, the title deriving from *prae ire*, meaning 'to go before'. The praetors were soon superseded by the two annually elected consuls. When the consuls were absent the praetor was in charge of the courts, acted as president of the Senate, and had the right to command armies. The main duties of the praetor were to deal with the administration of the law, and as business increased, two praetors were appointed, one for internal affairs and a second for dealing with foreigners. As the Republic expanded, more praetors were appointed, continually increased until Imperial times.

Proconsul: governor of one of the non-Imperial provinces. Ten of these were selected annually by lot rather than by direct appointment by the Emperor; of these ten, eight were ex-praetors, and two were consulars.

Protectores: a title used by Gallienus for his military entourage, not simply a bodyguard, but perhaps the foundation of a staff college formed from officers loyal to the Emperor.

Quaestor: originally the lowest-ranking magistrates of the Republic appointed to assist the consuls in financial matters. The office was held by young men at the start of their career, before they had entered the Senate. As the Empire expanded more quaestors were created to deal with provincial administration. Quaestors acted as deputies to consular governors, and could hold commands in the army. Sometimes in modern versions of ancient works, quaestor is translated in the military context as quartermaster, which is not strictly accurate.

Regio: region, used of the districts of Italy, but also applied to provincial areas, such as the *regio* controlled by the centurions commanding the auxiliary unit at Ribchester. See also *praepositus*.

Schola (plural *scholae*): late Roman cavalry guard unit; *scholae palatinae* were the Emperor's guard.

Sestertius: Roman silver coin; four *sestertii* equalled one *denarius*.

Seviri Augustales: literally six men for the cult of the Emperor. The Imperial cult spread through the provinces and helped to unify the Empire. The members of these groups were usually freedmen.

Stipendium: military pay, handed out three times each year. The term was also applied to a period of service, and often appears on military tombstones in the abbreviated form *stip.* followed by the number of years the soldier had served.

Tribunus angusticlavius: narrow-stripe tribune. There were five of these equestrian officers in a legion, usually just starting out on their careers. They would probably have commanded a quingenary cohort before being appointed to a legion.

Tribunus laticlavius: broad-stripe tribune, from the senatorial class, and second in command of a legion.

Triumph: during the Republic, a triumph was granted by the Senate to victorious generals, who valued this opportunity to show off their captives and the spoils of war by processing along the Via Sacra in Rome, to the Temple of Jupiter. The *triumphator* rode in a chariot with his face painted red, and was supposed to approach the Temple on his knees to dedicate the spoils, with a slave at his side constantly reminding him that he was mortal. Augustus recognised the inflammatory nature of the triumph and took steps to limit it to members of the Imperial family. Other generals were denied the procession, and were granted *ornamenta triumphalia*, or triumphal insignia.

Turma (plural *turmae*): a division of a cavalry unit (*ala* q.v.) containing thirty-two men, commanded by a decurion (q.v.).

Vicani: inhabitants of a *vicus* (q.v.). In Britain, this term usually denotes the people living in a civil settlement outside a fort. Some *vicani* from the forts set up communal inscriptions, suggesting that they had a corporate sense of identity; one inscription from Old Carlisle refers to a *magister* (literally a 'master') of the vicani.

Vicarius: governor of a diocese (q.v.), answerable to the Praetorian Prefects.

Vicesima hereditarum: inheritance tax, levied at 5 per cent of the total value of the inheritance, but only if it was bequeathed to people other than direct descendants.

Vicus: a term that could mean a subdivision of a town, or a rural village. In the military context it refers to the civilian settlement outside a Roman auxiliary fort, the most common usage of the term in Britain. See also *canabae*.

Vigiles: the fire brigade of the city of Rome, organised in military fashion by Augustus.

Roman Place Names

For a list of Roman names and detailed discussion of the sources for them, see A.L.F. Rivet and C. Smith, *The Place Names of Roman Britain*, London: Batsford, 1979.

Aldborough, Yorkshire: Isurium Brigantum
Ambleside: Galava
Anglesey: Mona
Bath: Aquae Sulis
Benwell: Condercum
Bewcastle: Fanum Cocidi
Binchester: Vinovia/Vinovium
Birrens: Blatobulgium
Bowes: Lavatris
Bowness-on-Solway: Maia
Bradwell: Othona
Brancaster: Branodunum
Brecon: Cicutium
Brougham: Brocavum
Brough-on-Humber: Petuaria
Brough-on-Noe: Navio
Burgh Castle: Garrianum
Buxton: Arnemetiae
Caerleon: Isca
Caerwent: Venta Silurum
Caistor-by-Norwich: Venta Icenorum
Canterbury: Durovernum Cantiacorum
Carlisle: Luguvallium
Carmarthen: Moridunum Demetarum
Carvoran: Magnis
Carrawburgh: Brocolitia
Castleshaw: Rigodunum
Catterick: Cataractonium
Chelmsford: Caesaromagus
Chester: Deva

Chichester: Noviomagus Reginorum (sometimes spelled Regnorum)
Cirencester: Corinium Dobunnorum
Colchester: Camulodunum, or Colonia Claudia Victricensis
Corbridge: Corstopitum
Dart River, Devon: Derventio (see also Littlechester, Malton, Papcastle and River Derwent)
Derwent River, Cumbria: Derventio (see also Littlechester, Malton, Papcastle and River Dart)
Dorchester, Dorset: Durnovaria Durotrigum
Dover: Dubris
Droitwich: Salinae (see also Middlewich)
Exeter: Isca Dumnoniorum
Godmanchester: Durovigutum
Gloucester: Glevum, or Colonia Nervia Glevensis
Great Chesters: Aesica
High Rochester: Bremenium
Housesteads: Vercovicium
Isle of Wight: Vectis
Leicester: Ratae Corieltavorum
Lincoln: Lindum, or Colonia Domitiana Lindenensis
Littlechester: Derventio (see also Malton, Papcastle and rivers Dart and Derwent)
London: Londinium, later Augusta
Lympne: Lemanis
Malton: Derventio (see also Littlechester, Papcastle and rivers Dart and Derwent)
Manchester: Mamucium
Maryport: Alauna (also used for several other sites and rivers)
Mersey River: Seteia
Middlewich: Salinae (see also Droitwich)
Monmouth: Blestium
Moresby: Gabrosentum
Newcastle-upon-Tyne: Pons Aelii
Newstead: Trimontium
Northwich: Condate
Orkney Islands: Orcades
Papcastle: Derventio (see also Littlechester, Malton and Dart and Derwent rivers)
Pevensey: Anderitum
Portchester: Portus Ardaoni (?)
Pumpsaint: Luentinum
Reculver: Regulbium
Ribchester: Bremetennacum Veteranorum
Richborough: Rutupiae
Risingham: Habitancum
Rochester: Durobrivae
St Albans: Verulamium
Silchester: Calleva Atrebatum
South Shields: Arbeia
Spey River: Tuesis
Stanwix: Uxelodunum

Tay River: Tavus
Thames River: Tamesis, or Tamesa
Tyne River: Tinea
Wall: Letocetum
Wallsend: Segedunum
Whitchurch, Shropshire: Mediolanum
Winchester: Venta Belgarum
Wroxeter: Viroconium
York: Eboracum, or Colonia Eboracensium

Places to Visit

This is not an exhaustive list of sites, but includes some of the places where there are interesting features to see. Useful books for finding these places are R.J.A. Wilson, *A Guide to the Roman Remains in Britain*, 4th edn, 2002, which gives locations, directions, with plans, guided tours and short historical overviews of all the Roman sites of England, Scotland and Wales. For Scotland see also Lawrence Keppie, *The Legacy of Rome: Scotland's Roman Remains*, 3rd edn, 2004. Opening times are given for many Roman sites in the annual volumes of *Hudson's Historic Houses and Gardens, Castles and Heritage Sites*, published by Heritage House Group. This publication includes sites owned by private individuals or charities, the National Trust, English Heritage, CADW, and Historic Scotland. These last organisations publish lists of their sites, and are accessible online.

ANTONINE WALL SITES
The Antonine Wall was built of turf and timber (though some forts were built in stone) in the reign of Antoninus Pius, and was occupied for only a short time. The visible remains are eroded and therefore less spectacular than those of Hadrian's Wall and its forts, but are still worth a visit. This list does not include all the excavated sites, but the main ones where there is something to see are listed here, running from east to west rather than alphabetically by site name.

EDINBURGH, MUSEUM OF SCOTLAND
Many of the finds associated with the Antonine Wall are on display here.

KINNEIL
Remains of an earth and timber milefortlet. This description suggests that like the milecastles of Hadrian's Wall, there was one fortlet every Roman mile on the Antonine Wall, but this is not proven. The internal buildings and gates are not visible, but their positions are marked out by timber posts, in the original postholes found during excavation, and modern paving stones mark the line of the Wall and the milefortlet defences. Open at any time.

WATLING LODGE AND TENTFIELD PLANTATION, NEAR FALKIRK
Impressive remains of the Wall and ditch, with display boards.

ROUGH CASTLE FORT
A small earth and timber fort, whose defences can still be traced. The most famous aspect here is the discovery of rows of *lilia* outside the fort. These were an effective addition to the defensive ditches and ramparts, consisting of pits each containing a sharp stake pointing upwards, covered over with branches to give the appearance of solid ground, and gruesomely impaling anyone who ventured over them. There were similar pits at Wallsend fort and Piercebridge in Durham. Open at any time.

SEABEGS WOOD, BETWEEN BONNYBRIDGE AND ALLANDALE, HISTORIC SCOTLAND
Another well preserved stretch of Wall and ditch, with informative display boards. Open at any time.

CASTLECARY FORT, HISTORIC SCOTLAND
Not much remains of this fort, but it is an important site because it was one of the stone forts of the Antonine Wall – the majority being of earth and timber. The defences are visible as mounds of earth, and information boards show the site plan. Open at any time.

CROY HILL, NEAR CROY VILLAGE, HISTORIC SCOTLAND
From this site, the traces of the ditch of the Antonine Wall can be traced for some distance, well preserved because it was dug through solid rock, and there is a clear view across the lower ground between the Wall and the hills further north. Open at any time.

BAR HILL FORT, HISTORIC SCOTLAND
The plan of this fort is visible on a display board. Unlike most of the other forts it was not attached to the Antonine Wall, but lay a short distance to the south, with the military road running between the fort and the Wall. The defences are not well preserved but the foundations of the headquarters building and the fort baths have been conserved. The baths of Roman forts were normally outside the defences, but here at Bar Hill, and also at some of the other Antonine Wall forts, the building was inside the fort, suggesting that there was a greater need for security along the Wall. Many examples of leather shoes, for men, women and children were found here, and are now in the Hunterian Museum in Glasgow. Bar Hill is open at any time.

BEARSDEN FORT
Most of the fort is hidden by modern housing, but excavations in the 1970s recovered the plan of the fort before the houses were built. The bath house is preserved, with walls standing to considerable height. As at Bar Hill fort, the baths building was located inside the fort, but a wall divided it off from the main buildings.

DUNTOCHER
There is not much to see here, save for a stretch of Wall on Golden Hill. The fortlet here was excavated from 1948 to 1951. A larger fort with an annexe replaced the fortlet, before the Wall was built in this sector.

GLASGOW, HUNTERIAN MUSEUM
Roman finds and inscriptions are on display. There is a gift shop.

Here ends the section on the Antonine Wall

ARBEIA ROMAN FORT, BARING STREET, SOUTH SHIELDS, TYNE AND WEAR, SOUTH TYNESIDE METROPOLITAN BOROUGH COUNCIL
Remains of different periods of the Roman fort are displayed, with granaries of the Severan supply base. The most spectacular feature is the reconstruction of a gateway. Entry is free except for the Time Quest Gallery.

ARDOCH ROMAN FORT, NEAR PERTH, SCOTLAND
This site was occupied by Agricola's troops in the first century and by Antonine Pius when the turf Wall was built to the south. There are several marching camps in the vicinity. The fort was one of the series that ran round the western edge of Fife, but the forts at Camelon and Strageath are not nearly so well preserved. The defences of Ardoch fort are traceable, but the most spectacular remains are those of the multiple ditches surrounding the fort. Since the site is not built over, it is possible to view the size of the fort. Open at any time.

BIGNOR ROMAN VILLA, PULLBOROUGH, WEST SUSSEX, PRIVATELY OWNED
Famous for its floor mosaics, all in situ but covered over for protection, and all visible. Visitors are advised to make an appointment.

BRANCASTER ESTATE, BRANCASTER, NORFOLK, NATIONAL TRUST
Among other attractions, the remains of the third-century fort of Branodunum, later incorporated into the forts of the Saxon Shore, are displayed.

BURGH CASTLE, NEAR GREAT YARMOUTH, NORFOLK, ENGLISH HERITAGE
Late third-century Saxon Shore fort on the River Yare. Most of the defences and projecting drum towers stand to a considerable height. Parts of the south wall have collapsed, and the east gate is now only a gap in the walls. Open at any time.

CAERLEON ROMAN LEGIONARY FORTRESS, AMPHITHEATRE AND LEGIONARY BATHS, HIGH STREET, CAERLEON, SOUTH WALES, CADW
The amphitheatre is on display and well worth a visit, and some legionary barracks can be seen nearby in a small conserved area of the fortress, which housed the II Augusta legion. These are the only legionary barracks, as opposed to those of an auxiliary fort, to be seen in Europe. The amphitheatre and barracks are free entry, but in the town there is a charge for visiting the foundations of the legionary baths, which have been conserved with excellent museum displays and holograms and sound effects of people using the baths. There is a shop selling books and gifts.

CAERNARVON, *SEE* SEGONTIUM ROMAN FORT

CAERWENT ROMAN TOWN, CAERWENT, SOUTH WALES, CADW
A must-see unmanned site, with free entry, and free car park and toilets, and a pub serving good, inexpensive food (2010). A complete Roman town, hardly built over except for a few modern buildings, with selected areas excavated and conserved, and explained by means of display boards with plans and reconstruction drawings. The defences can be traced all round the town, but the best part is the south wall with several projecting towers, all surviving to an impressive height. A Norman motte covers one corner of the defences.

CARVORAN FORT AND ROMAN ARMY MUSEUM, NEAR WALLTOWN CRAGS, NORTH OF HALTWHISTLE

This fort was not part of Hadrian's Wall, in that it pre-dates the Wall and was divided from it by the Vallum, or southern ditch of the Wall system, which diverts from its straight course to skirt the north ramparts. The fort itself is not visible except for mounds covering the defences, and the north-west angle tower has been excavated and conserved. The most important visitor attraction here is the Roman Army Museum with displays of some original finds, and life-size models. The museum has been refurbished (2011).

CHEDWORTH ROMAN VILLA, YANWORTH, NEAR CHELTENHAM, GLOUCESTERSHIRE, NATIONAL TRUST

One of the largest villas in Roman Britain, excavated in the nineteenth century, with continuing improvements and conservation programmes. There is a shrine in one corner of the villa, and it is now thought that the whole site may have been a religious complex rather than a villa and farm. There is a gift shop with an extensive range of books.

CHESTER AMPHITHEATRE, ENGLISH HERITAGE AND CHESTER CITY COUNCIL

This site, half of the legionary amphitheatre, has been excavated recently and conserved. Entry is free. Nearby there are the foundations of the fortress wall and corner tower, and the medieval walls follow a large part of the fortress defences. The Grosvenor Museum contains artefacts and stone inscriptions relating to the Roman occupation of Chester. The amphitheatre and walls are open at any reasonable time.

CIRENCESTER, GLOUCESTERSHIRE

This is the largest Roman town in Britain after London, and was the *civitas* capital of the Dobunni. The medieval and modern town do not come close to the size of the Roman town, but there is little to see, except for the amphitheatre with earth walls on the west and a stretch of the defences on the east side. The Corinium Museum contains splendid mosaics, tombstones, and sculptures with interpretive displays.

COLCHESTER, ESSEX

The pre-Roman British settlement here is not visible, nor are many of the Roman remains which have been excavated, because the modern town overlies them. The most spectacular locations to visit are the castle, which conceals the podium of the Temple of Claudius, and the museum inside the castle should not be missed. It contains many Roman finds, including the tombstones of the centurion Marcus Favonius Facilis, without whom no book on Roman Britain would be complete, and the cavalryman Longinus. On the west side of the city, the Balkerne Gate can be seen, and the defensive walls on both sides of it. The walls survive almost intact except for two sections, one on the north side and one on the south, and energetic visitors can walk round the whole circuit.

CRAMOND FORT, NEAR EDINBURGH

Situated on the River Almond at the junction with the Forth estuary, this fort may have been occupied under Agricola and his successors in the first century, and was certainly occupied in the Antonine and Severan periods. A short stretch of a wall of one of the Severan internal buildings is preserved, and partial ground plans of two granaries are marked out. The site would provide an important port for supply of the Antonine Wall troops and for Severus's northern campaigns.

DOLAUCOTHI ROMAN GOLD MINE, PUMPSAINT, LLANWRDA, CARMARTHEN, NATIONAL TRUST

The Romans mined for gold here, and the mine was still in use through Victorian times and up to the 1930s. There are guided tours through the underground works. There is also a gift shop.

DOVER CASTLE, ENGLISH HERITAGE

In the grounds of the castle there is the Roman lighthouse, the first four stages of which are preserved. It would have been much higher with about four more stages, but these have disappeared, despite the repairs carried out in medieval times. There is a museum and shop.

DOVER ROMAN PAINTED HOUSE, NEW STREET, DOVER, KENT, DOVER ROMAN PAINTED HOUSE TRUST

This building of the early third century is interpreted as a *mansio* or hostel for officials travelling on Imperial or provincial business. This site was preserved when the Saxon Shore fort was built, and the earthen rampart back covered the house. It yielded the largest painted wall in Britain.

FISHBOURNE ROMAN PALACE, SALTHILL ROAD, FISHBOURNE, CHICHESTER, SUSSEX, SUSSEX PAST

Notable for its grandiose size and wealth, the villa at Fishbourne was discovered in 1960. It has become possibly the most famous villa in Britain, but is not actually typical of a Roman villa. The Roman army occupied the site, then *c*.AD 50 a timber house was built with painted plaster walls and mortared floors, indicating the importance of the owner. The stone villa appeared about a decade later, and about twenty years after that the palace was built, with superb mosaic floors, and gardens.

GLOUCESTER, GLOUCESTERSHIRE

Like Lincoln the site was first occupied by legionary troops. The first fortress was at Kingsholm to the north of the city, and the Gloucester fort was probably established in the late AD 60s and occupied for thirty years or so, when the troops left and the fortress became a colony for veterans and their families. There are very few surviving remains, since the fortress and colony lie under the modern city, but the street plan preserves much of the Roman layout. The most important site to visit is the City Museum with sculptures, tombstones, mosaics and finds.

HADRIAN'S WALL SITES

Several forts are still visible on Hadrian's Wall, such as Halton and Greatchesters, where the ruins are mostly covered over with earth, but this list includes only those which are conserved. The forts are listed in order from the east to the west, rather than alphabetically.

SEGEDUNUM ROMAN FORT AND BATHS, BUDDLE STREET, WALLSEND, NEWCASTLE-UPON-TYNE

The most comprehensively excavated Roman fort in Britain, near the River Tyne where Hadrian's Wall ends. There is a museum, and a reconstructed section of wall, but perhaps the most important feature is the reconstruction of a complete bath house, based on the ruins at Chesters fort, with wall paintings.

NEWCASTLE-UPON-TYNE
The fort here is hidden underneath the modern city, but the ground plan of the granary is marked out in modern paving stones near the castle. The modern swing bridge is on the site of the Roman bridge across the Tyne. The Great North Museum houses many of the finds from Hadrian's Wall.

CHESTERS, CHOLLERFORD, NEAR HEXHAM, NORTHUMBERLAND, ENGLISH HERITAGE
Owned in the nineteenth century by John Clayton, who excavated the fort and saved it and other Roman sites from decay and destruction. The headquarters building of the fort, the commander's house, most of the defences and gates, and some barracks are on view, all contained inside fenced enclosures. The site is best studied by using an aerial view together with a plan. The site is most famous for the substantial remains of the bath house near the River Tyne. Across the river the foundations of the Roman bridge can be seen. There is a museum and shop.

LIMESTONE CORNER
On the B6318 between Chesters and Carrawburgh, to the right of the road, after coming up the hill and curving to the left, there is a small layby, and nearby an untidy heap of rocks, marking the point where the Romans ceased to dig the ditch to the north of the Wall, because of the hardness of the rock. On the other side of the road (take care if crossing it, as the traffic is life-threatening) the Vallum, the massive southern ditch with mounds on either side, was dug all through the rock, indicating its importance to the Romans. If only we knew exactly why it was so important!

CARRAWBURGH, NORTHUMBERLAND
The fort here was covered over after the latest excavations in the 1960s, but its outline and surrounding ditches can be seen. The most important site is on the other side of the fort, the temple of Mithras with replica altars. Open at any time.

HOUSESTEADS, NEAR HAYDON BRIDGE, NORTHUMBERLAND, OWNED BY THE NATIONAL TRUST AND ADMINISTERED BY ENGLISH HERITAGE
This is one of the most famous and most complete Roman forts, with a full circuit of defences and gates, and headquarters building, commander's house, hospital and granary conserved and on view. The site also has a block of late Roman barracks on display, called 'chalets' because unlike earlier barracks they are not joined up but consist of several closely spaced but individual houses, in which it has been suggested that soldiers lived with their families. Outside the fort there are foundations of some of the houses and shops of the *vicus* or civil settlement. There is a museum and shop on the site and a National Trust shop near the car park.

Vindolanda Roman fort and vicus pre-dates the Wall and was not part of the running barrier. See separate entry under Vindolanda.

STEEL RIGG
Going westwards, the road to Steel Rigg is on the right, opposite the road that leads to the Once Brewed Heritage Centre, and then to Vindolanda, on the left. The Wall is well conserved here for some distance on either side of the car park, and from Steel Rig there is famous view of the Wall and Crag Lough.

CAWFIELDS, NEAR HALTWHISTLE, NORTHUMBERLAND
By the side of the quarry and artificial lake, there is a short stretch of the Wall fully conserved, and the foundations of a milecastle. Open at any time.

Carvoran, like Vindolanda, was not actually on the Wall, but for some reason separated from it by the course of the Vallum, which skirts round it on its northern side. See separate entry under Carvoran.

POLTROSS BURN MILECASTLE, GILSLAND, NORTHUMBERLAND
At the eastern edge of Gilsland, the town is entered underneath the railway arch, and the sign on the arch shows the way to one of the best milecastle sites. The outline of the two barrack blocks can be seen, with an oven in one corner. In the opposite corner there are the remains of a staircase, suggesting that there was a rampart walk around the milecastle, if not a wall walk along the Wall itself. Open at any time.

BIRDOSWALD, CUMBRIA, ENGLISH HERITAGE
The gates and defences here are very well preserved, and the site is famous for the excavations that revealed fifth-century occupation on the site of the granary. Museum and shop.

CARLISLE, CUMBRIA
There were successive Roman forts and an important town here of which nothing is visible now, but the museum at Tullie House makes up for the lack of remains. The cavalry fort at Stanwix in the Carlisle suburbs was the largest fort on the Wall, housing the one and only thousand-strong mounted unit in Britain, the *Ala Petriana.*

SOLWAY FIRTH
Roman forts and towers guarded the estuary for some distance down the Cumbrian coast. See the entry under Maryport.

Here ends the section on Hadrian's Wall

LEICESTER, LEICESTERSHIRE
There was a pre-Roman settlement here, and an early Roman fort, but no details are known. The town was the *civitas* capital of the Corieltauvi, and the modern street plan reflects the second-century layout. Not much remains of the Roman town for visitors to see, except for the Jewry Wall, a large section of the walls of the baths complex, to be found near St Nicholas's church. Nearby there is the Jewry Wall Museum, containing mosaic floors and wall paintings from some of the houses that have been excavated.

LETOCETUM ROMAN BATHS AND MUSEUM, WATLING STREET, WALL, NEAR LICHFIELD,

STAFFORDSHIRE, OWNED BY THE NATIONAL TRUST, AND IN THE GUARDIANSHIP OF ENGLISH HERITAGE
The site includes a *mansio* and bath house, and a museum with limited opening hours.

LINCOLN, LINCOLNSHIRE
This site on top of the steep hill started out as a fortress for IX legion in the aftermath of the rebellion of Boudicca, and was converted into a colony when the legion moved to York. The defences of the fortress can be traced in part, together with parts of walls around the extension to the south for the inhabitants of the colony. The buildings inside the colony are known in part, but excavation has not been extensive. There are three extant gateways, the north gate known as the Newport Arch being the most spectacular, because the whole arch survives, thanks to the medieval inhabitants who kept it in good repair. The west gate of the fortress is buried in the castle mound, but the foundations of the lower west gate of the colony are conserved near the Municipal offices. The third gate, on the east side of the fortress is just north of the cathedral, approached by the road appropriately named Eastgate. The north tower of this gate is impressive, containing a doorway and a staircase to the upper levels.

LULLINGSTONE ROMAN VILLA, LULLINGSTONE LANE, EYNSFORD, KENT, ENGLISH HERITAGE
Well-appointed villa with mosaic floors and wall paintings, and famous for one of the very earliest private Christian chapels in Britain. The villa reached its peak of development in the mid-fourth century.

MARYPORT ROMAN FORT AND THE SENHOUSE ROMAN MUSEUM, MARYPORT, CUMBRIA
The remains of the fort can be clearly seen here, and it is the only fort of the Solway system that can still be traced on the ground. The *vicus* outside the fort was extensively surveyed in the 1990s, and the Senhouse Museum, named after the Senhouse family who collected the material from the sixteenth century, houses many inscriptions from the site, including the series of altars to Jupiter, seventeen in total. The names of no less than six unit commanders are known from the inscriptions, a unique feature.

PEVENSEY ROMAN FORT AND NORMAN CASTLE, PEVENSEY, SUSSEX, ENGLISH HERITAGE
The fort at Pevensey was a later addition to the Saxon Shore forts, possibly built by the usurper Carausius or his assassin Allectus towards the end of the third century. The fort was oval in shape rather than the classic rectangle, and the Normans used the defences as the outer bailey of a castle. There is a gift shop.

PORTCHESTER ROMAN FORT AND CASTLE, PORTSMOUTH, HAMPSHIRE, ENGLISH HERITAGE
The complete circuit of Roman defensive walls and towers still survive here. Portchester was one of the forts of the Saxon Shore, a truly massive fort, but not much is known about how it was manned or how it functioned, and as in many of the Saxon Shore forts, there seems to have been few internal buildings. A Norman castle in one corner is dwarfed by the fort. There is a gift shop.

RICHBOROUGH ROMAN FORT, RICHBOROUGH, SANDWICH, KENT, ENGLISH HERITAGE
This fort was occupied from the time of the Claudian conquest until the late Roman period.

The remains of the Saxon Shore fort are visible, with some of the earlier phases of the military occupation, including the foundations of the enormous monumental arch. There is a museum and shop.

ST ALBANS (VERULAMIUM)
Much of Roman Verulamium lies outside the modern town of St Albans. Excavations from the 1930s onwards have illustrated how the city grew to become one of the largest in Roman Britain. There are remains of several buildings to visit, including part of the defensive walls, but the most spectacular is the theatre, which was probably built during the reign of Hadrian, and continued in use until the fourth century. Roman theatres are known to have existed in other cities, but only at Verulamium can you gain an impression of what they were like. Don't miss the Museum, which contains an important collection of finds, well presented and interpreted.

SEGONTIUM ROMAN FORT, CAERNARFON, GWYNEDD, Owned by the National Trust and administered by CADW
The remains of the fort are on view, and there is a museum.

SILCHESTER ROMAN TOWN, ENGLISH HERITAGE
This was one of the earliest towns in Britain, preceded by a circuit of Iron Age earthworks. One section of these earthworks can still be seen, but the others were levelled when the Roman town was built. Silchester has the advantage of remaining free of modern buildings except for a farm and a church. The town defences are traceable, and on the south-east side a high stretch of wall is visible. The remains of the amphitheatre can be seen outside the town walls. Open at any time.

SOUTH SHIELDS, SEE ARBEIA ROMAN FORT

VINDOLANDA ROMAN FORT, BARDON MILL, HEXHAM, NORTHUMBERLAND, VINDOLANDA CHARITABLE TRUST
The visitor comes through the civil settlement (*vicus*) and into the fort where the remains of several buildings have been conserved. The museum, shop and café are further on down the hill, and there are reconstructions of Roman altars and inscriptions.

WALL, STAFFORDSHIRE, SEE LETOCETUM ROMAN BATHS AND MUSEUM

WALLSEND, SEE UNDER HADRIAN'S WALL, THE ENTRY FOR SEGEDUNUM ROMAN FORT AND BATHS

WROXETER ROMAN TOWN, SHROPSHIRE, ENGLISH HERITAGE
In its initial phases this site was a legionary base, for XIV Gemina and XX Valeria Victrix (a title earned in suppressing the Boudiccan revolt). When the legions departed, the town became the *civitas* capital of the Cornovii. The spectacular wall called the Old Work is one of the walls of the baths complex, and in a climate that is not kind to buildings it is an almost miraculous survival. The site is well displayed and explained, enhanced now by the reconstruction of a Roman villa, as seen on television. There is a museum and a shop for gifts and books.

York, Yorkshire

York was the legionary fortress of IX Hispana and then VI Victrix, with a substantial civil settlement outside the fortress walls and the settlement on the other side of the River Ouse which was made a colony in the third century. The medieval walls use much of the Roman defences and can be walked round. Coming into the city from the railway station and going towards the Minster, the late Roman sections of the defences of the fortress can be seen in the gardens on the left. The Multangular Tower is the surviving example of eight such projecting towers along the river frontage of the late Roman fortress. The Yorkshire Museum in the gardens displays Roman finds. In the undercroft of the Minster, parts of the legionary headquarters building can be seen with explanatory models, and a large section of painted wall plaster is on view. It was found in a fourth-century room added onto the back of the headquarters.

What the Ancient Authors Said About Roman Britain

This section contains brief information about the principal ancient authors who wrote about Roman Britain, and summarises what they said. The list follows a chronological order, not for events in Britain, but for the dates when each author was working. Square brackets are used for explanations of the context of the passages quoted and for further clarification of some words or sentences, for example where there is modern controversy over some details.

JULIUS CAESAR (100 BC TO 44 BC) *THE GALLIC WAR (DE BELLO GALLICO)*
Besides his work on the Gallic War, in which he describes what he saw in Britain in 55 and 54 BC, Gaius Julius Caesar produced two other works, on the civil war with the Pompeians, and on the Alexandrian, African and Spanish wars against the sons of Pompey the Great. The prime purpose of Caesar's writings was self-advertisement, to present his own point of view, or rather how he wanted to be seen by contemporaries and by posterity. While he was busy conquering Gaul, creating a military reputation and making a political name for himself, he was only too aware that in recent years Pompey the Great had failed to advertise himself sufficiently. Pompey's reputation and self-evident achievements ought to have carried all before him, but when he returned to Rome, the senators, especially those whose toes he had crushed in his efforts to obtain the eastern command, blocked his every move. Caesar intended that the people of Rome and Italy, and also the Senate, should not forget about him or ignore him while he was absent in Gaul, and that they should know more of him when he returned home.

Caesar's description of the battles in Gaul and Britain are vivid and detailed, and his description of the tribes in Britain contains useful information. The translator of the Loeb edition of *The Gallic War* considered that the work had been compiled from the information contained in Caesar's despatches to the Senate, which in turn would have incorporated the despatches of the various subordinate officers sent to Caesar at his headquarters. This would account for the immediacy and vigour of the accounts of military operations, which is enhanced by the fact that Caesar adhered to the present tense and the third person when he described his actions, never saying 'I did this', or 'I achieved that', but 'Caesar does this or achieves that'. Much of Roman literature, especially of this type, was meant to be read out loud, or almost performed as a dramatic work, just as modern raconteurs lapse into the present tense when telling their stories: 'so he goes down to the pub, and he says ...' etc.

Caesar's narratives of manoeuvres and battles are probably trustworthy, and the value of his works is not in doubt, not least because there is nothing else by any other author that covers the same period. Historically, there is very little detail concerning topography of Britain, and the chronology is sometimes questionable, but this should not detract from the overall worth of the details.

Summary of the reports about Britain by Julius Caesar in *The Gallic War* (*De Bello Gallico*). The narrative is reproduced in the present tense, just as Caesar wrote it, but the passages here are not direct translations:

2.4 Diviciacus, a great king in Gaul, rules over some tribes in Britain.

2.14 The tribe of the Bellovaci raise revolt against Caesar in Gaul, and when it fails, the leaders flee to Britain.

3.8 The Veneti of the west coast of Gaul possess numerous ships, which they use to sail to Britain.

3.9 The Veneti seek allies among the tribes of Gaul, including some tribes from Britain.

4.20–36; 38 The first expedition to Britain 55 BC
Caesar gathers information about Britain, leaves his legates in command in Gaul, and embarks from two different ports, to cross the Channel. The Britons had heard from Gallic merchants that Caesar was planning to invade, and they assemble their cavalry and chariots to meet him. The legions have to disembark in deep water because the ships cannot be brought right up to shore. They hesitate, then the standard bearer of the Tenth legion leaps down and the rest follow. After a desperate battle the Romans gain a foothold and Caesar makes camp. The Britons send deputies, offer hostages and make temporary peace, some of them remaining near the camp.

A storm disperses the cavalry transports, and at full moon the storm wrecks some of Caesar's ships. Seeing the difficulties that the Romans now face, the Britons start to melt away and surreptitiously gather their warriors, while Caesar repairs the ships. He loses twelve of them. Then he concentrates on collecting supplies. A foraging party is attacked, but Caesar brings up troops and beats off the attack. He describes in some detail how the Britons fight from their chariots, admiring the expert way in which they handle them.

After another battle, the Britons withdraw and Caesar extracts promises of hostages to be sent to him in Gaul. Only two of the tribes actually send any.

5.1–23 The second expedition to Britain 54 BC
Caesar prepares a fleet, ordering all the ships to assemble at Portus Itius (Boulogne); this port provides the most convenient passage to Britain, about 30 miles from the coast of Gaul. Sixty ships are prevented from reaching the port by bad weather. Caesar also assembles 4,000 Gallic cavalry from all the tribes, with their own chiefs to lead them. Dumnorix objects, and is arrested but escapes and is killed.

Five legions and the cavalry set off at sunset, and are blown off course, arriving on the coast of Britain at about midday. There are no Britons in sight. Caesar makes camp, and reconnoitres to find where the tribes are. Leaving ten cohorts and 300 cavalry to guard the ships he sets off to meet the Britons, who have erected fortifications in a wood using felled trees and branches. The Seventh legion forms a tortoise with shields over their heads and break in. Next day Cesar sends off some cavalry and infantry to pursue the Britons, but news arrives that a storm has once again wrecked some ships. Caesar chooses legionary craftsmen to effect repairs and sends a message to Titus Labienus commanding in Gaul to send equipment and build more ships.

In the meantime the Britons re-assemble and elect a leader called Cassivellaunus. He describes the tribes and their way of life, and the shape and dimensions of Britain. He notes that the tribes living in Kent are more advanced than others, and their farms are very similar to those of the Gauls. Caesar resumes the campaign, with the Britons harassing them on the march, and the Romans are attacked while making camp. Caesar sends in two legionary cohorts, which form up for the fighting with a slight interval between them. The Britons exploit this by dashing into the gap. Caesar admits that the legions are too heavily armed and could not move far from the standards, and are therefore not suited to this new kind of fighting, nor are the cavalry forces well adapted to combat with the Britons, who draw them on and then leap down from the chariots to fight on foot, separating the Roman cavalry from the rest of the troops. The Britons fight in small groups, never in close formation, and they always leave some warriors in reserve so that they can come into the battle fresh while the tired warriors retire to rest.

Cassivellaunus ambushes a foraging party and is beaten off with difficulty, but thereafter he resorts to the use of fortifications and guerrilla warfare instead of pitched battles. He adopts a scorched earth policy to prevent the Romans from gathering supplies. Caesar is forced to keep the legions together, and finds it difficult to feed the troops. Then the Trinovantes approach him, offering to give hostages and to provide supplies, because Cassivellaunus has done them great harm in the past.

Cassivellaunus contacts four kings of tribes in Kent, asking them to attack the Roman naval camp and the fleet, but the attack fails. This is Cassivellaunus's last hope, so he agrees to make peace. Caesar demands hostages, and forbids Cassivellaunus to make war on the Trinovantes. He makes preparations to sail back to Gaul, but there are not enough ships, so he has to make two journeys. On the second leg, there are so few ships that he is forced to load them beyond their capacity, but the sea remains calm and he withdraws to Gaul.

6.13 The Druids of Gaul go to Britain to improve their learning, for the cult originated in the island.

STRABO (c.64 BC TO AFTER AD 21) *GEOGRAPHY*

Strabo was born in Pontus, and came to Rome to study. He wrote in Greek, in the age of Augustus and Tiberius, collecting information from other authors whose works are now lost. He travelled widely, visiting Rome several times, and remaining in Egypt for some years, but not all his information was derived from personal observation. Some of the sources that he used were already out of date. But his work is important for the study of the early Roman Empire, how it developed, and its effect on the surrounding territories and kingdoms. Strabo was probably a Roman citizen, and he understood how the Empire was governed.

Summary of reports on Britain in Strabo's *Geography*:

1.4.3 Pytheas's description of Britain is unreliable. He describes Thule, whereas other writers who have seen Britain do not mention it at all. Also Pytheas says that the island is 2,300 miles long, and Kent is some days' sail from Gaul.

2.5.8 There is nothing to be gained from knowledge of northern Britain, since it is too isolated to endanger Rome. Britain could have been held but the idea was rejected because the Britons are not powerful enough to attack. There is no advantage in holding the island, because it provides more revenue from customs dues than tribute could bring in, especially if the cost of garrisoning is deducted from the total.

4.4.1 The Veneti wanted to prevent Caesar from going to Britain because they traded there.

4.5.2 There are four crossing points to Britain, from the Rhine, the Seine, the Loire and the Garonne. Those who cross from the Rhine do not sail from the estuary but from the territory of the Morini, who live next to the Menapii, where Itius [Boulogne] lies, the port used by Caesar. The island is flat and forested but there are also some hilly areas. It produces grain, cattle, gold, silver and iron, which are exported along with slaves and hunting dogs. The British men are taller than the Gauls, and not so fair-haired. Some British boys in Rome were taller than anyone else, but bow-legged and not graceful. In their customs the Britons are like the Gauls, but more barbaric. They have milk but do not make cheese, and they are not good at farming. They are ruled by chiefs. In war they fight from chariots. The forests protect them, where they use felled trees to build circular fortifications, with huts and animal compounds inside, but only for temporary use. There is more rain than snow, and on some days the fog obscures the sun all day.

4.5.3 Some of the British chiefs have become friends of Augustus through embassies, and they make offerings on the Capitol Hill, rendering the whole island almost Roman property. The Britons submit so readily to taxes on exports and imports to and from Gaul, items such as ivory chains, necklaces, amber and glassware. There is no need to garrison the island, because at least one legion and some auxiliaries would be necessary and the expense of the army would be equal to the amounts brought in. If tribute were to be demanded the customs dues would have to be reduced, and extracting tribute by force creates danger.

4.5.5 Information about Thule is uncertain. It is the most northerly place for which there is a name. What Pytheas says about it is not reliable, but he used his information reasonably well, in that the people of the northerly areas do not cultivate crops, nor do they rear domesticated animals, but live on millet, vegetables, fruit and roots. The people who do have grain and honey make a drink from them. They thresh grain in large barns where they store the ears because of the climate which lacks sunshine.

CORNELIUS TACITUS (c.AD 56 TO c.AD 120) *ANNALS; HISTORIES; AGRICOLA*
The life of Tacitus spanned the reigns of Nero, Galba, Otho, Vitellius, Vespasian, Titus, Domitian, Nerva, Trajan and Hadrian. He witnessed great events and changes, one of the most important being a serious civil war when he was a teenager in AD 69, when four Emperors came to power in one year, and the first three were killed in quick succession. The feature of Roman rule that made the most impression on Tacitus was living through the dreadful and uncertain later years of Domitian's reign, when no one

of the senatorial class felt safe, largely because the Emperor himself did not feel safe, and was therefore deeply suspicious of everyone else.

Tacitus's two main historical works, the *Annals* and the *Histories*, deal successively with the history of the Roman Empire from AD 14, when Augustus died, to the assassination of Domitian in AD 96. Since there was a great deal of military activity in the Roman Empire during these years, Tacitus is an invaluable source for the wars themselves and the politics behind them. He describes Britain at various periods in both the *Histories* and the *Annals*, but his main work with relevance to Roman Britain is the *Agricola*, the life of his father-in-law Gnaeus Julius Agricola, governor of Britain from AD 77 (or 78) to 84 (or 85). The book deals with the seven seasons of Agricola's campaigns in Britain, and it is the only source (apart from a fragmentary inscription from Verulamium, and a lead pipe from the legionary fortress at Chester inscribed with Agricola's name) that tells us who was the provincial governor during this enigmatic period of Romano-British history. The narrative informs us about the activities of the Roman army for each of the seven campaigning seasons, the first of them in north Wales and the rest in northern Britain. The main theatre of the war for the last five years of Agricola's governorship was in Scotland, but locations and place names are only grudgingly given by Tacitus, who was writing for an audience far away in Rome, where exact place names would mean nothing and the action would mean everything. The major problem has always been to marry the archaeological record from Scotland and northern Britain with the literary record, and make sense of it. Much ink has flowed, for example, over the unknown site of the major Battle of Mons Graupius, where Agricola won his final victory.

Summary of reports on Britain in Tacitus's *Histories*:

1.2 Britain was subdued and immediately let go [referring to the conquest of northern England and Scotland by Agricola, and the abandonment of Scotland by Domitian].

1.6 Nero had withdrawn detachments of troops from Germany, Britain and Illyricum for a campaign he was preparing against the Albani, but he recalled them to help suppress the revolt of Vindex.

1.9 [The context of this passage is the civil war of AD 69; the armies were divided in their loyalties between the rival contenders for the throne after Nero's death.] The army in Britain displayed no hostility to Galba, indeed through all the confusion of the civil war no other legions made less trouble, either because they were far away and separated from the Continent by the short stretch of sea, or because they had learned to hate the enemy [i.e. the natives] by preference. [But see 1.59 below when Britain joins Vitellius in sentiment if not physically.]

1.43 [The context is the rivalry between the Emperor Galba and Otho. Galba was chosen by the legions in Spain, but soon Otho rose against him. Galba himself, and many of his adherents were killed.] One of Galba's men, Piso, escaped and lay hidden, but he was discovered and Otho sent Sulpicius Florus of the British auxiliaries, who had recently been enfranchised by Galba, and Statius Murcus of the bodyguard, to kill Piso.

1.52 Vitellius was urged by his friends that if he made a bid for the Empire, Britain would support him.

1.59 Britain did not hesitate to join Vitellius.

1.60 Trebellius Maximus was governor of Britain, but was hated by the soldiers. Roscius Coelius, legate of XX Valeria Victrix, had long been at odds with Trebellius, and inflamed the army against him. As the hostility escalated, Coelius accused Trebellius of robbing the legions and impoverishing them. Discipline broke down altogether, and the auxiliaries joined Coelius. Trebellius fled to Vitellius, leaving the government of the province of Britain to the legionary legates, all of equal rank, though Coelius dominated the others.

1.61 The legions in Britain declared for Vitellius.

1.70 [Caecina Alienus gathered troops for Vitellius, for the struggle against Otho.] Caecina halted in the Alps, and to protect northern Italy he sent infantry ahead, consisting of Gauls, Lusitanians and Britons.

2.11 Otho brought troops from Dalmatia and Pannonia. He sent detachments of four legions ahead, and the main body of the legions followed later. These were the Seventh, only recently enrolled by Galba, and three veteran legions, the Eleventh, and the Thirteenth, and the Fourteenth from Britain. This legion enjoyed a great reputation for crushing the revolt in Britain [Boudicca]. Nero added to their fame by selecting them as his best soldiers, so they had long been loyal to him and they were enthusiastic for Otho. But their power and strength were matched by their self-confidence, which made them slow in marching.

2.27 The cohorts of XIV legion who had been withdrawn to help in the revolt against Nero were on their way back to Britain when they heard of the revolt of Vitellius, and so they stayed in the territory of the Lingones in Gaul and joined Fabius Valens.

2.32 and 2.37 Suetonius Paulinus, ex-governor of Britain, fought in Otho's army.

2.57 Vitellius supplemented his troops with 8,000 men picked from Britain.

2.65 [After the death of Otho] Vitellius sent Vettius Bolanus to govern Britain in place of Trebellius Maximus who had fled to join him.

2.66 XIV legion caused trouble in Italy, so Vitellius ordered it back to Britain, by way of the Little St Bernard pass, so as to avoid the town of Vienne. Before the legionaries left Turin where they were based they set some fires and left them burning, thus destroying a lot of the city, but the losses endured were not as great as the losses incurred during the fighting between Vitellius and Otho. Once they had crossed the Alps some of the mutinous soldiers from XIV wanted to sack the town of Vienne, but the more level-headed men prevented them from doing so, and the legion sailed back to Britain.

2.86 Cornelius Fuscus, drumming up support for Vespasian, wrote to the First legion in Spain and to XIV in Britain, because they had been opponents of Vitellius.

2.97 [To prepare for the war against the Flavian party] Vitellius summoned allies from

Germany, Britain and Spain … In Britain, Vettius Bolanus had never enjoyed peace and was wavering in his support for Vitellius.

2.100 Caecina Alienus occupied Cremona for Vitellius, with detachments from several legions, including those from the three legions of Britain.

3.1 In opposition to the Flavian party Vitellius had the German legions and the flower of the legions of Britain.

3.2 The Flavian general Antonius Primus advised the army commanders to attack Vitellius immediately, because Germany was not too far away, Britain was only just across a short stretch of sea, and Spain and Gaul were closer still, and a delay would afford Vitellius the chance to recruit more men and gather horses and money from these provinces.

3.15 Vitellius summoned auxiliaries from Britain, Gaul and Spain.

3.22 Detachments from XX Valeria, IX Hispana and II Augusta formed the centre of Vitellius's army fighting against Antonius Primus and the Flavians, in the Battle of Cremona.

3.35 The Flavian leaders sent messages to Britain and Spain with news of their victory over Vitellius at Cremona, but they knew that the civil war was not yet over.

3.41 Caecina had started to waver in his support of Vitellius, and Fabius Valens, dithering, managed to get himself blocked by the Flavians, so he wrote to Vitellius asking for extra troops to break out. Three cohorts and a squadron of cavalry from Britain arrived, too large to escape detection but too small to break through. Valens sent the infantry to Rimini, and ordered the cavalry to protect the rear of his army. These British troops were not wholly loyal to him.

3.44 In Britain the legions inclined towards Vespasian, because he had commanded II Augusta under the Emperor Claudius and had distinguished himself in the British campaigns. This secured the whole island for Vespasian, but only after resistance had been overcome from the other legions, because some of the centurions and other soldiers had received promotion from Vitellius, and they hesitated to change their allegiance.

3.45 While the Roman forces in Britain were divided in their support for the rival Emperors, the Britons rose up under Venutius of the Brigantes. In addition to his hatred of the Romans he was also resentful of his wife, Queen Cartimandua, who had strengthened her power when she surrendered Caratacus to the Romans. From this came all her wealth, and her strong spirit that success bred in her. She despised her husband Venutius, and chose as consort his shield bearer Vellocatus. Opposition to her grew after this scandalous event, while Venutius had the support of nearly all the tribesmen. He called in assistance from outside and helped by a revolt of the Brigantes, he endangered Cartimandua, who called for Roman assistance. Some infantry and cavalry were despatched, and after a few skirmishes in which they did not perform very well, they managed to rescue the queen. Tacitus comments: 'The throne was left to Venutius, and the war to us.'

4.12 Batavian auxiliaries had won fame in Britain, when according to their custom they were led by the noblest men among them.

4.15 After a brutal levy of troops from among the Batavians, Civilis rebelled against the Romans. He sent messages to the auxiliary troops from Britain and won them over.

4.68 Vespasian's friend and deputy Mucianus made arrangements for the war against Civilis. He summoned XIV legion from Britain, and two from Spain.

4.74 Petillius Cerialis, appointed one of the commanders in the war against Civilis, addressed the Treveri and Lingones, advocating the Roman cause. He pointed out that defence requires armies and armies require taxes and if they did not take the side of Rome, they would still pay for these things, for protection against the Germans and the Britons. [It is not clear what threat the Britons represented.]

4.76 Another reference to XIV legion from Britain.

4.79 Civilis marched towards the coast to try to prevent XIV legion and the fleet from Britain from attacking the population near the sea, but the Roman commander turned inland and the fleet was attacked by the Canninefates, and most of the ships were sunk or captured.

5.16 Cerialis made a speech before the battle against Civilis, and referred to XIV legion as the conquerors of Britain.

Summary of reports on Britain in Tacitus's *Annals*:

2.24 After his campaign in Germany, Germanicus brought his troops out of the country and put them in winter quarters. Some of the soldiers marched overland, while others accompanied Germanicus, who went by sea, sailing down the west coast. The North Sea was calm when they set out but a storm blew them all off course. Some ships were wrecked, many men were lost, but some ships were swept across to Britain, and were sent back by various chieftains [in Latin a diminutive term is used, *reguli*, meaning literally little kings].

In book 12, chapters 31 to 40, Tacitus describes what happened in Britain under the governors Publius Ostorius Scapula and Aulus Didius Gallus, covering the years AD 47 to 58. At the end of chapter 40, Tacitus explains that in relating these events in Britain, he purposely broke off from his chronological account in order to relate the events consecutively, since if he described them separately in their proper chronological slot, they would not have made such a memorable impression on his audience.

12.31 Ostorius found great disturbance in Britain when he arrived, since the Britons thought that he would not risk mounting a campaign with an army he did not know, and with winter coming on. He moved swiftly and dispelled the rebels, though the location of his swift campaign is not named, nor are the tribes against whom he fought. He decided to disarm suspect tribes, and the Iceni rebelled, because they had made an alliance with the Romans. They roused their neighbouring tribes, and chose a place with a narrow approach, protected by an embankment, and though Ostorius had only auxiliary units with him, he attacked. The Romans broke through the defences and the Britons were trapped by their own embankment, but fought bravely. In this battle, Ostorius's son Marcus saved a Roman soldier's life and earned the reward [the *corona civica*, or civic crown].

12.32 After the defeat of the Iceni the other tribes were dissuaded from war. Ostorius led the army against the Decangi [probably the Deceangli of north Wales]. The Romans devastated the countryside, but the Britons did not engage in battle. When Ostorius was within reach of the coast that faces Ireland, a rebellion broke out among the Brigantes, but they were calmed by the execution of the leaders. Then Ostorius attacked the Silures, who were not so easily calmed. They had to be controlled by the establishment of a legionary fort. To facilitate this project, Colchester was occupied by a colony of veterans, who were to serve as protection against revolt and teach the Britons their legal duties.

12.33 The Silures were emboldened by Caratacus, who was able to use the character of the country to his advantage even though he did not command as strong a force as the Romans. He involved the Ordovices in his struggle, and all men who objected to the Romans. He chose a place for battle that was very advantageous to him, with steep cliffs on one side, and where the land offered an easy ascent he built ramparts of stones. A river ran along the front of his defensive site.

12.34 The tribal chiefs and Caratacus himself visited all the tribes in the battle array, lifting their spirits and promising victory. Caratacus told them that this battle would bring either freedom or servitude. The tribesmen took an oath not to give in.

12.35 Ostorius was dismayed by the strength of the place, with the river in front and no single point which was not thronged with warriors. The soldiers and officers were more confident that courage would win through, despite the defences. Ostorius surveyed the ground to find any weak points, and crossed the river at the head of his troops. The soldiers formed the tortoise, and tore down the stones blocking access to the hilltops, and broke through, the legionaries in close order and the lighter-armed auxiliaries skirmishing opposite them, so the Britons broke down into chaos. It was a notable victory for the Romans. The wife and daughter of Caratacus were captured, and his brothers surrendered.

12.36 Caratacus fled north to the Brigantes, but Queen Cartimandua handed him over, 'in the ninth year from the commencement of the war in Britain'. Caratacus's fame had spread beyond Britain. He was known in Italy, and in Rome his name was not without honour. Claudius arranged a spectacular procession of the British spoils, and Caratacus and his family, through the streets of Rome. Some of the Britons were fearful, but not Caratacus, who made a speech.

12.37 [Tacitus invents a speech for Caratacus.] The king reminded the Romans of his distinguished ancestry, and said that if he had been more moderate he might have entered the city as a friend and not a captive. He asked why the whole world, if it was to be ruled by Rome, should accept servitude. Then he suggested that if he was spared from punishment, it would be a memorial to Imperial clemency. Claudius agreed and freed the Britons, who paid their respects to Agrippina, Claudius's wife. The presence of Agrippina on such an occasion was unprecedented, since no woman had ever sat in state before the Roman standards.

12.38 The senators made long speeches about the capture of Caratacus, and triumphal insignia were awarded to Ostorius. But his reputation was then tarnished by a near defeat of Roman troops who were building forts in Silurian territory. The camp prefect and eight centurions were killed, and if a relieving force had not arrived in the nick of time all the troops would have been annihilated. Then a foraging party was attacked and these men and the soldiers sent to relieve them were routed.

12.39 Ostorius sent in the auxiliaries but they could not restore order, until the legions joined the fighting. The Romans prevailed, but the Britons escaped with slight losses. Then they kept attacking from the woods and marshes, sometimes without orders from their chiefs. The Silures in particular were aroused to total obstinacy because they had heard that Ostorius had said that the name of the Silures should be extinguished. They cut off two auxiliary cohorts who were destroying the countryside. Ostorius was broken by the anxiety of his command, and died.

12.40 Claudius appointed Aulus Didius [Gallus] to the vacancy so as not to leave the province without a governor. Didius made a rapid crossing of the Channel, and when he arrived he found that a legion commanded by Manlius Valens had been defeated. The Britons exaggerated the defeat, but Didius also made more of it, so that he would earn great credit if he quelled the tribes, and would have a reasonable excuse if he did not succeed. He stopped the ravages of the Silures, but then Venutius of the Brigantes made war on his wife Cartimandua, but she captured some of his family. Venutius encouraged tribesmen to invade Cartimandua's kingdom, at which point Roman troops were sent in. The legion commanded by Caesius Nasica did most of the work, since Didius was getting old, and was content to act through his subordinates, keeping the enemy at a distance.

The rebellion of Boudicca is told in book 14, chapters 29 to 39:

14.29 In the consulship of Caesennius Paetus and Petronius Turpilianus [AD 61, though the Boudicca rebellion is traditionally dated to AD 60] a disaster occurred in Britain. The governor Aulus Didius merely held what had been won, and his successor Veranius made a few raids against the Silures, but was prevented from doing more by his death. In his will, flattering Nero, he said that if he had been granted two more years he could have conquered the province. Britain was now governed by Suetonius Paulinus, who was a rival in military skill and popular reputation to the general Corbulo who had conquered Armenia. Suetonius prepared for an attack on the island of Mona [Anglesey], which served as a haven for refugees. He built a fleet of boats with flat bottoms to negotiate the shallow channel, and the infantry crossed in them, while the cavalry found fording places or swam by the side of their horses.

14.30 On the beach there was an armed mass of men, and women were weaving in and out of the ranks, dressed in black robes, their hair all dishevelled, and they brandished flaming torches. A circle of Druids raised their hands and uttered curses, so that the soldiers were awestruck, and stood as though paralysed. The general reassured them, and they encouraged each other not to be afraid of a band of women and fanatics, then they charged and cut down everyone in their path. The next step was to establish a garrison, and destroy the sacred groves, because they [the Druids] consider it a sacred duty to spill the blood of their captives over their altars and to consult their gods over human entrails. While he was engaged in this the news of the rebellion in the province was brought to Suetonius.

14.31 Prasutagus, the king of the Iceni, had named as his heirs his two daughters and the Emperor. He thought that this would protect his kingdom, but the result was the opposite. His kingdom was pillaged by centurions, and slaves robbed his house as though it had been captured in war. The king's wife Boudicca was flogged and her daughters raped, and the leading men of the Iceni had their estates confiscated. Incensed by the outrage and fearing that worse was to come, the Iceni took up arms and roused the Trinovantes and other tribes who had not yet succumbed to slavery. The veterans had incurred the greatest hostility by their behaviour at Colchester. They had thrown the natives out of their homes and farms, and called them captives or slaves. Added to this the temple of Claudius was continually before them, and the priests chosen to serve it were losing their fortunes in the name of religion. There seemed to be no difficulty in destroying the colony, which was not protected by fortifications, because the leaders had thought more of amenities than useful projects.

14.32 The statue of Victory at Colchester fell down, with its back turned as if running away from the enemy. Cries and shrieks had been heard in the Senate and in the theatre. Someone had seen a vision of the colony destroyed, in the waters of the Thames estuary. The sea appeared to be blood-red and the ebbing tide left behind what looked like corpses. The veterans at Colchester sent to the procurator Catus Decianus for help. He sent two hundred men, not properly armed. There were a few troops in the town. They all retired to the temple, but built no defences and did not evacuate the women and the old people. The town was destroyed as the Britons rushed in, except for the temple which was besieged for two days and then was taken. Petillius Cerialis tried to rescue the town but was routed by the Britons and he escaped with the cavalry to the protection of his camp. Catus, who had caused all the problems, fled to Gaul.

14. 33 Suetonius marched through the enemy to London, which although it was not a *colonia* was a busy town, largely through its crowd of merchants. Suetonius decided not to defend the town at the expense of saving the country. He took with him all those who could march with him, leaving the old and infirm, who fell to the enemy. A similar disaster occurred at Verulamium, since the Britons avoided forts, preferring to go for plunder. Seventy thousand Romans and allies were killed. The Britons took no prisoners, but slaughtered, hanged, burnt and crucified, taking their revenge before they met their own day of reckoning.

14.34 Suetonius had the XIV legion, a detachment from XX and some of the auxiliaries from the nearest forts, altogether about ten thousand men when he decided to risk a pitched battle. He took up his position approached by a narrow defile and backed by a wood, first checking that there were no Britons except in front, and the flat ground offered no possibility of ambush. He put the legionaries in the centre, flanked by the auxiliaries, with the cavalry on both wings. The British infantry and cavalry moved

407

in all directions, mustering unprecedented numbers, and so confident that they placed their families in the wagons in the rear.

14.35 Boudicca rode in her chariot with her daughters, visiting every clan, making a speech. She reminded the warriors of the injustice done to herself and her daughters. The greed of the Romans had left no one unharmed, but one legion had been destroyed and the rest could not stand up to so many warriors.

14.36 Suetonius urged his men to treat the noise and bluster of the Britons with contempt, since they would break and run when they met the weapons and courage of the Romans. The soldiers should keep close order, and after throwing their javelins they should use their shield bosses and swords to pile up enemy dead. The troops were more than ready, especially the veterans who had seen so many battles. Suetonius gave the order.

14.37 The legionaries stood still, protected by the narrow defile while the Britons approached, and they only threw their javelins when they could be certain of hitting the enemy. Then they dashed forward in a kind of wedge, and so did the auxiliaries. The cavalry forced their way through any opposition. The Britons fled but their exit was blocked by the wagons, and the Romans spared nothing, killing the women and the baggage animals. The Britons lost eighty thousand men, but Romans lost only four hundred dead, and a similar number of wounded. Boudicca took poison, and Poenius Postumus, camp prefect of II Augusta, fell on his sword because he had ignored the orders of his commander [to march] and cheated his legion of a share in the victory. [This is the first mention of Postumus and his failure to join Suetonius.]

14.38 The Roman army was camped in tents. The Emperor sent two thousand legionaries, eight auxiliary cohorts and a thousand cavalry from Germany. The gaps in IX Hispana were filled, and the allied infantry and cavalry were put into new winter quarters. The Britons who showed signs of disaffection were put to fire and sword. They were also starving because they had been so confident of victory that they had not planted any crops. Julius Classicianus, who had replaced Catus, was not on good terms with Suetonius, and told the Britons that they would do well to wait for a new governor to be appointed, since a new man would not be so angry and bitter, and would be more lenient with the tribes which had surrendered. He also reported to Rome that the fighting would not end while Suetonius was still in command.

4.39 Nero sent an Imperial freedman, Polyclitus, hoping that he might be able to reconcile the governor and the procurator, and influence the Britons to agree to a peaceful settlement. Polyclitus caused immense trouble all the way through Italy and Gaul, and to the Britons he was an object of derision, because they did not understand why freedmen should possess such power and influence. The report carried back to Rome was favourable, and Suetonius was retained in post, until he lost some ships, and then he was ordered to relinquish his army command to Petronius Turpilianus, who did not provoke the enemy, preferring inactivity which he called peace.

16.15 Nero ordered the execution of Ostorius Scapula [the son of the elder Scapula who had died while governor of Britain] because this man had a great military reputation and had won a civic crown in Britain, and Nero was afraid of him.

408

What the Ancient Authors Said About Roman Britain

Summary of Tacitus's *Agricola*:

The first four chapters of the biography of Gnaeus Julius Agricola concern his early life. Chapter 5 describes how he learned his first lessons in military matters in Britain under Suetonius Paulinus, a diligent and moderate leader.

Chapters 6–9 Agricola's family and his early political career
Agricola served in the province of Asia as quaestor, and was then elected tribune of the plebs in Rome. During the civil wars of AD 69, his mother was killed, and Agricola was appointed legate of XX legion, serving first under Vettius Bolanus, who governed leniently but inappropriately for a wild province, so that Agricola had to restrain his energy and enthusiasm, being accustomed to obey. The next governor was Petillius Cerialis, the first of the Flavian governors. Under him there was more opportunity to display military talents. At first there was only hard work and danger, but later Cerialis shared the glory as well, giving Agricola command over part of the army. Before his consulship, Agricola governed the province of Aquitania, and after his term as consul he was appointed governor of Britain.

Chapters 10–12 A description of Britain
Other writers have described Britain, and Tacitus says he does not want to challenge them, but it was under Agricola that the conquest was completed. Britain is the largest island known to the Romans, facing Germany in the east, and Spain in the west [!]. The south coast faces Gaul. Earlier writers said it is shaped like an elongated shoulder blade. In the extreme north there is an irregular area tapering off into a wedge shape. Under Agricola, for the first time, the fleet sailed round the country and established that Britain is an island. The Orkneys and Shetland isles were discovered, where the seas were sluggish and heavy to the oars, and the ocean did not move as other seas, even when blown by the winds. The sea penetrates far inland among the mountains.

The inhabitants do not know whether they are indigenous to the island, or immigrants, but the people of Caledonia with red hair and large limbs probably came from Germany, and the Silures, with swarthy complexions and dark curly hair, may have come from Iberia. In the areas closest to Gaul, the people are like the Gauls, perhaps because the climate and the soils produce similar tribes, but the same religious beliefs and practices are found in both Gaul and Britain, and they speak a similar language. The Britons are fiercer than the Gauls, though the Gauls were once more warlike but have now become accustomed to a life of ease. The Britons conquered by Claudius have gone the same way.

The Britons have some infantry and some of them fight from chariots. The drivers are noblemen, and their warriors are the fighters. It is a great advantage to the Romans that the tribes do not plan their operations jointly, or work together against a common threat. The climate is wet and miserable, but the cold is not extreme. The summer days are longer than in Italy, and the nights are lighter. In the far north the nights are very short, and the sun does not set but skirts the horizon. The island produces grain and there is an abundance of cattle, but no olives or vines. There is also gold, silver and other metals, and on the shores the Britons harvest blue-black pearls. Tacitus prefers to believe that they lack value rather than the Romans do not desire them.

409

Chapters 13–17 An overview of Roman Britain up to Agricola's appointment as governor

Caesar was the first to meet the Britons, and he gained a foothold on the coasts, but he just showed what the island was like rather than bequeathing it to the Romans. The first governors were Aulus Plautius and Ostorius Scapula. The nearest part of Britain gradually became a province, and a colony of veterans was founded. Certain states were granted to Togidumnus as king, and he remained loyal up to Tacitus's own day. It was the Roman custom to use kings as instruments of enslavement.

Didus Gallus held on to what had been gained, but planted some forts in outlying regions so he could say he had expanded the province. Veranius succeeded him and died within a year. Suetonius had two successful years, and established some garrisons, and then attacked Mona [Anglesey] which he thought supported rebels, but while he was there he was open to attack from the rear. The Britons began to discuss their slavery while the governor was far away, saying that in previous times they had only one king but now they had two, the governor and the procurator, one using centurions to browbeat them and the other using slaves. Nothing was safe from their greed. The Romans were cowards, plundering their homes, kidnapping children and enforcing conscription.

When the rebellion of Boudicca broke out, Britain would have been lost if Suetonius had not acted quickly. A single battle restored submissiveness, but many Britons kept their weapons, fearing that the general would inflict severe punishment because he construed the rebellion as a personal insult. The Emperor sent out Turpilianus, not acquainted with what the Britons had done, and more conciliatory. He restored peace without risking anything else and handed over to Trebellius Maximus, who never tested the army at all. The civil wars gave him the excuse for inactivity, but the soldiers were not used to doing nothing and mutinied, but it ended without bloodshed.

After Trebellius fled, the next governor, Bolanus, did not restore discipline and during the civil wars the soldiers became unruly. Vespasian recovered Britain, employing his best generals, so the hopes of the Britons began to wane. Cerialis attacked the Brigantes, the most populous tribe in Britain. There were many battles, some of them bloody, and Cerialis took over large areas of the territory. Frontinus sustained the burden, and subdued the Silures, overcoming the courage of the enemy and the difficulties of the terrain.

Chapter 18 Agricola's first campaigns in Britain against the Ordovices, and the reconquest of Anglesey

Agricola crossed to Britain in midsummer, when the soldiers were already thinking of rest and going into winter quarters, but the Britons seized their opportunity. The Ordovices had destroyed a cavalry unit. The troops were dispersed, but Agricola took legionary vexillations and some auxiliaries and marched at the head of the column into the hills. The Ordovices were cut to pieces, as Agricola made an impression with his first act. Then he attacked Mona where Suetonius had conquered the island but could not retain it when the rebellion broke out. Agricola had no ships, but he got the troops across to Mona using auxiliaries who knew the fords and could swim in full kit alongside their horses. The Britons had expected a naval landing. They were defeated and surrendered.

Chapter 19 Agricola spent the winter investigating and stopping abuses

He decided to root out the causes of war, first establishing discipline in his own household, refusing to use slaves or freedmen on official business, or to be influenced in his choice of centurions and officers. He knew all that went on but reserved punishment for serious offences. For the civilians he alleviated the burdens of the levy of corn and the collection of taxes by distributing the burden fairly, removing the opportunities for profit that were resented more than the taxes themselves. People had to wait for ages outside locked granaries, and had to buy corn at high prices, or were told to deliver their grain to remote places, all of which profited a few individuals.

Chapter 20 The second campaigning season
By stopping the abuses in his first year he restored peace, which was previously feared just as much as war. Agricola led the army out on campaign. He was present everywhere on the march, choosing the places to make camps himself, and reconnoitring the terrain. The enemy were given no rest, and he inspired fear in them and then showed them the benefits of peace.

Chapter 21 Encouragement for civil communities
Agricola considered that tribesmen living in scattered farms were more prone to warlike tendencies, so he provided amenities for them, encouraging individuals and assisting communities to build temples, market places, and houses. He provided education for the sons of the leading Britons. He rated the abilities of the Britons above that of the Gauls. The Latin language spread, the Britons adopted Roman dress, and learned about baths and banquets. They called it civilisation, but really it marked their enslavement.

Chapter 22 The third campaigning season
In the third season Agricola met new peoples, advancing as far as the River Tay. The enemy did not harass the army even though the soldiers were hindered by storms. There was time to establish some forts. No general selected sites more wisely, and no fort established by Agricola was taken by storm or given up to the enemy, and the garrisons could withstand a siege, each having supplies for one year. The soldiers made frequent patrols so the Britons were frustrated because they were accustomed to recoup in the winter the losses of the summer.

Chapter 23 The fourth campaigning season
Agricola secured the territory that he had overrun, and if only the glory of the Roman name had permitted it, he could have found a frontier line and stopped the advance between the estuaries of the Forth and Clyde. He placed garrisons here and cleared the territory to the south.

Chapter 24 The fifth campaigning season
Agricola crossed in the first ship [there is much modern debate about where this action occurred], and defeated previously unknown tribes. He drew up his forces in the part of the country that faces Ireland, smaller than Britain, with a similar climate. Its harbours were known from traders. An Irish chief had come to Agricola, a refugee from his own country, and Agricola kept him close by in case an opportunity should arise. He thought that one legion and some auxiliaries would be sufficient for the conquest of Ireland.

Chapters 25 to 27 The sixth campaigning season
The army advanced beyond the Forth, and the fleet harassed the coasts, in case the

people rose up and threatened the land routes. The army and the fleet often shared the same camps. The Britons were astonished by the presence of the fleet, which removed their last refuges, so they prepared for war, and attacked some forts. Some of Agricola's companions suggested that he should retire south of the Forth, but he heard that the Britons were advancing in several columns, so he divided his own forces into three to avoid encirclement.

The Britons changed their plans and attacked IX legion, which was the weakest in numbers, but Agricola brought up legions and cavalry and attacked the rear of the enemy. The Britons were terrified, and the soldiers of IX, hard pressed until now, started to rally. The Britons were defeated by two armies, one claiming that it had marched to the rescue, and the other that it had not required rescue. The soldiers were now clamouring to march to the very end of the island. Even the cautious ones were now enthusiastic. The Britons armed themselves and moved their women and children to places of safety.

Chapter 28 The units of Usipi, which had been levied in Germany and sent to Britain, mutinied, killed their centurion and the soldiers who had been with them to teach them military discipline, and stole three galleys, forcing the pilots to serve them. Two of these they killed and followed the lead of the third one. They put into shore for water and food, but met some Britons who were determined to protect their property. Eventually the Usipi were forced to eat their own men, first the weakest and then those drawn by lot. As they were not sailors they lost their vessels, and some of them were captured by the Frisii and Suevi, and sold into slavery. Only when some of these were sold in Britain was the full story revealed.

Chapter 29 The seventh campaigning season
At the beginning of the summer, Agricola's infant son died, but he bore the tragedy and threw himself into the war. The fleet was used again to harass the coasts. The army marched light, reinforced by the bravest of the Britons, and those who had long been at peace and whose loyalty was proven. The enemy rallied all the tribes, mustering thirty thousand men. They took up a position at Mons Graupius, with Calgacus as their leader.

Chapters 30 to 34 [These chapters relate the set-piece speeches made by the two opposing leaders before the battle began. This is a customary literary device for the Roman audience, and the content of these speeches usually represents the political views of the authors rather than historical accuracy, but since Agricola was Tacitus's father–in–law, it is assumed that there ought to be some kernel of truth in what each commander is made to say.] Calgacus said that the Britons were at the end of the island, with no land behind them, and even the sea no longer provided a refuge. The Romans robbed the world and exhausted the land, through robbery, slaughter, and plunder. They make a desert and call it peace. The tribes of the north did not have fertile plains, mines or harbours, but the Romans enslaved them and taxed their harvests, and yet there were other Britons who supported the Romans, some of them fighting in the Roman army.

The Britons applauded Calgacus's speech, and the Romans were so eager for battle that they had to be restrained by Agricola. He reminded the soldiers that they had served for seven seasons and marched further than any other army. The end of Britain was in sight, and the Romans held the rest. They had crossed marshes, mountains, forests, rivers and estuaries, asking 'When shall we fight the battle?' They had driven off the tribesmen when they attacked the IX legion in their camp at night, and the bravest of the Britons had already been defeated, so the ones they faced now were those who had been driven back, consequently there was nothing to fear from them.

Chapters 35 to 38 The Battle of Mons Graupius

Eight thousand auxiliary infantry formed the centre of the battle line, with three thousand cavalry on the flanks, and the legions as a reserve in front of the ramparts of the camp. Agricola opened up the ranks in case the enemy should attack the front and the flanks at the same time, but he could not stretch the line far enough to oppose the enormous numbers of tribesmen. Agricola sent away his horse and took up a position in the front ranks.

The battle commenced with long-range fighting, the Britons easily deflecting the javelins of the Romans with their swords, or catching them on their shields, while they threw their spears. Agricola ordered the Batavian cohorts and two Tungrian cohorts to engage. The Britons on the hill came down and moved around the rear of the Romans, but Agricola sent the cavalry reserve to block them. The Britons eventually scattered into the woods, and Agricola ordered the cavalry to dismount and flush the tribesmen out of the forest, but night came on and stopped the operations. Ten thousand Britons were killed at a cost of only three hundred and sixty Romans.

On the following day there was no one to be seen, only desolation, and houses burning in the distance. As the summer was over Agricola led the army back, taking hostages, and marching slowly to intimidate the enemy with his leisurely progress. The fleet was ordered to sail around the island.

Chapters 39 to 46

The reaction of the Emperor Domitian to the conquest of Britain, and Agricola's recall to Rome. Agricola had hoped to be made governor of Asia, but was forced to live in retirement, and died in his fifty-sixth year, without receiving any further appointments, but he was spared from living through the worst years under the Emperor Domitian.

Cassius Dio (c.AD 164 to after AD 229) *Roman History*

Dio's history of Rome, written in Greek, filled eighty books, covering a vast time span from the earliest years to AD 229. He adopted the annalistic tradition, recounting events as far as possible in the order that they occurred, inserting discussions here and there but without breaking the chronological narrative. About twenty-five books of the original eighty survive, but many of the gaps can be filled by the epitomes of his work that were compiled by different Byzantine historians, so it is possible to discern at least the main thrust of Dio's argument via these other sources.

Dio was born in Nicaea in the province of Bithynia, possibly in AD 164 but his birth date has not been recorded and some authors suggest he was born about ten years earlier in c.AD 155. He lived most of his life as a Roman senator, but retired and went home to Nicaea in AD 229. It is not known in which year he died. His career was varied and distinguished. He reached the consulship twice, and held posts in several provinces. As governor of Upper Pannonia he dealt with troublesome and undisciplined soldiers, but his reputation went before him, and when he was about to take up his second consulship, he met with opposition from the Praetorians in Rome, who indicated to him that his measures as provincial governor had been harsh, and they would be rather displeased if he attended the inauguration ceremony in person. Dio's view of the Roman army was therefore perhaps distorted; he certainly thought that it cost too much and did not give value for money, and he disapproved of Septimius Severus's policies, giving the soldiers a pay rise and allowing them some privileges.

Summary of reports on Britain in Dio's *Roman History*:

39.51–53 [A synopsis of Caesar's first invasion.] The Britons were forewarned and massed to meet Caesar, who had to sail round a headland and make a landing. He defeated the Britons, secured a foothold in the island and repulsed an attack on the camp, but the Britons escaped in their chariots and on their horses. Caesar's own cavalry did not arrive. The Britons sent to the Morini to intercede on their behalf and arrange peace. Caesar took hostages, but when news came of the damage to the fleet the Britons went to war again, attacking a foraging party. Caesar came to the rescue. The Britons would not come to terms until they had suffered a few defeats, and though Caesar did not want to make terms, winter was coming on, the cavalry still had not arrived, and there were not enough soldiers to sustain the war. The Gauls were restless again, so Caesar made peace. He had gained nothing except glory, and the Romans made much of his exploits, voting him twenty days of thanksgiving in Rome.

40.1–4 [For the next invasion] Caesar built ships that were like a cross between cargo boats and warships, being of light construction to withstand the waves, and they could be left high and dry on shore without being damaged. Caesar said that the Britons had not given the hostages they promised, but if he had not been able to use this excuse to invade, he would have found another. He crossed the Channel in many ships, and there were no Britons to oppose him. The larger army alarmed the Britons who retired into the woods and built fortifications, using felled trees piled on top of each other. They began to attack foraging parties, or they drew the Romans on and on and then killed them near their stockades. A storm damaged the Roman ships, so Cassivellaunus the British leader sent messages to his allies to ask them to attack the naval camp. In the battle the Romans allowed the chariots to pass through and hurled javelins at their sides. The Britons defeated the Roman infantry but were driven off by the cavalry, and retired to the Thames, where they made camp, fortified by stakes driven into the river bank along the water line. Caesar defeated them, made peace, took hostages and levied tribute. It was too dangerous to leave a garrison behind in winter so he retired to Gaul.

49.38.2 [34 BC] Augustus planned an expedition to Britain and marched to Gaul, but there was a revolt in Dalmatia, and it was called off.

53.22.5 [27 BC] Augustus went to Gaul again, planning to invade Britain, but since the Gauls were unsettled, he remained there, considering it more likely that he would be able to make terms with the Britons.

53.25.2 [26 BC] The Britons would not come to terms, but there was no campaign against them because the Salassi tribe rebelled.

59.25.1–3 Caligula planned an expedition to Britain, but when he arrived at the coast of Gaul he ordered the soldiers to gather shells, and brought them to Rome in carts as if they were booty from his conquest of the Ocean.

60.19–23 When Aulus Plautius gave the order for the troops to embark for the invasion of Britain they were reluctant to leave Gaul. Claudius sent his Imperial freedman Narcissus who made a speech to the soldiers. At first they would not listen then someone shouted '*Io Saturnalia*' referring to the December festival where slaves are served by their masters. The soldiers embarked. Plautius sailed in three divisions, to avoid meeting the opposition that a single force might encounter. The ships were at first driven back, but then they landed and found no Britons. Plautius had to search for them. He defeated Caratacus and Togodumnus, the sons of Cunobelinus, who was now dead. The Bodunni (Dobunni), subjects of the Catuvellauni, surrendered to Plautius, who left a garrison in their territory and advanced to a river, which the Celtic troops crossed, swimming with their armour and weapons. Instead of attacking the Britons these troops attacked the horses, so the charioteers and mounted men could not quickly escape. Plautius ordered Vespasian, the future Emperor, and Vespasian's brother Sabinus, to cross the river, which they did and attacked the Britons, but although the tribesmen were beaten off they attacked again the next day. They then withdrew to the Thames, near the point where the river joins the sea. The Britons knew the ground and could cross easily but some of the Romans got into difficulties and were killed. The Celts swam across, and became bogged down in the marshes.

Togodumnus was dead, and the Britons were all inflamed, so Plautius called a halt, as instructed if he met strong opposition, and sent for Claudius. Equipment had already been assembled for this eventuality, including some war elephants. When Claudius arrived he took command and went straight to Colchester. He won over some tribes and others surrendered. He was hailed Imperator several times, which was unprecedented for a single campaign. After disarming the Britons, Claudius instructed Plautius to take the rest of the country. Claudius was awarded the title Britannicus. A triumph was voted, and an annual festival, and arches were to be built in Gaul and in Rome. Claudius was absent from Rome for six months, but spent only sixteen days in Britain. A law was passed to the effect that all treaties made by the Emperor or by his legates with the Britons would be binding, as if they had been arranged by the Senate and People of Rome.

62.1–12 There was a disaster in Britain that resulted in the deaths of eighty thousand Romans and provincials. All this was under the leadership of a woman. There had been omens in Colchester, submerged houses were seen in the Thames and the water turned red at high tide. The cause of the rebellion arose from the recall of the loans made by Claudius to the Britons, which were now to be repaid, or so Catus Decianus said. Seneca had lent 10 million drachmas [40 million *sestertii*] to the British leading men who did not really want it, but now this too was recalled. Boudouika led the Britons, collecting about 120,000 warriors, whom she addressed, standing on an earthen tribunal. She was tall, and had a grim aspect, with a piercing gaze and a harsh voice. Her hair was long and fair, and she wore a gold torque around her neck, and a coloured tunic fastened by a brooch.

In her speech she reminded the Britons of the abuses perpetrated on them, how they were deprived of nearly all their possessions and taxed on what was left. But they had driven out Julius Caesar, and foiled the attempts of Augustus and Caligula to invade. They were all kinsmen, inhabiting a single island and called by a common name. The Britons had courage, whereas the Romans, weighed down with equipment, took refuge in forts, and could not stand hunger or thirst as the Britons could. Boudouika called on the goddess Andraste, calling on the Britons to defeat this 'woman' Domitia Nero, the effeminate Emperor.

Paulinus was in Mona [Anglesey] when he heard the news of the rebellion. The Britons sacked two Roman cities and tortured and killed the inhabitants. Women were impaled on stakes, naked and with their breasts cut off and sewed into their mouths, while the Britons indulged in feasts and orgies in their sacred groves. Paulinus returned from Mona. He was reluctant to commit to a battle until he found a suitable time and place, but he was short of supplies and was forced to make a stand. The Britons had 230,000 warriors, so Paulinus divided his army into three divisions so that they could fight on several fronts if they were surrounded. He made a speech to the soldiers of each division, encouraging them not to fear the Britons [62.9–11]. Then the battle began. The Britons closed with great clamour, and the Romans remained quiet until the enemy was within javelin range, then they threw their weapons and charged, breaking the British ranks, while the archers took on the chariots. Some of the Britons escaped but then Boudouika fell ill and died, and the Britons disbanded.

66.20.1–3 Agricola overran all the territory of Britain. He was the first Roman to discover that Britain was surrounded by the sea. Some soldiers [the Usipi] mutinied, killed their officers and put to sea in boats. They sailed around the western part of Britain as the wind and currents took them, escaping detection on the east side as they landed near some forts. After this Agricola sent the fleet to circumnavigate the island. As a result of these exploits in Britain, Titus received his fifteenth Imperial salutation. But Agricola lived the rest of his life in disgrace and poverty because he had accomplished more than other generals. Even though Titus had awarded him triumphal honours, Domitian killed him.

72.16.2 [In the wars on the Danube] Marcus Aurelius sent 5,500 Iazyges [Sarmatians] to Britain.

73.8.1–6 Under Commodus, there were several wars with the people beyond Dacia, but the greatest war was against the Britons, when the tribes crossed the wall that separated them from the Roman army and did tremendous damage, killing a general. Commodus sent Ulpius Marcellus against the Britons, a frugal man who lived like the soldiers. He was incorruptible but not pleasant. He needed little sleep and each night he used to write out orders on lime-wood tablets, and have someone deliver them to different people through the night so they would think that he was always awake, and would be deprived of sleep themselves. He defeated the Britons.

72.9.1–4 The Praetorian Prefect caused great anger among the troops, and those in Britain chose Priscus, a legionary legate, as Emperor, but he refused the honour. The restless officers picked 1,500 men to go to Italy, and they met Commodus outside Rome, convincing him that Perennis was plotting against him. Commodus turned Perennis over to his own soldiers, who killed him.

74.15.1–2 [Of the three contenders for the Empire, Severus, Niger, and Albinus] Severus was the most shrewd. He knew he would have to fight his rivals, so he chose Niger first and sent a letter to Albinus, appointing him Caesar. Albinus remained in his province, believing he would share in the government with Severus.

76.4.1 Severus no longer accorded the rank of Caesar to Albinus, so the latter declared himself Augustus.

76.6.1–8 Severus and Albinus fought their final battle at Lugdunum [Lyon], with 150,000 men on each side. Both commanders were present, though Severus had not been present at any other battle. Albinus was the better connected of the two but Severus was the greater commander, though before this battle, Albinus had defeated Lupus, one of Severus's generals. When the battle started, Albinus's left wing crumbled, fell back and the soldiers were slaughtered. On the right wing, Albinus's men had dug trenches and disguised them, and advancing as far as the pits they threw their javelins and then turned back as if in flight, so Severus's men pursued them, falling into the trenches. The men behind them were annihilated by showers of arrows from Albinus's troops. Severus brought up the Praetorians but nearly succeeded in destroying them and himself. He lost his horse and was in danger of his life, but tore off his cloak and entered the front ranks, trying to turn back the fleeing soldiers. Then the cavalry under Laetus came up and turned the near defeat into victory. It was said that he had hung back waiting to see which would be the winning side.

76.5.4 The Caledonians did not keep their promises and were getting ready to help the Meaetae. Severus was attending to wars elsewhere, so [the governor] Lupus was forced to buy peace from the Maeatae, and in return he received some captives. [Note: the numbering of Dio's chapters is confused at this point, since the original work is lost and these chapters consist of epitomes made by later authors, arranged as far as possible in chronological order. For ease of reference, this passage can be found on pages 216–217 of volume 9 of the Loeb version of Dio's *Roman History*.]

77.10.6 Severus was angry because in Britain he was winning wars through other generals, while in Italy he could not defeat a robber [the bandit leader Bulla].

77.11.1–2 Severus saw that his sons were changing their way of life, and the legions were becoming idle, so he made a campaign against Britain, though he knew from various omens that he would not return from there. He took with him a large amount of money.

77.12.1–5 There are two main races of Britons, the Caledonians and the Maeatae, the other tribal names having been merged into these. The Maeatae live near the wall that divides the island into two, and the Caledonians dwell beyond them. Both tribes live in wild mountainous terrain, full of marshes. There are no cities or farms. The people live on flocks and game, and fruit. Though there is an abundance of fish they do not eat any. They live in tents, do not wear shoes, and they share their women, rearing the children all together. They are mostly democratic, addicted to plunder, and choose the boldest men as leaders. In battle they use chariots and infantry, who are fast runners. They use shields, spears with an 'apple' on the top which makes a terrifying noise when shaken, and daggers. They can endure cold and hunger, and stay in the marshes for days with their heads above water. They eat bark and roots, and make a food of which one piece staves off hunger. This is what the inhabitants of the hostile part of the island are like. It has been proved that Britain is an island, 950 miles long, 308 miles wide, and at its narrowest part only 40 miles wide. We hold slightly less than one half of this island.

77.13.1–77.15.4 Severus desired to subdue the whole island, and invaded Caledonia, enduring many hardships caused by the terrain, forests, mountains, swamps and rivers, with no enemy in sight. The Romans lacked water, and if they were separated they were attacked. Anyone unable to walk was killed by his comrades, so as to avoid capture. Severus reached the end of the island, where he observed the motion of the sun and the lengths of the days and nights. He was carried in a litter for most of the journey. He made terms with the Britons, forcing them to cede large tracts of their land.

Antoninus (Caracalla) was causing anxiety, clearly intending to kill his brother, and plotting against his father. When Severus and Caracalla were riding to meet the Caledonians to discuss terms, Caracalla reined in his horse and drew his sword as if to kill his father. The men riding with them shouted out, Severus turned and saw the sword but kept silence. Having finished the business with the Britons, he summoned Caracalla, placed a sword within reach, and told him to murder him there and then, or to order the Praetorian Prefect to do it. Though he often blamed Marcus Aurelius for not quietly ridding himself of Commodus, he did not harm Caracalla.

When the Britons revolted again, Severus summoned the soldiers and ordered them to invade their lands and kill everyone they met. The Caledonians joined the revolt, so Severus prepared for war, but he died in February, possibly assisted by Caracalla. Before his death he said to his sons 'live in harmony, pay the soldiers and ignore everyone else'. His body was dressed in military clothes, and burned on a pyre. His ashes were placed in an urn of purple stone which he had brought with him to Britain, and taken to Rome, to be deposited in the tomb of the Antonine Emperors.

78.1–2 Caracalla assumed sole power, though in reality he was to share it with his brother. He made terms with the enemy and withdrew from their lands, abandoning the forts.

HERODIAN *HISTORY OF THE EMPIRE*
Very little is known about Herodian's background. He may have been born in Antioch, but worked in Rome, possibly as an Imperial freedman in a low-grade official post. His work covers the period from the end of the reign of Marcus Aurelius to about AD 238. Much of what he says should be treated with caution, but his reliability improves when he describes events with which he was personally familiar.

Summary of reports on Britain in Herodian's *History*:

2.15.1–5 The army in Britain was large and powerful, and the soldiers were good fighters. The governor Albinus was a wealthy patrician who wanted to be Emperor. Severus tricked Albinus into supporting him, because as commander of a large army and with his influential connections in Rome, Albinus could capture Rome while Severus was in the east. He pretended to honour Albinus, sending many promises by letter. He made Albinus Caesar, giving him a share in power and permission to issue coins and have statues put up. This neutralised the potential danger from Albinus.

3.5.2–3.6.6 Albinus was arrogant, but because of his ancestry and his connections he was winning over the senators. Severus decided to break with him, sending messengers who were instructed to speak to Albinus in private, and then kill him. Albinus grew suspicious, and arrested the messengers. Severus determined to destroy him, and made an inflammatory speech to the army.

3.7.1–7 Albinus prepared for war and crossed to Gaul, asking other governors to send money and supplies. Some of them complied and were punished for it later. When Severus arrived there were a few skirmishes and then the battle at Lugdunum [Lyon]. The Britons fought bravely, proving to be bloodthirsty and courageous. In the fighting, Severus turned and fled but was knocked off his horse and had to tear off his cloak so as to be recognised by his troops. Laetus came up at last, with fresh troops. He was accused of waiting to see the outcome of the battle, and as Severus fell he arrived on the scene. He was not rewarded like the other generals. Herodian says that other writers vary in their estimates of numbers of men killed. Severus's troops sacked Lugdunum and burnt it. Albinus was captured and executed, and his head was sent to Severus.

3.8.1–2 Severus rooted out and eliminated the supporters of Albinus and confiscated their property. Having set Britain in order, he divided it into two provinces.

3.14.1–3.15.2 The governor of Britain reported that there was a serious rebellion and he needed either more troops, or the presence of the Emperor. This suited Severus because he desired glory and wished to win victories in Britain, after his conquests in the east. Besides he was upset by the behaviour of his sons and decided to take them away from Rome on an expedition to Britain. He crossed the seas and assembled the army for war. A delegation came from the Britons to discuss terms, but Severus wanted to delay going back to Rome, so he dismissed the Britons. He made preparations to cross the marshes by using pontoons – Britain is mostly marshland because it is flooded by the ocean tides. The Britons swim in these marshes or run through them up to their waists in water. They are virtually naked and do not mind the mud because they do not wear clothes. They value iron more than gold and adorn their necks and waists with it. They also tattoo their bodies with patterns and pictures of animals, so they do not wear clothes so as not to obscure these pictures. They are fierce fighters, using only a narrow shield and a spear, with a sword slung from their naked bodies. Breastplates and helmets are not used because they would impede them in the marshes. It is always gloomy in their lands because of the fog that arises from the marshes.

When the war preparations were completed, Severus placed his younger son Geta in charge of jurisdiction over the provincials, and the civil administration of the Empire, with a council of the Emperor's friends. He took Caracalla with him on campaign. After they had crossed the fortification marking the boundary of the province, the army was involved in several skirmishes in which the Britons were routed and fled, hiding in the forests and marshes. They knew their terrain well, but the Romans were hampered by it and the war was drawn out.

Severus was now an old man and remained in his quarters, sending Caracalla to fight the war, but he was more interested in winning over the soldiers, slandering his brother, and trying to persuade the doctors to do away with Severus. Eventually Severus died, worn out with grief. He had achieved greater military renown than any other Emperor.

Caracalla assumed power as soon as Severus died, and executed all the household attendants. He tried to persuade the army to declare for him alone, but the soldiers showed equal loyalty to Caracalla and Geta. After failing to win over the army, Caracalla made peace with the Britons, in return for guarantees, and he left their lands.

AMMIANUS MARCELLINUS (C.AD 330–395)

Ammianus was a Roman military officer serving on the staff of Ursicinus, *magister equitum* or commander of the cavalry, from AD 349 to 359, and commander of the infantry (*magister peditum*) from 359 to 360. Ursicinus was dismissed from his post after the fall of the besieged city of Amida to the Persians. The mid to late fourth century was a time of constant military activity, which took Ammianus to Gaul, Germany, Italy, Illyricum and Mesopotamia. He served under the Emperor Julian in Gaul, and came out of retirement to follow him to Persia, where Julian conducted a disastrous campaign which ended in the Emperor's defeat and death. Ammianus can be fairly accused of a bias towards Ursicinus and to Julian, but this does not necessarily detract from his worth as a historian. He wrote his history of Rome in Latin, in thirty-one books, the first thirteen of which are lost. His work consists of his own accounts of events which he had seen for himself, and he fills in the details which he did not personally witness with narrative history compiled from different sources. He started his history of Rome with the Emperor Nerva, perhaps consciously picking up the thread where Suetonius left off in *The Twelve Caesars*, but the only extant portions of his work from book fourteen onwards cover events from 353 to his own day.

Summary of reports on Britain in Ammianus's *Roman History*:

18.2.3–4 [The context is Julian's war against the Alamanni on the Rhine in 359.] Before engaging in battle Julian regained the cities that had been destroyed and abandoned. He repaired the fortifications and built granaries to store the grain regularly brought over from Britain. The granaries were rapidly built and a quantity of food stored in them.

20.1.1–2 In Britain, in the tenth consulship of Constantius and the third of Julian [360], the Scotti and Picts broke the peace that had been agreed and devastated the regions near the frontiers. The provincials were afraid, wearied as they were by past disasters. Julian was in Paris for the winter and burdened by many problems, so he could not cross the sea to help the Britons as Constans had done, because it would have meant leaving Gaul without a ruler at a time when the Alamanni were ready to wage war. Therefore he sent Lupicinus, the chief commander to settle the troubles either by negotiation or war. Lupicinus took light-armed auxiliaries, the Aeruli, Batavians and two units of Moesians, and set off in the middle of winter for Boulogne. He sailed to Richborough and then marched to London, intending to make his plans according to the situation that he found and then take the field.

22.3.3 [In 361 after the death of Constantius II] adherents of Constantius were condemned or exiled. Palladius, formerly the chief minister [*magister officiorum*] was banished to Britain.

27.8.1–10 [Concerning the years 367–368.] Valentinian was on his way to Trier when serious news came from Britain of a barbarian conspiracy. Nectaridus, *Comes maritimi tractus* [the Count of the Saxon Shore?] had been killed and the general Fullofaudes had been ambushed and taken prisoner. Severus, *comes domesticorum* or commander of the household troops, was sent to Britain, but soon recalled and Jovinus was sent instead. He returned quickly to ask for a stronger army. Theodosius, famous for his service in war, was despatched, enrolling legions and cohorts of young men on the way. Ammianus says that the situation of Britain and the ebb and flow of the tides was described in the passages about Constans, so there is no need to repeat it here [unfortunately these sections are lost].

The Scotti and the Picts, divided into the Dicalydones and the Attacotti, were devastating the frontier areas, and the Saxons and the Franks were attacking the coasts of Gaul. Theodosius arrived at Boulogne, separated from Britain by a short stretch of sea, prone to dreadful surges and flat calm. He crossed to Richborough, and when the units of Heruli, Jovi and Victores arrived he set off for London, which in later times was called Augusta. He divided his troops and attacked the groups of raiders, laden down with booty. The ones who were driving cattle and prisoners were routed and the stolen property restored to the owners, save for a small amount reserved for the tired soldiers.

The inhabitants of London rejoiced to see him. Theodosius made his plans, having heard from prisoners and deserters that the raiders were widely dispersed and could only be defeated by secret plans and surprise attacks. He proclaimed an amnesty for deserters and recalled soldiers on leave, and asked for Civilis to govern as deputy prefect [*rector pro praefectis*] and the general Dulcitius, distinguished for his skill in war.

28.3.1–9 Theodosius marched out of Augusta, which used to be called London. He secured suitable places for laying ambushes, and did not ask the soldiers to do anything he would not do himself. He routed some tribes, and restored cities and forts. Then the rebellion of Valentinus broke out. This man had been exiled to Britain for some crime, and now tried to rouse the other exiles. But Theodosius heard from one of his sources what was planned. He turned Valentinus over to Dulcitius for execution, but forbade any further investigation, so as not to disturb the recently pacified provinces. He restored cities and frontier defences, protecting them by means of forts and watchtowers. He had so completely recovered a province that had been lost that it was given its own governor and called Valentia in accordance with the Emperor's wishes.

During these events, the *areani*, a type of unit described earlier under the expedition of Constans, had become corrupted. Theodosius dismissed them because they had been tempted by receipt of goods or promises of them to betray Roman plans to the enemy. It was their duty to range widely over large areas to gather information for Roman generals about rebellions among the tribes.

Theodosius returned to Rome, leaving the provinces of Britain dancing for joy.

29.1.44 [Valens roots out accomplices of the usurper Theodorus.] Even Alypius, former *vicarius* of Britain, a gentle and amiable man living in retirement, was reduced to wretchedness. The man who informed on him was Diogenes, who was tortured to make him give evidence. Alypius had his property confiscated and was exiled, first rescuing his son at the last minute as he was being led to his death, but he was reprieved.

29.4.7 [In 372] Valentinian made Fraomarius king of the Bucinobantes, a branch of the

Alamanni living opposite Mainz. Then he transferred him to Britain to command the unit of Alamanni there, distinguished for its size and strength.

30.7.3 Valentinian's father Gratianus commanded the army in Africa with the title *comes*, but he was suspected of theft. Much later he commanded in Britain with the same rank.

30.7.9 [An assessment of Valentinian's reign.] When the Britons could not resist the hordes attacking them, he restored peace and freedom, and gave them hope of better conditions, allowing almost none of the plunderers to return to their homes.

Further Reading

ANCIENT SOURCES

Ammianus Marcellinus. Loeb
Caesar. *Gallic War*. Loeb
Dio. *Roman History*. Loeb
Herodian. *History of the Empire*. Loeb
Pliny. *Natural History*. Loeb
Scriptores Historiae Augustae. Loeb
Strabo. *Geography*. Loeb
Suetonius. *Twelve Caesars*. Loeb
Tacitus. *Agricola*. Loeb
Tacitus. *Annals*. Loeb
Tacitus. *Germania*. Loeb
Tacitus. *Histories*. Loeb
Vegetius. *Epitoma Rei Militaris*

MODERN WORKS

REFERENCE
Birley, A.R. *The Roman Government of Britain*. Oxford, 2005.
de la Bédoyère, G. *Companion to Roman Britain*. Stroud, 1999.
Frere, S.S. and St. Joseph, J.K.S. *Roman Britain from the Air*. Cambridge, 1983.
Ireland, S. *Roman Britain: a sourcebook*. London, 1996.
Jones, B. and Mattingley, D. *An Atlas of Roman Britain*. Oxford, 1990.
Rivet, A.L.F. and Smith, C. *The Place Names of Roman Britain*. London, 1979.
Wilson, R.J.A. *A Guide to Roman Remains in Britain*. London, 4th edn. 2002.

GENERAL ACCOUNTS
de la Bédoyère, G. *Roman Britain: a new history*. London, 2006.
Frere, S.S. *Britannia: a history of Roman Britain*. London, 3rd edn. 1987.
Salway, P. *The Oxford Illustrated History of Roman Britain*. Oxford, 1993.
Salway, P. *Roman Britain*. Oxford History of England Vol. 1. 1991.

SPECIFIC PERIODS

Cunliffe, B. *Iron Age Communities in Britain: an account of England, Scotland and Wales from the seventh century BC until the Roman conquest.* London, 3rd edn. 1991.

Casey, P. J. *Carausius and Allectus: the British usurpers.* London, 1994.

Dark, K. *Civitas to Kingdom: British political continuity 300–800.* Leicester, 1994

Dark, K. *Britain and the End of the Roman Empire.* Stroud, 2000.

Darvill, T. *Prehistoric Britain.* London, 1987.

Esmonde Cleary, A.S. *The Ending of Roman Britain.* London, 1989.

Faulkner, N. *The Decline and Fall of Roman Britain.* Stroud, 2000.

Hanson, W.S. *Agricola and the Conquest of the North.* London, 1987.

Jones, M.E. *The End of Roman Britain.* Ithaca, 1996.

Macready. S. and Thompson, F.H. (eds.) *Cross-Channel Trade Between Gaul and Britain in the Pre-Roman Iron Age.* London, 1984.

Sealey, P.R. *The Boudican Revolt Against Rome.* Princes Risborough, 1997.

SOCIAL HISTORY

Alcock, J.P. *Food in Roman Britain.* Stroud, 2001.

Alcock, J. P. *Life in Roman Britain.* Stroud, 2010.

Birley, A.R. *The People of Roman Britain.* London, 1979, reprinted 1988.

Croom, A.T. *Roman Clothing and Fashion.* Stroud, 2000.

Ellis, S. *Roman Housing.* London, 2000.

Liversidge, J. *Britain in the Roman Empire.* London, 1968.

Millett, M. *The Romanization of Britain.* Cambridge, 1990.

THE ROMAN ARMY

Bidwell, P. *Roman Forts in Britain.* London, 1997.

Birley, A.R. *Garrison Life at Vindolanda: a band of brothers.* Stroud, 2002.

Bowman, A.K. *Life and Letters on the Roman Frontier: the Vindolanda writing tablets.* London, rev. edn. 2003.

Breeze, D. and Dobson, B. *Hadrian's Wall.* London, 1987.

Crow, J. *Housesteads.* London, 1995.

de la Bédoyère, G. *Hadrian's Wall: a history and guide.* Stroud, 1998.

Dixon, K.R. and Southern, P. *The Roman Cavalry.* London, 1992.

Goldsworthy, A. *The Complete Roman Army.* London, 2003.

Hanson, W.S and Maxwell, G.S. *Rome's North-West Frontier: the Antonine Wall.* Edinburgh, 2nd edn. 1986.

Johnson, A. *Roman Forts.* London, 1983.

Johnson, S. *The Roman Forts of the Saxon Shore.* London, 1979.

Mason, D.J.P. *Roman Britain and the Roman Navy.* Stroud, 2003.

Pearson, A. *The Roman Shore Forts.* Stroud, 2002.

Pitts, L.F. and St. Joseph, J.K.S. *Inchtuthil: the Roman legionary fortress.* London, 1985.

Shotter, D. *The Roman Frontier in Britain.* Preston, 1996.

Southern, P. and Dixon, K.R. *The Late Roman Army.* London, 2000.

Wilmot, T. *Birdoswald Roman Fort.* Stroud, 2001.

TOWNS

Bidwell, P.T. *Roman Exeter: fortress and town.* Exeter, 1980.

Boon, G.C. *Silchester: the Roman town of Calleva.* Newton Abbot, 1974.

Brewer, R.J. *Caerwent Roman Town*. Cardiff, 1993.
Burnham, B.C. and Wacher, J. *The 'Small Towns' of Roman Britain*. London, 1990.
Crummy, P.J. *City of Victory: the story of Colchester, Britain's first Roman town*. Colchester, 1997.
Cunliffe, B. *Roman Bath Discovered*. London, 1984.
de la Bédoyère, G. *Towns of Roman Britain*. Stroud, 2003.
Jones, M.E. *Roman Lincoln*. Stroud, 1992.
Mason, D.J.P. *Roman Chester*. Stroud, 2001.
McCarthy, M. *Roman Carlisle and the Lands of the Solway*. Stroud, 2002.
Wacher, J. *Towns of Roman Britain*. London, 1995.
White, R. and Barker, P. *Wroxeter: life and death of a Roman city*. Stroud, 1998.

VILLAS

Branigan, K. and Miles, D. (eds) *The Economies of Romano-British Villas*. Sheffield, 1988.
de la Bédoyère, G. *Roman Villas and the Countryside*. London, 1993.
Meates, G.W. *The Lullingstone Roman Villa, Kent: vol. 1: the site*. Maidstone, 1979
Meates, G.W. *The Lullingstone Roman Villa, Kent: vol. 2: the wall paintings and finds*. Maidstone, 1987.
Percival, J. *The Roman Villa*. London, 1976.
Smith, J.T. *Roman Villas: a study in social structure*. London, 1997.
Todd, M. (ed.) *Studies in the Romano-British Villa*. Leicester, 1978.

RELIGION

Green, M.J. *Exploring the World of the Druids*. London, 1997.
Henig, M. *Religion in Roman Britain*. London, 1984.
Lewis, M.J.T. *Temples in Roman Britain*. Cambridge, 1965.
Rodwell, W. (ed.) *Temples, Churches and Religion in Roman Britain*. British Archaeological Reports, British series 77. Oxford, 1980.
Thomas, C. *Christian Celts*. Stroud, 1998.

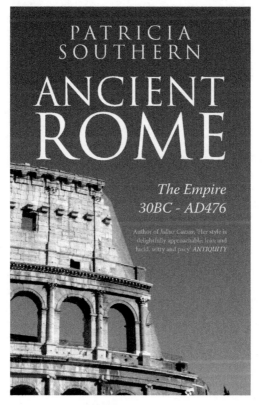

Index